Writing Your Own

OSF/Motif Widgets

Donald L. McMinds

Joseph P. Whitty

Hewlett-Packard Company

Prentice Hall PTR
Englewood Cliffs, NJ 07632

Library of Congress Cataloging-In-Publication Data

```
McMinds, Donald L.
    Writing Your Own OSF/Motif Widgets / Donald L. McMinds, Joseph P.
  Whitty.
       p.      cm.
    Includes bibliographical references and index.
    ISBN 0-13-104191-6
    1. X Window System (Computer system) 2. Motif (Computer file)
  I. Whitty, Joseph P., 1961-          .   II.  Title.
  QA76.76.W56M5217  1995
  005.13'3-dc20
                                                           94-2419
                                                              CIP
```

Editorial/production supervision: BooksCraft, Inc., Indianapolis, IN
Cover Designer: Wanda Lubelska
Acquisition editor: Karen Gettman
Manufacturing manager: Alexis R. Heydt

Published by Prentice Hall PTR
Prentice-Hall, Inc.
A Paramount Communications Company
Englewood Cliffs, NJ 07632

The publisher offers discounts on this book when ordered in bulk quantities. For more information contact: Corporate Sales Department, Prentice Hall PTR, 113 Sylvan Avenue, Englewood Cliffs, NJ 07632, Phone: 201-592-2863, FAX: 201-592-2249

Printed in the United States of America
10 9 8 7 6 5 4 3 2 1

ISBN: 0-13-104191-6

Prentice-Hall International (UK) Limited, *London*
Prentice-Hall of Australia Pty. Limited, *Sydney*
Prentice-Hall Canada Inc., *Torrent*
Prentice-Hall Hispanoamericana, S.A., *Mexico*
Prentice-Hall of India Private Limited, *New Delhi*
Prentice-Hall of Japan, Inc., *Tokyo*
Simon & Schuster Asia Pte. Ltd., *Singapore*
Editora Prentice-Hall do Brasil, Ltda., *Rio de Janeiro*

Contents

Preface

Motif is a graphical user interface (GUI) system consisting of a toolkit and a window manager. It was developed by the Open Software Foundation (OSF) beginning in 1988 and is based on the X Window System. OSF provides a comprehensive set of widgets,[1] which you can use to great advantage. These widgets provide the means to easily create very sophisticated, esthetically pleasing user interface applications. Many GUI applications have already been written using them.

A Need for Unique Widgets

Despite the number and variety of Motif widgets, there undoubtedly will come a time when your creative imagination needs a widget or gadget that doesn't exist in the Motif set. For example, what do you use if your application design calls for a dial or a knob? What if your company needs a unique set of widgets for financial or manufacturing applications? Because these devices currently don't exist in Motif, you probably have only three choices: try to combine some of the existing Motif widgets to achieve a user interface that is satisfactory for your application, redesign your application to use the existing Motif widgets, or write the widgets you need. Up to now, writing new widgets has been a difficult task except for programmers who are familiar with the OSF/Motif source code.

Key Features

This book is aimed at providing the knowledge you need to write your own widgets. We'll take you through the process step by step, from conception to the finished widget. You'll create three new widgets—a knob widget, a grid widget, and a special version of the knob widget called a knob gadget. A *gadget* is a widget without its own window, and it depends on its parent for its window. You'll learn how to connect each new widget to an existing superclass so that it

---

1. The term "widgets" is somewhat misleading because OSF/Motif is actually composed of widgets and gadgets. The difference between the two is explained in the book.

inherits behavior and resources of the superclass. We'll also describe programs that demonstrate the use of these new widgets. When you finish the book, you should be able to use what you've learned to design and create your own widgets and gadgets to augment the OSF/Motif library.

The source code for all the programs and header files used in this book is available free of charge by using anonymous ftp from either of the following sources:

- A machine at M.I.T. Use `ftp.x.org`. The programs are located in the file `contrib/wr_widgets.tar.Z`.

- A machine at the Hewlett-Packard plant in Corvallis, Oregon. You can use the machine name `hpcvaal.cv.hp.com` with the ftp command. The programs are located in the file `readonly/book_files/wr_widgets.tar.Z`

You may need to have your system administrator perform the anonymous ftp. Be sure to read the README file for current information about the programs.

If you have any questions, criticisms, or suggestions for improvement, please drop a line via e-mail to the following address:

`wr_widgets@cv.hp.com`

All comments and suggestions are welcome and very much appreciated.

Assumptions

Writing new widgets is not a task for beginners. To understand the information we provide, you should have an understanding of object-oriented programming, experience in C programming, and a good working knowledge of Motif, Xlib, and the Xt Intrinsics. This book is not an introduction to any of these, so without the necessary background you could find yourself very confused in a short time.

Related Books

Here's a list of books that provide information on Xlib, the Xt Intrinsics, and Motif:

- *Introduction to the X Window System*, by Oliver Jones, published by Prentice-Hall, Englewood Cliffs, NJ 07632.

- *The X Window System Programming and Applications with Xt* OSF/MotifEdition, by Douglas A. Young, published by Prentice-Hall, Englewood Cliffs, NJ 07632.

- *The X Window System Toolkit*, by Paul J. Asente and Ralph R. Swick, published by Digital Press, 12 Crosby Drive, Bedford, MA 01730.

- *OSF/Motif Reference Guide*, by Douglas A. Young, published by Prentice-Hall, Englewood Cliffs, NJ 07632.

- *Mastering OSF/Motif Widgets* (Second Edition), by Donald L. McMinds, published by Addison-Wesley, Reading, MA 01867.

- *The Definitive Guides to the X Window System, Volume 0: X Protocol Reference Manual*, edited by Adrian Nye, published by O'Reilly and Associates, Sebastopol, CA 95472.

- *The Definitive Guides to the X Window System, Volume 1: Xlib Programming Manual*, by Adrian Nye, published by O'Reilly and Associates, Sebastopol, CA 95472.

- *The Definitive Guides to the X Window System, Volume 2: Xlib Reference Manual*, edited by Adrian Nye, published by O'Reilly and Associates, Sebastopol, CA 95472.

- *The Definitive Guides to the X Window System, Volume 3: X Window System User's Guide*, by Valerie Quercia and Tim O'Reilly, published by O'Reilly and Associates, Sebastopol, CA 95472.

- *The Definitive Guides to the X Window System, Volume 4: X Toolkit Intrinsics Programming Manual*, by Adrian Nye and Tim O'Reilly, published by O'Reilly and Associates, Sebastopol, CA 95472.

- *The Definitive Guides to the X Window System, Volume 5: X Toolkit Intrinsics Reference Manual*, edited by Tim O'Reilly, published by O'Reilly and Associates, Sebastopol, CA 95472.

- *The Definitive Guides to the X Window System, Volume 6: Motif Programming Manual*, by Dan Heller, published by O'Reilly and Associates, Sebastopol, CA 95472.

Contents of the Book

Here's a brief summary of the contents of each chapter.

Chapter 1 reviews the X Window System, the Xt Intrinsics, and the OSF/Motif widgets and describes how all these systems work together. If you're familiar with X, the Xt Intrinsics, and OSF/Motif, you can skip this chapter without fear of missing anything.

Chapter 2 describes a generic step-by-step process you can use to create a new widget or gadget. Code segments from actual widgets should help you to understand the concepts being described. You'll use this process in subsequent chapters to create a knob and grid widget and a knob gadget.

Chapter 3 describes designing and writing the code for the knob widget, a widget that has the appearance and behavior of a knob control (like the volume control on many stereos, for example). The creation of the widget is covered step by step, with liberal use of code segments to explain what is happening and why. Complete code listings for both the widget (`knob.c`), associated header files (files ending in `.h`), and a sample program are given in Appendix A.

Chapter 4 describes designing and writing the code for the grid widget. The creation of the widget is covered step by step, with liberal use of code segments to explain what is happening and why. Code listings for both the widget (`grid.c`), associated header files, and a sample program are given in Appendix A.

Chapter 5 describes designing and writing a knob gadget. Describes a need for the knob gadget and the difference between it and the knob widget. The creation of the gadget is covered step by step, with liberal use of code segments to explain what is happening and why. Code listings for both the gadget, associated header files, and a sample program are given in Appendix A.

Chapter 6 provides some ideas for new widgets and gadgets that you might want to create.

Appendix A contains listings of all the programs, header files, sample programs, and a Makefile described in the book.

Appendix B contains a list of all the currently defined OSF/Motif representation types.

Appendix C contains a list of Motif functions used in writing widgets and gadgets.

Glossary provides definitions of terms used in the book, particularly those terms that may be unfamiliar to a programmer new to the Motif environment.

Acknowledgments

We acknowledge the superb efforts of Courtney Loomis for technical reviews and Patti Richey for formatting the table of contents and index and performing other document preparation chores.

Trademarks

Information contained in this document is subject to change without notice.

X Window System is a trademark of The Massachusetts Institute of Technology. UNIX is a registered trademark in the United States and other countries, licensed exclusively through X/Open Company Limited. HP-UX is a trademark of Hewlett-Packard Company. DEC is a trademark of Digital Equipment Corporation. The three-dimensional appearance of the widgets shown in this book is copyrighted by Hewlett-Packard Company. Motif, OSF/Motif, and Open Software Foundation are trademarks of the Open Software Foundation, Inc.

The following statement appears in M.I.T's X Window System documentation:

Copyright 1985, 1986, 1987, 1988 Massachusetts Institute of Technology, Cambridge, Massachusetts, and Digital Equipment Corporation, Maynard, Massachusetts.

Permission to use, copy, modify, and distribute this documentation for any purpose and without fee is hereby granted, provided that the above copyright notice appears in all copies and that both that copyright notice and this permission notice appear in supporting documentation, and that the name of M.I.T. or Digital not be used in advertising or publicity pertaining to distribution of the software without specific, written prior permission.

M.I.T. and Digital make no representations about the suitability of the software described herein for any purpose. It is provided "as is" without express or implied warranty.

Chapter 1 Introduction to OSF/Motif

This chapter provides some background on the OSF/Motif widgets and how they relate to the Unix operating system and the X Window System. If you're familiar with Motif, then you can skip this chapter and go right to Chapter 2.

X: The Beginning

The X Window System is a network transparent windowing system in which a client application can be run on one machine (called the X server) and displayed and controlled on the user's local machine. The two machines are connected to a network, and many applications can be run on the server and displayed on other machines. The X Application Programmer Interface (API), called *Xlib*, is designed for portability, allowing client applications to be ported to various platforms very easily. X also provides a foundation API for graphical user interface toolkits, such as OSF/Motif. This foundation API is called the *Xt Intrinsics*, and it is built on top of Xlib. Figure 1-1 shows this architecture.

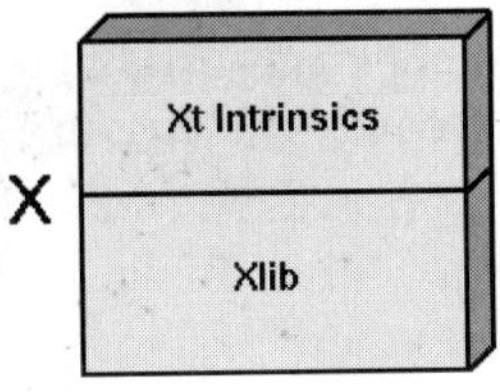

Figure 1-1 X Windows Architecture

The Xt Intrinsics provides an object-oriented C language framework for a graphical user interface toolkit. It does not provide an API that is in itself suited to be used by an application.

Enter Motif

Motif was developed by the Open Software Foundation (OSF), an organization committed to developing a standard, easy-to-use graphical user interface (GUI) development tool. Figure 1-2 shows how Motif is incorporated into the X architecture.

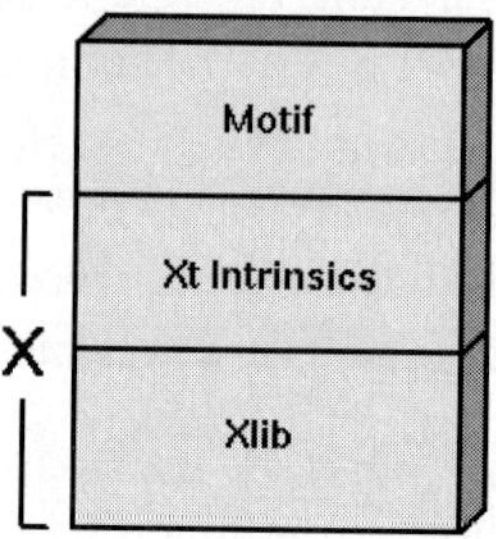

Figure 1-2 X and Motif Architecture

Motif is built on top of the Xt Intrinsics and Xlib, but unlike these two libraries, it allows you to create a graphics object with as little as one line of code. A graphics object is often generically referred to as a *widget*, although the term has a more specific meaning in the context of the Xt Intrinsics and Motif. For example, to create a Motif pushbutton widget, you could use a line like:

```
button = XmCreatePushButton(parent, "button", args, n);
```

It is true that you may need other lines to set the values of *resources* (attributes of a widget used to control behavior and visual characteristics of the widget) that you may want for the pushbutton. However, even allowing for that, it's much easier to create a pushbutton using the Motif widget or gadget than using Xlib and Xt Intrinsics code. Furthermore, there are several ways you can set the values of resources outside the Motif application, eliminating the need for some lines of code.

Introduction to OSF/Motif

What Are Widgets and Gadgets?

So now you know that Motif consists of widgets and gadgets that are GUI objects, but just exactly what are these objects?

Widget

A widget is a user interface object made up of data structures and functions[1] that use the Xlib and Xt Intrinsics APIs. It may or may not have a visible window, depending on its intended use. Examples of widgets that have a visible window are the pushbutton, toggle button, and frame. Examples of widgets that do not have a visible window are Shell, TopLevelShell, and ApplicationShell. Every widget belongs to a certain *class*, has its own resources, and can inherit the resources from the superclass from which the widget class was derived.

Gadget

A gadget is basically a widget that does not have its own window. Instead, it relies on its parent to supply the window, into which it renders its own visual image and through which it receives input events. As a result, a gadget can be more efficient than a widget, but the programmer has fewer choices concerning some of its attributes. Also, gadgets generate much more network traffic, which can cause performance degradation. Like widgets, every gadget belongs to a certain class, has its own resources, and can inherit the resources of gadgets belonging to its ancestral class.

Resources

Resources are attributes of a widget or gadget that are used to define parameters such as height, width, background color, and foreground color. You can set the value of a resource within a program, in a defaults file, in a command line, or from the resource manager window property.

Classes

Widgets and gadgets fall into various categories, called classes, depending on how they are used. Each class has special characteristics, and the classes form a *hierarchy*. This means that widgets or gadgets belonging to a lower class in the hierarchy inherit resources from the higher-level classes. Figure 1-3 shows the Motif widget class hierarchy.

---

1. Functions and procedures are called *methods* in object-oriented systems.

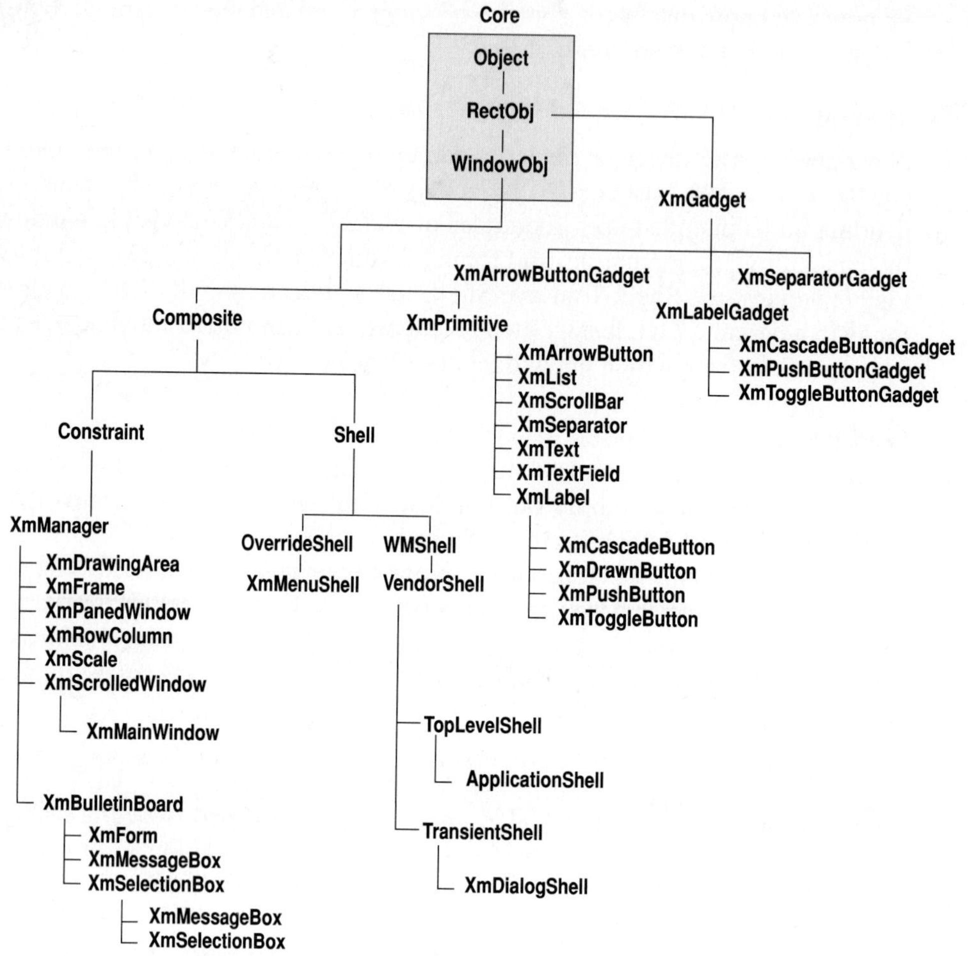

Figure 1-3 Widget and Gadget Hierarchy

Each of the higher widget classes has a set of resources that lower widget classes can inherit. For example, the drawing area widget, XmDrawingArea, is a subclass of XmManager, which is a subclass of Constraint, which is a subclass of Composite, which is a subclass of Core. The drawing area widget can therefore inherit resources from all the higher class widgets. Higher widget classes— particularly Core, Constraint, Composite, XmManager, and XmPrimitive—are often called *base classes*, and are used as the *superclass* of many widget classes. A lower widget class used by an application is often called a *leaf class*. Core is composed of three superclasses: Object, RectObj, and WindowObj. Note that all

widgets are subclassed from Core, but gadgets are subclassed from only Object
and RectObj.

A Sample Program

Figure 1-4 shows the output of a sample program we'll call (appropriately)
`sample.c`. This program doesn't do much, but it should refresh your memory
as to the composition of a Motif program and how the Motif widgets interact.

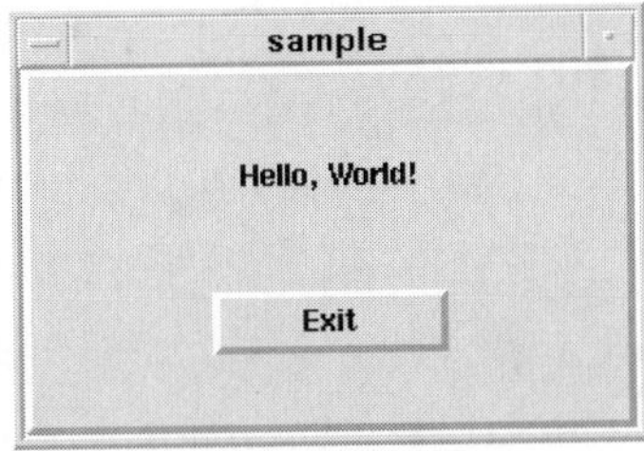

Figure 1-4 Window For sample.c

The `sample.c` window consists of a top-level shell, a bulletin board, a label,
and a pushbutton. When you click on the pushbutton, the program terminates.
You can find the listings for the program, its associated defaults file `Sample`, and
a Makefile in Appendix A.

You compile and link the program to the Xm, Xt, and X11 libraries and include
files. The Xm library contains all the code that defines the individual widgets.
For example, the code that creates the pushbutton is an object named
`PushButton.c`, and it is called by the Xt Intrinsics. We'll explain this in more
detail in the chapters that describe writing the new widgets.

Summary

This chapter presented a very brief review of the X Window System and the Motif
widgets. The next chapter presents a generic description of the process you'll use
to write new widgets.

Chapter 2 The Widget Writing Process

This chapter explains the basic process you need to follow when writing a new
widget. You should read this chapter thoroughly at least once. The process is
quite complicated, and you may find yourself getting confused very soon. If so,
be assured you are not alone. The best way to alleviate this problem is to stop
where you are as soon as you realize that you're lost and to go back and begin
again. Also, you may find that even though the generic process is confusing and
difficult to follow, once you apply the process and actually create a new widget, a
lot of things fall into place.

Introduction

You can break down the tasks you need to accomplish when writing a new widget
to a sequence of steps that we'll call the widget writing process. You may not
understand some of the process at this point, but you will as you become more
familiar with it.

The process essentially involves writing a source module and associated header
files that define the new widget class. Normally, the name is *<widgetname>*.c,
where *widgetname* is the name of the new widget. You include the widget's
private and public header files. You create an action table and a translation table
that handle events, and you specify the class record that identifies new methods,
class data, and inheritance from the superclass. The superclass is generally
XmManager, XmPrimitive, or XmGadget, depending on the purpose and type of
new widget you are writing. The new widget class is said to be subclassed from
the superclass. You could subclass a new widget from other classes such as Label,
but the widget examples we create are subclassed only from XmManager,
XmPrimitive, or XmGadget.

Figure 2-1 shows the components of the process.

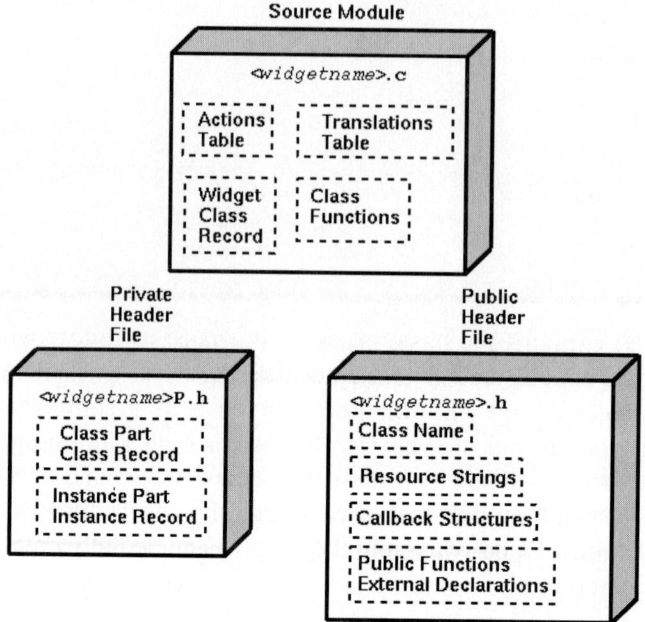

Figure 2-1   Components of the Widget Writing Process

Note that the action and translation tables are not used by gadgets. Their event handling is performed by the manager parent. The class and instance records are defined in the private header file and initialized in the program.

Process Outline

When you create a widget, you write an object that performs all the functions you want the widget to do. In addition to the code needed to perform the widget's functions, the object includes definitions and initializations that are common to all widgets. This common ground can be viewed as a process, and the outline that follows is a brief first look at the process. Subsequent sections of this chapter describe each step in detail.

1. Choose a superclass for the new widget: normally XmManager, XmPrimitive, or XmGadget.

2. Create the widget's private header file (*<widgetname>*P.h) and in it define:

a.   The class part structure

b.   Inheritance macros

c.   The class structure

d.   The instance part structure

e.   The instance structure

f.   Private utility functions, if any

g.   Extension parts and records, if any

h.   Constraint parts and record, if any

3.   Create the widget's public header file (*<widgetname>*.h), and in it define:

a.   Resource strings

b.   External declaration of the class record

c.   Callback structures

d.   Public utility convenience functions

4.   In the source module *<widgetname>*.c:

a.   Define the new widget's resources

b.   Define the action table (not applicable for gadgets)

c.   Define the translation table (not applicable for gadgets)

d.   Initialize the widget class record

e.   Define class method functions

f.   Define private and public utility and convenience functions

Choose a Superclass

You choose a superclass from which you want to subclass your new widget. All widgets are subclassed from Core. Subclasses of core include Composite, Constraint, XmManager, and XmPrimitive (see Figure 1-3 in Chapter 1).

If you want your new widget to contain children, then it should be a subclass of XmManager. Manager widgets, also called *container widgets*, provide the layout for other widgets. A row column container widget lays out its children vertically and horizontally in rows and columns. A form widget lays out its children in positions relative to each other.

If your new widget is not going to contain children, then it could be a subclass of XmPrimitive. Primitive widgets cannot have children and must be positioned by their parent. Primitive widgets have special functions such as pushbuttons, labels, text entry fields, and scrollbars.

If your new widget is a gadget, then it must be a subclass of XmGadget (a subclass of RectObj, a part of Core). Remember that a gadget is a widget that does not have its own window, thus handlings, translations, and visual attributes are all derived from its XmManager parent. The superclass you choose dictates the structures you'll need in the program. For example, the knob widget is subclassed from XmPrimitive (see Chapter 3), the grid widget is subclassed from XmManager (which automatically includes Composite and Constraint as well; see Chapter 4), and the knob gadget is subclassed from XmGadget (see Chapter 5).

Create the Private Header File

The private header file (*<widgetname>*P.h) is normally used only by other widget writers who want to subclass their widgets from yours. It is seldom, if ever, used by application programmers. The private header file consists of type definitions that define the class and instance structures for the new widget class. Appendix A contains a complete listing of the private header files for each of the widgets designed in this book.

Within the source module (see Figure 2-1), the widget class record is made up of parts, the exact number and type depending on the superclass from which the new widget class is to be subclassed. Each of these parts is defined in the corresponding widget's private header file. Every widget has a class part and an instance part, both of which are C data structures that contain data values and pointers to other structures and methods. Widgets that belong to the same class share the *class* part, but each widget created from this class has its own unique *instance* part. If you subclass a new widget from the XmPrimitive class, the superclass is XmPrimitive, and the widget class record consists of these parts:

- Core class part

- Primitive class part

- New widget class part

Figure 2-2 shows an example of how instances of the same widget class (XsmKnob, a subclass of XmPrimitive) have their own instance records but share the class record.

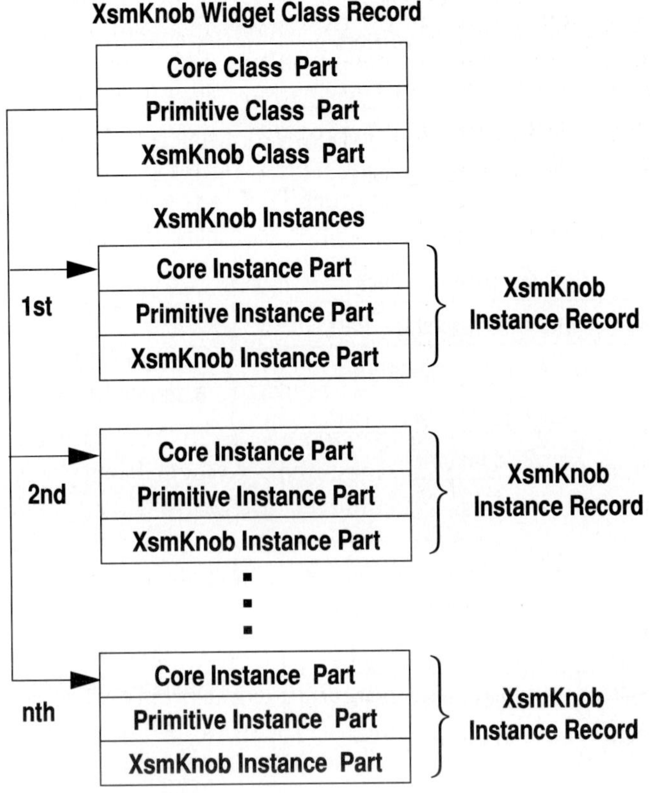

Figure 2-2   Primitive Widget Instances

Figure 2-3 shows an example of how two instances of the grid widget, a subclass of XmManager (see Chapter 4), have their own instance records but share the class record. Note the difference between Figure 2-3 and Figure 2-2.

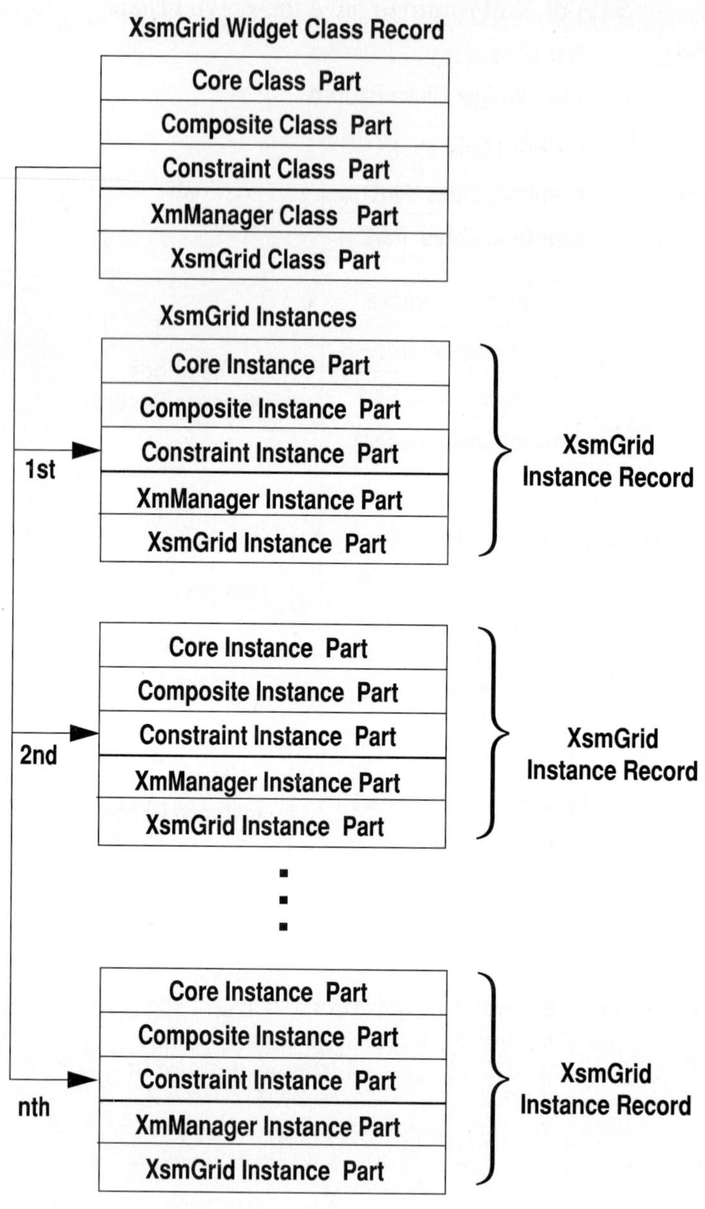

Figure 2-3   Manager Widget Instances

The difference exists because of the choice of superclass. When you subclass a widget from XmManager, you must include Composite and Constraint class parts as well as XmManager's class part.

Manage Multiple Inclusions

The first lines of the private header file are used to manage multiple inclusions:

```
#ifndef _XsmKnobP_h
#define _XsmKnobP_h
```

The associated `#endif` is the last line of the private header file:

```
#endif /* _XsmKnobP_h */
```

This prevents duplicate declarations and definitions when a header file has been included more than once.

Include Header Files

Next, include the new widget's public header and the superclass private header files:

```
#include "Knob.h"
#include <Xm/PrimitiveP.h>
```

The Core and XmPrimitive class parts are defined in their respective private header files to gain access to their definitions; you only have to define the new widget's class part. You do not need to include the Core private header file `CoreP.h`; that is done for you in `PrimitiveP.h`. Also, note the syntax used to include the public header file for the new widget class. If it is to be part of a library, and the header files are to be installed in a public place in a file system, then you need to select a unique prefix for the header files and use the syntax similar to that used for the Motif header files.

There are a number of different private and public header files that the new widget needs. Fortunately, you don't need to include all of them, as this is normally done for you. For example, consider a widget subclassed from Primitive. Its private header file includes `PrimitiveP.h` as described. `PrimitiveP.h` includes a file called `XmP.h`, which includes `IntrinsicP.h`, among others.

`IntrinsicP.h` includes `CoreP.h`, `CompositeP.h`, `ConstrainP.h`[1], and several others. The grid widget described in Chapter 4 is subclassed from

---

1. This is not a typographical error. Constraint class has two header files: `ConstrainP.h` and `Constraint.h`.

XmManager, and XmManager's private header file also includes `XmP.h`. Figure 2-4 shows the relationships between the various private and public header files.

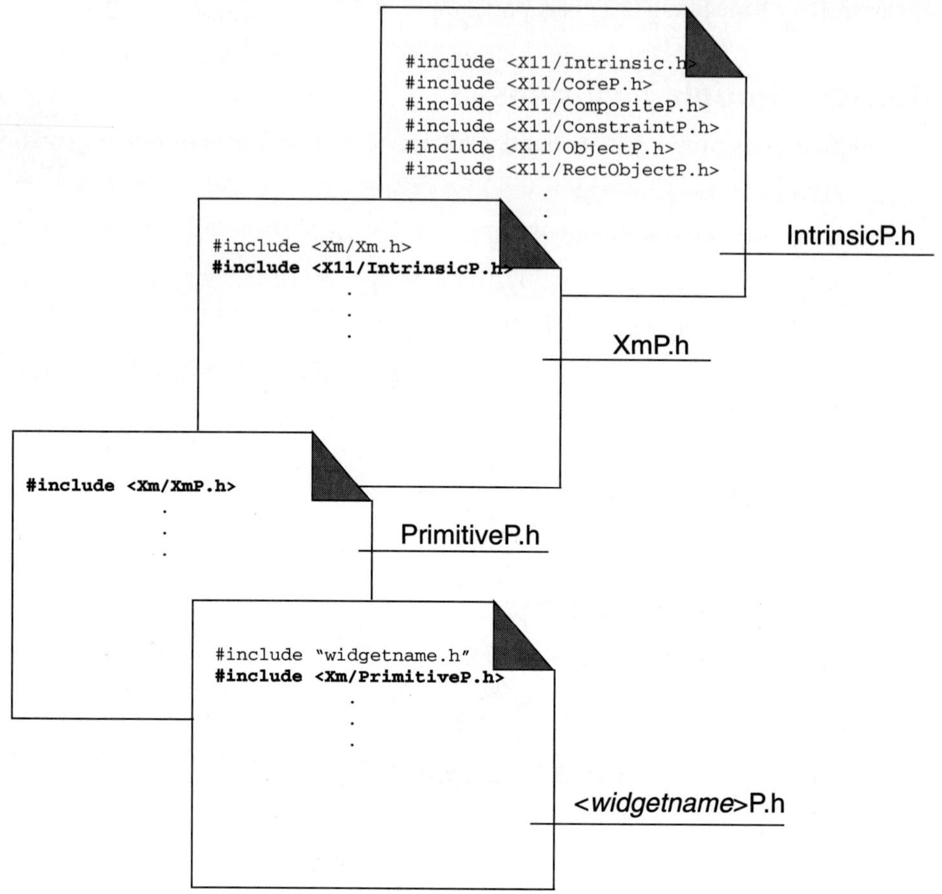

Figure 2-4   Private Header File Relationships

Define the Class Part Structure

Next, define the new widget's class part structure. At the end of this structure is a pointer to an extension record. The extension record is used for future enhancements. If there are class methods, they are included in the class part structure. Here's the class part structure for the knob widget. Note that it defines class methods in addition to the extension record.

```
typedef struct {

    XsmGetDiametersProc get_diameters;      /* procedure to draw inner
```

```
                                                    and outer circles */
    XtWidgetProc        create_segments; /* procedure used to
                                            create the knob
                                            handle line
                                            segments */
    XtWidgetProc        draw_indicator;  /* procedure for drawing
                                            the knob indicator */
    XtTimerCallbackProc turn;            /* timeout procedure used
                                            to turn knob */
    XtWidgetProc        draw;            /* procedure for drawing
                                            the knob */
    XtPointer           extension;       /* pointer to extension
                                            record used for future
                                            expansion */
} XsmKnobClassPart;
```

Define the Class Structure

Next, define the new widget's class structure. For a Primitive widget class, it
consists of the Core class part, the XmPrimitive class part, and the widget class
part:

```
typedef struct _XsmKnobClassRec {
  CoreClassPart          core_class;
  XmPrimitiveClassPart primitive_class;
  XsmKnobClassPart       knob_class;
} XsmKnobClassRec;
```

For a Manager widget class, the class structure consists of the Core class part, the
Composite class part, the Constraint class part, the XmManager class part, and the
widget class part:

```
typedef struct _XsmGridClassRec {
    CoreClassPart          core_class;
    CompositeClassPart     composite_class;
    ConstraintClassPart    constraint_class;
    XmManagerClassPart     manager_class;
    XsmGridClassPart       grid_class;
```

```
} XsmGridClassRec;
```

Define Inheritance Macros

Next, define inheritance macros. You can define an inheritance macro for each
method in the class structure. This characterization allows a subclass to inherit
any method from this class. The subclass has the option of using the inheritance
method or defining its own. Some widgets may not have any class methods and,
therefore, would not have any inheritance macros. The knob widget described in
Chapter 3 defines these inheritance macros:

```
#define XsmInheritGetDiameters ((XsmGetDiametersProc) _XtInherit)

#define XsmInheritCreateSegments ((XtWidgetProc) _XtInherit)

#define XsmInheritDrawIndicator ((XtWidgetProc) _XtInherit)

#define XsmInheritTurn ((XtTimerCallbackProc) _XtInherit)

#define XsmInheritDraw ((XtWidgetProc) _XtInherit)
```

Define the Instance Part Structure

Next, define the new widget's instance part structure. This is the widget's part of
the instance structure, the other parts being Core and either XmPrimitive or the
combination of Composite, Constraint, and XmManager. The widget resource
values are stored in the widget's instance part record. Here's the instance part
structure for the knob widget described in the next chapter:

```
typedef struct _XsmKnobPart {

    XtCallbackList value_changed_callback; /* resource - callback
                                                when value changes */

    int value;                  /* resource - value of the knob */

    int max_val;                /* resource - maximum value allowed */

    int min_val;                /* resource - minimum value allowed */

    int turn_delay;             /* resource - the delay before the next
                                    increment */

    Pixel knob_color;           /* resource - the color of the knob */

    Pixel indicator_color;      /* resource - the color of the
                                    indicator */

    Dimension margin_width;     /* resource - determines the outer
                                    edge of */

    Dimension margin_height;    /* the circle. Whichever value is
```

```
                                greater when the dimension is
                                subtracted from its margin
                                value determines the knob
                                diameter. */
    Dimension knob_margin;      /* resource - The percentage from the
                                   knob's outer edge to draw the inner
                                   circle. */
    Dimension orig_width;       /* saves the original dimension */
    Dimension orig_height;      /* saves the original dimension */
    Boolean move_clockwise;     /* indicates direction of turn */
    Boolean turning;            /* indicates whether turning is in
                                   progress */
    GC gc;                      /* graphics context use in graphic
                                   ops */
    XSegment *segments;         /* the line segments used for drawing
                                   the handle */
    int num_segments;           /* the number of segments in the above
                                   list */
    XtIntervalId timer_id;      /* the timer id of the timeout used in
                                   turning the knob */
    double angle_offset;        /* used to calculate the segment
                                   positions */
} XsmKnobPart;
```

Define the Instance Structure

Next, define the widget's instance structure. For a Primitive widget class such as
knob, this includes the instance parts from Core, XmPrimitive, and knob:

```
typedef struct _XsmKnobRec {
    CorePart            core;
    XmPrimitivePart  primitive;
    XsmKnobPart         knob;
} XsmKnobRec;
```

Notice that within this structure (XsmKnobRec), the field knob (type
XsmKnobPart) references the widget's instance part structure.

For a Manager widget class such as grid, the instance structure includes the instance parts from Core, Composite, Constraint, XmManager, and grid:

```
typedef struct _XsmGridRec {
    CorePart            core;
    CompositePart       composite;
    ConstraintPart      constraint;
    XmManagerPart       manager;
    XsmGridPart         grid;
} XsmGridRec;
```

Create the Public Header File

The public header file (*widgetname*.h) is used by application programmers, and contains the widget class name, resource strings, callback structures, and public function declarations.

Manage Multiple Inclusions

Like the private header file, the first lines manage multiple inclusions:

```
#ifndef _XsmKnobP_h
#define _XsmKnobP_h
```

The associated `#endif` is the last line of the private header file:

```
#endif /* _XsmKnobP_h */
```

This structure prevents multiple definitions when a header file is included more than once.

Include Xm.h

Next, include the Xm.h header file:

```
#include <Xm/Xm.h>
```

This header file has general definitions and inclusions needed by all widgets.

Define Resource Strings

Resource name macros define string values that are used to identify resources and resource classes.

Resource Names

Resource names consist of a special prefix, the letter *N*, and the name of the resource, the first letter of which is always lowercase. The name can include capitalization for word separation, however. Normal convention calls for the name to be the resource name with the first three or four characters of the defined name (XmN or XsmN, for example) dropped. See "Normal Resources" later in this chapter for more information. Here are the resource names for the knob's resources:

```
#define XsmNvalueChangedCallback    "valueChangedCallback"

#define XsmNindicatorColor          "indicatorColor"

#define XsmNmarginWidth             "marginWidth"

#define XsmNmarginHeight            "marginHeight"

#define XsmNknobMargin              "knobMargin"

#define XsmNknobColor               "knobColor"

#define XsmNmaxValue                "maxValue"

#define XsmNminValue                "minValue"

#define XsmNturnDelay               "turnDelay"

#define XsmNvalue                   "value"
```

Resource Class

The resource class name is very similar to the resource name. The class name uses a *C* instead of *N*, and the letter following the *C* is uppercase. Here are the resource class names for the knob's resources:

```
#define XsmCValueChangedCallback    "ValueChangedCallback"

#define XsmCIndicatorColor          "IndicatorColor"

#define XsmCMarginWidth             "MarginWidth"

#define XsmCMarginHeight            "MarginHeight"

#define XsmCKnobMargin              "KnobMargin"

#define XsmCKnobColor               "KnobColor"

#define XsmCMaxValue                "MaxValue"

#define XsmCMinValue                "MinValue"

#define XsmCTurnDelay               "TurnDelay"

#define XsmCValue                   "Value"
```

Define the Widget Class Name

The pointers to the widget instance and class structures in the public header file
are mainly used by applications that wish to have more specific type checking.
Instead of using the generic types Widget and WidgetClass for the widget instance
and class types, the application programmer may want to have a more specific
type for each widget instance and class.

```
externalref WidgetClass    xsmKnobWidgetClass;

   typedef struct _XsmKnobClassRec *XsmKnobWidgetClass;

   typedef struct _XsmKnobRec        *XsmKnobWidget;
```

Define Callback Structures

Next, define the new widget's callback structures:

```
typedef struct

{

   int       reason;

   XEvent   *event;

   int       value;

} XsmKnobCallbackStruct;
```

The variables *reason* and *event* are common to all callback structures, Other
variables, such as *value*, are unique to a specific callback. The number and type
of callback structures and the number of variables within the structures vary with
each widget, but the format is the same as that shown previously.

Define Public Function Declarations

Public functions belong to the widget class but are declared public so application
developers can access them. This assignment allows the application programmer
to interface directly with the widget. All Motif widgets have a "create"
convenience function. Also, many Motif widgets have convenience functions to
retrieve frequently reused resources because XtSetValues is quite involved and
inefficient. Here are the public function declarations for the knob widget
described in Chapter 3:

```
extern Widget XsmCreateKnob(

                    Widget    parent,

                    char     *name,

                    ArgList   arglist,
```

```
                    Cardinal argcount) ;
extern int XsmGetKnobValue(
                    Widget w) ;
extern void XsmSetKnobValue(
                    Widget w,
                    int    value) ;
```

Define New Resources

This occurs within the source module *widgetname*.c. You define resources for
the new widget and set default values for each resource. There are two types of
resources: normal and synthetic.

Normal Resources

The following code segment shows the resource definitions for two of the knob
widget's resources, XsmNturnDelay and XsmNknobColor.

```
static XtResource resources[] =
{
  {

  XsmNturnDelay, XsmCTurnDelay, XmRInt, sizeof(int),

  XtOffset(XsmKnobWidget, knob.turn_delay),

  XmRImmediate, (XtPointer) 50

  },


  {

  XsmNknobColor, XsmCKnobColor, XmRPixel, sizeof (Pixel),

  XtOffset (XsmKnobWidget, knob.knob_color),

  XmRCallProc, (XtPointer) DefaultKnobColor

  },

}
```

Note that *default_type* for XsmNturnDelay is XmRImmediate, meaning that
the value in *default_addr* (50 in this case) is the default value for the resource.
For XsmNknobColor, *default_value* is XsmRCallProc, so the default value is

determined by the procedure `DefaultKnobColor`, as specified in *default_addr*. Here's the listing of this procedure from `Knob.c`:

```c
static void

DefaultKnobColor( Widget g, int offset, XrmValue *value )

{

    XmManagerWidget  mw = (XmManagerWidget) XtParent (g);
    static Pixel     pixel;


    value->addr = (XtPointer) &pixel;
    value->size = sizeof (Pixel);


    /* Work around for bug in _XmBackgroundColorDefault callproc */
    _XmSetDefaultBackgroundColorSpec(XtScreen(g),
                                     XmDEFAULT_BACKGROUND);


    /* Motif callproc to get default color */
    _XmBackgroundColorDefault (g, offset, value);

}
```

Normal resources are defined in a record of type `XtResource`, which is defined in the Xt Intrinsics header file `Intrinsics.h`:

```c
 typedef struct _XtResource {
    String    resource_name;    /* Resource name     */
    String    resource_class;   /* Resource class    */
    String    resource_type;    /* Rep type desired */
    Cardinal  resource_size;    /* Size in bytes of rep */
    Cardinal  resource_offset;  /* Offset from base to put
                                   resource value */
    String    default_type;     /* representation type of
                                   specified default */
    XtPointer default_addr;     /* Addr of default resource */
 }XtResource, *XtResourceList;
```

resource_name — This field is a string that specifies the name of the resource. Macros for resource names consist of a special prefix, the letter *N*, and the name of the resource, the first letter of which is always lowercase. The name includes

The Widget Writing Process

capitalization for word separation, however. The prefix identifies the resource as belonging to a certain library. The Xt Intrinsics resources are identified with an Xt prefix, while Motif uses an Xm prefix. The widgets we create in this book use an Xsm prefix to denote Motif sample widgets. For example, the definition for the knob widget resource `XsmNindicatorColor` is:

```
#define  XsmNindicatorColor "indicatorColor"
```

The Xsm prefix is followed by an *N* and then *indicatorColor* with a lowercase *i* and an uppercase *C* in the word *Color*. Notice the string name is the same as the name following the *N*.

resource_class — This field is a string that specifies the class name of the resource class. Typically, it is similar to the resource name. The major differences are that instead of the uppercase *N* after the prefix, class names use an uppercase *C*. Also, the class name begins with an uppercase letter. Thus, the class name definition for the knob widget's indicator color is

```
#define  XsmCIndicatorColor "IndicatorColor"
```

The resource class name may be the same as other resources having similar functions and the same type. When choosing a class name, consider that users may set all resources with the same class to the same value from the resource environment.

resource_type — This field is a string that identifies the resource type, sometimes referred to as the *representation type*. Resource values from the resource environment always start as string values and some conversion is usually required to express the resource value as the proper type. Motif and the Xt Intrinsics supply a number of converters to accomplish this for the more common resource types. The naming convention for representation types is almost the same as the resource class name, but it uses an *R* after the prefix. Also, the resource type name begins with an uppercase letter. Motif specifies the Pixel resource type as

```
#define  XmRPixel "Pixel"
```

The Motif resource types are listed in Appendix B. If the type you desire is not among the types provided by Motif or the Xt Intrinsics, you need to define your unique type and create a resource converter that converts a string to the type used for the resource.

Motif 1.2 introduced a facility for managing resources with enumerated values. The representation types for these resources can be registered with Motif through the use of `XmRepType` functions, and cause the installation of a built-in converter for each of the registered representation types. In the resource initialization, the *resource_type* field specifies the name of the representation type. This name is used when registering the converter used to convert a string to the appropriate enumerated value.

Converters are registered in the `ClassInitialize()` class procedure (described later in this chapter). To register a resource converter that is an enumerated type you need to do the following:

1. Create a static list of strings that identify the valid strings setting for the resource.

   ```
   static char *HorizontalAlignmentNames[] =

                   {"align_center","align_left", "align_right"};
   ```

2. Create a NUM_NAMES() macro to determine the size of the resource list:

   ```
   #define NUM_NAMES(list)         (sizeof(list)/sizeof(char *))
   ```

3. In the `ClassInitialize()` procedure, call `XmRepTypeRegister()` passing to it the resource representation name, the list of strings specified previously, the list of values, and the number of values already specified. Here's an example from `ClassInitialize` in `Grid.c`:

   ```
   XmRepTypeRegister( XsmRHorizontalAlignment,

                   HorizontalAlignmentNames, NULL,

                   NUM_NAMES(HorizontalAlignmentNames));
   ```

If NULL is specified in the list of values, `XmRepTypeRegister( )` assumes the values are consecutive and begins at zero.

If a resource converter other than one for enumerated types is required, use the `XtSetTypeConverter( )` function to register the converter. See an Xt Intrinsics manual for information on this type of converter.

resource_size — This field specifies the size of the resource type in bytes. Use the `sizeof( )` function to determine the byte size. For example, the resource defined as type Pixel should be specified in this field as

`sizeof(Pixel)`

resource_offset — This field is an offset into the widget's instance structure. Use the `XtOffsetOf` macro to get the offset value. In Motif, the offset for the Xm-Primitive resource `highlightColor` is

`XtOffsetOf(XmPrimitiveRec, primitive.highlight_color)`

default_type — Any of the representation types listed in Appendix B are valid for this field; however, you would normally use one of these two types:

- `XmRImmediate` means that the value in the next field (*default_addr*) is the actual value to be used as the default value of the resource, and thus no conversion is required.

- `XmRCallProc` means that the value in the next field (*default_addr*) is a procedure pointer that is used to determine the default value of the resource.

default_addr — This field contains either the default value for the resource or a pointer to a procedure that is used to determine the default value (see previous discussion of *default_type*). If the default type is `XmRCallProc`, the procedure is defined as follows:

```
typedef void (*XtResourceDefaultProc)(Widget, int, XrmValue *);
    Widget     widget;
    int        offset;
    XrmValue *value;
```

`Knob.c` and `KnobG.c` both use this type of procedure for the default knob color (`DefaultKnobColor`).

Synthetic Resources

Motif includes support for the so-called synthetic resources, which allow for preprocessing resources prior to initialize, set values, and get values routines. It is used primarily to convert resolution-independent resources for a unit type of dimensions and positions other than pixel into pixel (the commonly used dimension) for use with X.   The Motif superclass widgets XmGadget, XmManager, and XmPrimitive each have a resource called `XmNunitType`, which provides the basic support for resolution independence.   It is used when converting values such as fractions of inches, millimeters, and font units into pixels for use as the internal representation. The following code segment shows the resource definitions for the knob widget's two synthetic resources, `XsmNmarginWidth` and `XsmNmarginHeight`.

```
static XmSyntheticResource syn_resources[] = {
    {
        XsmNmarginWidth,
        sizeof (Dimension),
        XtOffset( XsmKnobWidget, knob.margin_width),
        _XmFromHorizontalPixels,
        _XmToHorizontalPixels
    },

    {
```

```
            XsmNmarginHeight,

            sizeof (Dimension),

            XtOffset( XsmKnobWidget, knob.margin_height),

            _XmFromVerticalPixels,

            _XmToVerticalPixels
        }
    };
```

The structure used for the synthetic resources is defined as follows:

```
typedef struct _XmSyntheticResource

{
    String        resource_name;
    Cardinal      resource_size;
    Cardinal      resource_offset;
    XmExportProc export_proc;
    XmImportProc import_proc;
} XmSyntheticResource;
```

resource_name — This field specifies a resource previously declared in the *resource_name* field in the Core XtResource structure. Each synthetic resource must also be defined in the list of resources in the Core class field. Use the same name defined in the normal resources list.

resource_size — This field matches the size defined in the size field resource list. Typically, `sizeof( )` is used directly in this field to calculate the size.

resource_offset — This field matches the offset field defined in the offset field resource list. Use the `XtOffsetOf( )` macro to locate the offset into the instance record.

export_proc — This field holds the pointer to the procedure that converts the resource values for external consumption. In the case of resolution-independent resources, it converts internal pixels to the unit type specified in the `XmNunitType` resource. Export procedures are also used to copy data from internal string buffers of resources. Widgets use internal buffers to prevent direct exposure of the buffer to the application, in turn preventing possible corruption. The procedure specified in *export_proc* is used to provide the contents of the internal buffer to the application.

import_proc — This field holds the pointer to the function that is called when a resource is being set by the application. In the case of resolution independence, it converts a particular unit type to the Pixel type.

Define the Action Table

The *action table* defines the set of actions and maps action names to functions for the new widget. Actions are referenced in translation tables to map events to procedures. For example, a pushbutton has an "Arm" action that is mapped to a procedure that changes the color and appearance of the button. The action table has a string that maps the action to a procedure. In Motif, widgets have action tables, but gadgets do not. For this reason, the manager widgets must provide the action tables for their gadget children.

Here's a typical action table:

```
static XtActionsRec example_actions[] = {
    {"Arm",          ArmProc},
    {"Select",       SelectProc},
    {"SelectAll",    SelectAllProc},
    {"Release",      ReleaseProc},
    {"ReleaseAll",   ReleaseAllProc},
    {"Move",         MoveProc},
};
```

The table is an array of static structures. The structure itself is defined by the Xt Intrinsics in `Intrinsic.h`:

```
typedef struct _XtActionsRec *XtActionList;
typedef struct _XtActionsRec {
    String        string;
    XtActionProc proc;
} XtActionsRec;
```

string — The string used in the translation table to map to the procedure.

proc — The action procedure called when the event to which it is mapped occurs.

The `typedef` for the procedure defined in the action table is defined in `Intrinsic.h`:

```
typedef void (*XtActionProc)( Widget, XEvent *,
                 String *, Cardinal *);
  Widget       widget;
  XEvent       *event;
  String       *params;
  Cardinal     *num_params;
```

widget — The widget in which the event that triggered the action occurred.

event — The event that triggered the action.

params — The list of strings that contains the argument list.

num_params — The number of strings in *params*.

Here's an example of an actions procedure called `Select()`:

```
static void Select(Widget w, XEvent *event, String *params,
                 Cardinal *num_params)
{

    XsmExampleWidget exmpl = (XsmExampleWidget) widget;


   /* toggle selected state */
   if (exmpl->example.selected) {
      exmpl->example.selected = False;
      (*(((XmPrimitiveWidgetClass) XtClass(widget))
        ->primitive_class.border_unhighlight))(widget) ;
   } else {
      exmpl->example.selected = True;
      (*(((XmPrimitiveWidgetClass) XtClass(widget))
        ->primitive_class.border_highlight))(widget) ;
   }

}
```

Try to keep the action names short to save space, but at the same time keep the names readable for code maintenance.

Define the Translation Table

The *translation table* maps mouse and keyboard events to the actions defined in the action table. In Motif, widgets have translation tables, but gadgets do not. For this reason, manager widgets must provide the translation tables for their gadget children.

Here's an example of a translation table from `Knob.c`:

```
char defaultTranslations[] = "\
<Key>greater:    toggle-left()\n\
<Key>less:       toggle-right()\n\
<Key>:           release-knob()\n\
<Btn1Down>:      turn-left()\n\
<Btn3Down>:      turn-right()\n\
<Btn1Up>:        release-knob()\n\
<Btn3Up>:        release-knob()\n\
<FocusIn>:       Focus-in()\n\
<FocusOut>:      Focus-out()\n\
<EnterWindow>: enter()\n\
<LeaveWindow>: leave()";
```

The order of translation tables is important. The table is read from top to bottom. If there is a match with a translation higher in the table, the higher translation's action is called. Translations are separated by a newline character; a line continuation character (\) is needed to break the string constant into several lines for readability.

Relationship to the Action Table

Before we explain the translation table in detail, let's look at the relationship between the translation table and the action table described in the previous section. Figure 2-5 shows the relationship between the action and translation tables.

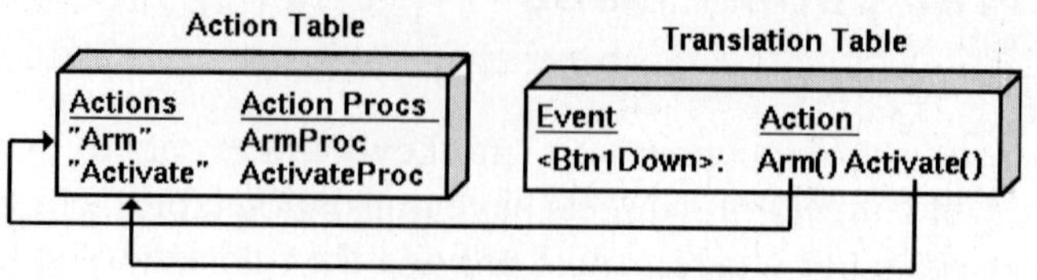

Figure 2-5   Action and Translation Table Relationships

Here, the action names are "Arm" and "Activate" and the corresponding action procedures are `ArmProc` and `ActivateProc`. The translation table shows that the event `<Btn1Down>` maps to the action names "Arm" and "Activate". The actions in the translation table are followed by a set of parentheses because they could have parameters.

Translation Table Parts

The translation table is a continuous string with each translation separated into three parts:

- Modifier

- Event

- Action name

Modifier

The modifier identifies the modifier keys that can be used in conjunction with the action. Motif uses four modifier keys:

- Ctrl

- Shift

- Meta

- Alt

The term *Meta* denotes a special modifier key. The actual key varies depending on the system you are using. Meta and Alt are treated in Motif as being semantically equivalent; translations should be written such that the use of either yields the same result. You can use the abbreviations c, s, m, and a, respectively, instead of the entire key name. For example, here's a line with the Shift modifier used:

```
s <Btn1Down>: Select()
```

This indicates that the Shift key must be pressed with the mouse button 1 press to call the Select action. Remember that the `Select( )` action maps to the action name, not the procedure name.

In addition to the modifiers, there is a syntax you can use to identify whether to require a modifier, preclude a modifier, or accept it whether it is used or not.

- If a tilde (~) precedes a modifier, it indicates that this action is *not* to be called when the modifier is pressed.

  ```
  ~s <Btn1Down>: Select()
  ```

  This translation indicates that the Select action is called only when mouse button 1 is pressed *without* the shift modifier.

- If an exclamation point (!) precedes the translation, it indicates that the action is to be called only when all the modifiers following the exclamation point are pressed.

  ```
  !s c <Btn1Down>: Select()
  ```

  This translation indicates that the Select action is called only when mouse button 1 is pressed with the Shift and Ctrl modifiers.

- If a colon (:) precedes the translation, it means that the case on the translation is evaluated.

  ```
  <Key> a: InsertA() \n\
  ```

  ```
  <Key> A: InsertCapitalA() \n\
  ```

  In this case only `InsertA` is called. With the use of the colon, the state of standard modifiers (such as Shift) is implicitly specified by the keysym in the translation:

  ```
  :<Key> a: InsertA() \n\
  ```

  ```
  :<Key> A: InsertCapitalA() \n\
  ```

  This example calls each translation based on the case, which depends on the state of the Shift modifier. Notice that even though Shift is not specified in the translation, its required state is implicitly specified and is not a "don't care" modifier.

- If the keyword Any is used, or no modifier is specified, any or all modifiers can be used with the translation.

  ```
  Any <Key>: InsertChar()
  ```

  is the same as

  ```
  <Key>: InsertChar()
  ```

which accepts all modifiers with the keypress. Only when the keyword None is used are the modifiers prevented from being used with this translation.

```
None <Key>: InsertChar()
```

Only a keypress without modifiers calls the `InsertChar` action.

- If a modifier is not specified, that modifier is accepted whether it is used or not ("don't care"). In the following example,

```
s <Btn1Down>: Select()
```

is essentially the same as

```
!s <Btn1Down>: Select()

!s c <Btn1Down>: Select()

!s m <Btn1Down>: Select()

!s a <Btn1Down>: Select()

!s c m <Btn1Down>: Select()

!s c a <Btn1Down>: Select()

!s c m a <Btn1Down>: Select()
```

- If you want the translation to require the Shift key to be the only modifier, either of the following is valid:

```
s ~c ~m ~a <Btn1Down>: Select()

!s <Btn1Down>: Select()
```

- If a less specific translation precedes a more specific translation, the less specific translation is called. For example,

```
s <Btn1Down>: Select()

s c <Btn1Down>: Select2()
```

The action `Select2()` is never called because a `<Btn1Down>` event with both Shift and Ctrl will always match the `Select( )` action; Shift and any other modifier that goes with it is less specific.

There are several possible solutions:

The easiest is to place the more specific translation first:

```
s c <Btn1Down>: Select2()

s <Btn1Down>: Select()
```

Or, you could use explicit translations:

```
s ~c <Btn1Down>: Select()

s c <Btn1Down>: Select2()
```

Event

An event can be the event name or a synonym for the event followed by a colon
(:). As a general rule, use the shortest possible synonyms whenever possible. Table 2-1 shows events and some corresponding alternate events.

Table 2-1 Events and Definitions

Event	Alt. Event
<KeyPress>	<Key>
	<KeyDown>
<KeyRelease>	<KeyUp>
<ButtonPress>	<BtnDown>
	<Btn1Down>
	<Btn2Down>
	<Btn3Down>
	<Btn4Down>
	<Btn5Down>
<ButtonRelease>	<BtnUp>
	<Btn1Up>
	<Btn2Up>
	<Btn3Up>
	<Btn4Up>
	<Btn5Up>
<MotionNotify>	<PtrMoved>
	<Motion>
	<MouseMoved>
Button<PtrMoved>	<BtnMotion>
	<Btn1Motion>
	<Btn2Motion>
	<Btn3Motion>
	<Btn4Motion>
	<Btn5Motion>
<EnterNotify>	<Enter>
	<EnterWindow>
<LeaveNotify>	<LeaveWindow>
	<Leave>
<FocusIn>	

Event	Alt. Event
<FocusOut>	
<KeymapNotify>	<Keymap>
<Expose>	
<GraphicsExpose>	<GrExp>
<NoExpose>	<NoExp>
<VisibilityNotify>	<Visible>
<CreateNotify>	<Create>
<DestroyNotify>	<Destroy>
<UnmapNotify>	<Unmap>
<MapRequest>	<MapReq>
<ReparentNotify>	<Reparent>
<ConfigureNotify>	<Configure>
<ConfigureRequest>	<ConfigReq>
<GravityNotify>	<Grav>
<ResizeRequest>	<ResReq>
<CirculateNotify>	<Circ>
<CirculateRequest>	<CircReq>
<PropertyNotify>	<Prop>
<SelectionClear>	<SelClr>
<SelectionRequest>	<SelReq>
<SelectionNotify>	<Select>
<ColormapNotify>	<Clrmap>
<ClientMessage>	<Message>
<MappingNotify>	<Mapping>

Key events are generally qualified by a particular keysym. In addition to the standard X keysyms, Motif has some specific keysyms for virtual keys. The mapping of these virtual keys may be different on different machines and can be altered by the user (see the *OSF/Motif Programmer's Reference*). With virtual keys, you can move the translations from system to system without concern for the differences in keyboards.

Table 2-2 shows the Motif keysyms and their default bindings.

Table 2-2 OSF Keysym Bindings

Virtual Key	Binding
osfCancel	<Key>Escape
osfLeft	<Key>Left
osfUp	<Key>Up
osfRight	<Key>Right
osfDown	<Key>Down
osfEndLine	<Key>End
osfBeginLine	<Key>Home
osfPageUp	<Key>Prior
osfPageDown	<Key>Next
osfBackSpace	<Key>BackSpace
osfDelete	<Key>Delete
osfInsert	<Key>Insert
osfAddMode	Shift<Key>F8
osfHelp	<key>F1
osfMenu	Shift<Key>F10
osfMenuBar	<Key>F10
osfSelect	<key>Select
osfActivate	<Key>KP_Enter
osfClear	<Key>Clear
osfUndo	<Key>Undo

Different vendors may have slight modifications to these bindings to tailor the OSF keysyms to the keyboard for the specific machine.

Action Name

The action name is the string value defined in the action table. The string value is always followed by a set of parentheses ( ). Don't confuse the action name with the procedure name.

For performance reasons, it is best to limit the number of spaces and characters in the translations. Use abbreviations for the modifiers whenever possible, because this will save time in parsing as well as static data space.

Initializing the Widget Class Record

The widget class record consists of the Core class part, a base class part (either XmManager, XmPrimitive, or XmGadget), and the new widget's class part.

Core Class Part

The Core class part is the heart of the widget class record. All widgets, regardless of their class, have a Core class part. All widgets of a given class have the same values for the Core class part fields, and may also have additional common fields.

The fields that are part of the subclass, as opposed to the fields that are part of the superclass, are called subclass fields. Many procedures are responsible only for the subclass fields and not for any superclass fields. The following listing is the Xt Intrinsics definition of a Core class part.

```
typedef struct _CoreClassPart {
    WidgetClass         superclass;         /* pointer to superclass
                                               ClassRec */
    String              class_name;         /* widget resource class
                                               name */
    Cardinal            widget_size;        /* size in bytes of widget
                                               record */
    XtProc              class_initialize;   /* class initialization
                                               proc */
    XtWidgetClassProc class_part_initialize; /* dynamic
                                               initialization */
    XtEnum              class_inited;       /* has class been
                                               initialized? */
    XtInitProc          initialize;         /* initialize subclass
                                               fields */
    XtArgsProc          initialize_hook;    /* notify that initialize
                                               called */
    XtRealizeProc       realize;            /* XCreateWindow for
                                               widget */
```

```c
    XtActionList      actions;              /* widget semantics name
                                               to proc map */
    Cardinal          num_actions;          /* number of entries in
                                               actions */
    XtResourceList    resources;            /* resources for subclass
                                               fields */
    Cardinal          num_resources;        /* number of entries in
                                               resources */
    XrmClass          xrm_class;            /* resource class
                                               quarkified */
    Boolean           compress_motion;      /* compress MotionNotify
                                               for widget */
    XtEnum            compress_exposure;    /* compress Expose events
                                               for widget*/
    Boolean           compress_enterleave;  /* compress enter and
                                               leave events */
    Boolean           visible_interest;     /* select for
                                               VisibilityNotify */
    XtWidgetProc      destroy;              /* free data for subclass
                                               pointers */
    XtWidgetProc      resize;               /* geom manager changed
                                               widget size */
    XtExposeProc      expose;               /* redisplay window */
    XtSetValuesFunc   set_values;           /* set subclass resource
                                               values */
    XtArgsFunc        set_values_hook;      /* notify that set_values
                                               is called */
    XtAlmostProc      set_values_almost;    /* set_values got
                                               Almost geometry reply */
    XtArgsProc        get_values_hook;      /* notify that get_values
                                               is called */
    XtVersionType     version;              /* version of intrinsics
```

```c
                                                   used */
    XtPointer              callback_private;      /* list of callback
                                                      offsets */
    String                 tm_table;              /* state machine   */
    XtGeometryHandler query_geometry;             /* return preferred
                                                      geometry */
    XtStringProc           display_accelerator;   /* display your
                                                      accelerator */
    XtPointer              extension;             /* pointer to extension
                                                      record */
} CoreClassPart;


typedef struct _WidgetClassRec {
    CoreClassPart core_class;
} WidgetClassRec, CoreClassRec;
```

We'll explain each of the fields in the Core class part in the following sections.

superclass Field

The superclass *field* is a pointer to the superclass record. The superclass is the class from which you are subclassing the new widget. Depending on the superclass you choose, the value of this field is normally one of these possibilities:

- `&XmManagerClassRec`
- `&xmPrimitiveClassRec`
- `&xmGadgetClassRec`

The value should be cast to `(WidgetClass)`.

class_name Field

The value of the *class_name* field is an ASCII string that describes the new widget class. Convention calls for it to be in the form *<library prefix><type>*. For example, Motif has `XmText` or `XmLabel`. Motif gadgets add the word Gadget at the end. For example, `XmSeparatorGadget` and `XmPushButtonGadget` are appropriate class names.

widget_size Field

The *widget_size* field specifies the size of the widget's instance record. Use the C expression

```
sizeof(XsmKnobRec)
```

to set the size.

class_initialize Field

The *class_initialize* field is a pointer to a method that is called the first time a widget of this class is initialized.   Any method or procedure that cannot be statically initialized or is registering a new resource-type converter requires a unique class initialize method. The syntax of this method is defined by the Xt Intrinsics:

```
typedef void (*XtProc) (void);
```

In Motif this method is used to create additional translation tables for later use. It is also used to merge translation tables that are too large to be compiled on some systems because of string length limitations and to add additional initialization of class extension records. For example, there is a field in the Core extension record called *record_type* that is initialized to XmQmotif.

If you create a Core class extension record using the Motif extension record structure, be sure to set the *record_type* of that structure here and set it to XmQmotif.

Here's an example of a class initialize method:

```
static void ClassInitialize( void )
{
char * event_bindings;

   event_bindings = (char *)XtMalloc(strlen(EventBindings1) +
      strlen(EventBindings2) + 1);
   strcpy(event_bindings, EventBindings1);
   strcat(event_bindings, EventBindings2);


   xmSExampleClassRec.core_class.tm_table = event_bindings;


   ExampleClassExtRec.record_type = XmQmotif;
}
```

class_part_initialize Field

The *class_part_initialize* field is a pointer to a method that is called when the first widget of this class or any subclass is initialized.

If there is a need to initialize a class field on a subclass-by-subclass basis, it should be done by this method. The syntax for this method is defined by the Xt Intrinsics:

```
typedef void (*XtWidgetClassProc) (WidgetClass)
    WidgetClass class;
```

class — The widget class that is being initialized.

Motif initializes some of its extension record data for baseline alignment and widget display records in this method.

This field in the class structure is set to NULL, unless you have fields in your class record that may need additional processing. For example, if you have procedure pointers with inheritance macros, you need to reassign the procedure pointers in this method. Here's the knob's `ClassPartInitialize` method:

```
static void ClassPartInitialize(WidgetClass wc)
{

    XsmKnobWidgetClass kc = (XsmKnobWidgetClass) wc;
    XsmKnobWidgetClass sc = (XsmKnobWidgetClass)
                                        wc->core_class.superclass;


/* assign procedures to the classes pointers that inherit these
    procedures */


    if (kc->knob_class.get_diameters == XsmInheritGetDiameters)
        kc->knob_class.get_diameters = sc->knob_class.get_diameters;


    if (kc->knob_class.create_segments == XsmInheritCreateSegments)
        kc->knob_class.create_segments =
            sc->knob_class.create_segments;


    if (kc->knob_class.draw_indicator == XsmInheritDrawIndicator)
        kc->knob_class.draw_indicator =
                sc->knob_class.draw_indicator;
```

```
if (kc->knob_class.turn == XsmInheritTurn)
    kc->knob_class.turn = sc->knob_class.turn;


if (kc->knob_class.draw == XsmInheritDraw)
    kc->knob_class.draw = sc->knob_class.draw;


}
```

class_inited Field

The *class_inited* field is an internal Xt Intrinsics flag that you should always initialize to False.

initialize Field

The *initialize* field specifies a method that initializes the widget's internal instance record fields; the internal fields are those fields in the instance structure that are *not* resource fields. This method also checks resource values set by the application for validity. If any values are invalid, the value of the new widget's instance field needs to be modified to a valid state, and a warning may be issued. Only the values changed in the `new_w` widget are retained.

The type of the method specified in this field is

```
typedef void (*XtInitProc) (Widget, Widget, ArgList, Cardinal*)
    Widget      request;
    Widget      new_w;
    ArgList     args;
    Cardinal * num_args;
```

request — Specifies the widget instance that was requested by the application prior to entering into the superclasses initialize methods. Any changes to this copy of the instance record are lost. Widget methods should never alter this record.

new_w — Specifies the current widget instance that may have been altered by superclass methods in superclass-to-subclass order. Any changes to the widget instance fields must be made to this widget record.

args — Specifies the argument list passed in an application's call to `XtCreateWidget()`.

---

num_args — Specifies the argument count passed in an application's call to `XtCreateWidget()`.

Motif widgets initialize graphics contexts (GC) for graphics and text drawing in the initialize method. They also verify all widget resources and initialize any internal instance fields in the procedure. Motif widgets check to see if the requested width and height of the widget is not equal to zero to see if the dimensions were not set by the application. If they weren't set, then the widget calculates a reasonable default dimension in the procedure. Note that the new widget contains a value set by the superclass widget's initialize method.

You should include these calculations when you reset the default height and width values. Motif adds shadow thickness and highlight thickness to the widget's height and width fields.

All subclass resources (those added by this widget class) should be checked for valid values.

Here's an example of an initialize method:

```
static void Initialize(Widget request, Widget new_w,
                       ArgList args, Cardinal *num_args )
{

  XsmExampleWidget req_ew = (XsmExampleWidget) request;

  XsmExampleWidget new_ew = (XsmExampleWidget) new_w;

  XGCValues values;

  unsigned long valuemask;

  Dimension st, ht;


/* verify valid values for resources */
  if (new_ew->example.resource1 <= 0) {

    XtWarning("Resource is must be greater than 0, Defaulting
             to 1");

    new_ew->example.resource1 = 1;

  }


  if (new_ew->example.resource2 > new_ew->example.resource1)
  {

    XtWarning("Resource 2 is must be less than resource 1");

    new_ew->example.resource2 = 0;
```

```
}

    st = new_ew->primitive.shadow_thickness;
    ht = new_ew->primitive.highlight_thickness;


/* verify requested height and width */
    if (req_ew->core.width == 0)
        new_ew->core.width = 100 + st + ht;
    if (req_ew->core.height == 0)
        new_ew->core.height = 100 + st + ht;


/* initialize fields */
    new_ew->example.flag1 = True;
    new_ew->example.flag2 = False;
    new_ew->example.timer_id = NULL;
    new_ew->example.count = 0;


/* Create Graphic Contexts */
    valuemask = (GCForeground | GCBackground);
    values.foreground = new_ew->primitive.foreground;
    values.background = new_ew->example.background;
    new_ew->example.gc = XCreateC(new_w, valuemask, &values);

}
```

initialize_hook Field

The *initialize_hook* field specifies a method that was used for passing the
argument list and argument count prior to the addition of these parameters in the
Initialize procedure in X11 Release 4. This method has been retained for
backward compatibility.

realize Field

The *realize* field specifies a method that creates the window for the widget. The
method is not chained.[1] This method is nearly always inherited from its parent's

---

1. A chained method is a method that exists in both superclasses and widget classes, and when one
is called, they all are called in sequence.

realize method using `XtInheritRealize`. You should never set this field to NULL in the class record initialization. Doing so will cause a fatal abort.

Here's the syntax for the Realize method:

```
typedef void (*XtRealizeProc) (Widget, XtValueMask *,
XSetWindowAttributes *)
    Widget                  widget;
    XtValueMask             *mask;
    XSetWindowAttributes    *attributes;
```

widget — The widget instance that is being realized.

mask — The mask indicating which fields are valid in the attributes structure.

attributes — The window attributes set by the Xt Intrinsics, to be passed to `XtCreateWindow()`.

Unless you need to have specialized X window attributes for this widget, set this field in `XtInheritRealize`.

actions Field

The *actions* field identifies the name of the action table to be used for the new widget. See "Define the Action Table" earlier in this chapter for detailed information on the action table. In `Knob.c`, the *actions* field of the Core class record is `knob_actions`, the name of the action table in `Knob.c`. Here's how it's defined:

```
static XtActionsRec knob_actions[] = {
    {"turn-left",      TurnLeft},
    {"turn-right",     TurnRight},
    {"toggle-left",    ToggleLeft},
    {"toggle-right",   ToggleRight},
    {"release-knob",   ReleaseKnob},
};
```

num_actions Field

Th *num_actions* field specifies the number of actions in the action table. Use `XtNumber` on the action table specified in the actions field. This results in the number of actions in the action table:

```
XtNumber(knob_actions)
```

resources Field

The *resources* field specifies the list of the new widget's resources that modify the look and behavior of the widget. See "Define New Resources" earlier in this chapter for detailed information. In `Knob.c`, this field is `resources`, which is the name of the knob's resource list. Here's a part of the knob's resource list from `Knob.c`:

```
static XtResource resources[] = {

 {

  XsmNvalueChangedCallback, XmCCallback, XmRCallback,

  sizeof(XtCallbackList),

  XtOffset (XsmKnobWidget, knob.value_changed_callback),

  XmRImmediate, NULL

  },
```

num_resources Field

The *num_resources* field specifies the number of resources in the resource list. Use `XtNumber` on the resource list. This results in the number of resources in the resource list:

```
XtNumber(resources)
```

xrm_class Field

The *xrm_class* field is another internal Xt Intrinsics flag. Always initialize it to `NULLQUARK`.

compress_motion Field

In *motion compression*, the Xt Intrinsics checks the event queue for motion events that involve the widget's window. If there is a match, widgets with compression turned on discard all motion events up to the most current event resulting in faster response to motion events. Widgets typically do turn on motion compression unless they need the intervening motion events to do drawing. You normally set this field to True, unless your new widget is a gadget or a widget that performs interactive drawing. Widgets should compress events as much as possible, unless there is a need to set all the events that are in the queue.

compress_exposure Field

Exposure compression is very similar to motion compression, in that a series of expose events intended for a widget is compressed into a single event. The X server generates an expose event for each rectangle of a widget that becomes

<hr>

exposed. Compression combines all the rectangles into an exposed region and sends one expose event to the widget.

There are several levels of compression. Setting the *compress_exposure* field to `XtExposeNoCompress` causes the Xt Intrinsics to send each expose event as it is received and set the *region* field to `NULL`. This results in slow redisplays and flashing because the widget must respond to each event. This is not recommended unless constant updating is required.

`XtExposeCompressSeries` looks at the count field of the event to determine a series of exposures. When the count field is zero, it marks an end of a series of expose events. The Xt Intrinsics combines this series into one expose event.

`XtExposeCompressMultiple` looks at the queue of events and, if there are several series of expose events together without another type of event in between, all the series of expose events are compressed to form one event to be sent.

`XtExposeCompressMaximal` takes it one step further. It looks in the entire event queue and compresses all expose events, regardless of whether there are any intervening nonexpose events between expose events. Motif uses this type of compression most often because it is the most efficient and reduces many unnecessary expose events. This is especially important if the widget does extensive redisplay during expose events.

There are instances where a widget needs to handle GraphicsExpose and NoExpose events. This is the case where an attempt to use `XCopyPlane` or `XCopyArea` from an area that is not available. The widget may need to fill these areas. To enable the sending of these events, the following values are OR'd into the *compress_exposure* field:

- `XtExposeGraphicsExpose` — Used for graphics expose events. The compression for these events will match the expose compression setting.

- `XtExposeGraphicsExposeMerged` — Combines graphics exposure and regular expose events. It is valid to use this event only when `XtExposeCompressMultiple` or `XtExposeCompressMaximal` are set. The event type is determined by the final expose event processed.

- `XtExposeNoExpose` — Causes NoExpose events to be delivered to the expose procedure. NoExpose events are never combined with other expose events.

Prior to X11 R4, *compress_exposure* was a Boolean field. Some of the Motif widgets set this field to True or False. This practice is still valid for backward compatibility. True maps to `XtExposeCompressSeries` and False to

                                                                                       The Widget Writing Process

`XtExposeNoCompress`. Under R4 and subsequent releases, it has the following possible values:

- `XtExposeNoCompress` - Performs no exposure compression.
- `XtExposeCompressSeries` - Compresses expose events from a single exposure.
- `XtExposeCompressMultiple` - Compresses all adjacent series of expose events in the event queue.
- `XtExposeCompressMaximal` - Compresses all expose events in the event queue. This value blocks the event queue during processing.

Most widgets use `XtExposeCompressMaximal`, and gadgets use `XtExposeNoCompress`.

compress_enterleave Field

In *enter/leave compression*, the Xt Intrinsics checks the event queue for a leave event after it detects an enter event. If it finds a leave event, it discards both events. Because Motif widgets perform focus handling and traversal highlighting, *compress_enterleave* is typically turned on to reduce highlight flashing. Therefore, set it to True, except for manager widgets that may contain a gadget child.

visible_interest Field

When the *visible_interest* field is True, the *visible_interest* field in the Core part of the instance structure is updated, indicating whether the widget is visible or not. This requires extra processing by having the Xt Intrinsics look for `VisibilityNotify` events from the X server. All Motif widgets currently set this field to False.

destroy Field

The *destroy* field specifies the destroy method used for freeing data allocated by the widget. Examples of allocated data include pixmaps, graphics contexts, internal buffers, data in XmString format, and fontlists. Also, timeouts, event handlers, and callbacks on other widgets should be removed here.

The type of the destroy method is defined by the Xt Intrinsics:

```
typedef void (*XtWidgetProc) (Widget)

    Widget widget;
```

widget — The widget instance that is being destroyed.

Examine the instance structure and verify that anything that is created with a `malloc` during initialization or operation of this widget is freed here.

Here's an example of a destroy method

```c
static void Destroy( Widget w )
{

    XsmKnobWidget kw = (XsmKnobWidget) w;


    /* Free graphics contexts */
    XtReleaseGC( w, kw->knob.gc);


    /* Free allocated data */
    XtFree((char *) kw->knob.segments);


    /* Remove any outstanding timeouts */
    if (kw->knob.timer_id) XtRemoveTimeOut(kw->knob.timer_id);


    /* Remove all callbacks */
    XtRemoveAllCallbacks (w, XsmNvalueChangedCallback);

}
```

resize Field

The *resize* field specifies a resize method called when a widget has been reconfigured to change its height or width. Widgets that have dimension-based information (such as a line count for scrolling) or that want to redraw themselves
dynamically in a different form or scale upon a change in size need to have a resize method.

The type of the resize method is defined by the Xt Intrinsics:

```c
typedef void (*XtWidgetProc) (Widget)
    Widget widget;
```

widget — The widget instance that is being resized.

Here are some examples of how Motif widgets use the resize method:

- Scrolled text and scrolled list use it to recalculate their line information and
  adjust their scrollbars appropriately.

- Scrollbar uses it to expand its sliders and arrows.

- Label uses it to reposition labels.

- Manager widgets use it to reorganize the size and locations of their children to

　　　　　　　　　　　　　　The Widget Writing Process

reflect a new size.

If you don't have any size-dependent visuals, you initialize this method to NULL in the class record definition. If you have size-dependent information, you need to have a resize method to recalculate that information. You do not need to call your expose method from the resize method, as this is done for you automatically.

It is very important that you do not make geometry requests from this method (or any functions or procedures called from this method, including calls to `XtGetValues` and `XtSetValues`). Doing so could result in an infinite geometry loop.

Here's an example of a resize method:

```
static void Resize( Widget w )
{
    XsmKnobWidgetClass kc = (XsmKnobWidgetClass) XtClass(w);


    /* Recreate any segments based on the new size */
    (*kc->knob_class.create_segments)(w);
}
```

expose Field

The *expose* field specifies the expose method, one of the most important methods in the widget. The expose method performs the drawing (or redrawing) of the widget visuals. It can be the key to how well the widget performs. It is called when an expose event on the widget occurs, when any of the `SetValues` methods of the class return True, and when a widget has been resized. It is usually named `Redisplay`, because naming it `expose` would conflict with an X event called Expose.

The type of the expose method is defined by the Xt Intrinsics:

```
typedef void (*XtExposeProc) (Widget, XEvent *, Region)
    Widget    widget;
    XEvent * event;
    Region    region;
```

widget — The widget instance that is to be redrawn.

event — The X event that generated the expose.

region — The region that has been exposed.

The expose method is passed a region that indicates the location of the expose event. Although many Motif widgets ignore the region information, it is more efficient to redraw only in the regions that were exposed, unless the calculations to do so would take more time than to redraw the whole widget.

As a first pass to see your visuals, redraw everything in this method, and then refine it to be more efficient about regions. In this way you can verify that you are getting the appropriate visuals.

Here's the knob widget's expose method. Note that it is named `Redisplay`, to avoid conflict with the X event named Expose.

```c
static void Redisplay( Widget w, XEvent *event, Region region)
{
    XsmKnobWidget kw = (XsmKnobWidget) w;
    XsmKnobWidgetClass kc = (XsmKnobWidgetClass) XtClass(w);


    /* Use the class pointer to redraw the knob itself */
    (*kc->knob_class.draw)(w);


    /* Use the class pointers to highlight or unhighlight the knob */
    if (kw->primitive.highlighted)
        (*kc->primitive_class.border_highlight)(w);
    else
        (*kc->primitive_class.border_unhighlight)(w);
}
```

set_values Field

The *set_values* field specifies the chained method called when an application calls `XtSetValues()`. It is used to verify and respond to changes to the widget's resources. Any changes made to the widget's resources need to be verified here. If changes to the widget's superclass resources directly affect variables in the widget's instance record, those resources should be used to update the instance record of the widget. For example, if the widget uses the XmPrimitive resource `foreground` when creating its graphics context, then the graphics context needs to be updated if the foreground resource changes. Any changes to the Core height, width, x, y, or border width resources generates a geometry request to the widget's parent automatically by the Xt Intrinsics. If the requested change in height or width is not acceptable to the parent of this widget, then the `SetValuesAlmost()` method is called to negotiate a compromise.

The return value for this method determines whether the expose method is called. Because this method is chained, if this or any of the superclass SetValues methods return True, the expose method is called.

The type of the SetValues method is defined by the Xt Intrinsics:

```
typedef Boolean (*XtSetValuesFunc) (Widget, Widget, Widget,
                                    ArgList, Cardinal *)
    Widget      old;
    Widget      request;
    Widget      new_w;
    ArgList     args;
    Cardinal    *num_args;
```

old — The widget instance prior to the request to have its resource values changed using *SetValues*.

request — The widget instance that faithfully reflects requested changes to its resources, as superclass *SetValues* methods must never alter the request instance.

new_w — The current widget instance that reflects the requested changes and that may also have been altered by a superclass *SetValues* method in superclass-to-subclass order. Any changes to the widget structure can be made to this widget instance only.

args — The argument list that is passed in the call to `XtSetValues()`.

num_args — The argument count that is passed in the call to `XtSetValues()`.

set_values_hook Field

The *set_values_hook* field specifies a set values hook method and has been obsolete since the release of X11 Version 4. It was used for passing the argument list and argument count and has been retained for backward compatibility.

set_values_almost Field

The *set_values_almost* field specifies a method called only when a change to the Core resources `height`, `width`, `x`, `y`, or `border_width` has been modified in the SetValues method and that modification is unacceptable to the widget's parent geometry manager. The `SetValuesAlmost` method is necessary if the widget needs to lay itself out based on the failed geometry request. Setting

```
*request = *reply
```

guarantees success in the next geometry request.

The type of the SetValuesAlmost method is defined by the Xt Intrinsics:

```
typedef void (*XtAlmostProc) (Widget, Widget, XtWidgetGeometry *,
        XtWidgetGeometry *)
    Widget     old;

    Widget     new_w;

    XtWidgetGeometry * request;

    XtWidgetGeometry * reply;
```

old — Specifies a copy of the widget instance before the `SetValues` methods were called.

new_w — Specifies the current widget instance that reflects resource changes and other alterations done by all `SetValues` methods.

request — Specifies the requested geometry that was sent to the geometry manager of this widget's parent. This structure must be modified to continue the geometry negotiations. If the reply structure contains acceptable values, the *request_mode* field of this structure needs to be set to zero.

reply — Specifies the geometry that is acceptable to the geometry manager of this widget's parent. If the *request_mode* field of this structure is zero, the geometry request was totally rejected; otherwise, this parameter is set to a compromise geometry by the `SetValuesAlmost` method.

Most Motif widgets set this field to `XtInheritSetValuesAlmost`, which generally accepts all compromises offered by the parent.

This field is almost always set to `XtInheritSetValuesAlmost`, unless there is a compelling reason for you to redo the layout yourself if the requested geometry fails. Setting this field to NULL causes all parents' compromises to be rejected.

get_values_hook Field

The *get_values_hook* field specifies a chained method used to provide data that must copy the original resource. This field is normally set to NULL, unless you need special processing of internal resources and don't do it through the Motif synthetic resource mechanism.

Widgets with resources that are pointers to data or that store the resource data in an internal format need to provide a GetValuesHook method.

The type of the GetValuesHook method is defined by the Xt Intrinsics:

```
typedef void (*XtArgsProc) (Widget, ArgList, Cardinal *);
    Widget     widget;

    ArgList    args;
```

```
Cardinal  *num_args;
```

widget — The widget instance that is being asked to take the focus.

args — The argument list passed in the call to `XtGetValues()`.

num_args — The argument count passed in the call to `XtGetValues()`.

Motif uses the set_values_hook and get_values_hook methods for its synthetic resource mechanism. The synthetic resources allow Motif to store cached resource
values in gadget instance records, convert values to appropriate units for resolution independent resources, and store and allocate duplicate records or strings for
use by the application. Most of Motif's use of the get_values_hook and
set_values_hook methods is done at the base class (XmPrimitive, XmManager,
and XmGadget) level, and the widget subclasses typically set this field to NULL.

Here's an example of a get_values_hook method:

```
static void GetValuesHook( Widget w, ArgList args, Cardinal
*num_args_ptr )
{
    XsmExampleWidget exmpl = (XsmExampleWidget) widget;

    Cardinal num_args = *num_args_ptr;

    char * temp_str;

    int length;

    int i;


    XtGetSubvalues((XtPointer)widget, example_subres,
                   XtNumber(example_subres), args, num_args);


    length = strlen(exmpl->example.str) + 1;

    for (i = 0; i < num_args; i++) {
        if (!strcmp(args[i].name, XmNstringValue)) {
            if (length > 1) {
                temp_str = (char *) XtMalloc((unsigned) length + 1);

                (void)memcpy((void*)temp_str,

                (void*)exmpl->example.str, length);

                *((XtPointer *)args[i].value) = temp_str;

            } else {

                *((XtPointer *)args[i].value) = XtNewString("");
```

```
            }
        }
      }
   }
```

accept_focus Field

The *accept_focus* field specifies a method that provides notification and allows
widget control of the receipt of the input focus. Motif doesn't use this field and
does not support subclasses that do use the accept focus method. Motif has its
own internal method for maintaining the focus, so Motif widgets typically set this
field to NULL.

version Field

The *version* field specifies the version of the Xt Intrinsics in use. You should set it
to `XtVersion`. You could set it to `XtVersionDontCare`, but then you run
the risk of encountering compatibility problems. Note that if this field is set to
`XtVersion`, upgrading to a new version of the Xt Intrinsics will require you to
recompile your program.

callback_private Field

The *callback_private* field is an internal Xt Intrinsics field, and you should always
set it to NULL.

tm_table Field

The *tm_table* field specifies the translation table for the new widget. See "Define
the Translation Table" earlier in this chapter for detailed information on the
translation table. In `Knob.c`, this field is set to `defaultTranslations`,
which is the name of the translation table for the knob. Here's the knob widget's
translation table:

```
char defaultTranslations[] = "\
<Key>greater:    toggle-left()\n\
<Key>less:       toggle-right()\n\
<Key>:           release-knob()\n\
<Btn1Down>:      turn-left()\n\
<Btn3Down>:      turn-right()\n\
<Btn1Up>:        release-knob()\n\
<Btn3Up>:        release-knob()\n\
```

```
<FocusIn>:      Focus-in()\n\

<FocusOut>:     Focus-out()\n\

<EnterWindow>: enter()\n\

<LeaveWindow>: leave()";
```

query_geometry Field

The *query_geometry* field specifies a query geometry method used in geometry negotiations. It allows a widget to give input to its parent on what the widget believes is its ideal size. Some composite (Manager) widgets use `XtQueryGeometry` (which calls a child's query_geometry method) to determine the ideal size of its children prior to laying them out. If there is no query geometry method, the current widget size is used as the widget's preferred size.

The type of the query geometry method is defined by the Xt Intrinsics:

```
typedef XtGeometryResult (*XtGeometryHandler) (Widget,
                        XtWidgetGeometry *,XtWidgetGeometry *);

    Widget              widget;

    XtWidgetGeometry    *request;

    XtWidgetGeometry    *reply;
```

widget — The widget instance that is being queried.

request — The requested geometry change.

reply — The returned reply geometry indicating its preferred size.

Motif uses this method to express the ideal sizes of child widgets for layout in a manager widget. The label and text widgets look at their fonts, contents, and spacing resources to determine their ideal sizes.

You should provide a function that determines the ideal size of your widget, and use this function in the Initialize, SetValues, and QueryGeometry methods to maintain a preferred size. Be sure to accommodate the application requests for the size of a particular widget. If you don't expect the size of your widget to change after it has been initially set up, then set this method to NULL.

Here's an example of a query geometry method:

```
static XtGeometryResult QueryGeometry( Widget widget,
XtWidgetGeometry *request,

                XtWidgetGeometry *reply )

{

    XsmExampleWidget exmpl = (XsmExampleWidget) widget;
```

```
    reply->width = exmpl->example.str_width +
        (2 * (exmpl->example.margin_width +
                exmpl->primitive.shadow_thickness +
                exmpl->primitive.highlight_thickness));


    reply->height = exmpl->example.font_height +
        (2 * (exmpl->example.margin_height +
                exmpl->primitive.shadow_thickness +
                exmpl->primitive.highlight_thickness));


    return _XmGMReplyToQueryGeometry(widget, request, reply) ;
}
```

display_accelerator Field

The *display_accelerator* field specifies a method used to display the widget's accelerators. This field is normally set to NULL.

If a widget wants to be notified if it has accelerators placed on it by an application, then use the display accelerators method to display these accelerators. If a widget does not need to be notified when accelerators are installed, then set this field to NULL.

The syntax of the display accelerators method is defined by the Xt Intrinsics:

```
typedef void (*XtStringProc) (Widget, String);
    Widget widget;
    String str;
```

widget — The widget instance that has had accelerators installed.

str — The sting representing the accelerators.

Motif does not use this method. The Motif label widget and its subclasses manage their own accelerator resource and set up the accelerators in the row column manager widget.

Here's an example of a display accelerator method:

```
static void DisplayAccelerator(Widget widget, String str)
{
    XsmExampleWidget exmpl = (XsmExampleWidget) widget;
```

```
    if (exmpl->example.acc_string != NULL)
        exmpl->example.acc_string = str;

}
```

extension Field

The *extension* field points to an extension record that you can use to extend a class
record in a manner that is compatible with a pre-existing version of the widget
class. You can't just add fields to a widget's class part structure, because doing so
would cause backward compatibility problems with widgets that are subclasses of
your widget class. Note that Motif extends the Core class structure with the base
class extension record.

If you don't want your widget subclasses to take advantage of the extension
record, set the *extension* field to NULL. Here's how the Core class extension
record is defined in Motif:

```
typedef struct _XmBaseClassExtRec{
    XtPointer               next_extension;
    XrmQuark                record_type;
    long                    version;
    Cardinal                record_size;
    XtInitProc              initializePrehook;
    XtSetValuesFunc         setValuesPrehook;
    XtInitProc              initializePosthook;
    XtSetValuesFunc         setValuesPosthook;
    WidgetClass             secondaryObjectClass;
    XtInitProc              secondaryObjectCreate;
    XmGetSecResDataFunc     getSecResData;
    unsigned char           flags[32];
    XtArgsProc              getValuesPrehook;
    XtArgsProc              getValuesPosthook;
    XtWidgetClassProc       classPartInitPrehook;
    XtWidgetClassProc       classPartInitPosthook;
    XtResourceList          ext_resources;
    XtResourceList          compiled_ext_resources;
    Cardinal                num_ext_resources;
```

```
Boolean                 use_sub_resources;

XmWidgetNavigableProc   widgetNavigable;

XmFocusChangeProc       focusChange;

XmWrapperData           wrapperData;
}XmBaseClassExtRec, *XmBaseClassExt;
```

The Xt Intrinsics requires all extension records to begin with the same four fields: *next_extension*, *record_type*, *version*, and *record_size*.

next_extension — This field specifies the next extension record. It is used to link extension records for all possible subclasses of your widget class. It is typically initialized to NULL, but is sometimes set dynamically in the `ClassPartInit` method.

record_type — This field specifies the quark that identifies this extension record. For Motif it is `XmQmotif`. This field is initialized in the `ClassInitialize` method of the class record because quarks are run time variables. In the static initialization of this field, set the field to NULLQUARK.

version — This field specifies the extension version. For Motif it is set to `XmBaseClassExtVersion`.

Record_Size — Specifies the size of the record. Use the C expression

```
sizeof(XmBaseClassExtRec)
```

to determine the size.

initializePrehook — Specifies a method used to update extension class fields prior to calling the initialize method. Motif uses it to dynamically override fields in the class structure for a given widget instance. Specifically, Motif dynamically changes the translation manager table (specified in *tm_table*) for the label and label subclass widgets that are children of row column widgets. This field is typically set to `XmInheritInitializePrehook`.

setValuesPrehook — Specifies a method used to update extension class fields prior to calling the SetValues method. Motif uses it to initialize its cache resource structures for resource caching. This field is set to `XmInheritSetValuesPrehook` for widgets without cached resources.

initializePosthook — Specifies a method used to clean up any temporary allocated data from the method specified in *secondaryObjectCreate,* or to do followup processing of extension data. Motif uses it to register cache resources and free subobjects used in resource caching. This field is typically set to `XmInheritInitializePosthook` for widgets without cached resources.

                                                    The Widget Writing Process

setValuesPosthook — Specifies a method used to clean up any temporary allocated data from the method specified in *setValuesPrehook*, or to do followup processing of extension data. Motif uses it to update cache resources and free temporary subobjects used in resource caching. This field is typically set to `XmInheritSetValuesPosthook` for widgets without cached resources.

secondaryObjectClass — Used for cached resources for gadgets. Motif widgets set this field to NULL. This field is typically set to `XmInheritClass` when cached resources are not used.

secondaryObjectCreate — This field specifies a method used to initialize the extension object data for use in the initialize method. In Motif, it is used to set up the cache resources for comparison in the Initialize and SetValues methods. This field is typically set to `XmInheritSecObjectCreate` when cached resources are not used.

getSecResData — Specifies a method used to copy secondary resource data for external use. Motif uses this method to copy cached resources and text widget subresources to make them available to application developers. The standard Xt intrinsics cannot transform the Motif internal resource values like cached resources, so Motif provides a way to make available these resources. This method is set to `XmInheritSecObjectCreate` if cached resources or subresources are not used.

flags — Used for the Motif fast subclassing. It is initialized in the class part initialize method class record. It is reserved for Motif widgets and cannot be used in custom widgets. You should always initialize it to {0}.

getValuesPrehook — Specifies a method used to set up extension objects used to retrieve cached resources prior to calling the GetValues method. Motif uses it to set up the extension objects used to get the cache resource information. This method is typically set to `XmInheritGetValuesPrehook` for widgets not introducing new cached resources.

getValuesPosthook — Specifies a method used to free data allocated in the method specified in the *getValuesPrehook* field. This method is typically set to `XmInheritGetValuesPosthook` for widgets not introducing new cached resources.

classPartInitPrehook— Specifies an internal Motif method. Always set it to NULL.

classPartInitPosthook — Specifies an internal Motif method. Always set it to NULL.

ext_resources — This field is an internal Motif extension class field. Always set it to NULL.

compiled_ext_resources — This field is an internal Motif extension class field. Always set it to NULL.

num_ext_resources — This field is an internal Motif extension class field. Always set it to 0.

use_sub_resources — This field is an internal Motif extension class field. Always set it to False.

widgetNavigable — Used to export the state of the widgets traversability based on certain internal conditions. This field is typically set to `XmInheritWidgetNavigable`.

focusChange — Used to handle changes in widget focus. This field is typically set to `XmInheritFocusChange`.

wrapperData — This field is an internal Motif extension class field. Always set it to NULL.

Summary

This chapter introduced the widget writing process. You'll use this process, or variations of it, to write any new widgets you need. You may not fully understand some parts of the process, or some of the terms used in the process now, but the next chapter uses the process to explain how to write the knob widget, so a lot of the mystery should be cleared up then.

Now that you have at least a general idea of what is involved in writing a new widget, let's proceed with the task of writing a primitive widget, the knob. This chapter describes how you write the source module and necessary header files to create the knob widget.

Introduction

Let's define the knob to act just like the volume control on a radio or television. Turn it clockwise and the volume increases; turn it counterclockwise and the volume decreases. The minimum value is at the knob's fully counterclockwise position, and the maximum value is at the knob's fully clockwise position. You can set both the maximum and minimum values in the applicable resources. Figure 3-1 shows a knob widget.

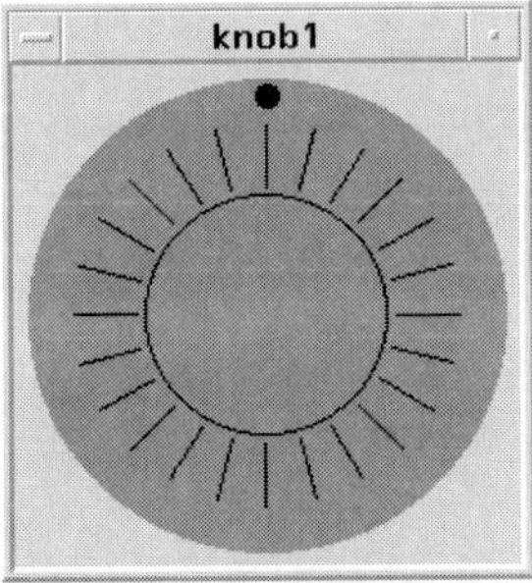

Figure 3-1 The Knob Widget

You can use the knob as a control similar to the existing Motif slider or scale widget. An example program, `knobcolors`, uses three knobs, one to vary each of the three primary colors. We'll describe `knobcolors` later in this chapter.

The Process

We'll use the widget writing process described in Chapter 2 to create the knob widget. This involves choosing the superclass, creating the private and public header files `KnobP.h` and `Knob.h`, and then writing the object `Knob.c`. You may see some duplication from Chapter 2 as we go through the widget writing process for the knob, but the more you go through it, the better you'll understand it. Throughout this chapter you'll see code segments from the files that make up the knob widget (`KnobP.h`, `Knob.h`, and `Knob.c`). Appendix A contains a complete listing of these files.

Choose the Superclass

We want the knob widget to have some of the characteristics of the existing Motif controls. We don't envision the knob to have any child widgets, so we'll subclass the knob from the XmPrimitive class instead of from XmManager. This means that XmPrimitive is the superclass, so we need to include XmPrimitive parts in the class instance records defined in the knob's private header file. Figure 3-2 shows the XmPrimitive portion of the widget hierarchy.

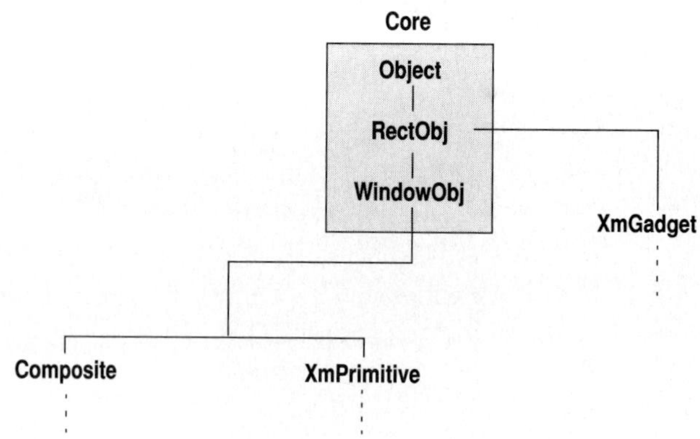

Figure 3-2 XmPrimitive Widget Hierarchy

Create the Private Header File

The knob widget's private header file `KnobP.h` is normally used only by other widget writers who want to subclass a new widget from knob.

Manage Multiple Inclusions

The first lines of the private header file are used to manage multiple definitions of the header file if it is included more than once:

```
#ifndef _XsmKnobP_h

#define _XsmKnobP_h
```

The associated `#endif` is the last line of `KnobP.h`.

Include Knob.h and PrimitiveP.h

Next, include the knob's public header file `Knob.h` and XmPrimitive's private header file `PrimitiveP.h`:

```
#include "Knob.h"

#include <Xm/PrimitiveP.h>
```

We include `Knob.h` because any public information contained therein may be used in the private structure definitions. We include `PrimitiveP.h` to obtain definitions of XmPrimitive's class and instance structures.

Define the Class Part Structure

Next, define the knob's class part structure. It defines fields to hold function pointers of class methods as well as a field to hold the extension record. Class methods are used when you determine that there are some internal procedures that a subclass may want to override. You don't need them to write a widget, but they make it easier for someone else to create a widget subclass from knob.

```
typedef struct {

  XsmGetDiametersProc get_diameters;   /* procedure to draw inner
                                          and outer circles */

  XtWidgetProc        create_segments; /* procedure used to
                                          create handle
                                          segments */

  XtWidgetProc        draw_indicator;  /* procedure for drawing
                                          knob indicator */

  XtTimerCallbackProc turn;            /* timeout procedure used
```

```
                                          to turn knob */
    XtWidgetProc          draw;           /* procedure for drawing
                                          the knob */
    XtPointer             extension;      /* pointer to extension
                                          record used for
                                          future expansion */
} XsmKnobClassPart;
```

Define the Class Structure

Next, define the knob's class structure. It is composed of segments from the Core class part, Primitive class part, and the knob class part.

```
typedef struct _XsmKnobClassRec {
   CoreClassPart        core_class;
   XmPrimitiveClassPart primitive_class;
   XsmKnobClassPart     knob_class;
} XsmKnobClassRec;
```

Define Procedure Pointers Not Defined in the Xt Intrinsics

Some local procedures need a pointer defined so that they can be inherited by a widget subclassing from knob. In this case, only the knob's `GetDiameters` procedure needs such a pointer:

```
typedef void (*XsmGetDiametersProc)(Widget, unsigned int *,
             unsigned int *);
```

Define Inheritance Macros

Next, define inheritance macros. These macros identify methods and procedures that widgets subclassing from knob can use instead of redefining them. The actual number of these macros corresponds to the number of methods in the class part structure, and some widgets may not have any. The knob widget defines these inheritance macros:

```
/* Define inheritance procedures for all knob class procedures. */
#define XsmInheritGetDiameters ((XsmGetDiametersProc) _XtInherit)
#define XsmInheritCreateSegments ((XtWidgetProc) _XtInherit)
#define XsmInheritDrawIndicator ((XtWidgetProc) _XtInherit)
#define XsmInheritTurn ((XtTimerCallbackProc) _XtInherit)
#define XsmInheritDraw ((XtWidgetProc) _XtInherit)
```

Note that _XtInherit is a "place holder" procedure that is redefined in knob's class part initialize method.

Define the Instance Part Structure

Next, define the knob's instance part structure. This structure is the part of the knob's instance record (defined next) that is specific for the knob widget class. The knob's resource values and internal widget instance fields are stored in its instance part record. Here's the instance record for the knob widget:

```
typedef struct _XsmKnobPart {
  XtCallbackList value_changed_callback; /* resource - callback
                                  when value changes */

    int value;                  /* resource - value of the knob */

    int max_val;                /* resource - maximum value allowed */

    int min_val;                /* resource - minimum value allowed */

    int turn_delay;             /* resource - the delay before the next
                                   increment */

    Pixel knob_color;           /* resource - the color of the knob */

    Pixel indicator_color;      /* resource - the color of the
                                   indicator */

    Dimension margin_width;     /* resource - determines the outer
                                   edge of */

    Dimension margin_height;    /* the circle. Whichever value is
                                   greater when the dimension is
                                   subtracted from its margin
                                   value determines the knob
                                   diameter. */

    Dimension knob_margin;      /* resource - The percentage from the
                                   knob's outer edge to draw the inner
                                   circle. */

    Dimension orig_width;       /* saves the original dimension */
    Dimension orig_height;      /* saves the original dimension */
    Boolean move_clockwise;     /* indicates direction of turn */
    Boolean turning;            /* indicates whether turning is in
                                   progress */
```

```
GC gc;                          /* graphics context use in graphic
                                   ops */
XSegment *segments;             /* the line segments used for drawing
                                   the handle */
int num_segments;               /* the number of segments in the above
                                   list */
XtIntervalId timer_id;          /* the timer id of the timeout used in
                                   turning the knob */
double angle_offset;            /* used to calculate the segment
                                   positions */
} XsmKnobPart;
```

Define the Instance Structure

Next, define the knob's instance structure:

```
typedef struct _XsmKnobRec {
    CorePart          core;
    XmPrimitivePart primitive;
    XsmKnobPart       knob;
} XsmKnobRec;
```

In this structure, the field knob (type XsmKnobPart) points to the knob's instance part record. Each of the types are defined in the respective class private
header file. For example, XmPrimitivePart is defined in PrimitiveP.h:

```
/*  The Primitive instance record  */


typedef struct _XmPrimitivePart
{

    Pixel    foreground;


    Dimension    shadow_thickness;
    Pixel    top_shadow_color;
    Pixmap    top_shadow_pixmap;
    Pixel    bottom_shadow_color;
    Pixmap    bottom_shadow_pixmap;
```


The Knob Widget

```
    Dimension    highlight_thickness;

    Pixel    highlight_color;

    Pixmap    highlight_pixmap;


    XtCallbackList help_callback;

    XtPointer        user_data;


    Boolean traversal_on;

    Boolean highlight_on_enter;

    Boolean have_traversal;


    unsigned char unit_type;

    XmNavigationType navigation_type;


    Boolean highlight_drawn;

    Boolean highlighted;


    GC        highlight_GC;

    GC        top_shadow_GC;

    GC        bottom_shadow_GC;
} XmPrimitivePart;
```

Create the Knob Public Header File

The public header file `Knob.h` is used by application programmers and contains the widget class name, resource strings, callback structures, and public function external declarations.

Manage Multiple Inclusions

Like the private header file, the first lines prevent multiple inclusions:

```
#ifndef _XsmKnob_h

#define _XsmKnob_h
```

The associated `#endif` is the last line of the private header file:

```
#endif /* _XsmKnob_h */
```

This allows a header file to be included more than once without errors associated with multiple definitions.

Include Xm.h

Next, include the `Xm.h` header file:

```
#include <Xm/Xm.h>
```

This header file has general definitions, declarations, and macros needed by all Motif widgets and applications.

Define Resource Name Macros

We define macros to map to the resource names. By convention, the words in the names are separated by differences in capitalization. The macro definition includes the two- or three-letter prefix (Xm or Xsm, for example) for the widget library, followed by an *N* that indicates a resource name. Here's the knob's resource name macros:

```
#define XsmNvalueChangedCallback    "valueChangedCallback"

#define XsmNindicatorColor          "indicatorColor"

#define XsmNmarginWidth             "marginWidth"

#define XsmNmarginHeight            "marginHeight"

#define XsmNknobMargin              "knobMargin"

#define XsmNknobColor               "knobColor"

#define XsmNmaxValue                "maxValue"

#define XsmNminValue                "minValue"

#define XsmNturnDelay               "turnDelay"

#define XsmNvalue                   "value"
```

Define Resource Class Name Macros

The resource class name macros also use capitalization to separate words. The class name macro uses an uppercase *C* instead of *N* and the letter following the *C* is always uppercase. Here's the resource class name macros for the knob's resources:

```
#define XsmCValueChangedCallback    "ValueChangedCallback"

#define XsmCIndicatorColor          "IndicatorColor"

#define XsmCMarginWidth             "MarginWidth"

#define XsmCMarginHeight            "MarginHeight"

#define XsmCKnobMargin              "KnobMargin"
```

```
#define XsmCKnobColor              "KnobColor"

#define XsmCMaxValue               "MaxValue"

#define XsmCMinValue               "MinValue"

#define XsmCTurnDelay              "TurnDelay"

#define XsmCValue                  "Value"
```

Define Callback Structures

The knob has only one callback structure:

```
typedef struct
{
   int     reason;
   XEvent *event;
   int     value;
} XsmKnobCallbackStruct;
```

The variables *reason* and *event* are common to all callback structures. Other variables, such as *value*, are unique to a specific callback. The knob defines a callback reason as a value for the *reason* field:

```
#define XsmCR_VALUE_CHANGED   0
```

Every callback has a specific reason associated with the cause of the callback's invocation. The reason can be associated with any widget event such as pressing a button or entering a window, but it doesn't have to be. A widget can execute a callback for virtually any reason. Some callbacks may have more than one reason for being called, and there is a definition for each reason.

Define the Widget Class Name

The pointers to the widget instance and class structures in the public header file are mainly used for applications that wish to have more specific type checking. Instead of using the generic types Widget and WidgetClass for the widget instance and class types, the application programmer may want to have a more specific type for each widget instance and class.

```
externalref WidgetClass   xsmKnobWidgetClass;

/*
 * To allow applications to use tight type checking, define
 * structures for the widget class and instance pointers
 * specific to this class of widget.
 */
```

```
typedef struct _XsmKnobClassRec * XsmKnobWidgetClass;
typedef struct _XsmKnobRec        * XsmKnobWidget;
```

Define Public Function Declarations

The knob has three public functions:

- `XsmCreateKnob` is a convenience function to simplify creating an instance of knob.

- `XsmGetKnobValue` obtains the current value of the knob setting.

- `XsmSetKnobValue` sets the knob's value to a specified figure.

Here are the function definitions as they appear in `Knob.h`:

```
extern Widget XsmCreateKnob(

                        Widget    parent,
                        char      *name,
                        ArgList   arglist,
                        Cardinal argcount);
extern int XsmGetKnobValue(

                        Widget w) ;
extern void XsmSetKnobValue(

                        Widget w,
                        int value) ;
```

Define New Resources

You define the knob's new resources in the program `knob.c`. You also set initial, or default, values for each resource at the same time. Table 3-1 shows the knob's resource names, classes, and default values.

Table 3-1 Knob Widget Resources

Resource Name	Resource Class Name	Default
XsmNvalueChangedCallback	XsmCValueChangedCallback	NULL
XsmNvalue	XsmCValue	0
XsmNmaxValue	XsmCMaxValue	100
XsmNminValue	XsmCMinValue	0
XsmNturnDelay	XsmCTurnDelay	50
XsmNknobColor	XsmCKnobColor	Dynamic

Table 3-1 Knob Widget Resources (Continued)

Resource Name	Resource Class Name	Default
XsmNindicatorColor	XsmCIndicatorColor	Dynamic
XsmNmarginWidth	XsmCMarginWidth	5
XsmNmarginHeight	XsmCMarginHeight	5
XsmNknobMargin	XsmCKnobMargin	50

The word *Dynamic* in the default column means that the default value is dependent on some other resource or procedure value.

The format you use to initialize the resources is defined by the Xt Intrinsics as described in Chapter 2. Here are the knob's resources as they are in defined in `knob.c`:

```
static XtResource resources[] = {
    {
        XmNvalueChangedCallback, XmCCallback, XmRCallback,
        sizeof(XtCallbackList),
        XtOffset (XsmKnobWidget, knob.value_changed_callback),
        XmRImmediate, NULL
    },


    {
        XsmNvalue, XsmCValue, XmRInt, sizeof(int),
        XtOffset (XsmKnobWidget, knob.value),
        XmRImmediate, (XtPointer) 0
    },


    {
        XsmNmaxValue, XsmCMaxValue, XmRInt, sizeof(int),
        XtOffset (XsmKnobWidget, knob.max_val),
        XmRImmediate, (XtPointer) 100
    },


    {
```

```c
    XsmNminValue, XsmCMinValue, XmRInt, sizeof(int),
    XtOffset (XsmKnobWidget, knob.min_val),
    XmRImmediate, (XtPointer) 0
  },

  {

    XsmNturnDelay, XsmCTurnDelay, XmRInt, sizeof(int),
    XtOffset(XsmKnobWidget, knob.turn_delay),
    XmRImmediate, (XtPointer) 50
  },

  {

    XsmNknobColor, XsmCKnobColor, XmRPixel, sizeof (Pixel),
    XtOffset (XsmKnobWidget, knob.knob_color),
    XmRCallProc, (XtPointer) DefaultKnobColor
  },

  {

    XsmNindicatorColor, XsmCIndicatorColor, XmRPixel,
       sizeof (Pixel),
    XtOffset (XsmKnobWidget, knob.indicator_color),
    XmRCallProc, (XtPointer) _XmForegroundColorDefault
  },

  {

    XmNmarginWidth, XmCMarginWidth, XmRHorizontalDimension,
    sizeof (Dimension),
    XtOffset (XsmKnobWidget, knob.margin_width),
    XmRImmediate, (XtPointer) DEFAULT_KNOB_MARGIN
  },

  {

    XmNmarginHeight, XmCMarginHeight, XmRVerticalDimension,
    sizeof (Dimension),
```

```
        XtOffset (XsmKnobWidget, knob.margin_height),

        XmRImmediate, (XtPointer) DEFAULT_KNOB_MARGIN

    },


    {

        XsmNknobMargin, XsmCKnobMargin, XmRDimension,

          sizeof (Dimension),

        XtOffset (XsmKnobWidget, knob.knob_margin),

        XmRImmediate, (XtPointer) DEFAULT_KNOB_MARGIN_PERCENTAGE

    },
```

The synthetic resource mechanism provides hooks that allow transformation
procedures to be called when you are setting or getting the various resources.
Note the definitions of these resources in the regular resource definition given
previously. There, the type fields have `XmRHorizontalDimension` and
`XmRVerticalDimension`, respectively. This indicates that they are
resolution independent resources.

```
static XsmyntheticResource syn_resources[] = {

        {

            XmNmarginWidth,

            sizeof (Dimension),

            XtOffset( XsmKnobWidget, knob.margin_width),

            _XmFromHorizontalPixels,

            _XmToHorizontalPixels

        },


        {

            XmNmarginHeight,

            sizeof (Dimension),

            XtOffset( XsmKnobWidget, knob.margin_height),

            _XmFromVerticalPixels,

            _XmToVerticalPixels

        }

    };
```

Define the Action Table

The action table defines the actions for the new widget. Actions work with translations to map events to procedures. The action table maps a string describing the action to a procedure. For example, the knob has a `turn-left` action that is mapped to a procedure called `TurnLeft` that causes the knob to rotate counterclockwise.

Here's the knob's action table:

```
static XtActionsRec knob_actions[] = {
    {"turn-left",        TurnLeft},
    {"turn-right",       TurnRight},
    {"toggle-left",      ToggleLeft},
    {"toggle-right",     ToggleRight},
    {"release-knob",     ReleaseKnob},
};
```

Define the Translation Table

The translation table maps mouse and keyboard events to the actions described in the action table.

Here's the knob's translation table:

```
char defaultTranslations[] = "\
<Key>greater:      toggle-left()\n\
<Key>less:         toggle-right()\n\
<Key>:             release-knob()\n\
<Btn1Down>:        turn-left()\n\
<Btn3Down>:        turn-right()\n\
<Btn1Up>:          release-knob()\n\
<Btn3Up>:          release-knob()\n\
<FocusIn>:         focus-in()\n\
<FocusOut>:        focus-out()\n\
<EnterWindow>:     enter()\n\
<LeaveWindow>:     leave()";
```

Let's review the relationship between the knob's translation and action tables described in the previous section. The translation table maps an event such as a keyboard press or mouse movement to an action and the action table maps an action to an action procedure. Thus, an event is tied to an action procedure. Figure 3-3 shows the relationship between the knob's action and translation tables.

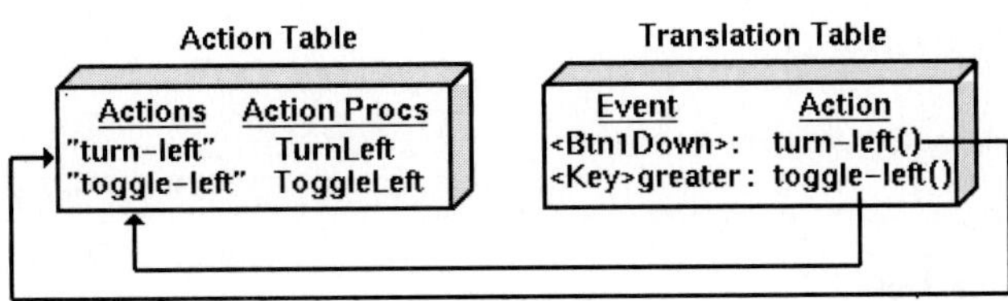

Figure 3-3   Action and Translation Tables Relationships

Here, the actions are "turn-left" and "toggle-left", and the corresponding action procedures are `TurnLeft` and `ToggleLeft`. The translation table shows that the event `<Btn1Down>` maps to the action "turn-left", and the event `<Key>greater` maps to the action "toggle-left".

Initialize the Widget Class Record

The knob's widget class record consists of the Core class part, a superclass part, and the knob widget's class part. The knob's superclass is the XmPrimitive class, which is a subclass of Core.

Core Class Part

The Core class part is the heart of the widget class record. All *widgets* (windowed objects), have a Core class part. All widget instances of a given class share exactly the same class record and have the same values for the Core class part fields, as well as all other class record fields.

Here's the listing of the knob's Core class part:

```
externaldef (xsmknobclassrec) XsmKnobClassRec xsmKnobClassRec = {

    {

    (WidgetClass) &xmPrimitiveClassRec, /* superclass          */

        "XsmKnob",                      /* class_name          */

        sizeof(XsmKnobRec),             /* widget_size         */

        NULL,                           /* class_initialize    */

        ClassPartInitialize,            /* class_part_initialize*/

        FALSE,                          /* class_inited        */
```

```c
    Initialize,                        /* initialize         */
    NULL,                              /* initialize_hook    */
    XtInheritRealize,                  /* realize            */
    knob_actions,                      /* actions            */
    XtNumber(knob_actions),            /* num_actions        */
    resources,                         /* resources          */
    XtNumber(resources),               /* num_resources      */
    NULLQUARK,                         /* xrm_class          */
    TRUE,                              /* compress_motion    */
    XtExposeCompressMaximal,           /* compress_exposure  */
    TRUE,                              /* compress_enterleave*/
    FALSE,                             /* visible_interest   */
    Destroy,                           /* destroy            */
    Resize,                            /* resize             */
    Redisplay,                         /* expose             */
    SetValues,                         /* set_values         */
    NULL,                              /* set_values_hook    */
    SetValuesAlmost,                   /* set_values_almost  */
    NULL,                              /* get_values_hook    */
    NULL,                              /* accept_focus       */
    XtVersion,                         /* version            */
    NULL,                              /* callback_private   */
    defaultTranslations,               /* tm_table           */
    QueryGeometry,                     /* query_geometry     */
    NULL,                              /* display accelerator*/
    NULL,                              /* extension          */
},
```

The settings for each of the Core class record fields are explained in the sections
that follow.

superclass Field

The *superclass* field is a pointer to the superclass record. Because we are subclassing knob from XmPrimitive, this field is set to `&XmPrimitiveClassRec`
and is cast to `(WidgetClass)`.

class_name Field

The value of the *class_name* field is an ASCII string that describes the new widget class. In keeping with the convention we established earlier, this field is set to "XsmKnob", which is the name of the new class.

widget_size Field

The *widget_size* is the size of the widget instance record, and is the value of the C expression

```
sizeof(XsmKnobRec)
```

where XsmKnobRec is the knob's instance structure defined in its private header file KnobP.h:

```
typedef struct _XsmKnobRec {
    CorePart          core;
    XmPrimitivePart primitive;
    XsmKnobPart       knob;
} XsmKnobClassRec;
```

class_initialize Field

The *class_initialize* field is a pointer to a method that is called the first time a widget of this class is initialized. This method is used only to initialize class record fields that cannot be statically initialized. This field is NULL because knob has no class fields that cannot be statically initialized.

class_part_initialize Field

The *class_part_initialize* field is a pointer to a method that is called when a widget of this class is initialized, and again each time a subclass of this widget is initialized. The method's purpose is to initialize the class part of class records that are subclasses of the knob widget class. For the knob, the method is ClassPartInitialize, and it is described later in this chapter.

class_inited Field

The *class_inited* field is an internal Xt Intrinsics flag that you should always set to False.

initialize Field

The *initialize* field specifies a method that initializes the widget's internal instance fields. For the knob, the method is called Initialize, and it is described later in this chapter.

initialize_hook Field

The *initialize_hook* field specifies a method that was used for passing the argument list and argument count prior to the addition of these parameters in the initialize method in X11 Release 4. The pointer to this method has been retained for backward compatibility. This field is set to NULL.

realize Field

The *realize* field specifies a method that creates the window for the knob widget. The method is not chained. Frequently this method is inherited from its superclass' realize method using `XtInheritRealize`. The knob needs nothing special or extra at realize time, so we set this field to `XtInheritRealize`.

actions Field

The *actions* field identifies the name of the action table to be used for the new widget. See "Define the Action Table" earlier in this chapter (and also in Chapter 2) for detailed information on the action table. In `knob.c`, the actions field is `knob_actions`, the name of the action table in `knob.c`.

num_actions Field

The *num_actions* field specifies the number of actions in the action table. `Knob.c` uses `XtNumber` on the action table specified in the *actions* field.

```
XtNumber(knob_actions)
```

resources Field

The *resources* field specifies the list of the knob's resources. In `knob.c` this field is `resources`. See "Define New Resources" earlier in this chapter (and in Chapter 2) for detailed information.

num_resources Field

The *num_resources* field specifies the number of resources in the resource list. `Knob.c` uses `XtNumber` on the resource list. This results in the number of resources in the resource list.

```
XtNumber(resources)
```

xrm_class Field

The *xrm_class* field is another internal Xt Intrinsics flag. Always set it to NULLQUARK.

compress_motion Field

The *compress_motion* field is normally set to True, unless your new widget is a gadget or a widget that performs interactive drawing. Because the knob has no need for interactive drawing, this field is set to True.

compress_exposure Field

The *compress_exposure* field is a flag that was a Boolean variable prior to X11 Release 4. Under R4 and subsequent releases, it has the following possible values:

- `XtExposeNoCompress` — Performs no exposure compression.
- `XtExposeCompressSeries` — Compresses expose events from a single exposure.
- `XtExposeCompressMultiple` — Compresses all adjacent series of expose events in the event queue.
- `XtExposeCompressMaximal` — Compress all expose events in the event queue. This value blocks the event queue during processing.

This field is set to `XtExposeCompressMaximal` because we want the maximum expose event compression.

compress_enterleave Field

The *compress_enterleave* field is normally set to True, unless your new widget is a gadget or a widget that performs interactive drawing. Because the knob is not a gadget and we want enter/leave event compression, this field is set to True.

visible_interest Field

The *visible_interest* field is set to False, as it is in all the Motif widgets. See the corresponding section in Chapter 2 for more information on this field.

destroy Field

The *destroy* field specifies the destroy method used for freeing data allocated by the widget. The knob's destroy method is called `Destroy()`. It is described later in this chapter.

resize Field

The *resize* field specifies a resize method called when a widget has been reconfigured to change it's height or width information. Widgets that have dimension-based information (such as a line count for scrolling) or that want to redraw themselves dynamically upon a change in size need to have a resize method. The knob's resize method is called `Resize()` and is described later in this chapter.

expose Field

The *expose* field specifies the expose method, one of the most important methods in the widget. The expose method performs the drawing (or redrawing) of the widget visuals. It can be the key to how well the widget performs. It is called when an expose event on the widget occurs, when any of the `SetValues` methods return True, and when a widget has been resized.   It is usually named `Redisplay()`, because there is an X event called Expose. For the knob, this method is called `Redisplay()`, and it is described later in this chapter.

set_values Field

The *set_values* field specifies the chained method called when an application calls `XtSetValues()`. It is used to verify changes to the widget's resources. For the knob, the method is called `SetValues`, and it is described later in this chapter.

set_values_hook Field

The *set_values_hook* field specifies a set_values_hook method that has been obsolete since the release of X11 Version 4. It was used for passing the argument list and argument count prior to the argument list being included in the `SetValues` method and has been retained for backward compatibility. This field is set to NULL.

set_values_almost Field

The *set_values_almost* field specifies a method called only when the Core resources `height`, `width`, `x`, `y`, or `border_width` have been modified in the `SetValues` method, and that modification is only partially acceptable to the widget's parent geometry manager.   For the knob, this method is called `SetValuesAlmost` and is described later in this chapter.

get_values_hook Field

The *get_values_hook* field specifies a chained procedure used to provide data that can't be obtained directly from the widget's instance record. This field is set to NULL.

accept_focus Field

The *accept_focus* field specifies a method that allows the setting of the input focus by means of a call to `XSetInputFocus()`. Motif doesn't use this field and does not support subclasses that do use the accept focus method. Motif has its

The Knob Widget

own internal method for maintaining the focus, so Motif widgets typically set this field to NULL, as does knob.

version Field
The *version* field specifies the version of the Xt Intrinsics in use. It is set to `XtVersion`.

callback_private Field
The *callback_private* field is an internal Xt Intrinsics field, and you should always set it to NULL.

tm_table Field
The *tm_table* field specifies the translation table for the new widget. See "Define the Translation Table" earlier in this chapter (and in chapter 2) for detailed information on the translation table. In `knob.c`, this field is `defaultTranslations`.

query_geometry Field
The *query_geometry* field specifies a query geometry method used in geometry negotiations. This field is set to `QueryGeometry`.

display_accelerator Field
The *display_accelerator* field specifies a method used to display the widget's accelerators. This field is normally set to NULL.

extension Field
The *extension* field points to an extension record that you use to extend a class record within an existing release of a Motif or Xt Intrinsics library. Knob uses no fields in the extension record, so the *extension* field is set to NULL.

XmPrimitive Class Part
The XmPrimitive class part is the second of the three class parts that make up the knob's class record. The XmPrimitive class part follows, with explanations for each field.

```
    {
        HighlightKnob,                      /* border_highlight   */
        UnhighlightKnob,                    /* border_unhighlight */
        XtInheritTranslations,              /* translations       */
        NULL,                               /* arm_and_activate   */
```

```
        syn_resources,                        /* syn resources       */

        XtNumber(syn_resources),               /* num syn_resources   */

        NULL,                                  /* extension           */

    },
```

border_highlight Field

The *border_highlight* field specifies a method that establishes border highlighting for the knob when it has the focus. The method is called `HighlightKnob`.

border_unhighlight Field

The *border_unhighlight* field specifies a method that removes the border highlight when the widget has lost the focus. The method is called `UnhighlightKnob`.

translations Field

The *translations* field specifies a translation table for the XmPrimitive class for Motif traversal translations. For the knob, we've chosen to inherit the existing traversal translations, so this field is set to `XtInheritTranslations`.

arm_and_activate Field

The *arm_and_activate* field specifies a method to arm and activate a control widget, such as a pushbutton. It is used mainly for accelerators in menus and dialogs. Because the knob does not need these features, this field is set to NULL.

syn_resources Field

The *syn_resources* field specifies synthetic resources. For the knob, this field is set to `syn_resources`, which is the array defined in `Knob.c` that contains the synthetic resources. See "Define New Resources" earlier in this chapter and in Chapter 2.

num_syn_resources Field

The *num_syn_resources* field specifies the number of synthetic resources. It is set to `XtNumber(syn_resources)`.

extension Field

The *extension* field specifies the extension record (if any) for the XmPrimitive class. Because knob does not need the fields in the extension record for the XmPrimitive class, this field is set to NULL.

Here's the XmPrimitive extension record:

```
typedef struct _XmPrimitiveClassExtRec{
    XtPointer                   next_extension;
    XrmQuark                    record_type;
    long                        version;
    Cardinal                    record_size;
    XmWidgetBaselineProc        widget_baseline;
    XmWidgetDisplayRectProc     widget_display_rect;
    XmWidgetMarginsProc         widget_margins;
}XmPrimitiveClassExtRec, *XmPrimitiveClassExt;
```

The first four fields are required by the Xt Intrinsics:

next_extension — a pointer to any follow on extension records. Initialize it to NULL.

record_type — always statically initialized to NULLQUARK and initialized in the `ClassInitialize` procedure to `XmQmotif`. Because `XmQmotif` is a run-time variable, it can't be statically initialized.

version — identifies the type of extension record. For gadgets, set it to `XmGadgetClassExtVersion`.

record_size — The size of this extension record (use `sizeof( )`).

widget_baseline — A class function that returns True if the widget has a computable baseline. It also determines the number of pixels from the y origin to the baseline of each line of text and returns the baseline values in the baseline array passed into the method.

```
typedef Boolean (*XmWidgetBaselineProc)(Widget, Dimension **,
                                        int *);

    Widget        widget;
    Dimension **baseline;
    int           *line_count;
```

where

widget is the instance pointer of the gadget,

baseline is the array of baselines to be passed back, and

line_count is the size of the array to be passed back.

widget_display_rect — A class function that returns the dimensions of the rectangle that encompasses the gadget's text or pixmap. It is used to provide information for the Motif function `XmWidgetGetDisplayRect()`. The class method returns True when the widget being passed in has a display rectangle associated with it.

widget_margins — Used in baseline alignment to get and set the margins of widgets that want to be realigned based on baselines. The margins are queried and later reset to align the widget baselines.

```
typedef void (*XmWidgetMarginsProc)(Widget, XmBaselineMargins *);

  Widget              widget;

  XmBaselineMargins  *margins_rec;
```

where
widget is the current widget instance record from (to) which the margins are retrieved (set), and

margins_rec is the structure that contains the margins to be returned
 or the margins to be used in resetting the widget's margins.

```
typedef struct _XmBaselineMargins

{

unsigned char get_or_set;   /* XmBASELINE_GET or XmBASELINE_SET */

Dimension margin_top;       /* height of the top margin */

Dimension margin_bottom;    /* height of the bottom margin */

Dimension shadow;           /* thickness */

Dimension highlight;        /* thickness */

Dimension text_height;      /* height of the text */

Dimension margin_height;    /* the margin height */

} XmBaselineMargins;
```

Knob Class Part

The Knob class part is the final class part that makes up the knob's class record. Here's the Knob class part:

```
{                                       /* knob class          */
    GetDiameters,                       /* get_diameters       */
    CreateSegments,                     /* create_segments     */
    DrawIndicator,                      /* draw_indicator      */
    TurnKnob,                           /* turn                */
    DrawKnob,                           /* draw                */
    NULL,                               /* extension           */
}
```

get_diameters Field

The *get_diameters* field specifies a method that determines the diameter of a knob. The method is called `GetDiameters`.

create_segments Field

The *create_segments* field specifies a method that creates the knob segments. The method is called `CreateSegments`.

draw_indicator Field

The *draw_indicator* field specifies a method that draws the knob indicator. The method is called `DrawIndicator`.

turn Field

The *turn* field specifies a method to turn the knob. The method is called `TurnKnob`.

draw Field

The *draw* field specifies a method that draws the knob. The method is called `DrawKnob`.

extension Field

The *extension* field specifies the extension record for the XmPrimitive class. Because we have no need to extend the knob class, we set this field to NULL.

Knob.c

Now let's take a look at the program `Knob.c`. Some parts of it have already been described as part of the widget writing process, but there's a lot more to the program that is unique to the knob widget.

Include Header Files

You already know about the knob's private header file, `KnobP.h`, but the standard math header file is also included:

```
#include <math.h>

#include "KnobP.h"
```

Variable Definitions

`Knob.c` defines a number of variables for its mathematical calculations needed in drawing and operating the knob.

```
#define   RADIANS(x)   (M_PI * 2.0 * (x) / 360.0)

#define   DEGREES(x)   ((x) / (M_PI * 2.0) * 360.0)

#define   MIN_ANGLE    225.0

#define   MAX_ANGLE    345.0

#define   NUM_SEGS     24

#define   MIN(a,b)     (((a) < (b)) ? (a) :  (b))

#define   MIN_KNOB_DIAMETER                3

#define   DEFAULT_DIAMETER                 100

#define   DEFAULT_KNOB_MARGIN              5

#define   DEFAULT_KNOB_MARGIN_PERCENTAGE   50
```

Method and Procedure Declarations

Following the variable definitions are the method and procedure declarations. You've already seen most of the names in our earlier discussions, and the purpose of most of them is self-explanatory.

```
/* core class methods */

static void ClassPartInitialize( WidgetClass widget_class) ;

static void Initialize( Widget request, Widget new_w, ArgList args,
                        Cardinal *num_args) ;

static void Destroy( Widget w) ;

static void Resize( Widget w) ;

static void Redisplay( Widget w, XEvent *event, Region region) ;

static Boolean SetValues( Widget old_w, Widget request, Widget
                          new_w, ArgList args, Cardinal *num_args) ;

static void SetValuesAlmost( Widget old_w, Widget new_w,
                             XtWidgetGeometry *request,
                             XtWidgetGeometry *reply);

static XtGeometryResult QueryGeometry( Widget w, XtWidgetGeometry
                             *request, XtWidgetGeometry *reply) ;


/* primitive class methods */
```

```c
static void HighlightKnob( Widget w) ;
static void UnhighlightKnob( Widget w) ;


/* knob class methods */
static void GetDiameters( Widget w, unsigned int *diameter,
                          unsigned int *inner_diameter) ;
static void CreateSegments( Widget w) ;
static void DrawIndicator( Widget w) ;


/* resource callprocs */
static void DefaultKnobColor( Widget, int, XrmValue *);


/* action procedures */
static void TurnKnob( XtPointer closure, XtIntervalId *id) ;
static void DrawKnob( Widget w) ;
static void TurnLeft( Widget w, XEvent *event, char **params,
                      Cardinal *num_params) ;
static void TurnRight( Widget w, XEvent *event, char **params,
                       Cardinal *num_params) ;
static void ToggleLeft( Widget w, XEvent *event, char **params,
                        Cardinal *num_params) ;
static void ToggleRight( Widget w, XEvent *event, char **params,
                         Cardinal *num_params) ;
static void ReleaseKnob( Widget w, XEvent *event, char **params,
                         Cardinal *num_params) ;
```

Method and Procedure Descriptions

This section describes the methods and procedures in `Knob.c`. They are divided
into six categories:

1. Core class methods
2. XmPrimitive class methods
3. Knob class methods
4. CallProcs

5. Action procedures

6. Convenience functions

Core Class Methods

Core class methods are called by the Xt Intrinsics.

ClassPartInitialize

`ClassPartInitialize` performs the initialization needed by the Core class part.   Knob uses `ClassPartInitialize` to set the class methods of the widget subclasses that inherit them. `ClassPartInitialize` checks each method to see if it has been set to the value requesting inheritance. If it is, it resets the method to its own class method pointer. Here's a portion of knob's `ClassPartInitialize`:

```
 static void ClassPartInitialize(WidgetClass wc)
{

  XsmKnobWidgetClass kc = (XsmKnobWidgetClass) wc;

  XsmKnobWidgetClass sc = (XsmKnobWidgetClass)

                          wc->core_class.superclass;


/* assign methods to the class pointers that inherit these

   methods */


    if (kc->knob_class.get_diameters == XsmInheritGetDiameters)

      kc->knob_class.get_diameters = sc->knob_class.get_diameters;



    .

    .

    .



    if (kc->knob_class.draw == XsmInheritDraw)

      kc->knob_class.draw = sc->knob_class.draw;

}
```

Initialize

`Initialize` is the main knob instance initialization method. It first examines knob's resources and verifies that the resource values are valid. It determines the minimum height and width necessary for the knob to be displayed correctly. Then it determines whether or not the application set the height and width by determining if the request widget's height and width are nonzero. If they are zero, `Initialize` sets them to a default value; otherwise it checks to see if they are within the minimum values. Next, it initializes internal instance fields. It creates line segments used for drawing the knob handle by calling the knob class method for creating segments. Finally, it creates a graphics context used in drawing the widget's graphics. All drawing is done in the expose method (`Redisplay`), not in `Initialize`.

```
static void Initialize( Widget request, Widget new_w, ArgList args,
                            Cardinal *num_args )
{
    XsmKnobWidget req_kw = (XsmKnobWidget) request;

    XsmKnobWidget new_kw = (XsmKnobWidget) new_w;

    XsmKnobWidgetClass kc = (XsmKnobWidgetClass) XtClass(new_w);

    Dimension min_width, min_height;

    XGCValues values;

    unsigned long valuemask;


  /* Verify resource values */


  /* verify that the maximum value is not less than or equal to
     zero */
   if (new_kw->knob.max_val <= 0) {
     XtWarning("MaxValue is must be greater than 0, Defaulting
               MaxValue to 1");
     new_kw->knob.max_val = 1;
   }



   .

   .

   .



     min_width = MIN_KNOB_DIAMETER +
               (2 * (new_kw->knob.margin_width +
```

```
                          new_kw->primitive.highlight_thickness));
      min_height = MIN_KNOB_DIAMETER +
                     (2 * (new_kw->knob.margin_width +
                            new_kw->primitive.highlight_thickness));


      .

      .

      .



      if (req_kw->core.width == 0)
         new_kw->core.width = DEFAULT_DIAMETER +
                               (2 * (new_kw->knob.margin_width +
                                new_kw->primitive.highlight_thickness));
      else
         if (new_kw->core.width < min_width)
            new_kw->core.width = min_width;


      if (req_kw->core.height == 0)


         .

         .

         .



   new_kw->knob.num_segments = NUM_SEGS;
   new_kw->knob.segments = (XSegment *) XtMalloc(sizeof(XSegment)
    * (new_kw->knob.num_segments + 1));
      .

      .

      .

   (*kc->knob_class.create_segments)(new_w);
      .

      .

      .
```


The Knob Widget

```c
    valuemask = (GCForeground | GCBackground);
    values.foreground = new_kw->primitive.foreground;
    values.background = new_kw->knob.knob_color;
    new_kw->knob.gc = XtGetGC(new_w, valuemask, &values);
}
```

Destroy

`Destroy` frees allocated resources when the knob is destroyed. The knob allocates data in the initialize procedure and during execution of an application using it. This includes the graphics context (GC), the segments, any timers it may need, and callbacks. The data need to be freed when the widget is destroyed.

```c
static void Destroy( Widget w )
{

    XsmKnobWidget kw = (XsmKnobWidget) w;


    /* Free graphics contexts */
    XtReleaseGC( w, kw->knob.gc);


    /* Free allocated data */
    XtFree((char *) kw->knob.segments);


    /* Remove any outstanding timeouts */
    if (kw->knob.timer_id) XtRemoveTimeOut(kw->knob.timer_id);


    /* Remove all callbacks */
    XtRemoveAllCallbacks (w, XsmNvalueChangedCallback);
}
```

Resize

`Resize` determines the appropriate new geometry for the knob when its size changes. Knob's resize method recreates the line segments used in drawing the knob lines. It uses the knob class method `create_segments` to recreate the segments. No drawing is performed in `Resize`; it is done in the expose method `Redisplay`.

```c
static void Resize( Widget w )
{
```

```
    XsmKnobWidgetClass kc = (XsmKnobWidgetClass) XtClass(w);


    /* Recreate any segments based on the new size */

    (*kc->knob_class.create_segments)(w);

}
```

Redisplay

`Redisplay` redraws a region when expose events occur, when the widget is resized, when the widget is initially drawn, or when changes in the `SetValues`
method warrant a redraw. The `Redisplay` method uses the knob class method
`DrawKnob` (invoked by referencing the `knob_class` *draw* field, which points
to the `DrawKnob` method) to accomplish the drawing of the knob. It also uses
the XmPrimitive class methods to accomplish any redrawing of the border high-
lights. Typically, the expose method needs to be able to highlight and unhighlight
the widget if the widget supports highlighting.

```
static void Redisplay( Widget w, XEvent *event, Region region)

{

    XsmKnobWidget kw = (XsmKnobWidget) w;

    XsmKnobWidgetClass kc = (XsmKnobWidgetClass) XtClass(w);


    /* Use the class pointer to redraw the whole knob */

    (*kc->knob_class.draw)(w);


    /* Use the class pointers to highlight or unhighlight the knob */

    if (kw->primitive.highlighted)

        (*kc->primitive_class.border_highlight)(w);

    else

        (*kc->primitive_class.border_unhighlight)(w);

}
```

SetValues

`SetValues` is invoked when `XtSetValues` is called by an application using
the knob when the application wants to set one or more knob resource values.
`SetValues` also looks at superclass resource values that would affect the knob's
drawing, such as the Core's height and width resources and XmPrimitive's
foreground and highlight thickness resources. If changes in the visual affect the
graphics context used for drawing, the GC needs to be updated. This method also

                                                    The Knob Widget

computes minimum width and heights, and verifies the height and width. If the height and width are modified, geometry negotiations are initiated between the knob and its parent. `SetValues` also recreates segments for drawing. It returns True if any redrawing needs to be performed, thus the need for the *redisplay* variable. Permanent changes to the knob's instance structure must be made in the *new_w* widget pointer. All other changes to any of the other widget pointers (*old_w, request*) are lost.

```c
static Boolean SetValues( Widget old_w, Widget request,
                          Widget new_w, ArgList args,
                          Cardinal *num_args )
{
   XsmKnobWidget old_kw = (XsmKnobWidget) old_w;
   XsmKnobWidget new_kw = (XsmKnobWidget) new_w;
   XsmKnobWidgetClass kc = (XsmKnobWidgetClass) XtClass(new_w);
   Dimension min_width, min_height;
   Boolean redisplay = False; /* flag to determine return value */


/* verify changes in resource settings */


/* verify that the maximum value is not less than or equal
   to zero */
   if (new_kw->knob.max_val <= 0) {
      XtWarning("MaxValue is must be greater than 0,
             MaxValue set to 1");
      new_kw->knob.max_val = 1;
   }



             .


             .


             .



   /* Don't allow a zero size to set */
      if (new_kw->core.width == 0)
         new_kw->core.width = old_kw->core.width;
```

```c
    if (new_kw->core.height == 0)
        new_kw->core.height = old_kw->core.height;


/* If the color resources change, the graphic context needs
   to be updated */
    if (new_kw->primitive.foreground !=
        old_kw->primitive.foreground ||
        new_kw->knob.knob_color != old_kw->knob.knob_color) {
            XGCValues values;
            unsigned long valuemask;


            valuemask = (GCForeground | GCBackground );
            values.foreground = new_kw->primitive.foreground;
            values.background = new_kw->knob.knob_color;
            XtReleaseGC( new_w, new_kw->knob.gc);
            new_kw->knob.gc = XtGetGC(new_w, valuemask, &values);
            redisplay = True;
    }


    min_width = MIN_KNOB_DIAMETER +
                (2 * (new_kw->knob.margin_width +
                    new_kw->primitive.highlight_thickness));
    min_height = MIN_KNOB_DIAMETER +
                (2 * (new_kw->knob.margin_width +
                    new_kw->primitive.highlight_thickness));
/* Try to retain a minimum height and width */

    if (new_kw->core.width < min_width)
    {
        new_kw->core.width = min_width;
        redisplay = True;
    }
```


The Knob Widget

```
if (new_kw->knob.margin_height != old_kw->knob.margin_height ||
    new_kw->knob.margin_width != old_kw->knob.margin_width ||
    new_kw->knob.knob_margin != old_kw->knob.knob_margin ||
    new_kw->knob.max_val != old_kw->knob.max_val ||
    new_kw->knob.min_val != old_kw->knob.min_val ||
    new_kw->core.height != old_kw->core.height ||
    new_kw->core.width != old_kw->core.width ||
    new_kw->primitive.highlight_thickness !=
    old_kw->primitive.highlight_thickness) {


    (*kc->knob_class.create_segments)(new_w);
    redisplay = True;

}
```

SetValuesAlmost

`SetValuesAlmost` is called when knob values have been modified and the resulting geometry changes are unacceptable to the knob's parent. Because `SetValues` may change the height and width values in Core, `SetValuesAlmost` is necessary for geometry negotiations in the cvent that the parent rejects the request for a different height and width. `SetValuesAlmost` checks to see if any of the values are valid. It first checks to see if the request failed. If so, it sets the request mode to zero, recreates the segments, and returns. Then, using the calculation for minimum height and width, it tries to compute a smaller size to accommodate the reply width by changing the margins (it can always accommodate a larger size). The recomputed width is set to the `request->width` field, and the negotiations continue. It recomputes the segments at the end because, if the request succeeds, it will not be called again.

```
static void SetValuesAlmost( Widget old_w, Widget new_w,
                             XtWidgetGeometry *request,
XtWidgetGeometry *reply)
{
    XsmKnobWidget new_kw = (XsmKnobWidget) new_w;
    XsmKnobWidget old_kw = (XsmKnobWidget) old_w;
    Dimension min_width, min_height;
```

```c
    /* If the request failed completely, reset old values and
       return */
 if (reply->request_mode == 0)
 {
     new_kw->knob.margin_width = old_kw->knob.margin_width;
     new_kw->knob.margin_height = old_kw->knob.margin_height;
     request->request_mode = 0;
     (*kc->knob_class.create_segments)(new_w);
     return;
 }

     .

     .

     .


 min_width = MIN_KNOB_DIAMETER +
                 (2 * (new_kw->knob.margin_width +
                         new_kw->primitive.highlight_thickness));
     .

     .

     .


 if ( reply->width < min_width )
 {
    new_kw->knob.margin_width--;
    min_width -= 2; /* minus one pixel on each side of knob */
    request->width = min_width;
 }
 else /* accept larger size */
 {
    request->width = reply->width;
 }
     .
```

```
      (*kc->knob_class.create_segments)(new_w);

}
```

QueryGeometry

If the parent wants to learn the preferred geometry of the knob widget, it makes a
request to QueryGeometry. This method computes the knob's ideal height and
width. QueryGeometry begins by initializing the reply width of the fields it is
interested in. If the request is for the height and width and the reply equals the request, QueryGeometry returns GeometryYes, indicating that the requested
geometry is the preferred geometry. If the reply is the original geometry, it returns
GeometryNo. Otherwise, it returns GeometryAlmost to begin negotiations.

```
static XtGeometryResult QueryGeometry( Widget w,

                                       XtWidgetGeometry *request,

                                       XtWidgetGeometry *reply)

{

    XsmKnobWidget kw = (XsmKnobWidget) w;


    reply->width = kw->knob.orig_width;

    reply->height = kw->knob.orig_height;

    reply->request_mode = CWWidth | CWHeight;


    /* return XtGeometryYes if the request matches the reply width

       and height */
    if (((request->request_mode & CWWidth) && request->width ==

            reply->width) &&

        ((request->request_mode & CWHeight) && request->height ==

          reply->height))

            return XtGeometryYes;


    /* return XtGeometryNo if reply matches our current width and

       height */
    if (reply->width == kw->core.width && reply->height ==
```

```
                kw->core.height)
            return XtGeometryNo;



    /* return XtGeometryAlmost if one of the reply fields doesn't
       match the current or request width or height. */
      return XtGeometryAlmost;

}
```

XmPrimitive Class Methods

XmPrimitive class methods are also called by the Xt Intrinsics, but they are specified by the XmPrimitive class.

HighlightKnob

`HighlightKnob` provides the highlighting visual around the knob. This could have been inherited if the knob had a rectangular shape, but because it is circular, we had to write a unique highlight method for it. `HighlightKnob` does the actual drawing of the highlight. It first gets the appropriate diameters, then it sets up the GC for drawing and draws the highlight. Next, it sets the XmPrimitive flag to save the highlighted state of the widget. At the end it resets the GC to its original state.

```
static void HighlightKnob( Widget w )
{
    XsmKnobWidget kw = (XsmKnobWidget) w;
    XsmKnobWidgetClass kc = (XsmKnobWidgetClass) XtClass(w);
    unsigned int outer_diameter, inner_diameter, diameter;
    XGCValues values;
    unsigned long valuemask;


  /* Get the diameter */
    (*kc->knob_class.get_diameters)(w, &outer_diameter,
                                    &inner_diameter);


    diameter = outer_diameter + (2 *
                                 kw->primitive.highlight_thickness);
```

```c
/* Change the graphic context to highlight the knob */
valuemask = (GCLineWidth | GCForeground);
values.foreground = kw->primitive.highlight_color;
values.line_width = kw->primitive.highlight_thickness;
XChangeGC(XtDisplay(kw), kw->knob.gc, valuemask, &values);


/* Draw the highlight */
XDrawArc(XtDisplay(kw), XtWindow(kw), kw->knob.gc,
        kw->knob.margin_width, kw->knob.margin_height,
        diameter, diameter, 0, 64*360);


/* Set flags to indicate that the highlight has been drawn */
kw->primitive.highlighted = True;
kw->primitive.highlight_drawn = True;


/* Change the graphic context back for drawing the knob */
values.foreground = kw->knob.knob_color;
values.line_width = 0;
XChangeGC(XtDisplay(kw), kw->knob.gc, valuemask, &values);
}
```

UnhighlightKnob

`UnhighlightKnob` removes the highlighting established by `HighlightKnob`. It is similar to the `HighlightKnob` method, except it erases the highlight and sets the flags to indicate that the highlight is not drawn.

```c
static void UnhighlightKnob( Widget w )
{

    .

    .

    .


/* Change the graphic context to unhighlight */
valuemask = (GCLineWidth | GCForeground);
values.foreground = kw->core.background_pixel;
values.line_width = kw->primitive.highlight_thickness;
```

```
        XChangeGC(XtDisplay(kw), kw->knob.gc, valuemask, &values);

        .

        .

        .


    kw->primitive.highlighted = False;
    kw->primitive.highlight_drawn = False;


        .

        .

        .

}
```

Knob Class Methods

These methods were created for the knob, but they can be inherited by a widget
subclassed from knob.

An interesting line of code that you'll see fairly often needs an explanation. For
example, consider this line in `CreateSegments`:

```
(*kc->knob_class.get_diameters)(w, &diameter, &inner_diameter);
```

The first part of the line dereferences the `kc->knob_class.get_diameters`
pointer. In effect, this calls the method pointed to by the *get_diameters* field of
the knob class record. In this case, the method is `GetDiameters`, so the
preceding line could have been written as:

```
GetDiameters(w, &diameter, &inner_diameter);
```

The code is written in this manner to allow the method to be replaced, if desired,
by a widget subclassing from knob. Calling the method directly, as in the preceding line, does not allow this.

GetDiameters

`GetDiameters` retrieves diameters of the inner and outer circles that are part of
the knob's visual appearance. This method uses the core height and width values,
the knob margin resources, and the highlight thickness to compute the knob's
diameters for the outer circle and the inner circle (the knob handle).

```
static void GetDiameters( Widget w, unsigned int *diameter,

                            unsigned int *inner_diameter)
```

```c
{
    XsmKnobWidget kw = (XsmKnobWidget) w;


    if (kw->core.height - (2 * kw->knob.margin_width) >=
        kw->core.width - (2 * kw->knob.margin_height))
        *diameter = kw->core.width - (2 * (kw->knob.margin_width +
                            kw->primitive.highlight_thickness));
    else
        *diameter = kw->core.height - (2 * (kw->knob.margin_height +
                            kw->primitive.highlight_thickness));


    if (*diameter < MIN_KNOB_DIAMETER) *diameter =
                                        MIN_KNOB_DIAMETER;


    *inner_diameter = (*diameter * kw->knob.knob_margin)/100;


    if (*inner_diameter < 1) *inner_diameter = 1;
}
```

CreateSegments

`CreateSegments` creates the lines that are drawn between the knob's inner and
outer circles and is used to show knob movement by redrawing the lines in a new
position. The segments enhance the knob's appearance. `CreateSegments`
uses the knob's outer and inner diameters and math functions to compute the end
points of the segments to be drawn.

```c
static void CreateSegments( Widget w )
{
    XsmKnobWidget kw = (XsmKnobWidget) w;

        .

        .

        .


    ptr = kw->knob.segments;


    angle_change = RADIANS(MAX_ANGLE)
```

```
                        /(float)(kw->knob.num_segments - 1);


    (*kc->knob_class.get_diameters)(w, &diameter, &inner_diameter);


      .

      .

      .


    for (i = 0; i < kw->knob.num_segments; i++) {
        cosine = cos(angle);
        sine   = sin(angle);
        ptr->x1   = (short)(center_x + radius * sine);
        ptr->y1 = (short)(center_y - radius * cosine);
        ptr->x2   = (short)(center_x + inner_radius * sine);
        ptr++->y2 = (short)(center_y - inner_radius * cosine);
        angle += angle_change;

    }

}
```

DrawIndicator

DrawIndicator draws the small colored dot on the knob face. This dot
identifies the knob's position relative to the minimum and maximum values.
DrawIndicator uses the get_diameters class method to obtain the
diameters for use in drawing the dot and filling it.

```
static void DrawIndicator( Widget w )

{

  Widget kw = (XsmKnobWidget) w;

    .

    .

    .



  (*kc->knob_class.get_diameters)(w, &diameter, &inner_diameter);


  angle = (RADIANS(MAX_ANGLE)  * kw->knob.value)/
                (kw->knob.max_val - kw->knob.min_val) ;
```

```
center_x = (diameter >> 1) + kw->knob.margin_width +
           kw->primitive.highlight_thickness;
center_y = (diameter >> 1) + kw->knob.margin_height +
           kw->primitive.highlight_thickness;



   .

   .

   .


XDrawArc(XtDisplay(w), XtWindow(w), kw->knob.gc,
         center_x, center_y, diameter, diameter, 0, 64*360);


XFillArc(XtDisplay(w), XtWindow(w), kw->knob.gc,
         center_x, center_y, diameter, diameter, 0, 64*360);


}
```

CallProcs

A CallProc is used to set the value of resources dynamically. The name *CallProc*
is derived from the type `XmRCallProc` used in the resource definition. For
example, the knob resource `XsmNknobColor` is defincd as

```
{

  XsmNknobColor, XsmCKnobColor, XmRPixel, sizeof(Pixel),

  XtOffset (XsmKnobWidget, knob.knob_color),

  XmRCallProc, (XtPointer) _XmBackgroundColorDefault

}
```

DefaultKnobColor

In Motif, the default background is the basis for all other default colors
(foreground, top shadow, bottom shadow, select color, etc.). If knob tries to get
the default background from the resource database and no entry is found, it uses a
default background color obtained by using an internal Motif 1.2 function
`_XmBackgroundColorDefault`. Due to a bug in this function, if the
resource value is found but has already been converted from a string value to a
pixel value, the default background is not set properly. The procedure

`DefaultKnobColor` solves this problem by calling the Motif 1.2 function
`_XmSetDefaultBackgroundColorSpec()`.

Action Procedures

The action procedures are called as the result of an action that takes place on the
knob widget.

TurnKnob

`TurnKnob` turns the knob either left or right, depending on which mouse button
was clicked. The rate of turn is specified by the resource `XsmNturnDelay`.
This method uses timers to keep the knob turning. It erases the old indicator and
old segments. It calls the value changed callback, because the value of the knob
changes. It uses the class method to recreate and draw the segments as well as to
redraw the indicator.

```
static void TurnKnob( XtPointer closure, XtIntervalId *id )
{
    Widget w = (Widget) closure;
    XsmKnobWidget kw = (XsmKnobWidget) w;
    XsmKnobWidgetClass kc = (XsmKnobWidgetClass) XtClass(w);
    XsmKnobCallbackStruct cb;

    if ((kw->knob.value < kw->knob.max_val - 1 &&
        kw->knob.move_clockwise) ||
        (kw->knob.value > 1 && !kw->knob.move_clockwise)) {
        kw->knob.timer_id =
                XtAppAddTimeOut(XtWidgetToApplicationContext(w),
                                (unsigned long) kw->knob.turn_delay,
                                kc->knob_class.turn, (XtPointer) kw);
    } else {
        kw->knob.turning = False;

    XSetForeground(XtDisplay(kw), kw->knob.gc, kw->knob.knob_color);
    (*kc->knob_class.draw_indicator)(w);

    XDrawSegments(XtDisplay(w), XtWindow(w), kw->knob.gc,
                kw->knob.segments, kw->knob.num_segments);
```

```c
    if (kw->knob.move_clockwise) kw->knob.value++;
    else kw->knob.value--;


    if (kw->knob.value_changed_callback) {
        cb.reason = XsmCR_VALUE_CHANGED;
        cb.event = NULL;
        cb.value = kw->knob.value;
        XtCallCallbackList(w, kw->knob.value_changed_callback,
                        (XtPointer) &cb);
    }


    kw->knob.angle_offset = (RADIANS(MAX_ANGLE) * kw->knob.value)/
                        (kw->knob.max_val - kw->knob.min_val) ;
    (*kc->knob_class.create_segments)(w);


    XSetForeground(XtDisplay(w), kw->knob.gc,
                kw->knob.indicator_color);
    (*kc->knob_class.draw_indicator)(w);


    XSetForeground(XtDisplay(w), kw->knob.gc,
                kw->primitive.foreground);
    XDrawSegments(XtDisplay(w), XtWindow(w), kw->knob.gc,
                kw->knob.segments, kw->knob.num_segments);


}
```

DrawKnob

`DrawKnob` draws the knob visual. It is invoked by the expose method
`Redisplay`. This class method uses X routines to draw and fill the knob,
indicator, and segments.

```c
static void DrawKnob( Widget w )
{
    XsmKnobWidget kw = (XsmKnobWidget) w;
    XsmKnobWidgetClass kc = (XsmKnobWidgetClass) XtClass(w);
```

```c
    unsigned int diameter, inner_diameter, top_knob_start;


    (*kc->knob_class.get_diameters)(w, &diameter, &inner_diameter);


    /* bottom of knob */
    XSetForeground(XtDisplay(kw), kw->knob.gc, kw->knob.knob_color);
    XFillArc(XtDisplay(kw), XtWindow(kw), kw->knob.gc,
            (kw->knob.margin_width +
             kw->primitive.highlight_thickness),
            (kw->knob.margin_height +
             kw->primitive.highlight_thickness),
            diameter, diameter, 0, 64*360);
    XSetForeground(XtDisplay(kw), kw->knob.gc,
                kw->primitive.foreground);


    XDrawArc(XtDisplay(kw), XtWindow(kw), kw->knob.gc,
            (kw->knob.margin_width +
             kw->primitive.highlight_thickness),
            (kw->knob.margin_height +
             kw->primitive.highlight_thickness),
            diameter, diameter, 0, 64*360);


    top_knob_start = (diameter - ((diameter *
                    kw->knob.knob_margin)/100))/2;


    /* top of knob */
    XDrawArc(XtDisplay(kw), XtWindow(kw), kw->knob.gc,
            (top_knob_start +
             kw->knob.margin_width +
             kw->primitive.highlight_thickness),
            (top_knob_start + kw->knob.margin_height +
             kw->primitive.highlight_thickness),
            inner_diameter, inner_diameter, 0, 64*360);
```

                                    The Knob Widget

```c
    XDrawSegments(XtDisplay(w), XtWindow(w), kw->knob.gc,
                    kw->knob.segments, kw->knob.num_segments);


    XSetForeground(XtDisplay(w), kw->knob.gc,
                    kw->knob.indicator_color);
    (*kc->knob_class.draw_indicator)(w);
    XSetForeground(XtDisplay(w), kw->knob.gc,
                    kw->primitive.foreground);


}
```

TurnLeft

TurnLeft is called when the user presses the left mouse button on the knob. It causes the knob to rotate to the left until the button is released or it reaches the minimum value. This is accomplished using a timer procedure.

```c
static void TurnLeft( Widget w, XEvent *event, char **params,
                    Cardinal *num_params )
{
    XsmKnobWidget kw = (XsmKnobWidget) w;
    XsmKnobWidgetClass kc = (XsmKnobWidgetClass) XtClass(w);


    /*
     * As long as the value has not reached the minimum value,
     * continue turning
     */


    if (kw->knob.value > kw->knob.min_val) {
        kw->knob.move_clockwise = False;
        kw->knob.timer_id =
            XtAppAddTimeOut(XtWidgetToApplicationContext(w),
                            unsigned long) kw->knob.turn_delay,
                            kc->knob_class.turn, (XtPointer) w);
    }
}
```

TurnRight

`TurnRight` is identical to `TurnLeft` except that it turns the knob to the right and stops when the mouse button is released or it reaches the maximum value.

ToggleLeft

`ToggleLeft` is called when the user presses the < key. It causes the knob to rotate to the left until it reaches the minimum value or the user presses the < key a second time. The knob starts turning the first time `ToggleLeft` is called, and stops turning the next time it is called or when it reaches its minimum value.

```
static void ToggleLeft( Widget w, XEvent *event, char **params,
                        Cardinal *num_params )
{
    XsmKnobWidget kw = (XsmKnobWidget) w;
    XsmKnobWidgetClass kc = (XsmKnobWidgetClass) XtClass(w);


    /* If the knob has not started turning, added the timeout */
    if (!kw->knob.turning) {
        if (kw->knob.value > kw->knob.min_val) {
            kw->knob.move_clockwise = False;
            kw->knob.timer_id =
                XtAppAddTimeOut(XtWidgetToApplicationContext(w),
                                (unsigned long) kw->knob.turn_delay,
                                kc->knob_class.turn, (XtPointer) w);
            kw->knob.turning = True;
        }
    } else {
        /* If it is already turning, remove the old timeout and
           continue turning with a new timeout */
        if (kw->knob.timer_id) XtRemoveTimeOut(kw->knob.timer_id);

        /* if it was turning left continue the turning, otherwise
           stop. */
        if (kw->knob.move_clockwise) {
            kw->knob.move_clockwise = False;
            kw->knob.timer_id =
```

```
XtAppAddTimeOut(XtWidgetToApplicationContext(w),

                    (unsigned long) kw->knob.turn_delay,

                    kc->knob_class.turn, (XtPointer) w);

        } else {

            kw->knob.turning = False;

        }

    }

}
```

ToggleRight

`ToggleRight` is called when the user presses the > key. It causes the knob to
rotate to the right until it reaches the maximum value or the user presses the > key
a second time.

ReleaseKnob

`ReleaseKnob` is called when the button is released.   This action procedure is
used to stop the knob turning when it was activated by the `TurnLeft` or
`TurnRight` action. It is called on a button release as specified in the translation
table. It removes the timeout used to turn the knob and sets a flag to indicate that
the knob is no longer turning.

```
static void ReleaseKnob( Widget w, XEvent *event, char **params,

                    Cardinal *num_params )

{

    XsmKnobWidget kw = (XsmKnobWidget) w;


    /* remove the timeout */
    if (kw->knob.timer_id) XtRemoveTimeOut(kw->knob.timer_id);


    kw->knob.turning = False;

}
```

Convenience Functions

Convenience functions exist for the convenience of the application developer.
We've created three convenience functions for the knob (remember that these are
public functions and were declared in `Knob.h`).

XsmCreateKnob

XsmCreateKnob is a convenience procedure used to create an instance of a
knob widget. It performs exactly like the convenience functions for creating existing Motif widgets.

```
Widget XsmCreateKnob( Widget parent, char *name, ArgList arglist,

                        Cardinal argcount )

{

    return (XtCreateWidget(name, xsmKnobWidgetClass,

                            parent, arglist, argcount));

}
```

XsmGetKnobValue

`XsmGetKnobValue` returns the value of the knob resource `XsmNvalue`. This
adjustment could be done using `XtGetValues`, but because `XsmNvalue` is a
resource that be may retrieved frequently, `XsmGetKnobValue` is provided to
avoid the performance overhead generated by `XtGetValues`.

```
int XsmGetKnobValue( Widget w )

{

    XsmKnobWidget kw = (XsmKnobWidget) w;


    return(kw->knob.value);

}
```

XsmSetKnobValue

`XsmSetKnobValue` sets the value of the knob resource `XsmNvalue`. This
adjustment could be done using `XtSetValues`, but because `XsmNvalue` is a
resource that be may set frequently, `XsmSetKnobValue` is provided to avoid
the performance overhead generated by `XtSetValues`. Like `SetValues`,
`XsmSetKnobValue` has to verify the value. Because the expose method is not
called, the knob must be redrawn here.

```
void XsmSetKnobValue( Widget w, int value )

{

    XsmKnobWidget kw = (XsmKnobWidget) w;
    XsmKnobWidgetClass kc = (XsmKnobWidgetClass) XtClass(w);


    /* return if the value doesn't change */
```

```c
    if (value == kw->knob.value) return;

/* verify the changed values */
  if (value > kw->knob.max_val) {
     XtWarning("Value is less than MaxValue, Defaulting to
               MaxValue");
     kw->knob.value = kw->knob.max_val;
  }


  if (value < kw->knob.min_val) {
     XtWarning("Value is greater than MinValue, Defaulting to
               MinValue");
     kw->knob.value = kw->knob.min_val;
  }


/*
 * If the knob is realized, redraw the knob segments and indicator
 * to indicate the new value
 */


  if (XtIsRealized(w)) {
     /* erase old indicator */
     XSetForeground(XtDisplay(kw), kw->knob.gc,
                    kw->knob.knob_color);
     (*kc->knob_class.draw_indicator)(w);
     XDrawSegments(XtDisplay(w), XtWindow(w), kw->knob.gc,
                   kw->knob.segments, kw->knob.num_segments);


     /* set new value */
     kw->knob.value = value;


     /* recreate segments */
     kw->knob.angle_offset = (RADIANS(MAX_ANGLE) *
```

```
                              kw->knob.value)/
                      (kw->knob.max_val - kw->knob.min_val) ;
          (*kc->knob_class.create_segments)(w);


      /* redraw indicator */
      XSetForeground(XtDisplay(w), kw->knob.gc,
                     kw->knob.indicator_color);
      (*kc->knob_class.draw_indicator)(w);


      /* redraw segments */
      XSetForeground(XtDisplay(w), kw->knob.gc,
                     kw->primitive.foreground);
      XDrawSegments(XtDisplay(w), XtWindow(w), kw->knob.gc,
                    kw->knob.segments, kw->knob.num_segments);
    } else {
      kw->knob.value = value;

    }

  }
```

Compiling Knob.c

You'll need a Makefile to compile the `knob.c` object. The Makefile listed in
Appendix A specifies specific paths for the include and library directories, and
you may need to change these to suit your system. Note that the Makefile creates
only an object file called `Knob.o`. The object file is then linked when an
application uses a knob widget. You normally access Motif widgets by linking
the Motif library `libXm`, which is composed of all the Motif widget object files.

Sample Programs

Now that you've created the knob, let's put it to use in an actual program. This
section briefly describes two programs, `knob1.c` and `knobcolors.c`. You
can find the listing for each of these programs in Appendix A.

knob1.c

knob1.c is a very simple program that produces a window with a single knob. No callbacks are included, so the program doesn't do anything, but you can get an idea of how the knob works by looking at this program and the next one. Figure 3-4 shows the window from knob1.c:

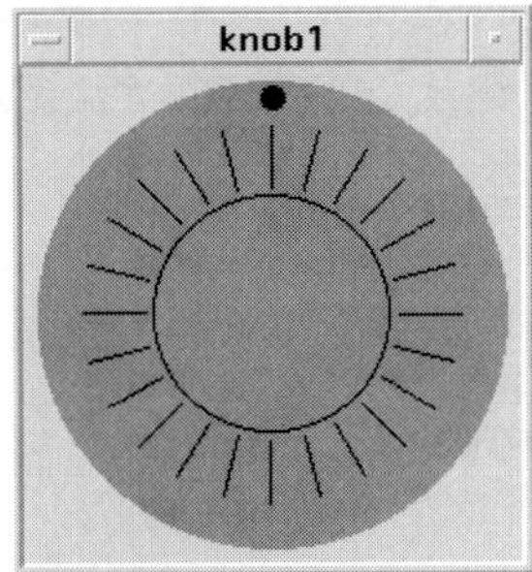

Figure 3-4 Window From knob1.c

knobcolors.c

knobcolors.c produces a window with three knobs, one to control each of the primary colors. Figure 3-5 shows the window from knobcolors.c:

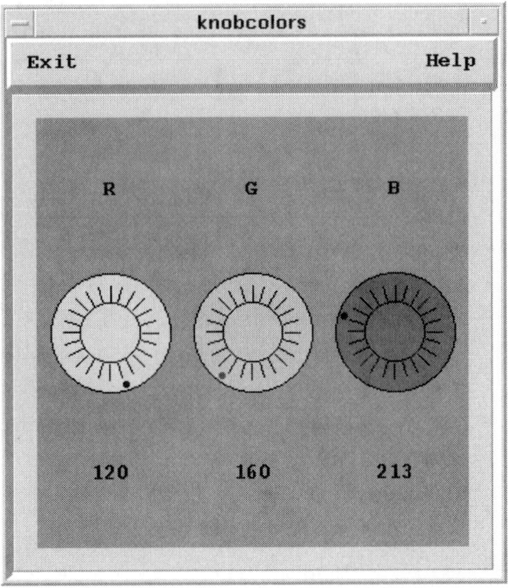

Figure 3-5 Window From knobcolors.c

As each knob is turned, the knob's value and the background color of the window change accordingly. The program uses a row column to hold the knobs. A similar program is used in the next chapter to demonstrate the grid widget, except that it uses the grid instead of the row column.

Summary

This chapter described the knob widget and took you through its creation. The next chapter describes the grid widget, a manager widget similar to the Motif row column widget, but with some important differences.

Chapter 4 The Grid Widget

The knob widget described in Chapter 3 is subclassed from XmPrimitive. Now, we'll show you a widget subclassed from XmManager. This widget, called the grid widget, is a manager that controls the layout of its children based on resource values that the user provides. There are some significant differences between writing the knob widget and writing the grid widget, because the grid is a manager.

Introduction

The grid widget is designed to be used as a container for other widgets. It is similar to the Motif row column widget but has these advantages:

- You can place a widget at a specific location within the grid widget; row column wants its children created in the order they are to be placed.

- The grid is more efficient because it does not have the overhead associated with menu use, as row column does.

- The user has the option of displaying lines on the grid by setting a resource.

The Process

We'll use the widget writing process described in Chapter 2 to create the grid widget. This involves choosing the superclass, creating the private and public header files `GridP.h` and `Grid.h`, and then writing the object `grid.c`. You may see some duplication from Chapter 2 as we go through the widget writing process for the grid, but the more you go through it, the better you'll understand it.

Throughout this chapter you'll see code segments from the files that make up the grid widget. Appendix A contains a complete listing of these files.

Choose the Superclass

Unlike the knob widget, which was subclassed from XmPrimitive, we want the grid widget to manage child widgets, so we'll subclass it from the XmManager class. This means that we'll include the XmManager, Composite, Constraint and Core class parts in the grid's private header file. The Composite and Constraint classes are included, because XmManager is a subclass of Constraint and Constraint is a subclass of Composite. Figure 4-1 shows the XmManager portion of the widget hierarchy

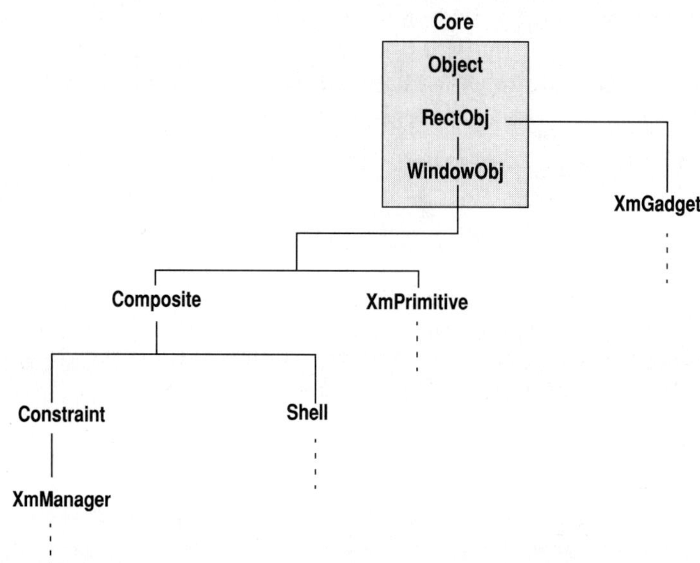

Figure 4-1   XmManager Widget Hierarchy

Create the Grid Private Header File

The grid widget's private header file, `GridP.h` describes details of the grid widget's implementation and is normally used only by other widget writers who want to subclass a new widget from the grid widget. See Appendix A.

Manage Multiple Inclusions

The first lines of the private header file are used to manage multiple inclusions of the header file without causing duplicate definitions:

```
#ifndef _XsmGridP_h
#define _XsmGridP_h
```

The associated `#endif` is the last line of `GridP.h`.

Include Grid.h and Manager.h

Next, include the grid's public header file `Grid.h` and the superclass XmManager's private header file `ManagerP.h`:

```
#include "Grid.h"
#include <Xm/ManagerP.h>
```

Figure 4-2 shows the relationships between the private and public header files.

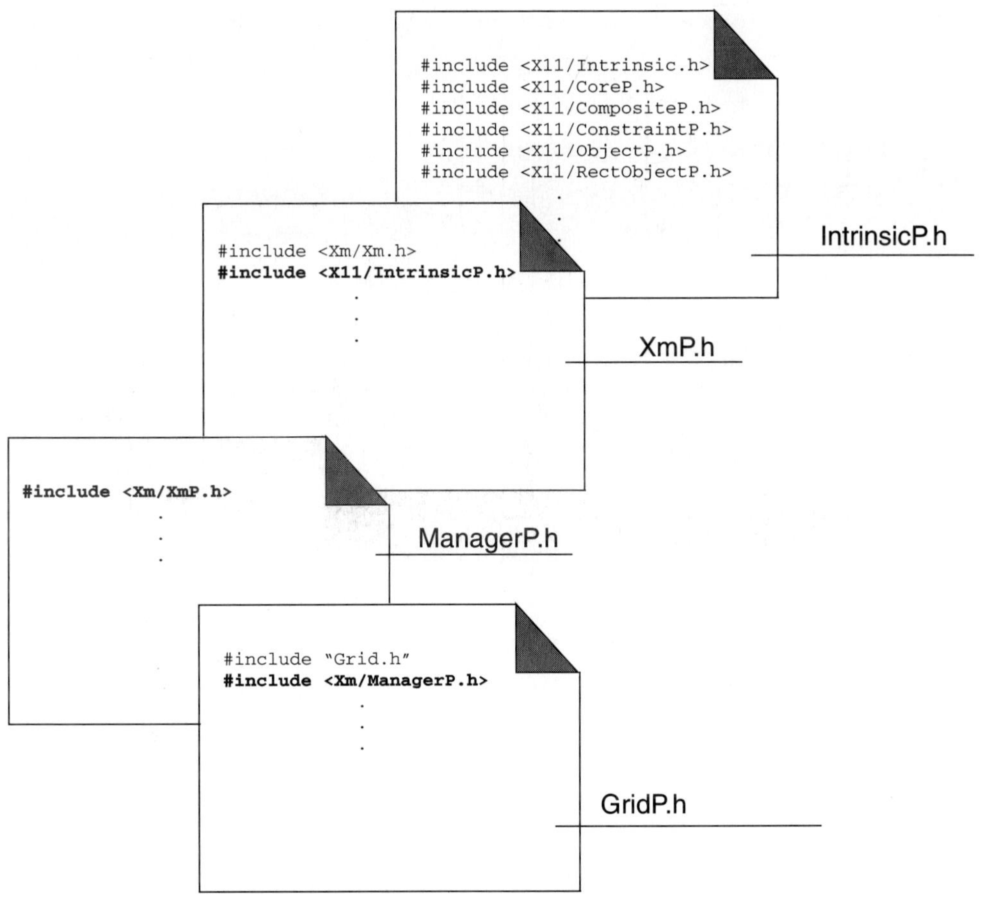

Figure 4-2   Private Header File Relationships

It's almost the same as Figure 2-4, except that in this case `ManagerP.h` is shown instead of `PrimitiveP.h`. `ManagerP.h` includes `XmP.h`, just as `PrimitiveP.h` does. This is how the Composite and Constraint header files are included. Because XmManager is a subclass of both of these classes (see Figure 4-1, the XmManager widget hierarchy), both are used here, unlike the XmPrimitive class, which is not a subclass of either Composite or Constraint.

Define the Class Part Structure

Next, define the grid's class part structure.

```
typedef struct {
    XsmUpdateGridProc   update_grid;       /* update grid dimensions */
    XsmAddChildProc     add_child;         /* Add child to grid */
    XtWidgetProc        layout_children;   /* Layout widget children */
    XtWidgetProc        draw_grid;         /* Draw grid lines */
    XtWidgetProc        erase_grid;        /* Erase grid lines */
    XtPointer           extension;         /* Pointer to extension
                                              record */
} XsmGridClassPart;
```

Note that the types of the first two procedures were defined earlier in `GridP.h`; they are not defined by the Xt Intrinsics.

Define the Class Structure

Next, define the grid's class structure:

```
typedef struct _XsmGridClassRec {
    CoreClassPart           core_class;
    CompositeClassPart      composite_class;
    ConstraintClassPart     constraint_class;
    XmManagerClassPart      manager_class;
    XsmGridClassPart        grid_class;
} XsmGridClassRec;
```

Note that it is composed of pointers to the Core class part, Composite class part, Constraint class part, XmManager class part, and grid class part. Recall that XmManager is a subclass of Constraint, which is a subclass of Composite, thus the need to include these two class parts in addition to the XmManager class part. The XmManager widget hierarchy in Figure 4-1 may help clarify this concept.

Define Procedure Pointer Types

Some local procedures need a pointer type defined so that they can be inherited by a widget subclassing from grid. The grid has two such procedures: `XsmUpdateGridProc` and `XsmAddChildProc`.

```
typedef void(*XsmUpdateGridProc)(Widget, Dimension *, Dimension *);

typedef void(*XsmAddChildProc)(Widget, Widget, Dimension,

          Dimension);
```

Define Inheritance Macros

Next, define inheritance macros. These are macros that identify methods and procedures that widgets subclassing from grid can use instead of providing their own implementation of the class method. The actual number of these macros corresponds to the number of methods in the class part structure, and some widgets may not have any. The grid widget defines these inheritance macros:

```
#define XsmInheritUpdateGridDimensions ((XsmUpdateGridProc)

                              _XtInherit)

#define XsmInheritAddChild ((XsmAddChildProc) _XtInherit)

#define XsmInheritLayoutChildren ((XtWidgetProc) _XtInherit)

#define XsmInheritDrawGrid ((XtWidgetProc) _XtInherit)

#define XsmInheritEraseGrid ((XtWidgetProc) _XtInherit)
```

Define the Instance Part Structure

Next, define the grid's instance part structure. Here's the grid's instance part structure:

```
typedef struct _XsmGridPart {

Dimension    columns;

Dimension    rows;

Dimension    margin_width;

Dimension    margin_height;

Dimension    orig_margin_width;

Dimension    orig_margin_height;

Dimension    h_spacing;

Dimension    v_spacing;

WidgetList *widget_grid;

Dimension    *row_height;

Dimension    *col_width;
```

```c
    XtEnum          horiz_alignment;

    XtEnum          vert_alignment;

    Boolean         show_grid_lines;

    Boolean         lines_visible;

    GC              gc;

} XsmGridPart;
```

This is a part of the grid's instance structure (defined next), the other parts being
Core, Composite, Constraint, and XmManager. The grid's resource values are
stored in its instance part record. The instance record contains resources and internal variables for each instance of the grid widget.

Define the Instance Structure

Next, define the grid's instance structure:

```c
typedef struct _XsmGridRec {

    CorePart            core;

    CompositePart       composite;

    ConstraintPart      constraint;

    XmManagerPart       manager;

    XsmGridPart         grid;

} XsmGridRec;
```

Notice that within this structure (XsmGridRec), the field *grid* (type
XsmGridPart) references the grid's instance part record. All the instance parts
(CorePart, CompositePart, ConstraintPart, XmManagerPart, and
XsmGridPart) form the grid widget instance record.

In addition to the grid instance record, we must also define the grid's Constraint
instance record. The Constraint part contains resources and internal variables that
are created for each of the grid's children.

```c
typedef struct _XsmGridConstraintPart

{

    Position    row_pos;

    Position    col_pos;

    Dimension   orig_row_pos;

    Dimension   orig_col_pos;

    Boolean     auto_placed;

} XsmGridConstraintPart;
```

```
/* Only the active constraint parts of a widget are       */
/* added here to form the constraint record. Neither      */
/* Core, Composite, or Constraint have active constraint */
/* parts.

typedef struct _XsmGridConstraintRec
{
    XmManagerConstraintPart manager;
    XsmGridConstraintPart   grid;
} XsmGridConstraintRec, * XsmGridConstraintPtr;
```

Create the Grid Public Header File

The public header file (`Grid.h`) is used by application programmers. It contains error messages, the widget class name, resource strings, callback structures, and external public function declarations.

Manage Multiple Inclusions

Like the private header file, the first lines manage multiple inclusions:

```
#ifndef _XsmGrid_h
#define _XsmGrid_h
```

The associated `#endif` is the last line of the private header file:

```
#endif /* _XsmGrid_h */
```

which prevents a header file from being included more than once.

Include Xm.h

Next, include the `Xm.h` header file:

```
#include <Xm/Xm.h>
```

This header file has general definitions and inclusions needed by all widgets.

Define Resource Name Macros

We define macros to map to the resource names. By convention, the words in the names are separated by differences in capitalization. The macro definition includes the two- or three-letter prefix (Xm or Xsm, for example) for the widget library, followed by an *N* that indicates a resource name. Here's the grid's resource name macros:

```
#define XsmNcolumnPosition           "columnPosition"

#define XsmNcolumns                  "columns"

#define XsmNhorizontalAlignment      "horizontalAlignment"

#define XsmNhorizontalSpacing        "horizontalSpacing"

#define XsmNmarginHeight             "marginHeight"

#define XsmNmarginWidth              "marginWidth"

#define XsmNrowPosition              "rowPosition"

#define XsmNrows                     "rows"

#define XsmNshowGridLines            "showGridLines"

#define XsmNverticalAlignment        "verticalAlignment"

#define XsmNverticalSpacing          "verticalSpacing"
```

Define Resource Class Name Macros

The resource class name macros also use capitalization to separate words. The class name macro uses an uppercase *C* instead of *N*, and the letter following the *C* is always uppercase. Here's the resource class name macros for the grid's resources:

```
#define XsmCColumnPosition           "ColumnPosition"

#define XsmCColumns                  "Columns"

#define XsmCHorizontalAlignment      "HorizontalAlignment"

#define XsmCHorizontalSpacing        "HorizontalSpacing"

#define XsmCMarginHeight             "MarginHeight"

#define XsmCMarginWidth              "MarginWidth"
```

Define the Widget Class Name

The pointers to the widget instance and class structures in the public header file are mainly used for applications that wish to have more specific type checking. Instead of using the generic types `Widget` and `WidgetClass` for the widget instance and class types, the application programmer may want to have a more specific type for each widget instance and class.

```
externalref WidgetClass        xsmGridWidgetClass;


typedef struct _XsmGridClassRec *XsmGridWidgetClass;

typedef struct _XsmGridRec       *XsmGridWidget;
```

Define Callback Structures

The grid has no callbacks, so you don't have to define a callback structure.

Define Public Function Declarations

The grid has only one public function, `XsmCreateGrid`. It is a convenience function to simplify creating an instance of grid. Here's the function definition as it appears in `Grid.h`:

```
extern Widget XsmCreateGrid(

                Widget parent,

                char *name,

                ArgList arglist,

                Cardinal argcount) ;
```

Define New Resources

You define the grid's new resources in `Grid.c`. You also set initial, or default, values for each resource at the same time. Table 4-1 shows the grid's resource names, classes, and default values.

Table 4-1 Grid Widget Resources

Resource Name	Resource Class Name	Default
XsmNcolumns	XsmCColumns	1
XsmNrows	XsmCRows	1
XsmNmarginWidth	XsmCMarginWidth	4
XsmNmarginHeight	XsmCMarginHeight	4
XsmNhorizontalSpacing	XsmCHorizontalSpacing	4
XsmNverticalSpacing	XsmCVerticalSpacing	4
XsmNhorizontalAlignment	XsmCHorizontalAlignment	XsmALIGN_CENTER
XsmNverticalAlignment	XsmCVerticalAlignment	XsmALIGN_MIDDLE
XsmNshowGridLines	XsmCShowGridLines	False

The format you use to define the resources is defined by the Xt Intrinsics as described in Chapter 2. Here's the grid's resources as they are defined in `Grid.c`:

```
static XtResource resources[] = {


    {

        XsmNcolumns,

        XsmCColumns,

        XmRDimension,

        sizeof(Dimension),
```

```
    XtOffset (XsmGridWidget, grid.columns),
    XmRImmediate, (XtPointer) 1
  },

  {
    XsmNrows,
    XsmCRows,
    XmRDimension,
    sizeof(Dimension),
    XtOffset (XsmGridWidget, grid.rows),
    XmRImmediate, (XtPointer) 1
  },

  {
    XsmNmarginWidth,
    XsmCMarginHeight,
    XmRHorizontalDimension,
    sizeof(Dimension),
    XtOffset (XsmGridWidget, grid.margin_width),
    XmRImmediate, (XtPointer) 4
  },

  {
    XsmNmarginHeight,
    XsmCMarginHeight,
    XmRVerticalDimension,
    sizeof(Dimension),
    XtOffset (XsmGridWidget, grid.margin_height),
    XmRImmediate, (XtPointer) 4
  },

  {
    XsmNhorizontalSpacing,
    XsmCHorizontalSpacing,
```

```c
      XmRHorizontalDimension,
      sizeof(Dimension),
      XtOffset (XsmGridWidget, grid.h_spacing),
      XmRImmediate, (XtPointer) 4
   },

   {

      XsmNverticalSpacing,
      XsmCVerticalSpacing,
      XmRVerticalDimension,
      sizeof(Dimension),
      XtOffset (XsmGridWidget, grid.v_spacing),
      XmRImmediate, (XtPointer) 4
   },

   {

      XsmNhorizontalAlignment,
      XsmCHorizontalAlignment,
      XsmRHorizontalAlignment,
      sizeof(unsigned char),
      XtOffset (XsmGridWidget, grid.horiz_alignment),
      XmRImmediate, (XtPointer) XsmALIGN_CENTER
   },

   {

      XsmNverticalAlignment,
      XsmCVerticalAlignment,
      XsmRVerticalAlignment,
      sizeof(unsigned char),
      XtOffset (XsmGridWidget, grid.vert_alignment),
      XmRImmediate, (XtPointer) XsmALIGN_MIDDLE
   },

   {
```

```
        XsmNshowGridLines,

        XsmCShowGridLines,

        XmRBoolean,

        sizeof(Boolean),

        XtOffset (XsmGridWidget, grid.show_grid_lines),

        XmRImmediate, (XtPointer) False
    },

};
```

The synthetic resource list initialization sets up resource procedures that are called when you are setting or getting the various resources. Synthetic resources change their values dynamically. As in Motif, our dimension resources change dynamically based on the `XmNunitType` resource. For example, if the unit type is in 1000ths of an inch, the conversion routines modify the resource values to convert the resource value in the given unit type into a number of pixels for use in displaying the widget in the stated dimensions.

```
static XmSyntheticResource syn_resources[] =
{
    {
        XmNmarginWidth,

        sizeof (Dimension),

        XtOffset( XsmGridWidget, grid.margin_width),

        _XmFromHorizontalPixels,

        _XmToHorizontalPixels
    },


    {
        XmNmarginHeight,

        sizeof (Dimension),

        XtOffset( XsmGridWidget, grid.margin_height),

        _XmFromVerticalPixels,

        _XmToVerticalPixels,
    },


    {
        XmNhorizontalSpacing,
```

```c
        sizeof (Dimension),
        XtOffset( XsmGridWidget, grid.h_spacing),
        _XmFromHorizontalPixels,
        _XmToHorizontalPixels
    },

    {
        XmNverticalSpacing,
        sizeof (Dimension),
        XtOffset( XsmGridWidget, grid.v_spacing),
        _XmFromVerticalPixels,
        _XmToVerticalPixels,
    },
};
```

There are also Constraint resources for children of the grid widget:

```c
static XtResource constraint_resources[] =
{

    {
        XsmNrowPosition,
        XsmCRowPosition,
        XmRPosition,
        sizeof(Position),
        XtOffsetOf( struct _XsmGridConstraintRec, grid.row_pos),
        XmRImmediate, (XtPointer) MAXDIMENSION
    },

    {
        XsmNcolumnPosition,
        XsmCColumnPosition,
        XmRPosition,
        sizeof(Position),
        XtOffsetOf( struct _XsmGridConstraintRec, grid.col_pos),
        XmRImmediate, (XtPointer) MAXDIMENSION
```

```
    },
};
```

Define the Action Table

The grid has no actions, so you don't need to define an action table.

Define the Translation Table

The grid has no new translations, so you don't need to define a translation table.

Initialize the Grid Widget Class Record

The widget class record consists of the Core class part, a superclass part, and the grid's class part. The grid's superclass is XmManager, but, as you have already seen, it inherits from the Composite and Constraint classes as well.

Core Class Part

The Core class part is the heart of the widget class record. All widgets, regardless of their class, have a Core class part[1]. All widgets of a given class have the same values for the Core class part fields, and may also have additional common fields.

Here's the listing of the grid's Core class part:

```
externaldef (xsmgridclassrec) XsmGridClassRec xsmGridClassRec = {
    {                                        /* core_class fields      */
      (WidgetClass) &xmManagerClassRec,   /* superclass              */
        "XsmGrid",                         /* class_name              */
        sizeof(XsmGridRec),                /* widget_size             */
        ClassInitialize,                   /* class_initialize        */
        ClassPartInitialize,               /* class_part_initialize   */
        FALSE,                             /* class_inited            */
        Initialize,                        /* initialize              */
        NULL,                              /* initialize_hook         */
        XtInheritRealize,                  /* realize                 */
        NULL,                              /* actions                 */
```

---

1. The term "widgets" as used here refers to windowed objects, which of course does not include gadgets. Gadgets do not have a Core class part.

                                                    The Grid Widget

```c
    0,                               /* num_actions          */
    resources,                       /* resources            */
    XtNumber(resources),             /* num_resources        */
    NULLQUARK,                       /* xrm_class            */
    TRUE,                            /* compress_motion      */
    XtExposeCompressMaximal,         /* compress_exposure    */
    TRUE,                            /* compress_enterleave  */
    FALSE,                           /* visible_interest     */
    Destroy,                         /* destroy              */
    Resize,                          /* resize               */
    Redisplay,                       /* expose               */
    SetValues,                       /* set_values           */
    SetValuesAlmost,                 /* set_values_hook      */
    XtInheritSetValuesAlmost,        /* set_values_almost    */
    NULL,                            /* get_values_hook      */
    NULL,                            /* accept_focus         */
    XtVersion,                       /* version              */
    NULL,                            /* callback_private     */
    NULL,                            /* tm_table             */
    QueryGeometry,                   /* query_geometry       */
    XtInheritDisplayAccelerator,     /* display_accel        */
    NULL,                            /* extension            */
},
```

The values for each of the Core class record fields are explained in the sections
that follow.

superclass Field

The *superclass* field is a pointer to the superclass record. Because we are subclassing grid from XmManager, this field is set to `&XmManagerClassRec` and
is cast to `(WidgetClass)`.

class_name Field

The value of the *class_name* field is an ASCII string that defines the name of the
new widget class. In keeping with the convention we established earlier, this field
is set to `"XsmGrid"`, which is the name of the new class.

---

widget_size Field

The widget size is the size of the grid's instance record and is the value of the C expression

```
sizeof(XsmGridPart)
```

where `XsmGridPart` is the grid's instance record defined in its private header file `GridP.h`:

```
typedef struct _XsmGridPart {
    Dimension       columns;
    Dimension       rows;
    Dimension       margin_width;
    Dimension       margin_height;
    Dimension       orig_margin_width;
    Dimension       orig_margin_height;
    Dimension       h_spacing;
    Dimension       v_spacing;
    WidgetList    *widget_grid;
    Dimension     *row_height;
    Dimension     *col_width;
    XtEnum          horiz_alignment;
    XtEnum          vert_alignment;
    Boolean         show_grid_lines;
    Boolean         lines_visible;
    GC              gc;
} XsmGridPart;
```

class_initialize Field

The *class_initialize* field is a pointer to a method that is called the first time a widget of this class is initialized. For the grid, the method is called `ClassInitialize`, and is described later in this chapter.

class_part_initialize Field

The *class_part_initialize* field is a pointer to a method that is called when a grid widget is initialized, and again each time a subclass of grid is initialized. The method is called `ClassPartInitialize`.

class_inited Field

The *class_inited* field is an internal Xt Intrinsics flag that you should always set to False.

initialize Field

The *initialize* field specifies a method that initializes the widget's internal instance fields. For the grid, the method is called `Initialize`, and it is described later in this chapter.

initialize_hook Field

The *initialize_hook* field specifies a method that was used for passing the argument list and argument count prior to the addition of these parameters in the initialize procedure in X11 Release 4. This method has been retained for backward compatibility. The grid sets this field to NULL.

realize Field

The *realize* field specifies a method that creates the window for the widget. The method is not chained. Frequently this method is inherited from its parent's realize method using `XtInheritRealize`. For the grid, we plan to inherit the realize method from its parent, so this field is set to `XtInheritRealize`.

actions Field

The *actions* field identifies the name of the action table to be used for the new widget. The grid has no actions, so this field is NULL.

num_actions Field

The *num_actions* field specifies the number of actions in the action table. Because the grid has no actions, this field is set to 0.

resources Field

The *resources* field specifies the list of the grid's resources. In `Grid.c` this field is `resources`. See "Define New Resources" earlier in this chapter (and in Chapter 2) for detailed information.

num_resources Field

The *num_resources* field specifies the number of resources in the resource list. `Grid.c` uses the macro `XtNumber` on the resource list. This macro returns the number of resources in the resource list.

```
XtNumber(resources)
```

xrm_class Field

The *xrm_class* field is another internal Xt Intrinsics flag. Always set it to NULLQUARK.

compress_motion Field

The *compress_motion* field is normally set to True, unless your new widget is a gadget or a widget that performs interactive drawing. Because the grid has no need for interactive drawing, this field is set to True.

compress_exposure Field

The *compress_exposure* field is a flag that was a Boolean variable prior to X11 Release 4. Under R4 and subsequent releases, it has the following possible values:

- `XtExposeNoCompress` — Performs no exposure compression.

- `XtExposeCompressSeries` — Compresses expose events from a single exposure.

- `XtExposeCompressMultiple` — Compresses all adjacent series of expose events in the event queue.

- `XtExposeCompressMaximal` — Compresses all expose events in the event queue. This blocks the event queue during processing.

The grid sets this field to `XtExposeCompressMaximal`.

compress_enterleave Field

The *compress_enterleave* field is normally set to True, unless your new widget is a gadget or a widget that performs interactive drawing. Because the grid is not a gadget, this field is set to True.

visible_interest Field

The grid sets the *visible_interest* field to False, as do all the Motif widgets. See the corresponding section in Chapter 2 for more information on this field.

destroy Field

The *destroy* field specifies the destroy method used for freeing data allocated by the widget. The grid's destroy method is called `Destroy`. It is described later in this chapter.

resize Field

The *resize* field specifies a resize method called when a widget has been reconfigured to change its height or width information. Widgets that have dimension-based information (such as a line count for scrolling) or that want to redraw themselves dynamically upon a change in size must have a resize method. The grid's resize method is called `Resize` and is described later in this chapter.

expose Field

The *expose* field specifies the expose method, one of the most important methods in the widget. The expose method performs the drawing (or redrawing) of the widget visuals. It can be the key to how well the widget performs. It is called when an expose event on the widget's window occurs, when any of the `SetValues` methods return True, and when a widget has been resized. Many widgets also use this method for all changes in visual appearance. The expose method is usually named `Redisplay`, because there is an X event called `Expose`. For the grid, this method is called `Redisplay`, and it is described later in this chapter.

set_values Field

The *set_values* field specifies the chained method called when an application calls `XtSetValues()`. It is used to verify changes to the widget's resources. For the grid, the method is called `SetValues`, and it is described later in this chapter.

set_values_hook Field

The *set_values_hook* field specifies a set_values_hook method that has been obsolete since the release of X11 Version 4. It was used for passing the argument list and argument count prior to X11 R4 and has been retained for backward compatibility. The grid sets this field to NULL.

set_values_almost Field

The *set_values_almost* field specifies a method called only when a change to the Core resources `height`, `width`, `x`, `y`, or `border_width` has been modified in the `SetValues` method, and that modification is unacceptable to the widget's parent geometry manager. For the grid, this method is `SetValuesAlmost`.

get_values_hook Field

The *get_values_hook* field specifies a chained procedure used to provide the data that must be a copy of the original resource. Grid sets this field to NULL.

accept_focus Field

The *accept_focus* field specifies a method that tracks the setting of the input focus by means of a call to `XSetInputFocus()`. Motif doesn't use this field and does not support subclasses that do use the accept focus method. Motif has its own internal method for maintaining the focus, so Motif widgets typically set this

field to NULL. Grid uses the Motif focus handling and, therefore, sets this field to
NULL.

version Field

The *version* field specifies the version of X in use. Grid sets it to `XtVersion`.

callback_private Field

The *callback_private* field is an internal Xt Intrinsics field, and you should always
set it to NULL.

tm_table Field

The *tm_table* field specifies the translation table for the new widget. The grid has
no translations, so this field is set to NULL.

query_geometry Field

The *query_geometry* field specifies a query geometry method used in geometry
negotiations. This method is `QueryGeometry` in the grid.

display_accelerator Field

The *display_accelerator* field specifies a method that is used to display a widget's
accelerators. This field is normally set to NULL. Grid sets it to NULL.

extension Field

The *extension* field points to an extension record that you use to extend a class
record within an existing release of a Motif or Xt Intrinsics library. Grid doesn't
need the extension record, so it sets the *extension* field to NULL.

Composite Class Part

The Composite class part specifies methods that allow communication with the
children of the grid widget. Here's the definition of the Composite class part:

```
    {                                       /* composite_class fields */
        GeometryManager,                    /* geometry_manager      */
        ChangeManaged,                      /* change_managed        */
        InsertChild,                        /* insert_child          */
        DeleteChild,                        /* delete_child          */
        NULL,                               /* extension             */
    },
```

The values for each of the Composite class record fields are explained in the sections that follow.

geometry_manager Field

The *geometry_manager* field is used to negotiate changes in the children's geometry. The child requests the change, and the manager widget determines if it can accommodate the request. If this function returns `XtGeometryNo`, the request is not granted. If the return value from this function is `XtGeometryAlmost`, it means that the parent has accepted part of the request and indicates in the reply parameter what is an acceptable compromise. If the child uses the values set in the reply pointer to make an additional geometry request, the geometry manager is obligated to accept that request.

Acceptable requests may return either `XtGeometryYes`, indicating that the request is acceptable but the requesting widget has not been reconfigured with the new values, or `XtGeometryDone`, indicating that the requesting widget has had its geometry changed. It is easier for manager widgets to have layout routines reconfigure all the widgets based on geometry changes and return `XtGeometryDone`, but widget sets must be consistent. Because Motif uses `XtGeometryYes` instead of `XtGeomtryDone`, it is best to remain consistent with Motif and set up your geometry manager method to use `XtGeometryYes`.

If a request causes the geometry of the parent to change, the parent must in turn make a request to its parent to be able to change its geometry to accommodate the child's geometry request. Thus, the geometry requests are chained all the way up to the shell or to the parent that can accommodate the request without changing its size.

A child can also make `QueryOnly` requests, which is just a "what if" query. Geometry managers must not permanently modify any child's geometry on `QueryOnly` requests. They then must make `QueryOnly` requests to their parents.

The definition of the geometry procedure is as follows:

```
typedef XtGeometryResult (*XtGeometryHandler)(
    Widget                  /* widget */,
    XtWidgetGeometry*       /* request */,
    XtWidgetGeometry*       /* reply */
);
```

widget — Specifies the child making the geometry request.

request — Specifies what is being requested.

reply — The pointer that holds the information that the geometry manager wants to relay back to the requestor.

The `XtWidgetGeometry` structure identifies the types of geometry changes:

```
typedef struct {
    XtGeometryMask request_mode;
    Position       x, y;
    Dimension      width, height, border_width;
    Widget         sibling;
    int stack_mode;    /* Above, Below, TopIf, BottomIf, Opposite,
                          DontChange */
} XtWidgetGeometry;
```

request_mode identifies what is being requested. It is a bit mask, and the values are OR'd into this field. The possible values for request mode are defined in `Xm.h`.

```
#define CWX              (1<<0)
#define CWY              (1<<1)
#define CWWidth          (1<<2)
#define CWHeight         (1<<3)
#define CWBorderWidth    (1<<4)
#define CWSibling        (1<<5)
#define CWStackMode      (1<<6)
```

The values in the other fields of the `XtWidgetGeometry` structure are valid only if the bit is set in the *request_mode* for that field.

When creating a geometry manager, it is up to the widget creator to decide how to handle geometry requests. Some accept only changes in width, height, and border width. Others might allow different changes.

request_mode is one of the main routines for adjusting layout, and it is typically not inherited, but it can inherit the applicable superclass geometry manager by setting `XtInheritGeometryManager` in the *geometry_manager* Composite class field. Grid has a geometry manager method called `GeometryManager`.

change_managed Field

The *change_managed* field specifies a procedure that is called when a child is managed or unmanaged, when the manager is first realized and contains managed children, and when managed children are destroyed.

This procedure is used when the child widgets are first laid out. In this procedure, the parent goes into geometry negotiations with its parent to accommodate the managed children.

The `ChangeManaged`, `InsertChild`, and `DeleteChild` procedures are all type `XtWidgetProc`, which is defined as follows:

```
typedef void (*XtWidgetProc)(

    Widget        /* widget */

);
```

The widget passed in is the parent widget, not the widget that is getting managed. Thus, the layout needs to go through all the managed children to reset the layout. This procedure is typically not inherited by the widget, although it can be inherited by placing `XtInheritChangeManaged` in the *change_managed* Composite class field. Grid has a change managed method called `ChangeManaged`.

insert_child Field

The *insert_child* field specifies a method called `InsertChild` that is invoked when each child is inserted into the grid. The widget passed to this routine is the child that is being inserted. It is called each time a child is added. `ChangeManaged` is not called until the parent is realized. Applications can also batch the managing of their children for performance improvement by using `XtManageChildren()`. When a child is created as a managed widget using `XtCreateManagedWidget()`, `InsertChild` is called first and then `ChangeManaged`.

This method can be inherited by setting `XtInheritInsertChild` in the *insert_child* Composite class field.

delete_child Field

The *delete_child* field specifies a method called `DeleteChild` that is invoked when a child is destroyed. The widget passed to this routine is the child that is being deleted. The grid may need to adjust its layout based on the child being deleted. If the child is a managed child, `ChangeManaged` is called first, indicating that the child is no longer managed, then `DeleteChild` is called. This method can be inherited by setting `XtInheritDeleteChild` in the *delete_child* composite class field.

extension Field

The *extension* field points to an extension record that you use to extend a Composite class record within an existing release of a Motif or Xt Intrinsics

library. Grid doesn't need the extension record, so it sets the *extension* field to
NULL.

Constraint Class Part

The Constraint class part is used to provide resources for the children of a
composite widget. These resources are typically used to allow the application to
specify where the children will be placed.

Here's the Constraint class part definition:

```
{                                            /* constraint_class fields */
    constraint_resources,                /* resource list          */
    XtNumber(constraint_resources),  /* num resources          */
    sizeof (XsmGridConstraintRec),    /* constraint size        */
    ConstraintInitialize,             /* init proc              */
    NULL,                             /* destroy proc           */
    ConstraintSetValues,              /* set values proc        */
    NULL,                             /* extension              */
},
```

constraint_resources Field

The *constraint_resources* field is the list of Constraint resource definitions. Note
that the resources are actually part of the children of the grid, not the grid itself.

num_resources Field

The *num_resources* field is the value of the C expression

```
XtNumber(constraint_resources)
```

constraint_size Field

The *constraint_size* field is the value of the C expression

```
sizeof(ConstraintRec)
```

initialize Field

The *initialize* field specifies a method similar to `Initialize()` except that this
method is for each child of the grid widget. If the grid had no Constraint resources, this field would be set to NULL. Because grid does have Constraint resources,
this field is set to `ConstraintInitialize`.

destroy Field

The *destroy* field specifies a method similar to `Destroy()` except that this method is for each child of the grid widget. Although grid has Constraint resources, it has no need to free Constraint resources allocated in `Initialize`, so this field is set to NULL.

set_values Field

The *set_values* field specifies a method similar to `SetValues` except that this method is for each child of the grid widget. If the grid had no Constraint resources, this field would be set to NULL. Because grid does have Constraint resources, this field is set to `ConstraintSetValues`.

extension Field

The *extension* field points to an extension record that you use to extend a Constraint class record within an existing release of a Motif or Xt Intrinsics library. Grid doesn't need the extension record, so it sets the *extension* field to NULL.

Manager Class Part

The Manager class part is the last of the three superclass parts in the grid's class record. The Manager class part follows, with explanations for each field.

```
    {                                       /* manager_class fields    */

        XtInheritTranslations,              /* translations            */

        syn_resources,                      /* syn_resources           */

        XtNumber(syn_resources),            /* num_syn_resources       */

        NULL,                               /* syn_cont_resources      */

        0,                                  /* num_syn_cont_resources  */

        XmInheritParentProcess,             /* parent_process          */

        NULL,                               /* extension               */

    },
```

translations Field

The *translations* field specifies the list of translations used for keyboard traversal. The existing translations are overwritten only if the manager has other plans for any of the Motif traversal keys. This is rarely the case, so this field is most often set to `XtInheritTranslations`, which is what grid does.

---

syn_resources Field

The *syn_resources* field is a list of synthetic resources for use with the Motif resolution independence functionality.   See "Synthetic Resources" in Chapter 2. The list for the grid is `syn_resources`.

num_syn_resources Field

The *num_syn_resources* field is the value of the C expression

```
XtNumber(syn_resources)
```

syn_constraint_resources Field

The *syn_constraint_resources* field is a list of synthetic resources on the children widgets for use with the Motif resolution independence functionality. See "Synthetic Resources" in Chapter 2. The grid has no constraint synthetic resources, so this field is set to NULL.

num_syn_constraint_resources Field

The *num_syn_constraint_resources* field is normally the value of the C expression

```
XtNumber(syn_constraint_resources)
```

However, because grid has no constraint synthetic resources, this field is set to 0.

parent_process Field

The *parent_process* field specifies a method used to process event handling for gadgets. The grid sets this field to `XmInheritParentProcess` to inherit its parent's method for event handling.

extension Field

Motif defines an extension record for manager widgets, but it is currently not being used. Set this field to NULL.

Grid Class Part

The grid class part is the last part of the grid's class record. The grid class part follows, with explanations for each field.

```
    {                                   /* grid_class fields    */
        UpdateGridDimensions,           /* update_grid          */
        AddChildToGrid,                 /* add_child            */
        LayoutChildren,                 /* layout_children      */
        DrawGridLines,                  /* draw_grid            */
```

```
            EraseGridLines,                    /* erase_grid          */

            NULL,                               /* extension           */

        }
```

update_grid Field

The *update_grid* field specifies a method called `UpdateGridDimensions`
that calculates the current total height and width of the grid.

add_child Field

The *add_child* field specifies a method called `AddChildToGrid`, which adds a
new child widget to the grid.

layout_children Field

The *layout_children* field specifics a method called `LayoutChildren`, which
lays out and aligns child widgets within the grid according to specified or empty
positions.

draw_grid Field

The *draw_grid* field specifies a method called `DrawGridLines`, which draws
the lines between the rows and columns of the grid.

erase_grid Field

The *erase_grid* field specifies a method called `EraseGridLines`, which erases
the lines between the rows and columns of the grid.

extension Field

The *extension* field points to an extension record that you use to extend a grid
class record within an existing release of a Motif or Xt Intrinsics library. Grid
doesn't need the extension record, so it sets the *extension* field to NULL.

Grid.c

Now let's take a look at the program `Grid.c`. Some parts of it have already been
described as part of the widget writing process, but there's a lot more to the program that is unique to the grid widget.

Include Header Files

You already know about the grid's private header file, `GridP.h`:

```
#include "GridP.h"
```

Warning Messages

The grid provides the application developer with warning messages when certain
programming transgressions occur.

```
#define MESSAGE1  "There must be at least one row."

#define MESSAGE2  "There must be at least one column."

#define MESSAGE3  "The row position can not be greater than the
                   number of rows."

#define MESSAGE4  "The column position can not be greater than  the
                   number of columns."

#define MESSAGE5  "The row and column position is already taken.\n
                   Defaulting to next available position."

#define MESSAGE6  "The grid is full.  The number of rows or columns
                   must be expanded."

#define MESSAGE7  "The row and column position is already taken.\n
                   Retaining old position."
```

Variable and Macro Definitions

There are two variables and several macro definitions in `Grid.c` to simplify the
code structure.

Variables

```
#define MAXDIMENSION  ((1 << 16)-1)

#define LINE_WIDTH    1
```

`MAXDIMENSION` is used as a flag for the default value to position a child in a row
or a column.

`LINE_WIDTH` specifies the width of the line used to draw the lines on the grid
separating the rows and columns.

Macros

The macros defined in `Grid.c` are used for coding shortcuts.

```
/* Macro to get constraint resource values */

#define GridInfo(w) ((XsmGridConstraintPtr)(w)->core.constraints)
```

                                                        The Grid Widget

```c
/* Macro for stack allocation */
#define StackAlloc(size, stack_array) \
    ((size) <= sizeof(stack_array) ? (XtPointer)(stack_array) \
                                   : XtMalloc((unsigned)(size)))


/* Macro to free stack allocation */
#define StackFree(pointer, stack_array) \
if ((pointer) != ((XtPointer)(stack_array))) \
    XtFree((char *)pointer);


/* Macro to get the line width if show_grid_lines is true */
#define GetLineWidth(gw) gw->grid.show_grid_lines ? LINE_WIDTH : 0


/* Macro to get the number of converter values in an enum list */
#define NUM_NAMES( list ) (sizeof( list) / sizeof( char *))
```

Method and Procedure Declarations

You've already seen most of the method and procedure names in our earlier discussions, and the purpose of most of them is self-explanatory. There are declarations for Core, Composite, Constraint, grid class, internal grid methods, and convenience functions. There are no XmManager class procedures declared, because grid inherits the ones it needs from its parent. See "Manager Class Part" earlier in this chapter.

```c
/* core class methods */
static void ClassInitialize( void );
static void ClassPartInitialize( WidgetClass );
static void Initialize( Widget request,
                        Widget new_w,
                        ArgList args,
                        Cardinal *num_args );
static void Destroy( Widget w );
static void Resize( Widget w );
static void Redisplay( Widget w,
                       XEvent *event,
```

```c
                        Region region );
    static Boolean SetValues( Widget old_w,
                              Widget request,
                              Widget new_w,
                              ArgList args,
                              Cardinal *num_args );
    static Boolean SetValuesAlmost( Widget old_w,
                                    Widget new_w,
                                    XtWidgetGeometry *request,
                                    XtWidgetGeometry *reply);
    static XtGeometryResult QueryGeometry( Widget wid,
                                    XtWidgetGeometry *request,
                                    XtWidgetGeometry *ret );


    /* composite class methods */
    static XtGeometryResult GeometryManager( Widget w,
                                    XtWidgetGeometry *request,
                                    XtWidgetGeometry *reply );
    static void ChangeManaged( Widget wid );
    static void InsertChild (Widget child);
    static void DeleteChild (Widget child);


    /* constraint methods */
    static void ConstraintInitialize( Widget rw,
                                 Widget nw,
                                 ArgList args,
                                 Cardinal *num_args );
    static Boolean ConstraintSetValues( Widget cw,
                             Widget rw,
                             Widget nw,
                             ArgList args,
                             Cardinal *num_args );


    /* grid class methods */
```

```c
static void UpdateGridDimensions( Widget w,
                                  Dimension * width,
                                  Dimension * height );
static void AddChildToGrid( Widget parent,
                            Widget child,
                            Dimension row_pos,
                            Dimension col_pos );
static void LayoutChildren( Widget w );
static void DrawGridLines( Widget w );
static void EraseGridLines( Widget w );


/* internal procedures */
static Dimension GetColumnWidth( XsmGridWidget gw,
                                 int col_pos );
static Dimension GetRowHeight( XsmGridWidget gw,
                               int row_pos );
static Boolean SetChildHorizPosition( XsmGridWidget parent,
                             Widget child,
                               XsmGridConstraintPart * grid_info,
                             Dimension row,
                             Dimension start_col );
static Boolean SetChildVertPosition( XsmGridWidget parent,
                             Widget child,
                               XsmGridConstraintPart * grid_info,
                             Dimension start_row,
                             Dimension col );
static Boolean SetChildPosition( XsmGridWidget parent,
                             Widget child,
                             XsmGridConstraintPart * grid_info,
                             Dimension start_row,
                             Dimension start_col );
static void SetInvGC( XsmGridWidget gw,GC gc );
static void SetNormGC( XsmGridWidget gw, GC gc );
static void LoadGC( XsmGridWidget gw, Pixel fg, Pixel bg );
```

```
static void ModifyGridLines( XsmGridWidget gw, Boolean draw_grid );
```

Grid Method and Procedure Descriptions

This section describes the various methods and procedures in `Grid.c`. They are divided into six categories:

1. Core class methods
2. Composite class methods
3. Constraint class methods
4. Grid class methods
5. Grid internal procedures
6. Convenience functions

Core Class Methods

Core class methods are called by the Xt Intrinsics.

ClassInitialize

Grid uses the `ClassInitialize` method to register converters for resource representation types that are not available in Motif.

```
static void

ClassInitialize( void )

{

    XmRepTypeRegister( XsmRHorizontalAlignment,

                        HorizontalAlignmentNames, NULL,

NUM_NAMES(HorizontalAlignmentNames));

    XmRepTypeRegister( XsmRVerticalAlignment,

                        VerticalAlignmentNames, NULL,

NUM_NAMES(VerticalAlignmentNames));

}
```

ClassPartInitialize

`ClassPartInitialize` performs the initialization needed by the Core class part. It is called to initialize this class and whenever a new subclass is created. Like the knob widget, grid uses `ClassPartInitialize` to set the class methods of the widget subclasses that inherit them. `ClassPartInitialize`

The Grid Widget

checks each method and looks for the setting of an inheritance macro. If one is found, it resets that method to its own class method pointer.

When a subclass uses an inheritance macro for one of the class methods, the procedure pointer in grid is placed in the subclass' class field for that method.

```
static void

ClassPartInitialize( WidgetClass wc )

{

    XsmGridWidgetClass gc = (XsmGridWidgetClass) wc;

    XsmGridWidgetClass sc = (XsmGridWidgetClass)
                              wc->core_class.superclass;


    /* assign procedures to the classes pointers that inherit these
        procedures */


    if (gc->grid_class.add_child == XsmInheritAddChild)
        gc->grid_class.add_child = sc->grid_class.add_child;



    .

    .

    .


}
```

Initialize

`Initialize` is the main grid instance initialization method. It verifies the values of the resources and the resources of its superclasses. It also initializes internal variables and sets up the graphics context.

```
static void

Initialize( Widget request, Widget new_w, ArgList args,
        Cardinal *num_args )

{

    XsmGridWidget new_m = (XsmGridWidget) new_w;

    XsmGridWidget req_m = (XsmGridWidget) request;

    unsigned int line_width = GetLineWidth(new_m); /* 0 if grid
                                              lines are off */

    int i;
```

```c
    /* verify resource values */
    if (new_m->grid.rows < 1)
    {
        _XmWarning( (Widget) new_w, MESSAGE1);
        new_m->grid.rows = 1;
    }

                .

                .

                .


    new_m->grid.row_height = (Dimension *) XtCalloc(new_m->grid.rows,
                                sizeof(Dimension));
    new_m->grid.col_width = (Dimension *)XtCalloc(new_m->grid.columns,
                                sizeof(Dimension));
            .

            .

            .



    LoadGC(new_m,new_m->core.background_pixel,new_m->manager.
        foreground);
}
```

Destroy

`Destroy` frees allocated resources when the grid is destroyed. The grid allocates
data in the initialize procedure and during execution of an application using it.
`Destroy` frees data when the grid is destroyed. This data includes the GC that
was created for drawing the grid lines.

```c
static void
Destroy( Widget w )
{
    XsmGridWidget gw = (XsmGridWidget) w;
    int i;
```

```c
    /* Free row_height and column_width arrays */
    XtFree((char *)gw->grid.row_height);
    XtFree((char *)gw->grid.col_width);


    /* Free two dimensional widget_grid array */
    for (i = 0; i < gw->grid.rows; i++)
        XtFree((char *)gw->grid.widget_grid[i]);
    XtFree((char *)gw->grid.widget_grid);


    if (gw->grid.gc != NULL)
        XtReleaseGC((Widget) gw, gw->grid.gc);

}
```

Resize

`Resize` redraws the grid when its size changes. In this method you must decide how to reposition the children to accommodate a change in size. Without a resize method, the children would be clipped from the window. The grid widget tries to keep the children centered by adjusting the margins. Upon shrinking, the grid widget shrinks the margins until they go to zero, then it allows the resize method to clip the children.

`Resize` first clears the grid lines if they are visible. Then, it determines the grid height and width based on the children's sizes and attempts to compute its best size. It saves the current margins for margin adjustment and adjusts the margin to accommodate the change in size. Lastly, it reaccomplishes the layout of the children based on the new margins and redraws the grid lines if they are required.

```c
static void
Resize( Widget w )
{
    XsmGridWidget gw = (XsmGridWidget) w;
    XsmGridWidgetClass gc = (XsmGridWidgetClass) XtClass(w);
    Dimension width, height, save_margin_width, save_margin_height;
    unsigned int line_width = GetLineWidth(gw); /* 0 if grid lines
                                                    are off */


    if (gw->grid.show_grid_lines && gw->grid.lines_visible &&
        XtIsRealized(w))
```

```c
        XClearWindow(XtDisplay(w), XtWindow(w));

    (*gc->grid_class.update_grid)(w, &width, &height);


    width += ((2 * (gw->grid.orig_margin_width + line_width)) +
             ((gw->grid.h_spacing + line_width) *
             gw->grid.rows));
    height += ((2 * (gw->grid.orig_margin_height + line_width)) +
             ((gw->grid.v_spacing + line_width) *
               gw->grid.columns));


    save_margin_width = gw->grid.margin_width;
    save_margin_height = gw->grid.margin_height;


    gw->grid.margin_width = gw->grid.orig_margin_width;
    gw->grid.margin_height = gw->grid.orig_margin_height;


    if (gw->core.width > width)
       gw->grid.margin_width += (gw->core.width - width)/2;
    if (gw->core.height > height)
       gw->grid.margin_height += (gw->core.height - height)/2;


    if (gw->grid.margin_width != save_margin_width ||
        gw->grid.margin_height != save_margin_height)
       (*gc->grid_class.layout_children)(w);


    if (gw->grid.show_grid_lines)
        (*gc->grid_class.draw_grid)(w);
}
```

Redisplay

`Redisplay` redraws a region that is exposed. It calls a Motif private function
`_XmRedisplayGadgets()` to determine if any gadget children need to be redisplayed and then calls the gadget's expose method. Remember that a gadget

does not handle events. Consequently, when an expose event occurs, a gadget must rely on its parent to notify it of event occurrences.

```c
static void
Redisplay( Widget w, XEvent *event, Region region )
{
    XsmGridWidget gw = (XsmGridWidget) w;
    XsmGridWidgetClass gc = (XsmGridWidgetClass) XtClass(w);


    /*  Redisplay gadgets.  */
     _XmRedisplayGadgets(w, event, region);


    if (gw->grid.show_grid_lines)
        (*gc->grid_class.draw_grid)(w);
    else if (gw->grid.lines_visible)
        (*gc->grid_class.erase_grid)(w);
}
```

SetValues

`SetValues` is called when `XtSetValues` is called by an application using the grid when the application wants to set one or more grid resource values. `SetValues` verifies any changes to grid resource values. If such changes affect the appearance of the grid, `SetValues` returns True, indicating that the expose method (`Redisplay`) should be called to redraw the grid and its children. Any changes to the grid's geometry generates a geometry request to its parent. If the `SetValues` method returns True, then the grid's expose method (`Redisplay`) is called. `SetValues` has a variable called *redisplay* that is set to True if there is a change in the grid's resources (or any of its superclass' resources) that would warrant a redraw. The variable *redisplay* is used as the return value for `SetValues`. Any changes in grid's geometry will cause geometry negotiations to be made. `SetValues` also updates its GC when a change has been made to its superclass' background or foreground. Permanent changes to the grid's instance structure must be made in the *new_w* widget pointer. All other changes to any of the other widget pointers (*old_w, request*) are lost.

```c
static Boolean
SetValues( Widget old_w, Widget request, Widget new_w,
           ArgList args, Cardinal *num_args )
{
```

```c
XsmGridWidget new_m = (XsmGridWidget) new_w;

.

.

.


if (new_m->grid.rows < 1)
{
    _XmWarning( (Widget) new_w, MESSAGE1);
    new_m->grid.rows = old_m->grid.rows;
}



.

.

.


if (new_m->grid.rows != old_m->grid.rows)
  /* Reallocate space for the list of row heights */
    new_m->grid.row_height = (Dimension *)
            XtRealloc((XtPointer)new_m->grid.row_height,
            sizeof(Dimension) * new_m->grid.rows);


.

.

.



if (new_m->grid.rows < old_m->grid.rows ||
     new_m->grid.columns < old_m->grid.columns)
{
    Widget child;
    Dimension width, height;

    for (i = 0; i < new_m->composite.num_children; i++)
    {
            child = new_m->composite.children[i];
```

```c
        grid_info = &(GridInfo(child)->grid);

        row_pos = grid_info->orig_row_pos;
        col_pos = grid_info->orig_col_pos;

        (*gc->grid_class.add_child)(new_w, child, row_pos,
            col_pos);
    }

    (*gc->grid_class.update_grid)(new_w, &width, &height);

    new_m->core.width = width +
                        ((2 * (new_m->grid.margin_width +
                         line_width)) +
                        ((new_m->grid.h_spacing  + line_width) *
                         new_m->grid.rows));

    new_m->core.height = height +
                         ((2 * (new_m->grid.margin_height +
                          line_width)) + ((new_m->grid.v_spacing
                          + line_width) * new_m->grid.columns));

    (*gc->grid_class.layout_children)(new_w);
}


if (new_m->core.background_pixel !=
    old_m->core.background_pixel ||
    new_m->manager.foreground != old_m->manager.foreground)
{
    LoadGC(new_m, new_m->core.background_pixel,
           new_m->manager.foreground);
    redisplay = True;
}
```

```
    if (new_m->grid.show_grid_lines != old_m->grid.show_grid_lines)
        redisplay = True;


    return (redisplay);
}
```

SetValuesAlmost

`SetValues` resets the grid's width and height when the row and column resources change. This change in width and height causes the Xt Intrinsics to generate a geometry request to the grid's parent to determine if the change is acceptable to the parent. If the parent doesn't completely accept the change in width and/or height, then `SetValueAlmost` is called with the instance structures of the new (current) and old (state of the widget prior to `SetValues` being called) grid instances. `SetValuesAlmost` is also passed the requested geometry structure, which contains the requested changes to the geometry, and the reply geometry structure that contains the grid's parent's geometry manager's reply to the geometry request.

If the *request_mode* field of the reply structure is set to zero, it means that the manager rejects all the parts of the geometry request (it replied `XtGeometryNo` to the request). In this case, grid resets the resources that affected the geometry to their original value, and does not change its geometry. If the geometry was partially accepted (`XtGeometryAlmost`), grid resets only the resources of the part of the geometry request that failed. If any of the resources get rolled back, the grid needs to be updated to reflect the rollback of the resources. The request structure is set to the reply structure indicating that it accepts the compromise geometry.

QueryGeometry

`QueryGeometry` makes geometry requests to the grid's children in order to calculate the grid's preferred geometry. The `QueryGeometry` method is more complex for manager widgets then for primitive widgets, because it has to get the geometries of its children to determine the appropriate size for itself. Once it has determined its appropriate geometry, it must reply `XtGeometryYes` if the requested geometry matches the preferred geometry. If the requested geometry matches the current geometry, it should return `XtGeometryNo`. Otherwise, it should return `XtGeometryAlmost`.

```
static XtGeometryResult

QueryGeometry( Widget wid, XtWidgetGeometry *request,
XtWidgetGeometry *reply )
```

```c
{
    XsmGridWidget gw = (XsmGridWidget) wid;

    .

    .

    .


    for (i = 0; i < gw->grid.rows; i++)
    {
        row_height = 0;

        for (j = 0; j < gw->grid.columns; j++)
        {
            child = gw->grid.widget_grid[i][j];

            if (child != NULL)
            {
                XtQueryGeometry(child, NULL, &desired);

                if (row_height < desired.height)
                    row_height = desired.height;

                if (max_col_width[j] < desired.width)
                    max_col_width[j] = desired.width;
            }
        }

        height += row_height;
    }

    .

    .

    .


    reply->width = width + ((2 * (gw->grid.margin_width +
```

```
            line_width)) + ((gw->grid.h_spacing +
            line_width) * gw->grid.rows));


    reply->height = height + ((2 * (gw->grid.margin_height +
            line_width)) + ((gw->grid.v_spacing +
            line_width) * gw->grid.columns));


    reply->request_mode = CWWidth | CWHeight;


    if ((request->request_mode & CWWidth && request->width ==
        reply->width) &&
        (request->request_mode & CWHeight && request->height ==
        reply->height))
            return XtGeometryYes;


    if (reply->width == gw->core.width &&
        reply->height == gw->core.height)
        return XtGeometryNo;


    return XtGeometryAlmost;
}
```

Composite Class Methods

Composite procedures are called by the Xt Intrinsics, but they are specified by the
Composite class.

GeometryManager

GeometryManager is used to negotiate changes in the children's geometry. A
child requests the change, and grid determines if it can accommodate the request.
GeometryManager is one of the more complex and most important methods of
the manager widgets. This method controls the geometry negotiations between
the children, the grid itself, and the grid's parent. It has to determine what changes
in geometry it will accept, whether it can accommodate the change and reconfigure the children, if necessary, to allow the child to change its geometry.

GeometryManager first determines the kind of geometry changes it will
accept. It only considers changes to width and height. Thus, if the request does

not include a change in width or height, it is rejected. If the request includes width or height as well as other requests, and the request values for the other geometry fields equal the reply values (i.e., effectively no change) `GeometryManager` returns `GeometryYes`.

Next, `GeometryManager` checks to see if the request is a `QueryOnly` request so that it won't try to reposition its other children. Then, it determines its new width and height based on the request. If the request would cause the grid to grow or shrink, it must make a geometry request to its parent to see if it can make the change.

Once it has been determined that the grid can grow or shrink (based on the reply from grid's parent), `GeometryManager` sets up its reply to the child making the request. If it can grant some of the request but not all, `XtGeometryAlmost` is returned. If it is a `QueryOnly` request, it must set the child back to its original values prior to making the geometry request and return the appropriate geometry value indicating whether the request is able to be granted. If the request can be granted completely and it is not a `QueryOnly` request, the grid lays out the other children to accommodate the child's request and returns `XtGeometryYes`. The Xt Intrinsics cause the requesting child's resize and redisplay methods to be called to make the change.

```
static XtGeometryResult

GeometryManager( Widget w, XtWidgetGeometry *request,

                 XtWidgetGeometry *reply )

{

    XsmGridWidget gw = (XsmGridWidget) XtParent(w);




    if (!(mask & (CWWidth | CWHeight)))

        return XtGeometryNo;




    if (mask & CWX && request->x != w->core.x)
```

```c
{
    reply->x = w->core.x;

    reply->request_mode |= CWX;

    set_almost = True;
}


    .

    .

    .


if ((mask & XtCWQueryOnly) || set_almost)
    geo_request.request_mode = XtCWQueryOnly;
else
    geo_request.request_mode = 0 ;


  .

  .

  .


if (mask & CWWidth)
{
  if (request->width > gw->grid.col_width[grid_info->col_pos] ||
     (w->core.width == gw->grid.col_width[grid_info->col_pos] &&
      request->width < gw->grid.col_width[grid_info->col_pos]))
  {
      save_width = w->core.width;
      w->core.width = request->width;

      for (j = 0; j < gw->grid.columns; j++)
         width += GetColumnWidth(gw, j);

      width += ((2 * (gw->grid.margin_width + line_width)) +
                   ((gw->grid.h_spacing  + line_width) *
                   gw->grid.rows));
```

```c
        if (gw->core.width != width)
        {
            make_request = True;
            geo_request.request_mode |= CWWidth;
            geo_request.width = width;
        }
    } else
        w->core.width = request->width;
}


if (mask & CWHeight)
{
    .
    .
    .


}


if (make_request)
{
    result = XtMakeGeometryRequest((Widget) gw, &geo_request,
            &geo_reply);

    .
    .
    .
}


if (set_almost)
    result = XtGeometryAlmost;


if ((mask & XtCWQueryOnly))
{
```

```
        if (mask & CWWidth)

            w->core.width = save_width;

        if (mask & CWHeight)

            w->core.height = save_height;

    }

    else

    {

        if (result == XtGeometryYes)

        {

            gw->grid.row_height[grid_info->row_pos] =

                GetRowHeight(gw, grid_info->row_pos);

            gw->grid.col_width[grid_info->col_pos] =

                GetColumnWidth(gw, grid_info->col_pos);

            (*gc->grid_class.layout_children)((Widget) gw);

        }

    }


    return (result);

}
```

ChangeManaged

`ChangeManaged` is called when any of these conditions exist:

- A child is managed.

- A child is unmanaged.

- A managed child is deleted.

- All managed children are realized for the first time.

- The grid is realized for the first time and has managed children.

`ChangeManaged` negotiates with its parent to accommodate the grid's children.
Grid uses this method to lay out its children. Because grid widget leaves room for
both managed and unmanaged children, the layout in this method could also be
done in the `InsertChild` and `DeleteChild` Composite class methods, but it
is more efficient to perform the layout once on the realize of the children
(typically all performed at once), rather than as each child is added and deleted.
Most applications that use widgets realize their shell just prior to going into the
main loop, and thus all the widget children are realized at once, so this method is

called only once. If the application created all its widgets, realized the shell, and then managed the widgets individually, `ChangeManaged` would be called each time a child is managed. Obviously, this would be far less efficient.

`ChangeManaged` first determines grid's height and width based on its children's geometry and its own margin and spacing resources. Then it makes a geometry request to grid's parent if it currently isn't large enough to accommodate the children. If the geometry request returns `XtGeometryAlmost`, it will make another geometry request with the return values just obtained (which is guaranteed to succeed). The grid adjusts its spacing and margins if the parent won't allow enough space to fit the margins and the children's sizes.

If the adjustments fail to provide all the space needed, grid must clip its children. Once a size has been settled on for the grid, it lays out the children.

One last thing that `ChangeManaged` must do is call the Motif private function `_XmNavigChangeManaged()` to ensure that the focus of a managed widget moves to another child if the child that currently has the focus is unmanaged or out of view. Motif will make this function public in Motif 2.0, and it will be called `XmeNavigChangeManaged()`.

```
static void
ChangeManaged( Widget w )
{
    XsmGridWidget gw = (XsmGridWidget) w;

    .

    .

    .


    (*gc->grid_class.update_grid)(w, &width, &height);


    width += ((2 * (gw->grid.margin_width + line_width)) +
                    ((gw->grid.h_spacing + line_width) *
                    gw->grid.rows));

    .

    .

    .


    if (gw->core.width != width)
```

```c
    {
        make_request = True;
        geo_request.request_mode |= CWWidth;
        geo_request.width = width;
    }


    .

    .

    .


    if (make_request)
    {
        result = XtMakeGeometryRequest(w, &geo_request, &geo_reply);

        if (result != XtGeometryYes)
        {

            .

            .

            .


            if (result == XtGeometryAlmost)
                result = XtMakeGeometryRequest(w, &geo_reply, NULL);

            .

            .

            .


            if (gw->core.width != width)
            {
                diff = (int) width - (int)gw->core.width;

                if (diff > 0)
                    if (gw->grid.margin_height >= diff)
                        gw->grid.margin_height -= diff;
                    else
```

```c
                    {
                        diff -= gw->grid.margin_height;
                        gw->grid.margin_height = 0;
                    }
                else
                    gw->grid.margin_width = gw->grid.margin_width +
                                        (gw->core.width - width)/2;
            }

            (*gc->grid_class.update_grid)(w, &width, &height);
        }
    }


    (*gc->grid_class.layout_children)(w);


    _XmNavigChangeManaged(w);
}
```

InsertChild

The `InsertChild` method is used when the children's managed state does not
affect the layout of the other children in the manager widget. `InsertChild`
marks the children's position as occupied whether the child is managed or not.
This means that the layout routine leaves room for unmanaged children. As
children are created, `InsertChild` inserts them into the widget grid, and their
height and width are used in computing the row's height and the column's width.

DeleteChild

The `DeleteChild` method is used when the children's managed state does not
affect the layout of the other children in the manager widget. When managed
children are deleted, the `ChangeManaged` method is called to indicate that the
managed child is becoming unmanaged. If the layout depends on both managed
and unmanaged children, then `DeleteChild` needs to be used to reposition the
remaining children after a child is deleted. Grid uses this method to remove the
child from the widget grid array (in `Grid.c`), and then it recomputes the row's
height and the column's width.

Constraint Class Methods

Constraint class methods are called by the Xt Intrinsics, and they are specified by the Constraint class.

ConstraintInitialize

`ConstraintInitialize` examines the grid's children's Constraint resource values, and determines their validity. It also initializes the necessary Constraint fields in each child's Constraint record. The `ConstraintInitialize` method is just like the `Initialize` method except that it verifies resources and initializes fields of grid's children's constraint records. This method is called each time a new child is created with the grid as a parent.

```
static void
ConstraintInitialize( Widget req_w, Widget new_w, ArgList args,
                      Cardinal *num_args )
{
    XsmGridWidget parent = (XsmGridWidget) XtParent(new_w);

    .

    .

    .


    if (row_pos > parent->grid.rows - 1 && row_pos != MAXDIMENSION)
    {
        _XmWarning( (Widget) parent, MESSAGE3);
        row_pos = parent->grid.rows - 1;
    }
}
```

ConstraintSetValues

`ConstraintSetValues` determines the validity of the grid's children's Constraint resource values.

Grid Class Methods

The grid class methods can be used by any widget that is subclassed from grid.

UpdateGridDimensions

`UpdateGridDimensions` updates the width and height of each row and column based on a change in the geometries of the children. It returns the total width and height of the grid based on the computed row widths and column heights.

```
static void

UpdateGridDimensions(Widget w, Dimension * width, Dimension *
height)

{

    XsmGridWidget gw = (XsmGridWidget) w;

    int i, j;


    *height = 0;
    *width = 0;


    for (i = 0; i < gw->grid.rows; i++)

    {

        gw->grid.row_height[i] = GetRowHeight(gw, i);

        *height += gw->grid.row_height[i];

    }


    for (j = 0; j < gw->grid.columns; j++)

    {

        gw->grid.col_width[j] = GetColumnWidth(gw, j);

        *width += gw->grid.col_width[j];

    }

}
```

AddChildToGrid

`AddChildToGrid` adds a child to the grid based on the row and column positions specified in the child's Constraint record. It checks to see if a child can be placed in the grid at a certain row and column position. If the location given is already occupied, it tries to find a new position by moving to the right and down, wrapping around when it reaches the last location in the grid. If it returns to the original location without finding a place to put the new child, it determines that the grid is full and returns False.

`AddChildToGrid` tries to retain a row or column position if only one of the two positions is set. For example, if a column is set but not a row, it searches for an open position in that column before moving to other rows.

```c
static void
AddChildToGrid( Widget parent, Widget child,
                Dimension row_pos, Dimension col_pos)
{
    XsmGridWidget gw = (XsmGridWidget) parent;
    .

    .

    .


    if (row_pos == MAXDIMENSION && col_pos == MAXDIMENSION)
        grid_info->auto_placed = True;
    else
        grid_info->auto_placed = False;


    if (row_pos == MAXDIMENSION) row_pos = 0;
    .

    .

    .


    if (gw->grid.widget_grid[row_pos][col_pos] == NULL)
    {
        gw->grid.widget_grid[row_pos][col_pos] = child;
    }
    else
    {
        if (!grid_info->auto_placed)
        {
            .

            .

            .


        if (!SetChildPosition(gw, child, grid_info, row_pos,
col_pos))

            _XmWarning( (Widget) parent, MESSAGE6);
```

```
    }
}
```

LayoutChildren

`LayoutChildren` examines the grid's rows and columns and moves the children to their appropriate x,y position based on their location in the widget grid array.

`LayoutChildren` positions the children based on their location in the internal grid array. Based on a resource setting, it aligns the children to the left, center, or right. It uses the private Motif procedure `_XmConfigureObject()` to reconfigure the children's location. This procedure will be made public in Motif 2.0 and will be called `XmeConfigureObject()`.

```
static void

LayoutChildren(Widget w)

{

    XsmGridWidget gw = (XsmGridWidget) w;

    .

    .

    .


    row_adj = 0;


    for (i = 0; i < gw->grid.rows; i++)

    {

        col_adj = 0;


        row_height = gw->grid.row_height[i];


        for (j = 0; j < gw->grid.columns; j++)

        {

            child = gw->grid.widget_grid[i][j];


            col_width = gw->grid.col_width[j];


            if (child != NULL)
```

```c
                {
                    x = gw->grid.margin_width + line_width +
                        (gw->grid.h_spacing + 1)/2 +
                        ((gw->grid.h_spacing + line_width) * j) + col_adj;

                        .

                        .

                        .


                    if (child->core.width != col_width)
                    {
                        if (gw->grid.horiz_alignment == XsmALIGN_CENTER)
                            x += (col_width - child->core.width)/2;
                        else if (gw->grid.horiz_alignment == XsmALIGN_RIGHT)
                            x += (col_width - child->core.width);
                    }


                        .

                        .

                        .




                    if (child->core.x != x || child->core.y != y)
                        _XmConfigureObject( child, x, y, child->core.width,
                                            child->core.height,
                                            child->core.border_width);
                }


            col_adj += col_width;
            }


        row_adj += row_height;
        }
    }
```

DrawGridLines

`DrawGridLines` draws the lines between the rows and columns of the grid if the resource `show_grid_lines` is true. It sets the *lines_visible* field in the grid instance structure to True to indicate that the lines have been drawn.

```
static void

DrawGridLines(Widget w)

{

    XsmGridWidget gw = (XsmGridWidget) w;


    ModifyGridLines(gw, True);

    gw->grid.lines_visible = True;

}
```

EraseGridLines

`EraseGridLines` erases the lines between the rows and columns of the grid. It sets the *lines_visible* field in the grid instance structure to False to indicate that the lines have been erased.

Grid Internal Functions and Procedures

The grid internl functions and procedures are internal to the grid and cannot be accessed by widgets that are subclassed from grid.

GetColumnWidth

`GetColumnWidth` dctermines the width of a specified column by finding the width of the widest child in that column.

```
static Dimension

GetColumnWidth(XsmGridWidget gw, int col_pos)

{

    Widget child;

    WidgetList * widget_grid = gw->grid.widget_grid;

    Dimension col_width = 0;

    int i;


    for (i = 0; i < gw->grid.rows; i++)


    {
```

```
        child = widget_grid[i][col_pos];


        if (child != NULL)
            if (child->core.width > col_width)
                col_width = child->core.width;
    }


    return (col_width);
}
```

GetRowHeight

`GetRowHeight` determines the height of a specified row by finding the height of the tallest child in that row.

SetChildHorizPosition

`SetChildHorizPosition` examines the current row looking for an unoccupied position. If one is found, it is assigned to the child that originated the request. It returns False if a position is not found in the current row. It is used by the `AddChildToGrid` class method to set a child to a position in a row.

```
static Boolean

SetChildHorizPosition( XsmGridWidget parent, Widget child,

                       XsmGridConstraintPart * grid_info,

                       Dimension row, Dimension start_col)

{

    XsmGridConstraintPart * cur_grid_info;

    Dimension cur_col;

    Widget cur_child;

    if (row >= parent->grid.rows)

        return False;

    if (start_col >= parent->grid.columns)

        start_col = parent->grid.columns - 1;

    cur_col = start_col++;

    while (cur_col != start_col)

    {

        if (cur_col == parent->grid.columns) cur_col = 0;
```

```c
    if (parent->grid.widget_grid[row][cur_col] == NULL)
    {
        parent->grid.widget_grid[row][cur_col] = child;

        grid_info->row_pos = row;
        grid_info->col_pos = cur_col;
        return True;
    }


    cur_col++;
  }

  return False;

}
```

SetChildVertPosition

`SetChildVertPosition` examines the current column looking for an unoccupied position. If one is found, it is assigned to the child that originated the request. It returns False if a position is not found in the current column. It is used by the `AddChildToGrid` class method to set a child to a position in a column.

SetChildPosition

`SetChildPosition` searches for an unoccupied position in the grid for a child. If no unoccupied position is found, the return value is set to False, indicating that the grid is full. It is used by the `AddChildToGrid` class method to set a child to a position in a column.

LoadGC

`LoadGC` creates the graphics context used in drawing the grid lines. If one already exists, it releases the GC and creates another one using the foreground and background values of the manager widget.

```c
static void
LoadGC( XsmGridWidget gw, Pixel fg, Pixel bg)
{
    unsigned long valueMask = (GCForeground | GCBackground);
    unsigned long dynamicMask;
    XGCValues values;
```

```
    if (gw->grid.gc != NULL)

        XtReleaseGC((Widget) gw, gw->grid.gc);

    values.background = bg;

    values.foreground = fg;

    dynamicMask = (GCForeground | GCBackground);

    gw->grid.gc = XtAllocateGC((Widget) gw, gw->core.depth,

                valueMask, &values, dynamicMask, 0);

}
```

ModifyGridLines

`ModifyGridLines` is used by `EraseGridLines` and `DrawGridLines` to erase and draw the grid lines.

Grid Convenience Functions

Convenience functions exist for the convenience of the application developer. We've created one convenience function for grid (remember that these are public functions and are defined in `Grid.h`).

XsmCreateGridWidget

`XsmCreateGridWidget` is a convenience procedure used to create an instance of a grid widget. It performs exactly like the convenience functions for existing Motif widgets.

```
Widget XsmCreateGrid( Widget parent, char *name, ArgList arglist,

                    Cardinal argcount)

{

  return (XtCreateWidget(name, xsmGridWidgetClass,

                    parent, arglist, argcount));

}
```

Compiling Grid.c

You'll need a Makefile to compile the `grid.c` object. The Makefile listed in Appendix A specifies paths for the include and library directories, and you'll probably need to change these to suit your system. Note that the Makefile only creates an object file called `Grid.o`. The object file is then linked when an

---

application uses a grid widget. You normally access Motif widgets by linking the Motif library `libXm.a`, which is composed of all the Motif widget object files.

Sample Program

Now that you've created the grid, let's put it to use in an actual program. This section briefly describes `gridcolors.c`. You can find the listing for each of these programs in Appendix A.

gridcolors.c

`gridcolors.c` produces a window with three knobs, one to control each of the primary colors. As the knobs are turned, the background color of the window changes accordingly, and the value of the knob displayed below it is also changed. The knobs are managed by a grid widget instead of a row column widget as was used in `knobcolors.c` described in Chapter 3. Figure 4-3 shows the window from `gridcolors.c`:

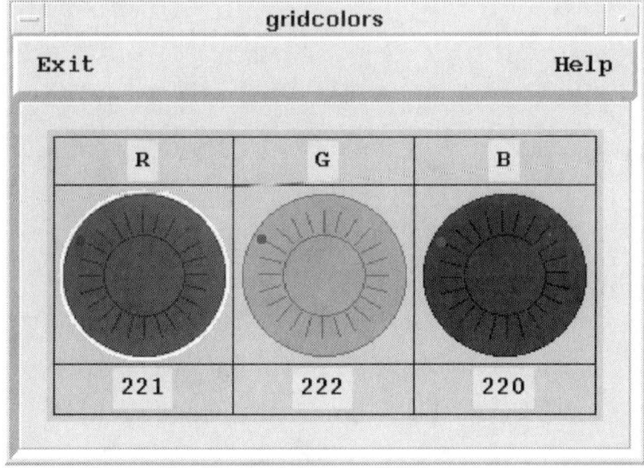

Figure 4-3   gridcolors.c Window

Summary

This chapter described the grid widget and took you through it's creation. The next chapter describes a knob gadget, very similar to the knob widget described in

Chapter 1. This discussion will help you to understand the differences between a widget and a gadget.

Chapter 5

The Knob Gadget

A gadget is a widget that relies on its manager parent to provide the necessities that govern its appearance and behavior. This chapter describes how to write the object and necessary header files to create a knob gadget. It will be especially useful for you to compare the code here with that of the knob widget described in Chapter 3.

Introduction

The knob gadget looks just like the knob widget we created in Chapter 3. Turn it clockwise, and its value increases; turn it counterclockwise and its value decreases. Although it looks just like the knob widget, there are internal differences that we'll describe as we go through the process. Figure 5-1 shows a knob gadget. As you can see, it doesn't look any different than the knob widget.

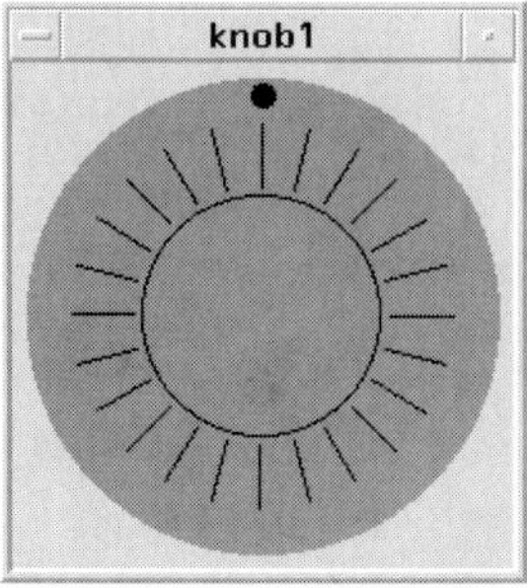

Figure 5-1 The Knob Gadget

The minimum value is at the knob gadget's fully counterclockwise position, and the maximum value is at the knob gadget's fully clockwise position. You can set both the maximum and minimum values in the applicable resources. You can use the knob gadget as a control, just the same as the knob widget. An example program `knobgcolors.c` uses three knobs, one to vary each of the three primary colors. It's exactly the same as `knobcolors.c` except that it uses the knob gadget instead of the knob widget.

The Process

We'll use the widget writing process described in Chapter 2 to create the knob gadget. This involves choosing the superclass, creating the private and public header files `KnobGP.h` and `KnobG.h`, and then writing the object `KnobG.c`. You may see some duplication from Chapters 2 and 3 as we go through the process for the knob gadget.

Throughout this chapter you'll see code segments from the files that make up the knob gadget . Appendix A contains a complete listing of these files.

Choose the Superclass

Because this version of knob is a gadget and not a widget, we must subclass it from the XmGadget class. This means that we'll include the XmGadget class part in the knob gadget's private header file. The XmGadget class part is defined in `GadgetP.h`:

```
typedef struct _XmGadgetClassPart
{
    XtWidgetProc          border_highlight;
    XtWidgetProc          border_unhighlight;
    XtActionProc          arm_and_activate;
    XmWidgetDispatchProc  input_dispatch;
    XmVisualChangeProc    visual_change;
    XmSyntheticResource * syn_resources;
    int                   num_syn_resources;
    XmCacheClassPartPtr   cache_part;
    XtPointer             extension;
} XmGadgetClassPart;
```

Figure 5-2 shows the XmGadget portion of the widget hierarchy shown in Figure 1-3.

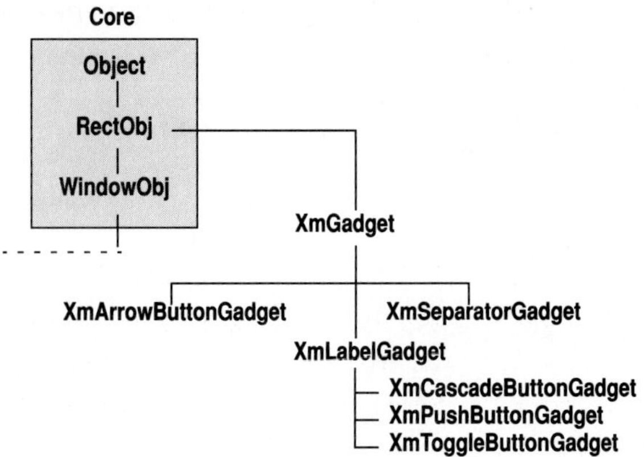

Figure 5-2 XmGadget Widget Hierarchy

Create the Private Header File

The knob gadget's private header file `KnobGP.h` is normally used only by other widget writers who want to subclass a new widget from the knob gadget. You can find the complete listing for `KnobGP.h` in Appendix A.

Manage Multiple Inclusions

The first lines of the private header file are used to manage multiple inclusions:

```
#ifndef _XsmKnobGP_h

#define _XsmKnobGP_h
```

The associated `#endif` is the last line of `KnobGP.h`.

Include KnobG.h and GadgetP.h

Next, include the knob's public header file `Knob.h` and gadget's private header file `GadgetP.h`:

```
#include "KnobG.h"

#include <Xm/GadgetP.h>
```

Define the Class Part Structure

Next, define the knob gadget's class part structure.

```
typedef struct {
  XsmGetDiametersProc get_diameters;    /* procedure to draw inner
                                           and outer circles */
  XtWidgetProc        create_segments; /* procedure used to
                                          create handle segments */
  XtWidgetProc        draw_indicator;  /* procedure for drawing
                                          knob indicator */
  XtTimerCallbackProc turn;             /* timeout procedure used
                                           to turn knob */
  XtWidgetProc        draw;             /* procedure for drawing
                                           the knob */
  XtPointer           extension;        /* pointer to extension
                                           record used for future
                                           expansion */
} XsmKnobGadgetClassPart;
```

Define the Class Structure

Next, define the knob gadget's class structure:

```
typedef struct _XsmKnobGadgetClassRec {
  RectObjClassPart        rect_class;
  XmGadgetClassPart       gadget_class;
  XsmKnobGadgetClassPart knobg_class;
} XsmKnobGadgetClassRec;
```

Note that it is composed of pointers to the RectObj class part, XmGadget class part, and the knob gadget class part.

Define Procedure Pointers

Some local procedures need a pointer defined so that they can be inherited by a widget subclassing from the knob gadget. The knob gadget has one such procedure: `XsmGetDiametersProc`.

```
typedef void (*XsmGetDiametersProc)(Widget, unsigned int *,
                                    unsigned int *) ;
```

Define Inheritance Macros

Next, define inheritance macros. These macros identify methods and procedures that widgets subclassing from the knob gadget can use instead of redefining the methods and procedures. The actual number of these macros corresponds to the number of methods in the class part structure, and some widgets may not have any. The knob gadget defines these inheritance procedures:

```
#define XsmInheritGetDiameters ((XsmGetDiametersProc) _XtInherit)

#define XsmInheritCreateSegments ((XtWidgetProc) _XtInherit)

#define XsmInheritDrawIndicator ((XtWidgetProc) _XtInherit)

#define XsmInheritTurn ((XtTimerCallbackProc) _XtInherit)

#define XsmInheritDraw ((XtWidgetProc) _XtInherit)
```

Define the Instance Part Structure

Next, define the knob gadget's instance part structure, which is a part of the knob gadget's instance record (defined next). The other parts are Object, RcctObj, and XmGadget. The knob gadget's resource values are stored in its instance part structure. Here's the instance part structure for the knob gadget:

```
typedef struct _XsmKnobGadgetPart {

  XtCallbackList value_changed_callback; /* resource - callback
                                        when value changes */

    int value;                  /* resource - value of the knob */

    int max_val;                /* resource - maximum value allowed */

    int min_val;                /* resource - minimum value allowed */

    int turn_delay;             /* resource - the delay before the
                                   next increment */

  Pixel knob_color;             /* resource - the color of the knob */

  Pixel indicator_color;        /* resource - the color of the
                                   indicator */

  Dimension margin_width;       /* resource - determines the outer
                                   edge of */

  Dimension margin_height;      /* the circle. Whichever value is
                                   greater when the dimension is
                                   structured from its margin
                                   value determines the knob
                                   diameter. */

  Dimension knob_margin;        /* resource - The percentage from the
                                   knob's outer edge to draw the inner
                                   circle. */
```

```
    Dimension orig_width;        /* saves the original dimension */

    Dimension orig_height;       /* saves the original dimension */

    Boolean move_clockwise;      /* indicates direction of turn */

    Boolean turning;             /* indicates whether turning is in
                                    progress */

    GC gc;                       /* graphics context use in graphic
                                    ops */

    XSegment *segments;          /* the line segments used for drawing
                                    the handle */

    int num_segments;            /* the number of segments in the above
                                    list */

    XtIntervalId timer_id;       /* the timer id of the timeout used in
                                    turning the knob */

    double angle_offset;         /* used to calculate the segment
                                    positions */

} XsmKnobGadgetPart;
```

Define the Instance Structure

Next, define the knob gadget's instance structure:

```
typedef struct _XsmKnobGadgetRec {
    ObjectPart          object;
    RectObjectPart      rectangle;
    XmGadgetPart        gadget;
    XsmKnobGadgetPart   knob;
} XsmKnobGadgetRec;
```

Notice that within this structure (XsmKnobGadgetRec), the field *knob* (type
XsmKnobGadgetPart) points to the knob gadget's instance part record. Each
of the types are defined in the respective class private header file. For example,
XmGadgetPart is defined in GadgetP.h:

```
/*  The Gadget instance record  */


typedef struct _XmGadgetPart
{
    Dimension shadow_thickness;

    Dimension highlight_thickness;
```



```
    XtCallbackList help_callback;
    XtPointer       user_data;

    Boolean traversal_on;
    Boolean highlight_on_enter;
    Boolean have_traversal;

    unsigned char unit_type;
    XmNavigationType navigation_type;

    Boolean highlight_drawn;
    Boolean highlighted;
    Boolean visible;

    Mask event_mask;
} XmGadgetPart;
```

Create the Public Header File

The public header file (`knobG.h`) is used by application programmers and contains the XmGadget class name, resource strings, callback structures, and public function external declarations.

Prevent Multiple Inclusions

Like the private header file, the first lines prevent multiple inclusions:

```
#ifndef _XsmKnobG_h
#define _XsmKnobG_h
```

The associated `#endif` is the last line of the private header file:

```
#endif /* _XsmKnobG_h */
```

This line prevents a header file from being included more than once.

Include Xm.h

Next, include the `Xm.h` header file:

```
#include <Xm/Xm.h>
```

This header file has general definitions, declarations, and macros needed by all widgets and gadgets.

Define Resource Name Macros

We define macros to map to the resource names. By convention, the words in the names are separated by differences in capitalization. The macro definition includes the two- or three-letter prefix (Xm or Xsm, for example) for the widget library, followed by an *N* that indicates a resource name. Here's the knob gadget's resource name macros:

```
#define XsmNvalueChangedCallback    "valueChangedCallback"

#define XsmNindicatorColor          "indicatorColor"

#define XsmNmarginWidth             "marginWidth"

#define XsmNmarginHeight            "marginHeight"

#define XsmNknobMargin              "knobMargin"

#define XsmNknobColor               "knobColor"

#define XsmNmaxValue                "maxValue"

#define XsmNminValue                "minValue"

#define XsmNturnDelay               "turnDelay"

#define XsmNvalue                   "value"
```

Define Resource Class Name Macros

The resource class name macros also use capitalization to separate words. The class name macro uses an uppercase *C* instead of *N*, and the letter following the *C* is always uppercase. Here's the resource class name macros for the knob gadget's resources:

```
#define XsmCValueChangedCallback    "ValueChangedCallback"

#define XsmCIndicatorColor          "IndicatorColor"

#define XsmCMarginWidth             "MarginWidth"

#define XsmCMarginHeight            "MarginHeight"

#define XsmCKnobMargin              "KnobMargin"

#define XsmCMaxValue                "MaxValue"

#define XsmCMinValue                "MinValue"

#define XsmCTurnDelay               "TurnDelay"

#define XsmCValue                   "Value"
```

Define Callback Structures

The knob gadget has only one callback structure:

```
typedef struct
{
    int     reason;
    XEvent *event;
    int     value;
} XsmKnobCallbackStruct;
```

The variables *reason* and *event* are common to all callback structures, Other variables, such as *value*, are unique to a specific callback. The knob gadget defines a callback reason as a value for the *reason* field:

```
#define XsmCR_VALUE_CHANGED  0
```

Every callback has a specific reason be executed. The reason can be associated with any widget event such as pressing a button or entering a window, but it doesn't need to be. A widget can execute a callback for virtually any reason.

Define the Widget Class Name

The pointers to the widget instance and class structures in the public header file are mainly used for applications that wish to have more specific type checking. Instead of using the generic types `Widget` and `WidgetClass` for the widget instance and class types, the application programmer may want to have a more specific type for each widget instance and class.

```
externalref WidgetClass   xsmKnobGadgetClass;


/*
 * To allow applications to use tight type checking, define
 * structures for the gadget class and instance pointers
 * specific to this class of widget.
 */


typedef struct _XsmKnobGadgetClassRec * XsmKnobWidgetClass;
typedef struct _XsmKnobGadgetRec        * XsmKnobWidget;
```

Define Public Function Declarations

The knob gadget has three public functions:

*   `XsmCreateKnobGadget` is a convenience function to simplify creating an

instance of knob.

- `XsmGetKnobGadgetValue` obtains the current value of the knob setting.
- `XsmSetKnobGadgetvalue` sets the knob gadget's value to a specified figure.

Here are the function definitions as they appear in `KnobG.h`:

```
extern Widget XsmCreateKnobGadget(

                    Widget    parent,

                    char      *name,

                    ArgList   arglist,

                    Cardinal argcount);
extern int XsmGetKnobValue(

                    Widget w) ;
extern void XsmSetKnobValue(

                    Widget w,

                    int value) ;
```

Define New Resources

You define the knob gadget's new resources in the program `knobG.c`. You also set default values for each resource at the same time. Table 5-1 shows the knob gadget's resource names, classes, and default values.

Table 5-1 Knob Gadget Resources

Resource Name	Resource Class Name	Default
XsmNvalueChangedCallback	XsmCValueChangedCallback	NULL
XsmNvalue	XsmCValue	0
XsmNmaxValue	XsmCMaxValue	100
XsmNminValue	XsmCMinValue	0
XsmNturnDelay	XsmCTurnDelay	50
XsmNknobColor	XsmCKnobColor	Dynamic
XsmNindicatorColor	XsmCIndicatorColor	Dynamic
XsmNmarginWidth	XsmCMarginWidth	5
XsmNmarginHeight	XsmCMarginHeight	5
XsmNknobMargin	XsmCKnobMargin	50

The format you use to define the resources is defined by the Xt Intrinsics as described in Chapter 2. Here are the knob gadget's resources as they are in defined in `knobG.c`:

```
static XtResource resources[] = {
    {
        XsmNvalueChangedCallback, XmCCallback, XmRCallback,
        sizeof(XtCallbackList),
        XtOffset (XsmKnobGadget, knob.value_changed_callback),
        XmRImmediate, NULL
    },

    {
        XsmNvalue, XsmCValue, XmRInt, sizeof(int),
        XtOffset (XsmKnobGadget, knob.value),
        XmRImmediate, (XtPointer) 0
    },

    {
        XsmNmaxValue, XsmCMaxValue, XmRInt, sizeof(int),
        XtOffset (XsmKnobGadget, knob.max_val),
        XmRImmediate, (XtPointer) 100
    },

    {
        XsmNminValue, XsmCMinValue, XmRInt, sizeof(int),
        XtOffset (XsmKnobGadget, knob.min_val),
        XmRImmediate, (XtPointer) 0
    },

    {
        XsmNturnDelay, XsmCTurnDelay, XmRInt, sizeof(int),
        XtOffset(XsmKnobGadget, knob.turn_delay),
        XmRImmediate, (XtPointer) 50
    },
```

```c
    {
      XsmNknobColor, XsmCKnobColor, XmRPixel, sizeof (Pixel),
      XtOffset (XsmKnobGadget, knob.knob_color),
      XmRCallProc, (XtPointer) _XmBackgroundColorDefault
    },

    {
      XsmNindicatorColor, XsmCIndicatorColor, XmRPixel,
      sizeof (Pixel),
      XtOffset (XsmKnobGadget, knob.indicator_color),
      XmRCallProc, (XtPointer) _XmForegroundColorDefault
    },

    {
      XsmNmarginWidth, XmCMarginWidth, XmRHorizontalDimension,
      sizeof (Dimension),
      XtOffset (XsmKnobGadget, knob.margin_width),
      XmRImmediate, (XtPointer) DEFAULT_KNOB_MARGIN
    },

    {
      XsmNmarginHeight, XmCMarginHeight, XmRVerticalDimension,
      sizeof (Dimension),
      XtOffset (XsmKnobGadget, knob.margin_height),
      XmRImmediate, (XtPointer) DEFAULT_KNOB_MARGIN
    },

    {
      XsmNknobMargin, XsmCKnobMargin, XmRDimension,
      sizeof (Dimension),
      XtOffset (XsmKnobGadget, knob.knob_margin),
      XmRImmediate, (XtPointer) DEFAULT_KNOB_MARGIN_PERCENTAGE
    },
```

```
};
```

The word Dynamic in the default column means that the default value depends on the setting of other resources. The resources `XsmNknobColor` and `XsmNknobIndicatorColor` have CallProcs to set their values dynamically.

The synthetic resource list initialization sets up resource procedures that are called when you are setting or getting the various resources. These synthetic resources are used in resolution independence.

```
static XsmyntheticResource syn_resources[] = {
        {
          XmNmarginWidth,
          sizeof (Dimension),
          XtOffset( XsmKnobGadget, knob.margin_width),
          _XmFromHorizontalPixels,
          _XmToHorizontalPixels
        },


        {
          XmNmarginHeight,
          sizeof (Dimension),
          XtOffset( XsmKnobGadget, knob.margin_height),
          _XmFromVerticalPixels,
          _XmToVerticalPixels
        }
};
```

Define the Action Table

A gadget cannot have actions or translations. It relies on its parent to supply actions and translations.

Define the Translation Table

A gadget cannot have actions or translations. It relies on its parent to supply actions and translations.

Initialize the Knob Gadget Class Record

The knob gadget class record consists of the XmGadget class part and the knob gadget's class part.

RectObj Class Part

The RectObj class part is the heart of the knob gadget class record. It corresponds to the Core class part that all widgets have. All gadgets, regardless of their class, have a RectObj class part. All gadgets of a given class have the same values for the RectObj class part fields, and may also have additional common fields.

Here's the listing of the knob gadget's RectObj class part:

```
        /* RectObj Class Rec    */
(WidgetClass) &xmGadgetClassRec,     /* superclass              */
"XsmKnobGadget",                     /* class_name              */
sizeof(XsmKnobGadgetRec),            /* widget_size             */
NULL,                                /* class_initialize        */
ClassPartInitialize,                 /* class_part_initialize   */
FALSE,                               /* class_inited            */
Initialize,                          /* initialize              */
NULL,                                /* initialize_hook         */
NULL,                                /* realize                 */
NULL,                                /* actions                 */
0,                                   /* num_actions             */
resources,                           /* resources               */
XtNumber(resources),                 /* num_resources           */
NULLQUARK,                           /* xrm_class               */
FALSE,                               /* compress_motion         */
XtExposeNoCompress,                  /* compress_exposure       */
FALSE,                               /* compress_enterleave     */
FALSE,                               /* visible_interest        */
Destroy,                             /* destroy                 */
Resize,                              /* resize                  */
Redisplay,                           /* expose                  */
SetValues,                           /* set_values              */
NULL,                                /* set_values_hook         */
```

```
    SetValuesAlmost,                    /* set_values_almost   */

    NULL,                               /* get_values_hook     */

    NULL,                               /* accept_focus        */

    XtVersion,                          /* version             */

    NULL,                               /* callback_private    */

    NULL,                               /* tm_table            */

    QueryGeometry,                      /* query_geometry      */

    NULL,                               /* display accelerator*/

    NULL,                               /* extension           */
  },
```

The settings for each of the RectObj class part fields are explained in the sections that follow.

superclass Field

The *superclass* field is a pointer to the superclass record. Because we are subclassing a knob gadget from XmGadget, this field is set to `&XmGadgetClassRec` and is cast to `(WidgetClass)`.

class_name Field

The value of the *class_name* field is an ASCII string that describes the new widget class. In keeping with the convention we established earlier, this field is set to `"XsmKnobGadget"`, which is the name of the new class.

widget_size Field

The widget size (or in this case, the gadget size) is the value of the C expression

`sizeof(XsmKnobGadgetRec)`

where `XsmKnobGadgetRec` is the knob gadget's class record defined in its private header file `KnobGP.h`:

```
typedef struct _XsmKnobGadgetClassRec {

  RectObjClassPart          rect_class;

  XmGadgetClassPart         gadget_class;

  XsmKnobGadgetClassPart    knob_class;

} XsmKnobClassRec;
```

class_initialize Field

The *class_initialize* field specifies a method that is called the first time a gadget of this class is initialized. This method is used only to initialize methods or procedures that cannot be statically initialized and to register resource converters when new resource types are used. This field is NULL, because the knob gadget has no methods or procedures that cannot be statically initialized and does not introduce new resource types.

class_part_initialize Field

The *class_part_initialize* field specifies a method that is called when a gadget of this class is initialized, and again each time a subclass of this gadget is initialized. For the knob gadget, the method is `ClassPartInitialize`, and it is described later in this chapter.

class_inited Field

The *class_inited* field is an internal Xt Intrinsics flag that you should always set to False.

initialize Field

The *initialize* field specifies a method that initializes the widget's internal instance fields. For the knob gadget, this method is called `Initialize`, and it is described later in this chapter.

initialize_hook Field

The *initialize_hook* field specifies a method that was used for passing the argument list and argument count prior to the addition of these parameters in the initialize procedure in X11 Release 4. This method has been retained for backward compatibility. This field is set to NULL.

realize Field

The *realize* field specifies a method that creates the windows for widgets. Because gadgets do not have their own windows, this field is set to NULL.

actions Field

The *actions* field identifies the name of the action table to be used for widgets. Because gadgets do not have actions, this field is set to NULL.

num_actions Field

The *num_actions* field specifies the number of actions in the action table. The knob gadget has no actions, so this field is 0.

resources Field

The *resources* field specifies the list of the knob gadget's resources. In `knobG.c` this field is `resources`. See "Define New Resources" earlier in this chapter (and in Chapter 2) for detailed information.

num_resources Field

The *num_resources* field specifies the number of resources in the resource list. `KnobG.c` uses `XtNumber` on the resource list. This results in the number of resources in the resource list.

```
XtNumber(resources)
```

xrm_class Field

The *xrm_class* field is another internal Xt Intrinsics flag. Always set it to NULLQUARK.

compress_motion Field

The *compress_motion* field is normally set to True, unless your new widget is a gadget or a widget that performs interactive drawing. Because this knob is a gadget, this field is set to False.

compress_exposure Field

The *compress_exposure* field is a flag that was a Boolean variable prior to X11 Release 4. Under R4 and subsequent releases, it has the following possible values:

- `XtExposeNoCompress` — Performs no exposure compression.
- `XtExposeCompressSeries` — Compresses exposure events from a single exposure.
- `XtExposeCompressMultiple` — Compresses all adjacent series of exposure events in the event queue.
- `XtExposeCompressMaximal` — Compress all exposure events in the event queue, which blocks the event queue during processing.

This field is set to `XtExposeNoCompress`, because this knob is a gadget, and as such does not handle events.

compress_enterleave Field

The *compress_enterleave* field is normally set to True, unless your new widget is a gadget or a widget that performs interactive drawing. Because this knob is a gadget, this field is set to False.

visible_interest Field

The *visible_interest* field is set to False, because it is in all the Motif widgets. See the corresponding section in Chapter 2 for more information on this field.

destroy Field

The *destroy* field specifies the destroy method used for freeing data allocated by the widget. The knob gadget's destroy method is called `Destroy`. It is described later in this chapter.

resize Field

The *resize* field specifies a resize method called when a widget has been reconfigured to change its height or width information. Widgets that have dimension-based information (such as a line count for scrolling) or that want to redraw themselves dynamically upon a change in size need to have a resize method. The same is true of gadgets. Even though they don't have their own window, gadgets do perform the drawing needed. The knob gadget's resize method is called `Resize` and is described later in this chapter.

expose Field

The *expose* field specifies the expose method, one of the most important methods in the widget. The expose method performs the drawing (or redrawing) of the widget visuals. It can be the key to how well the widget performs. The parent calls the expose method called when an expose event on the parent occurs in a region that includes the knob gadget, when any of the set values methods return True, and when a widget has been resized. Many widgets also use this method for all changes in visual appearance. It is usually named `Redisplay`, because there is an X event called `Expose`. For the knob gadget, this method is called `Redisplay`, and it is described later in this chapter.

set_values Field

The *set_values* field specifies the chained method called when an application calls `XtSetValues()`. It is used to verify changes to the widget's resources. For the knob gadget, this method is called `SetValues`, and it is described later in this chapter.

set_values_hook Field

The *set_values_hook* field specifies a set values hook method that has been obsolete since the release of X11 Version 4. It was used for passing the argument list and argument count prior to the argument list being included in the `SetValues` method and has been retained for backward compatibility. This field is set to NULL.

---

set_values_almost Field

The *set_values_almost* field specifies a method called only when a change to the RectObj resources `height`, `width`, `x`, `y`, or `border_width` has been modified in the set values method, and that modification is unacceptable to the widget's parent geometry manager. For the knob gadget, this method is called `SetValuesAlmost` and is described later in this chapter.

get_values_hook Field

The *get_values_hook* field specifies a chained method used to provide the data that must be a copy of the original resource. This field is set to NULL.

accept_focus Field

The *accept_focus* field specifies a method that tracks the setting of the input focus by means of a call to `XSetInputFocus()`. Motif doesn't use this field and does not support subclasses that do use the accept focus method. Motif has its own internal method for maintaining the focus, so Motif widgets and gadgets set this field to NULL, as does the knob gadget.

version Field

The *version* field specifies the version of X in use. It is set to `XtVersion`.

callback_private Field

The *callback_private* field is an internal Xt Intrinsics field, and you should always set it to NULL.

tm_table Field

The *tm_table* field specifies the translation table for the knob gadget. Because gadgets do not have translations, this field is NULL.

query_geometry Field

The *query_geometry* field specifies a query geometry method used in geometry negotiations. This field is set to `QueryGeometry`.

display_accelerator Field

The *display_accelerator* field specifies a method used to display the widget's accelerators. The knob gadget sets this field to NULL.

extension Field

The *extension* field points to an extension record that you use to extend a class
record within an existing release of a Motif or Xt Intrinsics library. The knob gadget doesn't need to use the extension record, so the *extension* field is set to NULL.

XmGadget Class Part

The XmGadget class part is the second part of the gadget class record. All
gadgets have an XmGadget class part. All gadgets of a given class have the same
values for the XmGadget class part fields and may also have additional common
fields. Here's the listing of the knob gadget's XmGadget class part:

```
typedef struct _XmGadgetClassPart

{

    XtWidgetProc            border_highlight;

    XtWidgetProc            border_unhighlight;

    XtActionProc            arm_and_activate;

    XmWidgetDispatchProc input_dispatch;

    XmVisualChangeProc    visual_change;

    XmSyntheticResource *syn_resources;

    int                     num_syn_resources;

    XmCacheClassPartPtr   cache_part;

    XtPointer               extension;

} XmGadgetClassPart;
```

The settings for each of the XmGadget class record fields are explained in the sections that follow.

border_highlight Field

The *border_highlight* field specifies a method that provides border highlighting
for the knob when it has the focus. This method is called `HighlightKnob`. It
is the same method specified in the Primitive class record used by the knob
widget.

border_unhighlight Field

The *border_unhighlight* field specifies a method that removes the border highlight
when the widget has lost the focus. This method is called `UnhighlightKnob`.
It is the same method specified in the Primitive class record used by the knob
widget.

arm_and_activate Field

The *arm_and_activate* field specifies a method to arm and activate a control widget, such as a pushbutton. In this case, the arm and activate method is called when the manager receives a return, spacebar, or a select key (in the default Motif configuration).   It normally has a keyboard equivalent to the button click action. For gadgets to catch a key event meant to identify arm and activate, the arm and activate class method needs to be defined. Treat it like an action procedure for return and spacebar key events.

```
typedef void (*XtActionProc)( Widget, XEvent *, String *,
                Cardinal *);
    Widget          widget;
    XEvent*         event;
    String*         params;
    Cardinal*       num_params;
```

widget — Specifies the widget where the event occurred that triggered the action.

event — The event that triggered the action.

params — The list of strings that contains the argument list.

num_params — The number of strings in the *params* field.

input_dispatch Field

The *input_dispatch* field specifies a method that forwards event notices from a gadget's parent to the gadget. Because a gadget does not have translations, its XmManager parent sets up the translations. Each gadget child registers its interest in certain events in its `Initialize()` and `SetValues()` class methods through the *event_mask* field of the XmGadget instance structure .

```
new_kg->gadget.event_mask = XmARM_EVENT | XmACTIVATE_EVENT |
                XmFOCUS_IN_EVENT | XmFOCUS_OUT_EVENT |
                XmENTER_EVENT | XmLEAVE_EVENT |
                XmKEY_EVENT;
```

Motif allows a limited set of events that can be forwarded to a gadget by its manager parent. Here is the list of events:

```
#define XmNO_EVENT              0x000   /* No events */
#define XmENTER_EVENT           0x001   /* Enter event */
#define XmLEAVE_EVENT           0x002   /* Leave event */
#define XmFOCUS_IN_EVENT        0x004   /* Focus In event */
```

```
#define XmFOCUS_OUT_EVENT            0x008   /* Focus Out event */

#define XmMOTION_EVENT              0x010   /* Button Motion event */

#define XmARM_EVENT                 0x020   /* Button 1 Press event */

#define XmACTIVATE_EVENT            0x040   /* Button 1 Release event */

#define XmHELP_EVENT                0x080   /* Help (F1) Key event */

#define XmKEY_EVENT                 0x100   /* Any Key event */

#define XmMULTI_ARM_EVENT           0x200   /* Double Button 1 Press
                                               event */

#define XmMULTI_ACTIVATE_EVENT 0x400   /* Double Button 1 Release
                                               event*/

#define XmBDRAG_EVENT               0x800   /* Button 2 Press event */

#define XmALL_EVENT                 0xFFF   /* All the above events */
```

Because of this limited set of events, the knob gadget can't perform actions on mouse button 2 or 3. This is one of the limitations of gadgets.

visual_change Field

The *visual_change* field specifies a method that allows a gadget's manager parent to notify the gadget that the parent has undergone a visual change. A gadget that uses the visual information from its parent widget needs to register this method. When the visual for the parent changes, the gadget must determine whether it needs to redraw itself. The gadget needs to compare the old and new manager values to determine if it (the gadget) needs to be redisplayed.   If so, the gadget returns True; otherwise, it returns False, and no redisplay is done. Here's the definition of the visual change method:

```
typedef Boolean (*XmVisualChangeProc)( Widget, Widget, Widget) ;
    Widget gadget;
    Widget cur_mgr;
    Widget new_mgr;
```

gadget — The instance pointer to this gadget.

cur_mgr — The instance pointer to the manager parent prior to the visual change.

new_mgr — The instance pointer to the manager parent after the visual change.

syn_resources Field

The *syn_resources* field specifies synthetic resources. For the knob gadget, this field is set to `syn_resources`, which is the array defined in `KnobG.c` that contains the synthetic resources. See "Define New Resources" earlier in this chapter and in Chapter 2.

num_syn_resources Field

The *num_syn_resources* field specifies the number of synthetic resources. It is set to `XtNumber(syn_resources)`.

cache_part Field

The *cache_part* field is used in resource caching. The knob gadget sets this field to NULL. Resource caching is an advanced topic that is beyond the scope of this book.

extension Field

The *extension* field specifies the extension record (if any) for the XmGadget class structure. Because the knob gadget does not need to extend the XmGadget class, this field is set to NULL.

Knob Gadget Class Part

The knob gadget class part is the final class part that makes up the knob gadget's class record. Here's the knob gadget class part:

```
    {                                       /* Knob Gadget Class Rec */

    GetDiameters,                           /* get_diameters        */

    CreateSegments,                         /* create_segments      */

    DrawIndicator,                          /* draw_indicator       */

    TurnKnob,                               /* turn                 */

    DrawKnob,                               /* draw                 */

    NULL,                                   /* extension            */

  }
```

get_diameters Field

The *get_diameters* field specifies a method that determines the diameter of a knob. This method is called `GetDiameters`.

create_segments Field

The *create_segments* field specifies a method that creates the knob segments. This method is called `CreateSegments`.

draw_indicator Field

The *draw_indicator* field specifies a method that draws the knob indicator. This method is called `DrawIndicator`.

turn Field

The *turn* field specifies a method to move the knob. This method is called `TurnKnob`.

draw Field

The *draw* field specifies a method that draws the knob. The method is called `DrawKnob`.

extension Field

The *extension* field specifies the extension record for the knob gadget class. Because we have no need to extend it, we set this field to NULL.

KnobG.c

Now let's take a look at the program `KnobG.c`. Some parts of it have already been described as part of the widget writing process, but there's a lot more to the program that is unique to the knob gadget.

Include Header Files

You already know about the knob gadget's private header file, `KnobGP.h`, but the standard math header file is also included:

```
#include <math.h>

#include <X11/keysym.h>

#include <Xm/ManagerP.h>

#include "KnobGP.h"
```

Variable Definitions

`KnobG.c` defines a number of variables for its mathematical calculations needed in drawing and operating the knob.

```
/* defines for mathematic functions used in drawing */
#define  RADIANS(x)  (M_PI * 2.0 * (x) / 360.0)
```

```c
#define  DEGREES(x)   ((x) / (M_PI * 2.0) * 360.0)
#define  MIN_ANGLE    225.0
#define  MAX_ANGLE    345.0
#define  NUM_SEGS     24
#define  MIN(a,b)     (((a) < (b)) ? (a) :  (b))
#define  MIN_KNOB_DIAMETER                 3
#define  DEFAULT_DIAMETER                  100
#define  DEFAULT_KNOB_MARGIN               5
#define  DEFAULT_KNOB_MARGIN_PERCENTAGE    50
```

Method and Procedure Declarations

Following the variable definitions are the method and procedure declarations.
You've already seen most of the names in our earlier discussions, and the purpose
of most of them is self-explanatory.

```c
/* rectobj methods */
static void ClassPartInitialize( WidgetClass widget_class) ;
static void Initialize( Widget request, Widget new_w, ArgList args,
                        Cardinal *num_args) ;
static void Destroy( Widget w) ;
static void Resize( Widget w) ;
static void Redisplay( Widget w, XEvent *event, Region region) ;
static Boolean SetValues( Widget old_w, Widget request, Widget
                          new_w, ArgList args, Cardinal *num_args) ;
static void SetValuesAlmost( Widget old_w, Widget new_w,
                             XtWidgetGeometry *request,
                             XtWidgetGeometry *reply);
static XtGeometryResult QueryGeometry( Widget w,
                             XtWidgetGeometry *request,
                             XtWidgetGeometry *reply) ;


static void GetDiameters( Widget w, unsigned int *diameter,
                          unsigned int *inner_diameter) ;


/* gadget methods */
```

```c
static void HighlightKnob( Widget w) ;
static void UnhighlightKnob( Widget w) ;
static void InputDispatch( Widget wid, XEvent *event,
                           Mask event_mask) ;
static void ArmAndActivate( Widget wid, XEvent *event,
                            String *params,
                            Cardinal *num_params) ;
static Boolean VisualChange( Widget wid, Widget cmw, Widget nmw) ;


/* resource callprocs */
static void DefaultIndicatorColor( Widget, int, XrmValue *);
static void DefaultIndicatorColor( Widget, int, XrmValue *);


/* knob methods */
static void CreateSegments( Widget w) ;
static void DrawIndicator( Widget w) ;
static void TurnKnob( XtPointer closure, XtIntervalId *id) ;
static void DrawKnob( Widget w) ;


/* action procs */
static void HandleKey( Widget w, XEvent *event, char **params,
                       Cardinal *num_params) ;
static void ToggleLeft( Widget w, XEvent *event, char **params,
                        Cardinal *num_params) ;
static void ToggleRight( Widget w, XEvent *event, char **params,
                         Cardinal *num_params) ;
static void ToggleKnob( Widget w, XEvent *event, char **params,
                        Cardinal *num_params) ;
static void StartKnobTurn( Widget w, XEvent *event, char **params,
                           Cardinal *num_params) ;
static void ReleaseKnob( Widget w, XEvent *event, char **params,
                         Cardinal *num_params) ;
```


The Knob Gadget

Method and Procedure Descriptions

This section describes the various methods and procedures in `KnobG.c`. They are divided into six categories:

1. RectObj class methods

2. Xmgadget class methods

3. Knob gadget methods

4. CallProcs

5. Action procedures

6. Convenience functions

RectObj Methods

RectObj methods are called by the Xt Intrinsics.

ClassPartInitialize

`ClassPartInitialize` performs the initialization needed by the Core class part. It is exactly like the knob widget `ClassPartInitialize` method. See Chapter 3 for more information.

```
static void ClassPartInitialize(WidgetClass wc)

{

    XsmKnobGadgetClass kc = (XsmKnobGadgetClass) wc;

    XsmKnobGadgetClass sc = (XsmKnobGadgetClass)

                            wc->core_class.superclass;


    if (kc->knobg_class.get_diameters == XsmInheritGetDiameters)

        kc->knobg_class.get_diameters =

            sc->knobg_class.get_diameters;



    .


    .


    .



}
```

Initialize

`Initialize` is the main knob gadget instance initialization routine. It is essentially the same as that of the knob widget with a few notable exceptions. References to the width and height of the superclass use the RectObj part instead of the Core part used in the knob widget. The knob gadget uses the XmManager parent's foreground when setting up the graphics context instead of the XmPrimitive's foreground. Also, for event handling, the knob gadget must set up an event mask to indicate the events it wants to have forwarded to its `InputDispatch` class method.

```
static void Initialize( Widget request, Widget new_w, ArgList args,
                        Cardinal *num_args )
{

    XsmKnobGadget req_kg = (XsmKnobGadget) request;

    .

    .

    .


    if (req_kg->rectangle.width == 0)
        new_kg->rectangle.width = DEFAULT_DIAMETER +
            (2 * (new_kg->knobg.margin_width +
            new_kg->gadget.highlight_thickness));
    else
        if (new_kg->rectangle.width < min_width)
            new_kg->rectangle.width = min_width;



    .

    .

    .


    /* Set up graphic context for use in drawing the knob */

    valuemask = (GCForeground | GCBackground);
    values.foreground = mw->manager.foreground;
    values.background = new_kg->knobg.knob_color;
    new_kg->knobg.gc = XtGetGC((Widget)mw, valuemask, &values);
```

```
        new_kg->gadget.event_mask = XmARM_EVENT | XmACTIVATE_EVENT |
                                XmFOCUS_IN_EVENT | XmFOCUS_OUT_EVENT |
                                XmENTER_EVENT | XmLEAVE_EVENT |
XmKEY_EVENT;

}
```

Destroy

`Destroy` frees allocated resources when the knob gadget is destroyed. It is
exactly the same as the knob widget's `Destroy` method. See Chapter 3 for more
information.

```
static void Destroy( Widget w )

{

    XsmKnobGadget kg = (XsmKnobGadget) w;


    XtReleaseGC( w, kw->knobg.gc);

        .

        .

        .

}
```

Resize

`Resize` redraws the knob gadget when its size changes. It is exactly the same as
the knob widget's `Resize` method. See Chapter 3 for more information.

```
static void Resize( Widget w )

{

    XsmKnobGadgetClass kc = (XsmKnobGadgetClass) XtClass(w);


    /* Recreate any segments based on the new size */
    (*kc->knobg_class.create_segments)(w);

}
```

Redisplay

`Redisplay` redraws a region that is exposed. It is exactly the same as the knob widget's `Redisplay` method except that it looks at the XmGadget class record to get the highlight methods. See Chapter 3 for more information.

```
static void Redisplay( Widget w, XEvent *event, Region region)
{
    XsmKnobGadget kg = (XsmKnobGadget) w;
    XsmKnobGadgetClass kc = (XsmKnobGadgetClass) XtClass(w);


    /* Use the class pointer to redraw the whole knob */
     (*kc->knobg_class.draw)(w);


    /* Use the class pointers to highlight or unhighlight the knob */
     if (kg->gadget.highlighted)
        (*kc->gadget_class.border_highlight)(w);
     else
        (*kc->gadget_class.border_unhighlight)(w);
}
```

SetValues

`SetValues` is called when `XtSetValues` is called by an application using the knob gadget when it wants to set one or more knob resource values. It is almost the same as the knob widget's `SetValues` method with a few exceptions. Like the `Initialize` method, the gadget's `SetValues` uses the RectObj instance part for height and width information instead of the Core instance part. It uses the XmGadget instance part for *highlight_thickness*. It also sets the *event_mask* for the events that it wants to receive in the `InputDispatch` class method.

```
static Boolean SetValues( Widget old_w, Widget request, Widget
new_w,

                          ArgList args, Cardinal *num_args )
{
    XsmKnobGadget old_kg = (XsmKnobGadget) old_w;
          .

          .

          .
```


The Knob Gadget

```c
        if (new_kg->rectangle.width == 0)
            new_kg->rectangle.width = old_kg->rectangle.width;
        if (new_kg->rectangle.height == 0)
            new_kg->rectangle.height = old_kg->rectangle.height;


            .

            .

            .


        if (new_kg->knobg.margin_height != old_kg->knobg.margin_height ||
            new_kg->knobg.margin_width != old_kg->knobg.margin_width ||
            new_kg->knobg.knob_margin != old_kg->knobg.knob_margin ||
            new_kg->knobg.max_val != old_kg->knobg.max_val ||
            new_kg->knobg.min_val != old_kg->knobg.min_val ||
            new_kg->rectangle.height != old_kg->rectangle.height ||
            new_kg->rectangle.width != old_kg->rectangle.width ||
            new_kg->gadget.highlight_thickness !=
            old_kg->gadget.highlight_thickness) {

            (*kc->knobg_class.create_segments)(new_w);
            redisplay = True;
        }


            .

            .

            .


        new_kg->gadget.event_mask = XmARM_EVENT | XmACTIVATE_EVENT |
                            XmFOCUS_IN_EVENT | XmFOCUS_OUT_EVENT |
                            XmENTER_EVENT | XmLEAVE_EVENT |
    XmKEY_EVENT;
        return(redisplay);
```

}

SetValuesAlmost

`SetValuesAlmost` is called when knob gadget values have been modified, and
the resulting geometry changes are unacceptable to the knob gadget's parent. It is
exactly the same as the knob widget's `SetValuesAlmost` method. See Chapter 3 for more information.

```
static void SetValuesAlmost( Widget old_w, Widget new_w,
                             XtWidgetGeometry *request,
                             XtWidgetGeometry *reply)
{
    XsmKnobGadget new_kg = (XsmKnobGadget) new_w;
    .
    .
    .

}
```

QueryGeometry

The knob Gadget's QueryGeometry method is just like the knob widget's
QueryGeometry method. See Chapter 3 for more information.

```
static XtGeometryResult QueryGeometry( Widget w, XtWidgetGeometry
                                    *request,
  XtWidgetGeometry *reply)
{
    XsmKnobGadget kg = (XsmKnobGadget) w;
    .
    .
    .

}
```

XmGadget Methods

XmGadget methods are also called by the Xt Intrinsics, but they are specified by
the XmGadget class.

HighlightKnob

`HighlightKnob` provides the highlighting visual around the knob gadget. This
could have been inherited if the knob gadget had a rectangular shape, but because

it is circular, we had to write a unique highlight procedure for it. The knob
gadget's `Highlight` method has some notable changes that must be reviewed.
Like the knob widget, it retrieves the diameters for drawing, but unlike the knob
widget it needs to get its highlight colors from its parent, and its
highlight_thickness from the XmGadget instance part. It draws the arc relative to
its parent so the x and y parameters in the call to `XDrawArc()` must include the
x and y from the RectObj instance part along with the margin width and the
margin height. The highlighted and highlight drawn fields of the gadget instance
part need to be set, and the GC should be returned to it's previous state.

```c
static void HighlightKnob( Widget w )
{
    XsmKnobGadget kg = (XsmKnobGadget) w;

    .

    .

    .


    valuemask = (GCLineWidth | GCForeground);

    values.foreground = mw->manager.highlight_color;

    values.line_width = kg->gadget.highlight_thickness;

    XChangeGC(XtDisplay(kg), kg->knobg.gc, valuemask, &values);


    XDrawArc(XtDisplay(kg), XtWindow(kg), mw->manager.highlight_GC,
            kg->rectangle.x + kg->knobg.margin_width,

            kg->rectangle.y + kg->knobg.margin_height, diameter,

            diameter, 0, 64*360);


    kg->gadget.highlighted = True;

    kg->gadget.highlight_drawn = True;



    .

    .

    .


}
```

UnhighlightKnob

UnhighlightKnob removes the highlighting established by HighlightKnob. It is exactly the same as the HighlightKnob method except that it erases the highlight and sets the flags to indicate that the highlight is not drawn.

```c
static void UnhighlightKnob( Widget w )
{
    XsmKnobGadget kg = (XsmKnobGadget) w;

    .

    .

    .


    /* Change the graphic context to unhighlight */
    valuemask = (GCLineWidth | GCForeground);
    values.foreground = mw->core.background_pixel;
    values.line_width = kg->gadget.highlight_thickness;
    XChangeGC(XtDisplay(kg), kg->knob.gc, valuemask, &values);


    .

    .

    .



    kg->gadget.highlighted = False;
    kg->gadget.highlight_drawn = False;


    .

    .

    .


}
```

ArmAndActivate

The ArmAndActivate method is called when the Select, Return, or Spacebar key is pressed and released. It is usually used with accelerators in menus and dialogs. The knob gadget uses this method to change the direction of the knob turning. This is done because the Motif manager widgets don't dispatch the

The Knob Gadget

button 3 press and release that was used in the knob widget to turn the knob clockwise. Knob gadget would have to switch the clockwise knob turning to button 2, but Motif manager widgets don't dispatch button 2 release events to the gadget. So knob gadget uses the `ArmAndActivate` method to toggle the direction of the knob turning with mouse button 1. It simply calls the `ToggleKnob` action procedure to do the toggling.

```
static void
ArmAndActivate( Widget wid, XEvent *event, String *params,
                Cardinal *num_params )
{
    ToggleKnob(wid, event, NULL, NULL);
}
```


InputDispatch

The `InputDispatch` method gets the events that are dispatched from the manager parent and calls the appropriate action procedure. This is the way gadgets handle events, because they don't have a window to use with translations or event handlers.

```
static void
InputDispatch( Widget wid, XEvent *event, Mask event_mask )
{
    XsmKnobGadget kg = (XsmKnobGadget) wid;
    XsmKnobGadgetClass kc = (XsmKnobGadgetClass) XtClass(wid);

    if (event_mask & XmARM_EVENT)
        StartKnobTurn(wid, event, NULL, NULL);
    else if (event_mask & XmACTIVATE_EVENT)
        ReleaseKnob(wid, event, NULL, NULL);
    else if (event_mask & XmKEY_EVENT)
        HandleKey(wid, event, NULL, NULL);
    else if (event_mask & XmENTER_EVENT)
        _XmEnterGadget ((Widget) kg, event, NULL, NULL);
    else if (event_mask & XmLEAVE_EVENT)
        _XmLeaveGadget ((Widget) kg, event, NULL, NULL);
    else if (event_mask & XmFOCUS_IN_EVENT)
```

```
            _XmFocusInGadget( (Widget) kg, event, NULL, NULL);
        else if (event_mask & XmFOCUS_OUT_EVENT)
            _XmFocusOutGadget( (Widget) kg, event, NULL, NULL);

}
```

VisualChange

The `VisualChange` method is called from XmManager class `SetValues`
when the managers visuals have changed. The gadget regenerates any GC based
on the visual changes and returns True indicating a redraw is needed. Otherwise,
False is returned.

```
static Boolean

VisualChange( Widget wid, Widget cmw, Widget nmw )

{

    XsmKnobGadget kg = (XsmKnobGadget) wid ;

    XmManagerWidget curmw = (XmManagerWidget) cmw ;

    XmManagerWidget newmw = (XmManagerWidget) nmw ;


    if (curmw->manager.foreground != newmw->manager.foreground)

    {

        XSetForeground(XtDisplay(kg), kg->knobg.gc,

                        newmw->manager.foreground;

    )

        return (True);

    }


    if (curmw->manager.highlight_color !=

        newmw->manager.highlight_color ||

        curmw->core.background_pixel !=

        newmw->core.background_pixel ||

        curmw->manager.highlight_pixmap !=

        newmw->manager.highlight_pixmap)

            return (True);


        return (False);
```

Knob Gadget Methods

The knob gadget methods were created for the knob gadget, but they can be inherited by a widget subclassed from knob.

An interesting line of code that you'll see fairly often needs an explanation. For example, consider this line in the procedure `CreateSegments`:

```
(*kc->knobg_class.get_diameters)(w, &diameter, &inner_diameter);
```

In effect, this calls the method pointed to by the *get_diameters* field of the knob gadget class record. In this case, the procedure is `GetDiameters`, so the foregoing line could have been written as

```
GetDiameters(w, &diameter, &inner_diameter);
```

The code is written in this manner to allow the method to be replaced, if desired, by a widget subclassing from knob. Calling the procedure directly, as in the foregoing line, does not allow this.

GetDiameters

`GetDiameters` retrieves diameters of the inner and outer circles that are part of the knob gadget's visual appearance. This method is the same as the knob widget with one notable exception. It gets its height and width information from the RectObj instance part of its instance record. See Chapter 3 for more information.

```
static void GetDiameters( Widget w, unsigned int *diameter,

                          unsigned int *inner_diameter)

{

    XsmKnobGadget kg = (XsmKnobGadget) w;


    if (kg->rectangle.height - (2 * kg->knobg.margin_width) >=

        kg->rectangle.width - (2 * kg->knobg.margin_height))

            *diameter = kg->rectangle.width - (2 *

                    (kg->knobg.margin_width +

                    kg->gadget.highlight_thickness));

    else

        *diameter = kg->rectangle.height - (2 *
                (kg->knobg.margin_height +
                kg->gadget.highlight_thickness));

        .

        .

        .
```

```
}
```

CreateSegments

`CreateSegments` create the lines that are drawn between the knob gadget's
inner and outer circles. The segments enhance the knob's appearance. This
method is that same in knob gadget as it is in knob widget.

See Chapter 2 for a detailed description of this method.

```c
static void CreateSegments( Widget w )
{
    XsmKnobGadget kg = (XsmKnobGadget) w;

    .

    .

    .


}
```

DrawIndicator

`DrawIndicator` draws the small colored dot on the knob face. The dot
identifies the knob's position relative to its minimum and maximum value. This
method is exactly the same as the `DrawIndicator` in the knob widget except
that the formulas for calculating the *center_x* and *center_y* include the RectObj
instance part's x and y values to indicate the offset into the managers window. See
Chapter 3 for more information.

```c
static void DrawIndicator( Widget w )
{
    Widget kw = (XsmKnobWidget) w;

    .

    .

    .


    center_x = kg->rectangle.x + (diameter >> 1) +
            kg->knobg.margin_width +
            kg->gadget.highlight_thickness;

    center_y = kg->rectangle.y + (diameter >> 1) +
            kg->knobg.margin_height +
            kg->gadget.highlight_thickness;
```

```c
        .
        .
        .

    XDrawArc(XtDisplay(w), XtWindow(w), kg->knobg.gc,
            center_x, center_y, diameter, diameter, 0, 64*360);

    XFillArc(XtDisplay(w), XtWindow(w), kg->knobg.gc,
            center_x, center_y, diameter, diameter, 0, 64*360);


}
```

TurnKnob

TurnKnob turns the knob either left or right, depending on the toggle of the
Spacebar. Unlike the knob widget, the knob gadget cannot recognize mouse
button 2 or 3 actions. Therefore, a different behavior scheme had to be devised
for the knob gadget. The Spacebar is used as a toggle to switch between
clockwise and counterclockwise movement of the knob. The rate of turn is
specified by the resource XsmNturnDelay.   This method is the same in knob
gadget as it is in knob widget except when setting the foreground for drawing the
segments of the knob handle, the manager parent's foreground is used.   See
Chapter 3 for more information.

```c
static void TurnKnob( XtPointer closure, XtIntervalId *id )
{
    Widget w = (Widget) closure;
    XsmKnobGadget kg = (XsmKnobGadget) w;
    XsmKnobGadgetClass kc = (XsmKnobGadgetClass) XtClass(w);
    XmManagerWidget mw = (XmManagerWidget) XtParent(w);

        .

        .

        .


    XSetForeground(XtDisplay(kg), kg->knobg.gc,
                kg->knobg.indicator_color);
```

```
        .

        .

        .

}
```

DrawKnob

DrawKnob actually draws the knob visual. This method is the same in knob gadget as it is in knob widget except that it uses the rectangle instance part fields to offset into the parent's window when drawing the circles. See Chapter 2 for a detailed description of this method.

```
static void DrawKnob( Widget w )
{
    XsmKnobGadget kg = (XsmKnobGadget) w;

        .

        .

        .

    XFillArc(XtDisplay(kg), XtWindow(kg), kg->knobg.gc,
            kg->rectangle.x +
           (kg->knobg.margin_width +
            kg->gadget.highlight_thickness),
            kg->rectangle.y +
           (kg->knobg.margin_height +
            kg->gadget.highlight_thickness),
            diameter, diameter, 0, 64*360);
    XSetForeground(XtDisplay(kg), kg->knobg.gc,
                mw->manager.foreground);

    XDrawArc(XtDisplay(kg), XtWindow(kg), kg->knobg.gc,
             kg->rectangle.x +
            (kg->knobg.margin_width +
             kg->gadget.highlight_thickness),
             kg->rectangle.y +
            (kg->knobg.margin_height +
```

```c
                 kg->gadget.highlight_thickness),
        diameter, diameter, 0, 64*360);

    .

    .

    .


    XDrawArc(XtDisplay(kg), XtWindow(kg), kg->knobg.gc,
            kg->rectangle.x +
           (kg->knobg.margin_width +
            kg->gadget.highlight_thickness),
            kg->rectangle.y +
           (kg->knobg.margin_height +
            kg->gadget.highlight_thickness),
            diameter, diameter, 0, 64*360);

    top_knob_start = (diameter - ((diameter *
                     kg->knobg.knob_margin)/100))/2;

    /* top of knob */
    XDrawArc(XtDisplay(kg), XtWindow(kg), kg->knobg.gc,
            kg->rectangle.x + (top_knob_start +
            kg->knobg.margin_width +
            kg->gadget.highlight_thickness),
            kg->rectangle.y + (top_knob_start +
            kg->knobg.margin_height +
            kg->gadget.highlight_thickness),
            inner_diameter, inner_diameter, 0, 64*360);

    .

    .

    .


}
```

CallProc

A CallProc is used to set the value of resources dynamically. The name *CallProc* is derived from the type `XmRCallProc` used in the resource definition. For example, the knob gadget resource `XsmNknobColor` is defined as

```
{

  XsmNknobColor, XsmCKnobColor, XmRPixel, sizeof(Pixel),

  XtOffset (XsmKnobWidget, knob.knob_color),

  XmRCallProc, (XtPointer) _XmBackgroundColorDefault

}
```

DefaultKnobColor

The `DefaultKnobColor` CallProc attempts to get the parent's background if the parent is a manager widget; otherwise, it uses the workaround described in Chapter 2 to get the default knob color.

DefaultIndicatorColor

The `DefaultIndicatorColor` CallProc attempts to get the parent's foreground if the parent is a manager widget; otherwise, it uses the private Motif CallProc `XmForegroundColorDefault()` to get the default foreground color. OSF has no plans to make this public for Motif 2.0.

Action Procedures

These procedures are called as the result of an action that takes place on the knob gadget.

HandleKey

`HandleKey` is called when the user presses any key on the keyboard. This procedure handles key events and calls the appropriate knob turning procedure based on the keysym of the event. It looks at the event using `XLookupString()` to get the keysym. If the keysym is for the < key, it calls the `ToggleLeft` action procedure. If the keysym is for the > key, it calls the `ToggleRight` action procedure.

```
static void HandleKey( Widget w, XEvent *event, char **params,

                      Cardinal *num_params )

{

    KeySym keysym;


    /* Get the keysym from the event */
```


The Knob Gadget

```
        XLookupString((XKeyEvent *) event, (char *)NULL, 0, &keysym,
                NULL);


    if (keysym == XK_less)
        ToggleLeft( w, event, params, num_params );
    else if (keysym == XK_greater)
        ToggleRight( w, event, params, num_params );
}
```

ToggleLeft

`ToggleLeft` is called when the user presses the < key. It causes the knob to rotate to the left until it reaches the minimum value or the user presses the < key a second time.This method is the same in knob gadget as it is in knob widget.

See Chapter 2 for a detailed description of this procedure.

```
static void ToggleLeft( Widget w, XEvent *event, char **params,
                    Cardinal *num_params )
{
    XsmKnobGadget kg = (XsmKnobGadget) w;

        .

        .

        .


}
```

ToggleRight

`ToggleRight` is called when the user presses the > key. It causes the knob to rotate to the right until it reaches the maximum value or the user presses the > key a second time. This procedure is just like the previous procedure except that it causes the knob to turn clockwise on a > key event instead of counterclockwise on a < key event as determined in the `HandleKey` procedure. It will continue to turn unless it is toggled off or it reaches the maximum value.

ToggleKnob

`ToggleKnob` is called when the user presses the Spacebar, which toggles the direction the knob gadget is turning.

StartKnobTurn

The `StartKnobTurn` procedure is called on a mouse button press and uses a timeout to keep the knob turning. This procedure is called when the left mouse button is pressed. It causes the knob to rotate in the direction determined by the `ArmAndActivate` class method. The `ArmAndActivate` method toggles the direction of the turn. If the knob is turning counterclockwise, it continues until the mouse button is released or when it reaches the minimum value.

If the knob is turning clockwise, it continues until the mouse button is released or it reaches the maximum value.

```
static void StartKnobTurn( Widget w, XEvent *event, char **params,
                           Cardinal *num_params )
{
    XsmKnobGadget kg = (XsmKnobGadget) w;
    XsmKnobGadgetClass kc = (XsmKnobGadgetClass) XtClass(w);


    /*
     * As long as the value has not reached the minimum value,
     * continue turning
     */
    if (kg->knobg.move_clockwise)
    {
      if (kg->knobg.value < kg->knobg.max_val)
        kg->knobg.timer_id =
          XtAppAddTimeOut(XtWidgetToApplicationContext(w),
          (unsigned long) kg->knobg.turn_delay,
          kc->knobg_class.turn, (XtPointer) w);
    }
    else
    {
      if (kg->knobg.value > kg->knobg.min_val)
        kg->knobg.timer_id =
          XtAppAddTimeOut(XtWidgetToApplicationContext(w),
          (unsigned long) kg->knobg.turn_delay,
          kc->knobg_class.turn, (XtPointer) w);
    }
```

}

ReleaseKnob

The `ReleaseKnob` procedure is called on a mouse button release event and removes a timeout to stop the knob from turning. This procedure is essentially the same as the action procedure in the knob widget. See Chapter 3 for more information.

```c
static void ReleaseKnob( Widget w, XEvent *event, char **params,
                         Cardinal *num_params )
{
    XsmKnobGadget kg = (XsmKnobGadget) w;


    /* remove the timeout */
    if (kg->knobg.timer_id) XtRemoveTimeOut(kg->knobg.timer_id);


    kg->knobg.turning = False;
}
```

Convenience Functions

Convenience functions exist for the convenience of the application developer. There are three convenience functions for the knob gadget (remember that these are public functions and were defined in `KnobG.h`).

XsmCreateKnobGadget

`XsmCreateKnob` is a convenience procedure used to create an instance of a knob widget. It performs exactly like the convenience functions for existing Motif widgets.

```c
Widget XsmCreateKnobGadget( Widget parent, char *name, ArgList
                            arglist,
                            Cardinal argcount )
{
    return (XtCreateWidget(name, xsmKnobGadgetClass,
                           parent, arglist, argcount));
}
```

XsmGetKnobGadgetValues

`XsmGetKnobGadgetValues` retrieves the value of a specified knob resource. This function is the same as the knob widget's XsmGetKnobValue. See Chapter 3 for more information.

```c
int XsmGetKnobGValue( Widget w )
{
    XsmKnobGadget kg = (XsmKnobGadget) w;


    return(kg->knobg.value);
}
```

XsmSetKnobGadgetValues

`XsmSetKnobGadgetValues` sets the value of a specified knob gadget resource. This function is essentially the same as the knob widget's `XsmSetKnobValue`. The only difference is that `XsmSetKnobGadgetValues` uses the manager parent's foreground when setting the foreground for drawing the handle segments. See Chapter 3 for more information.

```c
void XsmSetKnobGValue( Widget w, int value )
{
    XsmKnobGadget kg = (XsmKnobGadget) w;
    XsmKnobGadgetClass kc = (XsmKnobGadgetClass) XtClass(w);
    XmManagerWidget mw = (XmManagerWidget) XtParent(w);

    .

    .

    .


    XSetForeground(XtDisplay(kg), kg->knobg.gc,
                   mw->manager.foreground);

    .

    .

    .

}
```

Compiling Knobg.c

You'll need a Makefile to compile the `Knobg.c` object. The Makefile listed in Appendix A specifies specific paths for the include and library directories, and you may need to change these to suit your system. Note that the Makefile only creates an object file called `Knobg.o`. The object file is then linked when an application uses a knob gadget. You normally access Motif widgets by linking the Motif library `libXm.a`, which is composed of all the Motif widget object files.

Now that you've created the knob, let's put it to use in an actual program, `knobgcolors.c`. You can find the listing for this program in Appendix A.

knobgcolors.c

`knobgcolors.c` produces a window with three knob gadgets, one to control each of the primary colors. As the knobs are turned, the background color of the window changes accordingly. This is the same as `knobcolors.c` described in Chapter 3, except that here we use the knob gadget.

Summary

This chapter described the knob gadget and took you through its creation. The next chapter looks at where you can go from here and offers some ideas on widgets that you can create using the knowledge you've gained.

Chapter 6 Where Do You Go from Here?

Now that you have completed the main part of the book, you may wonder what you should do next. This chapter presents some ideas on new widgets and gadgets that you can create.

Some Ideas for New Widgets

More than likely you already have some ideas of your own about the new widgets you'd like to write, but just in case you need some help, here are a few possibilities for you to consider.

Thermostat

This could be a widget or a gadget with the visual appearance of a thermometer. A callback could be invoked when the temperature reaches a certain value. Maximum and minimum values could be established by resources. The thermostat could also be used as a thermometer.

Dial

This widget could be used in many applications. You could design its visual to be a complete circle or a semicircle, based on a resource setting. Maximum and minimum values could be established by resources. You could use this widget as the basis for a clock widget.

Spreadsheet

A spreadsheet widget could be based on the grid widget described in Chapter 4. You could use small Motif text field widgets for cells, arranging them within the grid manager.

Book

A book widget could consist of two pages, left and right, on which text could be displayed. Clicking a mouse button on either page would flip the page.

Calendar Page

This widget would display the current month's calendar. It could also be based on the grid widget, perhaps with Motif label widgets used as the day and date display boxes.

Indicator

The indicator could be a widget or a gadget. Its appearance could vary: round, square, or rectangular, determined by a resource. You could have the indicator flash or change colors on the occurrence of some event. A callback could be invoked when the indicator flashes or its color changes.

Clock

You could design a clock widget based on the dial widget suggested previously. You could use a resource value to switch between analog and digital appearance, and use other resources to set an alarm.

Summary

This chapter concludes the book. We hope that you have learned enough to get you started writing your own widgets. Like any other endeavor, practice makes perfect, and the more widgets you write, the more you'll understand the underlying concepts. Use your imagination and the knowledge you've gained to come up with your own new widgets.

Appendix A Program Listings

This appendix contains listings of all the programs, header files, and Makefiles used to create and demonstrate the widgets described in this book. All the files are listed alphabetically, and the Makefiles are cross-referenced to the programs to which they apply.

Grid.c

Grid.c is the object for the grid widget described in Chapter 4.

```c
#include "GridP.h"


/* Error Messages */
#define MESSAGE1 "There must be at least one row."
#define MESSAGE2 "There must be at least one column."
#define MESSAGE3 "The row position can not be greater than the
                  number of rows."
#define MESSAGE4 "The column position can not be greater than the
                  number of columns."
#define MESSAGE5 "The row and column position is already taken.\n
                  Defaulting to next available position."
#define MESSAGE6 "The grid is full.  The number of rows or columns
                  must be expanded."
#define MESSAGE7 "The row and column position is already taken.\n
                  Retaining old position."
```

```c
#define MAXDIMENSION ((1 << 16)-1)
#define LINE_WIDTH    1


/* Macro to get constraint resource values */
#define GridInfo(w) ((XsmGridConstraintPtr)(w)->core.constraints)


/* Macro for stack allocation */
#define StackAlloc(size, stack_array) \
        ((size) <= sizeof(stack_array) ? \
         (XtPointer)(stack_array) \
        :    XtMalloc((unsigned)(size)))


/* Macro to free stack allocation */
#define StackFree(pointer, stack_array) \
        if ((pointer) != ((XtPointer)(stack_array))) \
            XtFree((char *)pointer);


/* Macro to get the line width if show_grid_lines is true */
#define GetLineWidth(gw) gw->grid.show_grid_lines ? LINE_WIDTH : 0


/* Macro to get the number of converter values in an enum list */
#define NUM_NAMES( list ) (sizeof( list) / sizeof( char *))


/********       Static Function Declarations     ********/


/* core class procedures */
static void ClassInitialize( void );
static void ClassPartInitialize( WidgetClass );
static void Initialize( Widget request,
                        Widget new_w,
                        ArgList args,
                        Cardinal *num_args );
static void Destroy( Widget w );
```

```
        static void Resize( Widget w );
        static void Redisplay( Widget w,
                            XEvent *event,
                            Region region );
        static Boolean SetValues( Widget old_w,
                            Widget request,
                            Widget new_w,
                            ArgList args,
                            Cardinal *num_args );
        static XtGeometryResult QueryGeometry( Widget wid,
                                    XtWidgetGeometry *request,
                                    XtWidgetGeometry *ret );


        /* composite class procedures */
        static XtGeometryResult GeometryManager( Widget w,
                                    XtWidgetGeometry *request,
                                    XtWidgetGeometry *reply );
        static void ChangeManaged( Widget wid );


        /* constraint procedures */
        static void ConstraintInitialize( Widget rw,
                            Widget nw,
                            ArgList args,
                            Cardinal *num_args );
        static Boolean ConstraintSetValues( Widget cw,
                            Widget rw,
                            Widget nw,
                            ArgList args,
                            Cardinal *num_args );


        /* grid class procedures */
        static void UpdateGridDimensions( Widget w,
                            Dimension * width,
                            Dimension * height );
```

```
static void AddChildToGrid( Widget parent,

                            Widget child,

                            Dimension row_pos,

                            Dimension col_pos );
static void LayoutChildren( Widget w );
static void DrawGridLines( Widget w );
static void EraseGridLines( Widget w );


/* internal procedures */
static Dimension GetColumnWidth( XsmGridWidget gw,

                                 int col_pos );
static Dimension GetRowHeight( XsmGridWidget gw,

                               int row_pos );
static Boolean SetChildHorizPosition( XsmGridWidget parent,

                             Widget child,

                               XsmGridConstraintPart * grid_info,

                             Dimension row,

                             Dimension start_col );
static Boolean SetChildVertPosition( XsmGridWidget parent,

                             Widget child,

                               XsmGridConstraintPart * grid_info,

                             Dimension start_row,

                             Dimension col );
static Boolean SetChildPosition( XsmGridWidget parent,

                             Widget child,

                               XsmGridConstraintPart * grid_info,

                             Dimension start_row,

                             Dimension start_col );
static void SetInvGC( XsmGridWidget gw,

                  GC gc );
static void SetNormGC( XsmGridWidget gw,

                  GC gc );
static void LoadGC( XsmGridWidget gw,

                Pixel fg,
```

```c
                    Pixel bg );
static void ModifyGridLines( XsmGridWidget gw, Boolean draw_grid );




/********      End Static Function Declarations      ********/




static char *HorizontalAlignmentNames[] =
          {"align_center","align_left", "align_right"};
static char *VerticalAlignmentNames[] =
          {"align_center","align_top", "align_bottom"};




/* This is the static initialization of the resources for the
 * Grid widget.  Note: the synthetic resources are also included
 * in this resource list as well as in the synthetic resource list.
 * The synthetic resource list includes additional information
 * about the synthetic resource.
 */

static XtResource resources[] = {

     {

        XsmNcolumns,
        XsmCColumns,
        XmRDimension,
        sizeof(Dimension),
        XtOffset (XsmGridWidget, grid.columns),
        XmRImmediate, (XtPointer) 1
     },


     {
```

```c
    XsmNrows,
    XsmCRows,
    XmRDimension,
    sizeof(Dimension),
    XtOffset (XsmGridWidget, grid.rows),
    XmRImmediate, (XtPointer) 1
},

{
    XsmNmarginWidth,
    XsmCMarginWidth,
    XmRHorizontalDimension,
    sizeof(Dimension),
    XtOffset (XsmGridWidget, grid.margin_width),
    XmRImmediate, (XtPointer) 4
},

{
    XsmNmarginHeight,
    XsmCMarginHeight,
    XmRVerticalDimension,
    sizeof(Dimension),
    XtOffset (XsmGridWidget, grid.margin_height),
    XmRImmediate, (XtPointer) 4
},

{
    XsmNhorizontalSpacing,
    XsmCHorizontalSpacing,
    XmRHorizontalDimension,
    sizeof(Dimension),
    XtOffset (XsmGridWidget, grid.h_spacing),
    XmRImmediate, (XtPointer) 4
},
```

```c
    {
      XsmNverticalSpacing,
      XsmCVerticalSpacing,
      XmRVerticalDimension,
      sizeof(Dimension),
      XtOffset (XsmGridWidget, grid.v_spacing),
      XmRImmediate, (XtPointer) 4
    },

    {

      XsmNhorizontalAlignment,
      XsmCHorizontalAlignment,
      XsmRHorizontalAlignment,
      sizeof(unsigned char),
      XtOffset (XsmGridWidget, grid.horiz_alignment),
      XmRImmediate, (XtPointer) XsmALIGN_CENTER
    },

    {

      XsmNverticalAlignment,
      XsmCVerticalAlignment,
      XsmRVerticalAlignment,
      sizeof(unsigned char),
      XtOffset (XsmGridWidget, grid.vert_alignment),
      XmRImmediate, (XtPointer) XsmALIGN_MIDDLE
    },

    {

      XsmNshowGridLines,
      XsmCShowGridLines,
      XmRBoolean,
      sizeof(Boolean),
      XtOffset (XsmGridWidget, grid.show_grid_lines),
```

```c
            XmRImmediate, (XtPointer) False
        },
};


/* Synthetic resources change their values dynamically.
 * As in Motif, our dimension resources change dynamically
 * based on the XmNunitType resource.  For example, if the unit
 * type is in 1000ths of an inch, the conversion routines will
 * modify the resource values to convert the resource value in the
 * given unit type into a number of pixels for use in displaying the
 * the widget in the stated dimensions.
 */
static XmSyntheticResource syn_resources[] =
{
    {
        XmNmarginWidth,
        sizeof (Dimension),
        XtOffset( XsmGridWidget, grid.margin_width),
        _XmFromHorizontalPixels,
        _XmToHorizontalPixels
    },

    {
        XmNmarginHeight,
        sizeof (Dimension),
        XtOffset( XsmGridWidget, grid.margin_height),
        _XmFromVerticalPixels,
        _XmToVerticalPixels,
    },

    {
        XmNhorizontalSpacing,
        sizeof (Dimension),
        XtOffset( XsmGridWidget, grid.h_spacing),
```

```c
            _XmFromHorizontalPixels,
            _XmToHorizontalPixels
        },


        {

            XmNverticalSpacing,
            sizeof (Dimension),
            XtOffset( XsmGridWidget, grid.v_spacing),
            _XmFromVerticalPixels,
            _XmToVerticalPixels,
        },
    };


/* Constraint resources for children of the Grid widget */
static XtResource constraint_resources[] =
{

        {

            XsmNrowPosition,
            XsmCRowPosition,
            XmRPosition,
            sizeof(Position),
            XtOffsetOf( struct _XsmGridConstraintRec, grid.row_pos),
            XmRImmediate, (XtPointer) MAXDIMENSION
        },


        {

            XsmNcolumnPosition,
            XsmCColumnPosition,
            XmRPosition,
            sizeof(Position),
            XtOffsetOf( struct _XsmGridConstraintRec, grid.col_pos),
            XmRImmediate, (XtPointer) MAXDIMENSION
        },
```

```c
};


/* This is the initialization of the class record.  The core class
 * part is initialized first, followed by the Composite,
 * Constraint, Manager, and Grid class parts.
 */
externaldef (xsmgridclassrec) XsmGridClassRec xsmGridClassRec = {
    {                       /* core_class fields       */
      (WidgetClass) &xmManagerClassRec,   /* superclass            */
        "XsmGrid",                        /* class_name            */
        sizeof(XsmGridRec),               /* widget_size           */
        ClassInitialize,                  /* class_initialize      */
        ClassPartInitialize,              /* class_part_initialize */
        FALSE,                            /* class_inited          */
        Initialize,                       /* initialize            */
        NULL,                             /* initialize_hook       */
        XtInheritRealize,                 /* realize               */
        NULL,                             /* actions               */
        0,                                /* num_actions           */
        resources,                        /* resources             */
        XtNumber(resources),              /* num_resources         */
        NULLQUARK,                        /* xrm_class             */
        TRUE,                             /* compress_motion       */
        XtExposeCompressMaximal,          /* compress_exposure     */
        TRUE,                             /* compress_enterleave   */
        FALSE,                            /* visible_interest      */
        Destroy,                          /* destroy               */
        Resize,                           /* resize                */
        Redisplay,                        /* expose                */
        SetValues,                        /* set_values            */
        NULL,                             /* set_values_hook       */
        XtInheritSetValuesAlmost,         /* set_values_almost     */
```

```c
    NULL,                                   /* get_values_hook      */
    NULL,                                   /* accept_focus         */
    XtVersion,                              /* version              */
    NULL,                                   /* callback_private     */
    NULL,                                   /* tm_table             */
    QueryGeometry,                          /* query_geometry       */
    XtInheritDisplayAccelerator,            /* display accel        */
    NULL,                                   /* extension            */
    },


    {               /* composite_class fields   */
    GeometryManager,                        /* geometry_manager     */
    ChangeManaged,                          /* change_managed       */
    XtInheritInsertChild,                   /* insert_child         */
    XtInheritDeleteChild,                   /* delete_child         */
    NULL,                                   /* extension            */
    },


    {               /* constraint_class fields */
    constraint_resources,                   /* resource list        */
    XtNumber(constraint_resources),         /* num resources        */
    sizeof (XsmGridConstraintRec),          /* constraint size      */
    ConstraintInitialize,                   /* init proc            */
    NULL,                                   /* destroy proc         */
    ConstraintSetValues,                    /* set values proc      */
    NULL,                                   /* extension            */
    },


    {               /* manager_class fields     */
    XtInheritTranslations,                  /* translations         */
    syn_resources,                          /* syn resources        */
    XtNumber(syn_resources),                /* num syn_resources    */
    NULL,                                   /* syn_cont_resources   */
```

```c
        0,                              /* num_syn_cont_resources*/
        XmInheritParentProcess,         /* parent_process     */
        NULL,                           /* extension          */
    },

    {               /* grid_class fields       */
        UpdateGridDimensions,           /* update_grid        */
        AddChildToGrid,                 /* add_child          */
        LayoutChildren,                 /* layout_children    */
        DrawGridLines,                  /* draw_grid          */
        EraseGridLines,                 /* erase_grid         */
        NULL,                           /* extension          */
    }
};


/* external definition of the grid class record */
externaldef(xsmgridwidgetclass) WidgetClass xsmGridWidgetClass =
                                (WidgetClass)
&xsmGridClassRec;




/*******************************************************************
 * Core Class Methods
 *******************************************************************/


/*******************************************************************
 *
 *  ClassInitialize() -
 *  The widget class initialization routine.
 *  Representation types are registered here for new types
 *  not previously registered by Motif or the Intrinsics.
 *
 *******************************************************************/
```

```c
static void
ClassInitialize( void )
{
    /* Register the representation types.  This can be used only with
     * resources that are enum types.  Other types must use
     * XtSetTypeConverter().
     */
    XmRepTypeRegister( XsmRHorizontalAlignment,
                       HorizontalAlignmentNames, NULL,
                       NUM_NAMES(HorizontalAlignmentNames));
    XmRepTypeRegister( XsmRVerticalAlignment,
                       VerticalAlignmentNames, NULL,

NUM_NAMES(VerticalAlignmentNames));
}


/**********************************************************************
 *
 *  ClassPartInitialize() -
 *  The initialization routine for class parts.  It is called for
 *  the initialization of this class and each time a new subclass is
 *  created for this widget class.  It is called only once per
 *  subclass.
 *
 **********************************************************************/

static void
ClassPartInitialize( WidgetClass wc )
{
    XsmGridWidgetClass gc = (XsmGridWidgetClass) wc;
    XsmGridWidgetClass sc = (XsmGridWidgetClass)
                            wc->core_class.superclass;

    /* assign procedures to the class pointers that inherit these
```

```c
    procedures */

    if (gc->grid_class.add_child == XsmInheritAddChild)
        gc->grid_class.add_child = sc->grid_class.add_child;

    if (gc->grid_class.layout_children == XsmInheritLayoutChildren)
        gc->grid_class.layout_children =
                sc->grid_class.layout_children;

    if (gc->grid_class.draw_grid == XsmInheritDrawGrid)
        gc->grid_class.draw_grid = sc->grid_class.draw_grid;

    if (gc->grid_class.erase_grid == XsmInheritEraseGrid)
        gc->grid_class.erase_grid = sc->grid_class.erase_grid;
}




/******************************************************************
 *
 *  Initialize() -
 *  The main widget instance initialization routine.  Initialize
 *  the instance variables here, and verify the resources values.
 *
 ******************************************************************/

static void
Initialize( Widget request, Widget new_w, ArgList args, Cardinal
            *num_args )
{
    XsmGridWidget new_m = (XsmGridWidget) new_w;
    XsmGridWidget req_m = (XsmGridWidget) request;
    unsigned int line_width = GetLineWidth(new_m); /* 0 if grid
                                                    lines are off */
    int i;
```

```c
    /* verify resource values */
    if (new_m->grid.rows < 1)
    {
        _XmWarning( (Widget) new_w, MESSAGE1);
        new_m->grid.rows = 1;
    }


    if (new_m->grid.columns < 1)
    {
        _XmWarning( (Widget) new_w, MESSAGE2);
        new_m->grid.columns = 1;
    }


    /* Ensure a minimum size */
    if (req_m->core.width == 0)
        new_m->core.width = (2 * (new_m->grid.margin_width +
                            line_width)) +  ((new_m->grid.h_spacing ?
                        new_m->grid.h_spacing : 10) + line_width) *
                            new_m->grid.columns;

    if (new_m->core.height == 0)
        new_m->core.height = (2 * (new_m->grid.margin_height +
                            line_width)) +((new_m->grid.v_spacing ?
                        new_m->grid.v_spacing : 10) + line_width)
                        * (new_m->grid.rows - 1);

    /* Allocate space for the list of row heights */
    new_m->grid.row_height = (Dimension *)
                        XtCalloc(new_m->grid.rows,
                        sizeof(Dimension));

    /* Allocate space for the list of column widgets */
    new_m->grid.col_width = (Dimension *)
```

```c
                                XtCalloc(new_m->grid.columns,
                                sizeof(Dimension));


    /* Allocate space for the grid of widgets */
    new_m->grid.widget_grid = (WidgetList *)
                                XtMalloc(sizeof(WidgetList) *
                                new_m->grid.rows);


    for (i = 0; i < new_m->grid.rows; i++)
    {
      new_m->grid.widget_grid[i] =
        (WidgetList)XtCalloc(new_m->grid.columns, sizeof(Widget));
    }


    /* Save original margins for use in Resize() */
    new_m->grid.orig_margin_width = new_m->grid.margin_width;
    new_m->grid.orig_margin_height = new_m->grid.margin_height;


    new_m->grid.lines_visible = False;


    LoadGC(new_m, new_m->core.background_pixel,
           new_m->manager.foreground);
}




/****************************************************************
 *
 *   Destroy() -
 *   Clean up allocated resources when the widget is destroyed.
 *   Anything that is malloc'd by the widget should be freed here.
 *
 ****************************************************************/
```

```c
static void
Destroy( Widget w )
{
    XsmGridWidget gw = (XsmGridWidget) w;
    int i;

   /* Free row_height and column_width arrays */
   XtFree((char *)gw->grid.row_height);
   XtFree((char *)gw->grid.col_width);

   /* Free two-dimensional widget_grid array */
    for (i = 0; i < gw->grid.rows; i++)
       XtFree((char *)gw->grid.widget_grid[i]);
   XtFree((char *)gw->grid.widget_grid);
}




/***************************************************************
 *
 *  Resize() -
 *  Redraw according to size changes.  Adjust only the margins to
 *  account for growth.  Clip children if the dimensions are too
 *  small.
 *
 ***************************************************************

static void
Resize( Widget w )
{
    XsmGridWidget gw = (XsmGridWidget) w;
    XsmGridWidgetClass gc = (XsmGridWidgetClass) XtClass(w);
    Dimension width, height, save_margin_width, save_margin_height;
```

```c
    unsigned int line_width = GetLineWidth(gw); /* 0 if grid lines
                                                   are off */


    /* Clear window if grid lines are visible */
    if (gw->grid.show_grid_lines && gw->grid.lines_visible &&
        XtIsRealized(w))
            XClearWindow(XtDisplay(w), XtWindow(w));


    /* Get grid height and width */
    (*gc->grid_class.update_grid)(w, &width, &height);


    /* Add in the margin widths and inter-column spacing */
    width += ((2 * (gw->grid.orig_margin_width + line_width)) +
            ((gw->grid.h_spacing + line_width) * gw->grid.rows));


    /* Add in the margin widths and inter-column spacing */
    height += ((2 * (gw->grid.orig_margin_height + line_width)) +
            ((gw->grid.v_spacing + line_width) *
             gw->grid.columns));


    /* Save current margins */
    save_margin_width = gw->grid.margin_width;
    save_margin_height = gw->grid.margin_height;


    /* Set to resource settings for margins */
    gw->grid.margin_width = gw->grid.orig_margin_width;
    gw->grid.margin_height = gw->grid.orig_margin_height;


    /* If there is a resize growth, reset the margins */
    if (gw->core.width > width)
        gw->grid.margin_width += (gw->core.width - width)/2;


    if (gw->core.height > height)
        gw->grid.margin_height += (gw->core.height - height)/2;
```

```c
    /* Redo geometry if the margins changed */
    if (gw->grid.margin_width != save_margin_width ||
        gw->grid.margin_height != save_margin_height)
        (*gc->grid_class.layout_children)(w);


    if (gw->grid.show_grid_lines)
        (*gc->grid_class.draw_grid)(w);
}




/***************************************************************************
 *
 *  Redisplay() -
 *  Redraw region that gets exposed.
 *
 ***************************************************************************/

static void
Redisplay( Widget w, XEvent *event, Region region )
{
    XsmGridWidget gw = (XsmGridWidget) w;
    XsmGridWidgetClass gc = (XsmGridWidgetClass) XtClass(w);

    /*  Redisplay gadgets.  */
    _XmRedisplayGadgets(w, event, region);

    if (gw->grid.show_grid_lines)
        (*gc->grid_class.draw_grid)(w);
    else if (gw->grid.lines_visible)
        (*gc->grid_class.erase_grid)(w);
}
```

```c
/******************************************************************
 *
 *  SetValues() -
 *  The procedure is used to verify changes to the resource values.
 *  If the resource changes affect the visuals of the widget, the
 *  return value of the procedure should be set to True indicating
 *  that the expose procedure will be called to redraw the widget.
 *  Any changes to the widget's geometry in this procedure will
 *  generate a geometry request to its parent.
 *
 ******************************************************************/

SetValues( Widget old_w, Widget request, Widget new_w,
           ArgList args, Cardinal *num_args )
{
    XsmGridWidget new_m = (XsmGridWidget) new_w;
    XsmGridWidget old_m = (XsmGridWidget) old_w;
    XsmGridWidgetClass gc = (XsmGridWidgetClass) XtClass(new_w);
    XsmGridConstraintPart * grid_info;
    unsigned int line_width = GetLineWidth(new_m); /* 0 if grid
                                                      lines are off */
    Boolean redisplay = False;
    Dimension col_pos;
    Dimension row_pos;
    int i, j;

    /* Verify resource values */
    if (new_m->grid.rows < 1)
    {
        _XmWarning( (Widget) new_w, MESSAGE1);
        new_m->grid.rows = old_m->grid.rows;
    }
```

```c
        if (new_m->grid.columns < 1)
        {
            _XmWarning( (Widget) new_w, MESSAGE2);
            new_m->grid.columns = old_m->grid.columns;
        }


    /* Reset arrays if rows or columns change. */
    if (new_m->grid.rows != old_m->grid.rows)
        /* Reallocate space for the list of row heights */
        new_m->grid.row_height = (Dimension *)XtRealloc((XtPointer)

new_m->grid.row_height,

sizeof(Dimension) *

new_m->grid.rows);

    if (new_m->grid.columns != old_m->grid.columns)
        /* Reallocate space for the list of column widgets */
        new_m->grid.col_width = (Dimension *) XtRealloc((XtPointer)

new_m->grid.col_width,

sizeof(Dimension) *

new_m->grid.columns);
    if (new_m->grid.rows != old_m->grid.rows ||
        new_m->grid.columns != old_m->grid.columns)
    {
      /* Free up old grid of widgets */
      for (i = 0; i < old_m->grid.rows; i++)
      {
          XtFree((char *)new_m->grid.widget_grid[i]);
      }
```

```c
        /* Reallocate space for the grid of widgets */
        new_m->grid.widget_grid = (WidgetList *)XtRealloc((XtPointer)

new_m->grid.widget_grid,

sizeof(WidgetList) *

new_m->grid.rows);


    /* Reallocate space for the grid of widgets */
     for (i = 0; i < new_m->grid.rows; i++)
        new_m->grid.widget_grid[i] =
            (WidgetList) XtCalloc(new_m->grid.columns,

sizeof(Widget));
     redisplay = True;
  }


  /* Reset children's positions in the position arrays when the
   * rows or columns change.
   */
  if (new_m->grid.rows < old_m->grid.rows ||
     new_m->grid.columns < old_m->grid.columns)
  {
    Widget child;
    Dimension width, height;

    for (i = 0; i < new_m->composite.num_children; i++)
    {
        child = new_m->composite.children[i];
        grid_info = &(GridInfo(child)->grid);

        row_pos = grid_info->orig_row_pos;
        col_pos = grid_info->orig_col_pos;
```

```c
        (*gc->grid_class.add_child)(new_w, child, row_pos,
                                col_pos);
    }


    /* Get grid height and width */
    (*gc->grid_class.update_grid)(new_w, &width, &height);


    /* Update width and height.  If they change, this will
     * automatically cause a geometry request to the grid's parent.
     */
    new_m->core.width = width +
                        ((2 * (new_m->grid.margin_width +
                            line_width)) + ((new_m->grid.h_spacing
                            + line_width) * new_m->grid.rows));


    new_m->core.height = height +
                        ((2 * (new_m->grid.margin_height +
                            line_width)) + ((new_m->grid.v_spacing
                            + line_width) * new_m->grid.columns));


    (*gc->grid_class.layout_children)(new_w);
    }


/* Save changes in margins for use in Resize() */
new_m->grid.orig_margin_width = new_m->grid.margin_width;
new_m->grid.orig_margin_height = new_m->grid.margin_height;


if (new_m->core.background_pixel !=
    old_m->core.background_pixel ||
    new_m->manager.foreground != old_m->manager.foreground)
{
    LoadGC(new_m, new_m->core.background_pixel,
            new_m->manager.foreground);
    redisplay = True;
```

```
        }

        if (new_m->grid.show_grid_lines != old_m->grid.show_grid_lines)
            redisplay = True;


        return (redisplay);
    }




/*****************************************************************
 *
 *  QueryGeometry() -
 *  When manager widgets have a query geometry procedure it should
 *  make query geometry requests to their children to calculate its
 *  preferred geometry.  Once this is done, set the reply fields
 *  and determine the appropriate XtGeometryResult to return.
 *
 *****************************************************************/

static XtGeometryResult
QueryGeometry( Widget wid, XtWidgetGeometry *request,
XtWidgetGeometry *reply )
{
    XsmGridWidget gw = (XsmGridWidget) wid;
    Widget child;
    Dimension col_stack[50];
    Dimension *max_col_width;
    Dimension row_height, width = 0, height = 0;
    unsigned int line_width = GetLineWidth(gw); /* 0 if grid lines
                                                   are off */
    XtWidgetGeometry desired;
    int i, j;
```

```c
/* Set up an array to save the max width of each column.
 * The StackAlloc macro will allocate space if the space
 * required is more than was allocated on the stack.
 */
max_col_width = (Dimension *) StackAlloc(gw->grid.columns,
                    col_stack);


/* Initialize the max_col_width array to zero */
 for (j = 0; j < gw->grid.columns; j++)
     max_col_width[j] = 0;


/* Go through the rows caluclating the height of each row
 * from the desired height of each child.  Also use the
 * values from the QueryGeometry to figure out the max width
 * of each column.
 */
 for (i = 0; i < gw->grid.rows; i++)
 {
     row_height = 0;

     for (j = 0; j < gw->grid.columns; j++)
     {
         child = gw->grid.widget_grid[i][j];

         if (child != NULL)
         {
             XtQueryGeometry(child, NULL, &desired);

             if (row_height < desired.height)
                 row_height = desired.height;

             if (max_col_width[j] < desired.width)
                 max_col_width[j] = desired.width;
         }
```

```c
        }

        height += row_height;
    }


    for (j = 0; j < gw->grid.columns; j++)
        width += max_col_width[j];


    /* Free the array.  The StackFree macro frees space only if it
     * is not allocated on the stack.
     */
    StackFree(max_col_width, col_stack);


    /* Set up the reply to the query */
    reply->width = width + ((2 * (gw->grid.margin_width +
                            line_width)) + ((gw->grid.h_spacing +
                            line_width) * gw->grid.rows));


    reply->height = height + ((2 * (gw->grid.margin_height +
                            line_width)) + ((gw->grid.v_spacing +
                            line_width) * gw->grid.columns));


    reply->request_mode = CWWidth | CWHeight;


    /* XtGeometryYes indicates that the requested geometry is the
     * same as reply geometry.
     */
    if ((request->request_mode & CWWidth && request->width ==
            reply->width) &&  (request->request_mode & CWHeight &&
            request->height == reply->height))
            return XtGeometryYes;


    /* XtGeometryNo indicates that our current geometry is the same
     * as reply geometry.
```

```c
     */
    if (reply->width == gw->core.width &&
        reply->height == gw->core.height)
            return XtGeometryNo;


   /* XtGeometryAlmost indicates that at least one of the fields
    * in the reply geometry differs from the request geometry.
    */
    return XtGeometryAlmost;
}


/**************************************************************************
 * Composite Class Methods
 **************************************************************************/




/**************************************************************************
 *
 * GeometryManager() -
 * Sets up geometry negotiations between the grid widget, the
 * child requesting a change in geometry, and the grid widget's
 * parent.  This function determines whether a child is allowed to
 * grow or shrink. (Other Geometry Managers also allow their
 * children to reposition themselves and change their border
 * widths.)
 *
 **************************************************************************/


static XtGeometryResult
GeometryManager( Widget w, XtWidgetGeometry *request,
XtWidgetGeometry *reply )
{
    XsmGridWidget gw = (XsmGridWidget) XtParent(w);
```

```c
    XsmGridConstraintPart * grid_info = &(GridInfo(w)->grid);
    XsmGridWidgetClass gc = (XsmGridWidgetClass)
                              XtClass((Widget)gw);
    unsigned int line_width = GetLineWidth(gw); /* 0 if grid lines
                                                   are off */
    Dimension width = 0, height = 0;
    Dimension save_width, save_height;
    XtGeometryResult result = XtGeometryYes;
    XtWidgetGeometry geo_request;
    XtWidgetGeometry geo_reply;
    Boolean set_almost = False;
    Boolean make_request = False;
    XtGeometryMask mask = request->request_mode;
    int i, j;

    /* Reject attempts that do not want to adjust height or width */
    if (!(mask & (CWWidth | CWHeight)))
        return XtGeometryNo;

    /* Adjustments to x, y or border width are not allowed.
     * Continue with the request for height and width but be
     * sure to return XtGeometryAlmost if x, y or border_width
     * are requested.
     */
    if (mask & CWX && request->x != w->core.x)
    {
        reply->x = w->core.x;
        reply->request_mode |= CWX;
        set_almost = True;
    }


    if (mask & CWY && request->y != w->core.y)
    {
        reply->y = w->core.y;
```

                                                      Program Listings

```c
        reply->request_mode |= CWY;
        set_almost = True;
    }


    if (mask & CWBorderWidth && request->border_width !=
        w->core.border_width)
    {
        reply->y = w->core.border_width;
        reply->request_mode |= CWBorderWidth;
        set_almost = True;
    }


    /* Check for query only or requests other than width and height.
     * If the request is for more than just width and height, we must
     * return GeometryAlmost. This means the request to our parent
     * must be a query only request to prevent our parent from
     * reconfiguring our geometry.
     */
    if ((mask & XtCWQueryOnly) || set_almost)
        geo_request.request_mode = XtCWQueryOnly;
    else
        geo_request.request_mode = 0 ;


    if (mask & CWWidth)
    {
        /* If the request width causes the column to grow or
         * the request width causes the column to shrink,
         * see if the change will affect the grid's geometry.
         * Otherwise accept the request and change the child's width.
         */
        if (request->width > gw->grid.col_width[grid_info->col_pos]
            ||(w->core.width == gw->grid.col_width[grid_info->col_pos]
            && request->width < gw->grid.col_width[grid_info->col_pos]))
```

```c
{
    /* Save the child's width in case of a failure to acquire a
     * new width from the grid's parent or in case the request
     * is a query.  Set the width to the requested value  for
     * use in computations.
     */
    save_width = w->core.width;
    w->core.width = request->width;


    /* Find total width for the columns */
    for (j = 0; j < gw->grid.columns; j++)
    {
        width += GetColumnWidth(gw, j);
    }


    /* Add in the margin widths, line_widths and inter-column
       spacing */
    width += ((2 * (gw->grid.margin_width + line_width)) +
              ((gw->grid.h_spacing  + line_width) *
              gw->grid.rows));


    /* If the computed width is not equal to the current grid
     * width, make the request to the parent of the grid widget
     * for a new size.
     */
    if (gw->core.width != width)
    {
        make_request = True;
        geo_request.request_mode |= CWWidth;
        geo_request.width = width;
    }
} else
    w->core.width = request->width;
}
```

```c
    if (mask & CWHeight)
    {
        /* If the request height causes the row to grow or
         * the request height causes the row to shrink,
         * see if the change will affect the grid's geometry.
         * Otherwise accept the request and change the child's height.
         */
        if (request->height > gw->grid.row_height[grid_info->row_pos] ||
            (w->core.height == gw->grid.row_height[grid_info->row_pos] &&
             request->height < gw->grid.row_height[grid_info->row_pos]))
        {
            /* Save the child's width in case of a failure to acquire a
             * new width from the grid's parent or in case the request
             * is a query.  Set the width to the requested value  for
             * use in computations.
             */
            save_height = w->core.height;
            w->core.height = request->height;

            /* Find total width for the columns */
            for (i = 0; i < gw->grid.rows; i++)
            {
                height += GetRowHeight(gw, i);
            }

            /* Add in the margin widths and inter-column spacing */
            height != ((2 * gw->grid.margin_height) +
                    (gw->grid.v_spacing * (gw->grid.columns - 1)));

            /* If the computed width is not equal to the current grid
             * width, make the request to the parent of the grid widget
             * for a new size.
             */
```

```c
        if (gw->core.height != height)
        {
            make_request = True;
            geo_request.request_mode |= CWHeight;
            geo_request.height = height;
        }
    } else
        w->core.height = request->height;
}


if (make_request)
{
    /* Ask the grid's parent if it is allowed to change size */
    result = XtMakeGeometryRequest((Widget) gw, &geo_request,
            &geo_reply);

    /* Request failed */
    if (result == XtGeometryNo)
    {
        w->core.width = save_width;
        w->core.height = save_height;
        return(result);
    }

    /* Part of the request failed, and part succeeded */
    if (result == XtGeometryAlmost)
    {
        reply->request_mode = mask;

        /* If the child is making a request to change its width */
        if (mask & CWWidth)
        {
            /* If the grid also needed to make a request to change
```

```c
                           its width */
        if (geo_request.request_mode & CWWidth)
        {
            /* If the request will be granted for width */
            if (geo_request.width == reply->width)
                reply->width = w->core.width;
            else
                /* If the request failed, reset the width to the
                 * difference between the parent's reply and
                 * request.
                 */
                reply->width = w->core.width +
                              (reply->width - geo_request.width);
        }
        else
        {
            /* If the parent didn't need to make a request for a
             * change in width, the new child width must be o.k.
             */
            reply->width = w->core.width;
        }

        w->core.width = save_width;
    }

    /* If the child is making a request to change its height */
    if (mask & CWHeight)
    {
        /* if the grid also needed to make a request to change
           its height */
        if (geo_request.request_mode & CWHeight)
        {
            /* If the request will be granted for height */
            if (geo_request.height == reply->height)
```

```
                      reply->height = w->core.height;
                  else
                      /* If the request failed, reset the height to the
                       * difference between the parent's reply and
                       * request.
                       */
                      reply->height = w->core.height +
                                  (reply->height - geo_request.height);
              }
              else
              {
                  /* If the parent didn't need to make a request for a
                   * change in height, the new child height must be o.k.
                   */
                  reply->height = w->core.height;
              }


              w->core.height = save_height;
          }
      }
      return (XtGeometryAlmost);
  }


  /* If there was a change in x, y, of border_width that we couldn't
     grant */
  if (set_almost)
      result = XtGeometryAlmost;


  if ((mask & XtCWQueryOnly))
  {
      if (mask & CWWidth)
          w->core.width = save_width;
      if (mask & CWHeight)
          w->core.height = save_height;
```

```c
    }
    else
    {
       /* If we succeeded, change the row_height and col_width arrays
        * and redo geometry for the children.
        */
       if (result == XtGeometryYes)
       {
          gw->grid.row_height[grid_info->row_pos] =
                 GetRowHeight(gw, grid_info->row_pos);
          gw->grid.col_width[grid_info->col_pos] =
                 GetColumnWidth(gw, grid_info->col_pos);
          (*gc->grid_class.layout_children)((Widget) gw);

       }
    }


    return (result);
}




/********************************************************************
 *
 *   ChangeManaged
 *   Something changed in the set of managed children, so place
 *   the children and change the grid widget size to reflect new
 *   size, if possible.
 *
 ********************************************************************/

static void
ChangeManaged( Widget w )
{
```

```
XsmGridWidget gw = (XsmGridWidget) w;
XsmGridWidgetClass gc = (XsmGridWidgetClass) XtClass(w);
unsigned int line_width = GetLineWidth(gw); /* 0 if grid lines
                                              are off */
XtGeometryResult result = XtGeometryYes;
XtWidgetGeometry geo_request, geo_reply;
Boolean make_request = False;
Dimension width, height;


/* Update the col_width and row_height arrays and return the
 * grid's new height and width.
 */
(*gc->grid_class.update_grid)(w, &width, &height);


/* Add in the margin widths and inter-column spacing */
width += ((2 * (gw->grid.margin_width + line_width)) +
          ((gw->grid.h_spacing + line_width) *
           gw->grid.rows));


/* Add in the margin widths and inter-column spacing */
height += ((2 * (gw->grid.margin_height + line_width)) +
          ((gw->grid.v_spacing + line_width) *
           gw->grid.columns));


/* If the width changed, request a new width */
if (gw->core.width != width)
{
    make_request = True;
    geo_request.request_mode |= CWWidth;
    geo_request.width = width;
}


/* If the height changed, request a new height */
if (gw->core.height != height)
```



```c
        {
            make_request = True;
            geo_request.request_mode |= CWHeight;
            geo_request.height = height;
        }

        if (make_request)
        {
            /* Make a request from the grid's parent for a new size */
            result = XtMakeGeometryRequest(w, &geo_request, &geo_reply);

            if (result != XtGeometryYes)
            {
                int diff;

                /* Make a second request, which is guaranteed to succeed
                 * because the request is using the geo_reply values in the
                 * request.
                 */
                if (result == XtGeometryAlmost)
                    result = XtMakeGeometryRequest(w, &geo_reply, NULL);

                /* If we couldn't change width */
                if (gw->core.width != width)
                {
                    diff = (int) width - (int)gw->core.width;

                    /* If couldn't grow, adjust margins and then clip if
                     * necessary */
                    if (diff > 0)
                    {
                        /* First reduce margins as much as possible */
                        if (gw->grid.margin_height >= diff)
                        {
```

```c
                    gw->grid.margin_height -= diff;
                }
                else
                {
                    diff -= gw->grid.margin_height;
                    gw->grid.margin_height = 0;
                }
            }
        /* If couldn't shrink, adjust margins */
        else
            gw->grid.margin_width = gw->grid.margin_width +
                                (gw->core.width - width)/2;
    }


    /* If we couldn't grow in height */
    if (gw->core.height != height)
    {
        diff = (int) height - (int)gw->core.height;

        /* If couldn't grow, adjust margins and then clip if
           necessary */
        if (diff > 0)
        {
            /* First reduce margins as much as possible */
            if (gw->grid.margin_height >= diff)
            {
                gw->grid.margin_height -= diff;
            }
            else
            {
                diff -= gw->grid.margin_height;
                gw->grid.margin_height = 0;
            }
        }
```


Program Listings

```c
                    /* If couldn't shrink, adjust margins */
                    else
                        gw->grid.margin_height += (gw->core.height -
                                        height)/2;
                }

            /* Update the col_width and row_height to account for the
             * adjustments */
            (*gc->grid_class.update_grid)(w, &width, &height);
        }
    }


    /* Lay out children based on the adjustments made */
    (*gc->grid_class.layout_children)(w);


    /* Call Motif routine that handles focus changes when children
     * are unmanaged.
     */
    _XmNavigChangeManaged(w);
}


/*****************************************************************
 * Constraint Class Methods
 *****************************************************************/



/*****************************************************************
 *
 *
 *  ConstraintInitialize() -
 *  Like the Initialize procedure, this goes through the children's
 *  constraint resource values and determines their validity.  It
 *  also initializes necessary constraint fields in each child
 *  constraint record and updates the parents instance fields that
```

 * are affected by changes in the children's constraint resources.
 *
 ***/

```c
static void
ConstraintInitialize( Widget req_w, Widget new_w, ArgList args,
                      Cardinal *num_args )
{
    XsmGridWidget parent = (XsmGridWidget) XtParent(new_w);
    XsmGridConstraintPart * grid_info = &(GridInfo(new_w)->grid);
    XsmGridWidgetClass gc = (XsmGridWidgetClass)
                                XtClass((Widget)parent);
    Dimension row_pos = grid_info->row_pos;
    Dimension col_pos = grid_info->col_pos;
    Boolean auto_pos = False;

    grid_info->orig_row_pos = row_pos;
    grid_info->orig_col_pos = col_pos;

  /* Verify constraint resources */
   if (row_pos > parent->grid.rows - 1 && row_pos != MAXDIMENSION)
   {
      _XmWarning( (Widget) parent, MESSAGE3);
      row_pos = parent->grid.rows - 1;
   }

   if (col_pos > parent->grid.columns - 1 && col_pos !=
       MAXDIMENSION)
   {
      _XmWarning( (Widget) parent, MESSAGE4);
      col_pos = parent->grid.columns - 1;
   }
   (*gc->grid_class.add_child)((Widget)parent, new_w, row_pos,
                              col_pos);
```

```c
}


/******************************************************************
 *
 *  ConstraintSetValues() -
 *  Like the SetValues procedure, this goes through the children's
 *  constraint resource values and determines their validity.
 *  It also updates the parents instance fields that are affected
 *  by changes in the children's constraint resources.
 *
 ******************************************************************/

static Boolean
ConstraintSetValues( Widget old_w, Widget request, Widget new_w,
                     ArgList args, Cardinal *num_args )
{
    XsmGridWidget parent = (XsmGridWidget) XtParent(new_w);

    XsmGridConstraintPart * new_grid_info =
            &(GridInfo(new_w)->grid);
    XsmGridConstraintPart * old_grid_info =
            &(GridInfo(new_w)->grid);
    Dimension col_pos = new_grid_info->col_pos;
    Dimension row_pos = new_grid_info->row_pos;
    Dimension old_col_pos = old_grid_info->col_pos;
    Dimension old_row_pos = old_grid_info->row_pos;
    Boolean redisplay = False;

    if (new_grid_info->row_pos > parent->grid.rows - 1)
    {
        _XmWarning( (Widget) parent, MESSAGE3);
```

```c
        new_grid_info->row_pos = old_row_pos;
    }


    if (new_grid_info->col_pos > parent->grid.columns - 1)
    {
        _XmWarning( (Widget) parent, MESSAGE4);
        new_grid_info->col_pos = old_col_pos;
    }


    if (row_pos != old_row_pos || col_pos != old_col_pos)
    {
        if (parent->grid.widget_grid[row_pos][col_pos] == NULL)
        {
            parent->grid.widget_grid[row_pos][col_pos] = new_w;
            parent->grid.widget_grid[old_row_pos][old_col_pos] = NULL;
            redisplay = True;
        }
        else
        {
            _XmWarning( (Widget) parent, MESSAGE7);
            new_grid_info->row_pos = old_row_pos;
            new_grid_info->col_pos = old_col_pos;
        }
    }


    new_grid_info->orig_row_pos = new_grid_info->row_pos;
    new_grid_info->orig_col_pos = new_grid_info->col_pos;


    return (redisplay);
}
```

```c
/***************************************************************
 * Grid Class Methods
 ***********************************************************/


/**************************************************************
 *
 * UpdateGridDimensions() -
 *         Update the width and height of each row_height and
 *         col_width array and return the total width and height
 *         of the grid widget.
 *
 ***********************************************************/

static void
UpdateGridDimensions(Widget w, Dimension * width,
                     Dimension * height)
{
   XsmGridWidget gw = (XsmGridWidget) w;
   int i, j;

   *height = 0;
   *width = 0;


   /* Update height for each row and keep track of total grid
      height */
   for (i = 0; i < gw->grid.rows; i++)
   {
      gw->grid.row_height[i] = GetRowHeight(gw, i);
      *height += gw->grid.row_height[i];
   }


   /* Initialize width for each column and keep track of total grid
      width */
   for (j = 0; j < gw->grid.columns; j++)
```

```c
    {
        gw->grid.col_width[j] = GetColumnWidth(gw, j);
        *width += gw->grid.col_width[j];
    }
}



/*****************************************************************
 *
 * AddChildToGrid() -
 *   Add the child to the grid based on the row and column
 *   positions.  If the position was not set, track it as
 *   being auto set and initialize the position to 0.
 *
 ***************************************************************/

static void
AddChildToGrid( Widget parent, Widget child,
                Dimension row_pos, Dimension col_pos)
{
    XsmGridWidget gw = (XsmGridWidget) parent;
    XsmGridConstraintPart * cur_grid_info;
    XsmGridConstraintPart * grid_info = &(GridInfo(child)->grid);
    Boolean place_column = False;
    Boolean place_row = False;
    Widget cur_child;

    if (row_pos == MAXDIMENSION && col_pos == MAXDIMENSION)
        grid_info->auto_placed = True;
    else
        grid_info->auto_placed = False;
```


Program Listings

```c
    /* If the row position was not originally set, set them to 0 */
 if (row_pos == MAXDIMENSION) row_pos = 0;


 /* If the row position was not originally set, set them to 0 */
 if (col_pos == MAXDIMENSION) col_pos = 0;


 /* Assign widgets to the widget_grid */
 if (gw->grid.widget_grid[row_pos][col_pos] == NULL)
 {
    gw->grid.widget_grid[row_pos][col_pos] = child;
 }
 else
 {
    /* If this widget has not been auto placed, replace any
     * widget that was auto placed and occupies this position.
     */
    if (!grid_info->auto_placed)
    {
   /* If the the row or column position were not set by
    * by the grid widget, issue a warning message about the
    * conflicting positions.
    */
       if (grid_info->orig_col_pos != MAXDIMENSION &&
           grid_info->orig_row_pos != MAXDIMENSION)
          _XmWarning( parent, MESSAGE5);

       cur_child = gw->grid.widget_grid[row_pos][col_pos];
       cur_grid_info = &(GridInfo(cur_child)->grid);

       /* Move the child that has been auto placed */
       if (cur_grid_info->auto_placed)
       {
          gw->grid.widget_grid[row_pos][col_pos] = cur_child;
```

```c
            child = cur_child;
            grid_info = cur_grid_info;
        }
    }


    if (!grid_info->auto_placed)
    {

        /* Try to place the child to a valid horizontal position
         * when the row_pos was set but the col_pos was not.
         */

        if (grid_info->orig_col_pos == MAXDIMENSION)
        {
            if (SetChildHorizPosition(gw, child, grid_info,
                                      row_pos, col_pos))
                return;
        }


        /* Try to place the child to a valid vertical position
         * when the col_pos was set but the row_pos was not.
         */

        if (grid_info->orig_row_pos == MAXDIMENSION)
        {
            if (SetChildVertPosition(gw, child, grid_info,
                                     row_pos, col_pos))
                return;
        }
    }


    /* Auto place the child to a valid position and issue
     * a warning message if the grid is full.
     */
```

```c
        if (!SetChildPosition(gw, child, grid_info, row_pos,
            col_pos))
            _XmWarning( (Widget) parent, MESSAGE6);
    }
}


/*****************************************************************
 *
 * LayoutChildren() -
 *          Run through the row and column arrays and move the
 *          children to their appropriate x,y position based on their
 *          location in the widget_grid array.  Align the children
 *          based on the setting of the child_alignment resource.
 *          This layout routine leaves holes for grid positions not
 *          filled with children, or filled with unmanaged children.
 *
 *****************************************************************/

static void
LayoutChildren(Widget w)
{
    XsmGridWidget gw = (XsmGridWidget) w;
    Widget child;
    Dimension col_adj, row_adj, col_width, row_height;
    unsigned int line_width = GetLineWidth(gw); /* 0 if grid lines
                                                    are off */
    Position x, y;
    int i, j;

    /* Set the adjustment for the first row */
    row_adj = 0;
```

```c
/* Move through the rows, setting the position of the widget
 * in each column for each row.
 */
for (i = 0; i < gw->grid.rows; i++)
{
    /* Set the adjustment for the first column */
    col_adj = 0;

    /* Get the row height */
    row_height = gw->grid.row_height[i];

    /* Set the position of the widget in each column in
       this row */
    for (j = 0; j < gw->grid.columns; j++)
    {
     /* Get the child at this row/column location */
      child = gw->grid.widget_grid[i][j];

     /* Get the column width */
      col_width = gw->grid.col_width[j];

     /* If there is a child at that location, move it to the
      * appropriate position.
      */
     if (child != NULL)
     {
        /* Adjust the x and y using margins, spacing, and
           adjustments */
        x = gw->grid.margin_width + line_width +
            (gw->grid.h_spacing + 1)/2 +
            ((gw->grid.h_spacing + line_width) * j) + col_adj;
        y = gw->grid.margin_height + line_width +
            (gw->grid.v_spacing + 1)/2 +
            ((gw->grid.v_spacing + line_width) * i) + row_adj;
```

```c
        /* Adjust x,y if center_children resource is True and
         * if this is not the widest child in its current column.
         */
        if (child->core.width != col_width)
        {
            if (gw->grid.horiz_alignment == XsmALIGN_CENTER)
                x += (col_width - child->core.width)/2;
            else if (gw->grid.horiz_alignment == XsmALIGN_RIGHT)
                x += (col_width - child->core.width);
        }


        /* Adjust x,y if center_children resource is True and
         * if this is not the tallest child in its current row.
         */
        if (child->core.height != row_height)
            if (gw->grid.vert_alignment == XsmALIGN_CENTER)
                y += (row_height - child->core.height)/2;
            else if (gw->grid.vert_alignment == XsmALIGN_BOTTOM)
                y += (row_height - child->core.height);


        /* Change the widgets location */
        if (child->core.x != x || child->core.y != y)
            _XmMoveObject (child, x, y);
    }


    /* Change adjustment for the next column */
    col_adj += col_width;
    }


    /* Change adjustment for the next row */
    row_adj += row_height;
    }
}
```

```c
/*****************************************************************
 *
 * DrawGridLines() -
 * A grid class procedure that draws the lines in between the
 * rows and columns of the grid.
 *
 *****************************************************************/

static void
DrawGridLines(Widget w)
{
    XsmGridWidget gw = (XsmGridWidget) w;

    ModifyGridLines(gw, True);
    gw->grid.lines_visible = True;
}


/*****************************************************************
 *
 * EraseGridLines() -
 *     A grid class procedure that erases the lines in between the
 *     rows and columns of the grid.
 *
 *****************************************************************/

static void
EraseGridLines(Widget w)
{
    XsmGridWidget gw = (XsmGridWidget) w;

    ModifyGridLines(gw, False);
    gw->grid.lines_visible = False;
}
```

```c
/****************************************************************

 * Internal Non-Class Functions

 ****************************************************************/


/**********************************************************

 *

 * GetColumnWidth() -
 * Get the width of the specified column by finding the
 * width of the widest child.
 *

 **********************************************************/


static Dimension
GetColumnWidth(XsmGridWidget gw, int col_pos)
{
    Widget child;
    WidgetList * widget_grid = gw->grid.widget_grid;
    Dimension col_width = 0;
    int i;


    for (i = 0; i < gw->grid.rows; i++)


    {
        child = widget_grid[i][col_pos];


      /* Find the widest child in this column. */
        if (child != NULL)
            if (child->core.width > col_width)
                col_width = child->core.width;
    }
```

```
    return (col_width);
}




/****************************************************************
 *
 * GetRowHeight() -
 *   Get the height of the specified row by finding the
 *   height of the tallest child.
 *
 ****************************************************************/

static Dimension
GetRowHeight(XsmGridWidget gw, int row_pos)
{
    Widget child;
    WidgetList * widget_grid = gw->grid.widget_grid;
    Dimension row_height = 0;
    int i;

    for (i = 0; i < gw->grid.columns; i++)
    {
        child = widget_grid[row_pos][i];

      /* Find the tallest child in this row. */
        if (child != NULL)
            if (child->core.height > row_height)
                row_height = child->core.height;
    }

    return (row_height);
}
```

```c
/*****************************************************************
 *
 * SetChildHorizPosition() -
 *   Run through the current row to find a position that is
 *   not occupied, and assign that position to the child.
 *   Return False if a position is not found in the current row.
 *
 *****************************************************************/

static Boolean
SetChildHorizPosition( XsmGridWidget parent, Widget child,
                       XsmGridConstraintPart * grid_info,
                       Dimension row, Dimension start_col)
{
    XsmGridConstraintPart * cur_grid_info;
    Dimension cur_col;
    Widget cur_child;

    if (row >= parent->grid.rows)
       return False;

    if (start_col >= parent->grid.columns)
       start_col = parent->grid.columns - 1;

    cur_col = start_col++;

    while (cur_col != start_col)
    {
       /* If we are past the last column in this row,
        * move to the first column.
        */
       if (cur_col == parent->grid.columns) cur_col = 0;
```

```c
        /* If a position in the grid is not occupied by a widget,
         * assign the child to this position and return True.  This
         * indicates that a position was found for the child.
         */
        if (parent->grid.widget_grid[row][cur_col] == NULL)
        {
            parent->grid.widget_grid[row][cur_col] = child;

            /* Update grid_info */
            grid_info->row_pos = row;
            grid_info->col_pos = cur_col;

            return True;
        }

        cur_col++;
    }

    /* Return False if a place was not found in this row */
    return False;
}




/******************************************************************
 *
 *
 * SetChildVertPosition() -
 *        Run through the current column to find a position that is
 *        not occupied, and assign that position to the child.
 *        Return False if a position is not found in the current
 *        column.
 *
```

```c
 *************************************************************/

static Boolean
SetChildVertPosition( XsmGridWidget parent, Widget child,
                      XsmGridConstraintPart * grid_info,
                      Dimension start_row, Dimension col)
{
   XsmGridConstraintPart * cur_grid_info;
   Dimension cur_row;
   Widget cur_child;

   if (col >= parent->grid.columns)
      return False;

   if (start_row >= parent->grid.rows)
      start_row = parent->grid.rows - 1;

   cur_row = start_row++;

   while (cur_row != start_row)
   {
     /* If we are past the last column in this row,
      * move to the first column.
      */
     if (cur_row == parent->grid.rows) cur_row = 0;

     /* If a position in the grid is not occupied by a widget,
      * assign the child to this position and return True.  This
      * indicates that a position was found for the child.
      */
     if (parent->grid.widget_grid[cur_row][col] == NULL)
     {
         parent->grid.widget_grid[cur_row][col] = child;
```

```c
        /* Update grid_info */
        grid_info->row_pos = cur_row;
        grid_info->col_pos = col;

        return True;
    }


    cur_row++;
  }

  /* Return False if a place was not found in this row */
  return False;
}




/*****************************************************************
*
 *
 * SetChildPosition() -
 *       Run through the widget grid to find a position that is
 *       not occupied and assign that position to the child.  If
 *       a position is not found, return False to indicate that the
 *       grid is full.
 *
 ****************************************************************/

static Boolean
SetChildPosition( XsmGridWidget parent, Widget child,
                  XsmGridConstraintPart * grid_info,
                  Dimension start_row, Dimension start_col)
{
    XsmGridConstraintPart * cur_grid_info;
```

```c
Dimension cur_col, cur_row;
Widget cur_child;

if (start_row >= parent->grid.rows)
   start_row = parent->grid.rows - 1;

if (start_col >= parent->grid.columns)
   start_col = parent->grid.columns - 1;

cur_row = start_row;
cur_col = start_col;



/* Search for next available grid position.  Begin at the column
 * next to the current position. Continue until we hit the end of
 * the grid; wrap to the beginning of the grid.  If we get back
 * to the original start position, break out of the loop.
 */
while (cur_row < parent->grid.rows)
{
   cur_col++;

  /* If we are past the last column in this row,
   * move to the first column in the next row.
   */
   if (cur_col == parent->grid.columns)
   {
      cur_col = 0;
      cur_row++;
   }

  /* If we are past the last row in this column,
   * move to the first row in the grid.
   */
```

```c
    if (cur_row == parent->grid.rows)
        cur_row = 0;


/* Break out of loop if the original start position
   is found. */
if (cur_row == start_row && cur_col == start_col)
    break;


/* If a position in the grid is not occupied by a widget,
 * assign the child to this position and return True.  This
 * indicates that a position was found for the child.
 */
if (parent->grid.widget_grid[cur_row][cur_col] == NULL)
{
    parent->grid.widget_grid[cur_row][cur_col] = child;

    /* Update grid_info */
    grid_info->row_pos = cur_row;
    grid_info->col_pos = cur_col;

    return True;
}
else
{
    if (!grid_info->auto_placed)
    {
        cur_child = parent->grid.widget_grid[cur_row][cur_col];
        cur_grid_info = &(GridInfo(cur_child)->grid);

        if (cur_grid_info->auto_placed)
        {
            parent->grid.widget_grid[cur_row][cur_col] =
                cur_child;
            child = cur_child;
```



```c
                grid_info = cur_grid_info;
            }
        }
    }
}


    /* Because no position was found for the child, the grid must be
     * full.  Return False to indicate a position was not found for
     * the child.
     */


    return False;
}



static void
SetInvGC( XsmGridWidget gw, GC gc)
{
    unsigned long valueMask = (GCForeground | GCBackground);
    XGCValues values;

    values.foreground = gw->core.background_pixel;
    values.background = gw->manager.foreground;

    XChangeGC(XtDisplay((Widget)gw), gc, valueMask, &values);
}


static void
SetNormGC( XsmGridWidget gw, GC gc)
{
    unsigned long valueMask = (GCForeground | GCBackground);
    XGCValues values;

    values.background = gw->core.background_pixel;
```

```c
        values.foreground = gw->manager.foreground;

        XChangeGC(XtDisplay((Widget)gw), gc, valueMask, &values);
}


static void
LoadGC( XsmGridWidget gw, Pixel fg, Pixel bg)
{
    unsigned long valueMask = (GCForeground | GCBackground);
    unsigned long dynamicMask;
    XGCValues values;

    if (gw->grid.gc != NULL)
        XtReleaseGC((Widget) gw, gw->grid.gc);

    values.background = gw->core.background_pixel;
    values.foreground = gw->manager.foreground;

    dynamicMask = (GCForeground | GCBackground);
    gw->grid.gc = XtAllocateGC((Widget) gw, gw->core.depth,
                    valueMask, &values, dynamicMask, 0);
}


static void
ModifyGridLines(XsmGridWidget gw, Boolean draw_grid)
{
    Widget widget = (Widget) gw;
    Dimension col_width, row_height;
    Position x, y, x2, y2;
    Position old_x, old_y;
    int i;

/* Move through the columns, drawing a line between each column */
```

```c
/* Set y positions */
 y = gw->grid.margin_height;
 y2 = gw->core.height - (gw->grid.margin_height + LINE_WIDTH);


/* Initialize x position */
 x = gw->grid.margin_width;


XDrawLine(XtDisplay(widget), XtWindow(widget), gw->grid.gc, x,
          y, x, y2);


old_x = gw->grid.margin_width + LINE_WIDTH +
        ((gw->grid.h_spacing + 1)/2);

/* Set the position of the widget in each column in this row */
 for (i = 0; i < gw->grid.columns - 1; i++)
 {
  /* Get the column width */
   col_width = gw->grid.col_width[i];


  /* Add spacing, and col_width to x position */
   x = old_x + ((gw->grid.h_spacing + 1)/2) + col_width;


   if (draw_grid)
      SetNormGC(gw, gw->grid.gc);
   else
      SetInvGC(gw, gw->grid.gc);


   XDrawLine(XtDisplay(widget), XtWindow(widget), gw->grid.gc,
             x, y, x, y2);


   old_x = old_x + gw->grid.h_spacing + col_width + LINE_WIDTH;
 }


 x = (gw->core.width - (gw->grid.margin_width + LINE_WIDTH));
```

```c
    XDrawLine(XtDisplay(widget), XtWindow(widget), gw->grid.gc, x,
            y, x, y2);


    /* Move through the rows, drawing a line between each row */


    /* Set x positions */
    x = gw->grid.margin_width;
    x2 = (gw->core.width - (gw->grid.margin_width + LINE_WIDTH));


    /* Initialize y position */
    y = gw->grid.margin_height;


    XDrawLine(XtDisplay(widget), XtWindow(widget), gw->grid.gc,
            x, y, x2, y);


    old_y = gw->grid.margin_height + LINE_WIDTH +
        ((gw->grid.v_spacing + 1)/2);


    for (i = 0; i < gw->grid.rows - 1; i++)
    {
      /* Get the row height */
       row_height = gw->grid.row_height[i];


      /* Add spacing and row_height to y position */
       y = old_y + ((gw->grid.v_spacing + 1)/2) + row_height;


       if (draw_grid)
          SetNormGC(gw, gw->grid.gc);
       else
          SetInvGC(gw, gw->grid.gc);


       XDrawLine(XtDisplay(widget), XtWindow(widget), gw->grid.gc,
            x, y, x2, y);
```

```c
        old_y = old_y + gw->grid.v_spacing + LINE_WIDTH + row_height;
    }


    y = (gw->core.height - (gw->grid.margin_height + LINE_WIDTH));
    XDrawLine(XtDisplay(widget), XtWindow(widget), gw->grid.gc, x,
            y, x2, y);
}




/***************************************************************************
 * Public Functions
 ***************************************************************************/


/*************************************************
 *
 * XsmCreateGrid -
 *   Grid widget creation convienence routine.
 *
 *************************************************/


Widget
XsmCreateGrid( Widget parent, char *name, ArgList arglist, Cardinal
argcount )
{
    return (XtCreateWidget(name, xsmGridWidgetClass,
                        parent, arglist, argcount));
}
```

Grid.h


```c
#ifndef _XsmGrid_h
#define _XsmGrid_h


#include <Xm/Xm.h>


#ifdef __cplusplus
extern "C" {
#endif


/*****************
 * Resource Names *
 *****************/
#define XsmNcolumnPosition        "columnPosition"
#define XsmNcolumns               "columns"
#define XsmNhorizontalAlignment   "horizontalAlignment"
#define XsmNhorizontalSpacing     "horizontalSpacing"
#define XsmNmarginHeight          "marginHeight"
#define XsmNmarginWidth           "marginWidth"
#define XsmNrowPosition           "rowPosition"
#define XsmNrows                  "rows"
#define XsmNshowGridLines         "showGridLines"
#define XsmNverticalAlignment     "verticalAlignment"
#define XsmNverticalSpacing       "verticalSpacing"


#define XsmCColumnPosition        "ColumnPosition"
#define XsmCColumns               "Columns"
#define XsmCHorizontalAlignment   "HorizontalAlignment"
#define XsmCHorizontalSpacing     "HorizontalSpacing"
#define XsmCMarginHeight          "MarginHeight"
#define XsmCMarginWidth           "MarginWidth"
#define XsmCRowPosition           "RowPosition"
```

```c
#define XsmCRows                "Rows"
#define XsmCShowGridLines       "ShowGridLines"
#define XsmCVerticalAlignment   "VerticalAlignment"
#define XsmCVerticalSpacing     "VerticalSpacing"


/* Enums for the above resource types */
enum{ XsmALIGN_CENTER, XsmALIGN_LEFT, XsmALIGN_RIGHT};
enum{ XsmALIGN_MIDDLE, XsmALIGN_TOP, XsmALIGN_BOTTOM};




/* -------------- *
 * Extern class   *
 * -------------- */
externalref WidgetClass       xsmGridWidgetClass;


typedef struct _XsmGridClassRec *XsmGridWidgetClass;
typedef struct _XsmGridRec       *XsmGridWidget;




/********     Public Function Declarations     ********/
extern Widget XsmCreateGrid(
                Widget    parent,
                char      *name,
                ArgList   arglist,
                Cardinal argcount) ;
/********     End Public Function Declarations     ********/


#ifdef __cplusplus
}  /* Close scope of 'extern "C"' declaration which encloses file.
*/
#endif
```

```c
#endif /* _XsmGrid_h */
/* DON'T ADD STUFF AFTER THIS #endif */
```

```c
#ifndef _XsmGridP_h
#define _XsmGridP_h


/* Include the public header as well as the superclass private
   header */


#include "Grid.h"
#include <Xm/ManagerP.h>


/*---------------------------------------------------------------*/
/************************
 * THE GRID CLASS RECORD *
 ************************/


/* The Grid widget's part of the widget class record. */


typedef struct {
    XsmUpdateGridProc   update_grid;        /* update grid dimensions */
    XsmAddChildProc     add_child;          /* Add child to grid */
    XtWidgetProc        layout_children;    /* Layout widget children */
    XtWidgetProc        draw_grid;          /* Draw grid lines */
    XtWidgetProc        erase_grid;         /* Erase grid lines */
    XtPointer           extension;          /* Pointer to extension
                                               record */
} XsmGridClassPart;



/* All the widget class parts together form */
/* the widget class record.                 */


typedef struct _XsmGridClassRec {
```

```c
    CoreClassPart           core_class;
    CompositeClassPart      composite_class;
    ConstraintClassPart     constraint_class;
    XmManagerClassPart      manager_class;
    XsmGridClassPart        grid_class;
} XsmGridClassRec;


/* Define procedure pointers not defined in the Intrinsics. */

typedef void(*XsmUpdateGridProc)(Widget, Dimension *, Dimension *);
typedef void(*XsmAddChildProc)(Widget, Widget, Dimension,
            Dimension);


/* Define inheritance procedures for all grid class procedures. */

#define XsmInheritUpdateGridDimensions ((XsmUpdateGridProc)
                                        _XtInherit)
#define XsmInheritAddChild ((XsmAddChildProc) _XtInherit)
#define XsmInheritLayoutChildren ((XtWidgetProc) _XtInherit)
#define XsmInheritDrawGrid ((XtWidgetProc) _XtInherit)
#define XsmInheritEraseGrid ((XtWidgetProc) _XtInherit)



/*-------------------------------------------------------------------*/
/***************************
 * THE GRID INSTANCE RECORD *
 ***************************/


/* The Grid widget's instance record.  It includes resource */
/* and internal variables.                                   */

typedef struct _XsmGridPart {
    Dimension       columns;
    Dimension       rows;
```

```c
    Dimension      margin_width;
    Dimension      margin_height;
    Dimension      orig_margin_width;
    Dimension      orig_margin_height;
    Dimension      h_spacing;
    Dimension      v_spacing;
    WidgetList     *widget_grid;
    Dimension      *row_height;
    Dimension      *col_width;
    XtEnum         horiz_alignment;
    XtEnum         vert_alignment;
    Boolean        show_grid_lines;
    Boolean        lines_visible;
    GC             gc;
} XsmGridPart;


/* All the widget instance parts together form */
/* the widget instance record.                 */


typedef struct _XsmGridRec {
    CorePart         core;
    CompositePart    composite;
    ConstraintPart   constraint;
    XmManagerPart    manager;
    XsmGridPart      grid;
} XsmGridRec;


/*-------------------------------------------------------------------*/
/***************************************
 * THE GRID CONSTRAINT INSTANCE RECORD *
 ***************************************/


/* Used only with constraint managers, the constraint part */
/* contains resources and internal variables that are to   */
```

```c
    /* be placed on each instance of children of this manager  */
    /* widget.                                                  */

    typedef struct _XsmGridConstraintPart
    {
        Dimension row_pos;
        Dimension col_pos;
        Dimension orig_row_pos;
        Dimension orig_col_pos;
        Boolean   auto_placed;
    } XsmGridConstraintPart;


    /* Only the active constraint parts of widget are         */
    /* added here to form the constraint record. Neither      */
    /* Core, Composite, or Constraint have active constraint  */
    /* parts.  Manager does have an active constraint part,   */
    /* so it must be added for constraint widgets.  Not       */
    /* all managers are constraint widgets.                   */

    typedef struct _XsmGridConstraintRec
    {
        XmManagerConstraintPart manager;
        XsmGridConstraintPart   grid;
    } XsmGridConstraintRec, * XsmGridConstraintPtr;


    #endif /* _XsmGridP_h */
    /* DON't ADD STUFF AFTER THIS #endif */
```


Program Listings

gridcolors.c

This program is virtually identical to `knobcolors.c` except that it uses a grid widget as the manager instead of a row column widget used in `knobcolors.c`. The appearance of the `gridcolors.c` window is slightly different than `knobcolors.c` because the grid's `showGridLines` resource is set to True.

```
/*  Xm headers  */
#include <Xm/DialogS.h>
/*
#include <Xm/RowColumn.h>
*/
#include "Grid.h"
#include <Xm/RowColumn.h>
#include <Xm/Frame.h>
#include <Xm/Label.h>
#include <Xm/PushBG.h>
#include <Xm/CascadeB.h>
#include <Xm/MessageB.h>
#include <Xm/MainW.h>
#include "Knob.h"


/* Geometry */
#define HORIZONTAL_SPACING          (Dimension) 30
#define VERTICAL_SPACING            5
#define TOP_OFFSET                  (Dimension) 5
#define KNOB_HIGHLIGHT_THICKNESS    (Dimension) 2


#define RED         1
#define GREEN       2
#define BLUE        3
#define ALL_COLORS  4


#define BUFFERSZ        1000
```

```
Widget   appshell;
Widget   frame;
Widget   grid;
Widget   redLabel;
Widget   greenLabel;
Widget   blueLabel;
Widget   redKnob;
Widget   greenKnob;
Widget   blueKnob;
Widget   redValueLabel;
Widget   greenValueLabel;
Widget   blueValueLabel;

XColor  bg_color; /* color structure for the background color */
XColor  fg_color; /* color structure for the foreground color */
XColor  ts_color; /* color structure for the top shadow color */
XColor  bs_color; /* color structure for the bottom shadow color */
XColor  sc_color; /* color structure for the select color (arm)
                     color */

XmColorProc calcRGB;

Display *display;

Colormap colormap;

/* Forward Declarations */
static Widget CreateHelp(Widget);
static void HelpCB(Widget, XtPointer, XtPointer);
static void QuitCB(Widget, XtPointer, XtPointer);
static XtArgVal GetColor(char *);
static void CreateColorEditor(void);
static void ChangeRGB_CB(Widget, XtPointer, XtPointer);
static void SetKnobs(XColor *, int);
```

```c
static void GenerateColors(void);
static void SetColors(Widget, char *);

Pixel GetPixel(Widget, char *);

char *tmpbuf = "#78a0d5";
/***************************************/
/* Main                                */
/***************************************/
void main(int argc, char ** argv)
{
    register int n;
    Arg args[4];
    Widget main_window, menu_bar, menu_pane, cascade;
    Widget button;
    Boolean status;
    unsigned long plane_mask;
    unsigned long *color_cells;
    XtAppContext app_context;

  /* Initialize the toolkit and open the display */
    n = 0;
    XtSetArg (args[n], XmNallowShellResize, True); n++;
    appshell = XtAppInitialize(&app_context, "Knobcolors", NULL, 0,
              &argc, argv, NULL, args, n);

  /* Get the display */
    display = XtDisplay(appshell);

  /* Get the default colormap for this display */
    colormap = XDefaultColormap(display, XDefaultScreen(display));

  /* Allocate 4 color cells for use with this program: background,
     foreground, top shadow, and bottom shadow.  The select color
```

```c
     won't be used, so we don't need to allocate for it */
   color_cells = (unsigned long *)XtMalloc (4 *
                   sizeof (unsigned long));
   status = XAllocColorCells (display, colormap,
                         0, &plane_mask, 0, color_cells, 4);


   if(status == False)
   {
      printf(" couldn't allocate enough color cells\n");
      exit(1);
   }
   else
   {
/* Assign the allocated color cells to the correct structure */
      n = 0;
      bg_color.pixel = color_cells[n++];
      bg_color.flags = DoRed | DoGreen | DoBlue;
      fg_color.pixel = color_cells[n++];
      fg_color.flags = DoRed | DoGreen | DoBlue;
      bs_color.pixel = color_cells[n++];
      bs_color.flags = DoRed | DoGreen | DoBlue;
      ts_color.pixel = color_cells[n];
      ts_color.flags = DoRed | DoGreen | DoBlue;
   }


/* Get the RGB value (XColor) of the background */
   XParseColor(display, colormap, tmpbuf, &bg_color);


/* Create main window. */
   main_window = XmCreateMainWindow (appshell, "main1", args, 0);
   XtManageChild (main_window);


/* Create menu bar in main window. */
   menu_bar = XmCreateMenuBar (main_window, "menu_bar", args, 0);
```

```c
    XtManageChild (menu_bar);

/* Create "Exit" pulldown menu. */
    menu_pane = XmCreatePulldownMenu (menu_bar, "menu_pane",
                args, 0);


    button = XmCreatePushButtonGadget (menu_pane, "Quit", args, 0);
    XtManageChild (button);
    XtAddCallback (button, XmNactivateCallback, QuitCB, NULL);


    n = 0;
    XtSetArg (args[n], XmNsubMenuId, menu_pane); n++;
    cascade = XmCreateCascadeButton (menu_bar, "Exit", args, n);
    XtManageChild (cascade);

/* Create "Help" button. */
    cascade = XmCreateCascadeButton (menu_bar, "Help", args, 0);
    XtManageChild (cascade);
    XtAddCallback (cascade, XmNactivateCallback, HelpCB, NULL);


    n = 0;
    XtSetArg (args[n], XmNmenuHelpWidget, cascade); n++;
    XtSetValues (menu_bar, args, n);

/*
 * Create a frame widget
 */
    n = 0;
    XtSetArg(args[n], XmNmarginWidth, 15); n++;
    XtSetArg(args[n], XmNmarginHeight, 15); n++;
    frame = XmCreateFrame (main_window, "frame", args, n);
    XtManageChild(frame);

/*  Set main window areas  */
```

```c
    XmMainWindowSetAreas (main_window, menu_bar, NULL, NULL,
                          NULL, frame);

    /* Generate the foreground, top shadow, and bottom shadow colors
       based on the background color which was set by XParseColor above
     */
    GenerateColors();

    /* Create the sliders with labels using the generated colors */
    CreateColorEditor();

    XtRealizeWidget (appshell);

    XtAppMainLoop (app_context);
}



/*********************************************
 *  HelpCB       - callback for help button *
 ********************************************/
static void
HelpCB(Widget w, XtPointer client_data, XtPointer call_data)
{
    Widget    message_box;  /*  message box              */

  /*  Create help window. */
    message_box = CreateHelp (w);

  /*  Display help window. */
    XtManageChild (message_box);
}



/*********************************************
```

```c
 *  CreateHelp    - create help window
 ******************************************/
static Widget
CreateHelp(Widget parent)
{
    Widget          button;
    Widget          message_box;        /*  Message Dialog  */
    Arg             args[4];            /*  arg list        */
    register int  n;                    /*  arg count       */

    static char     message[BUFFERSZ]; /*  help text       */
    XmString        title_string = NULL;
    XmString        message_string = NULL;
    XmString        button_string = NULL;


  /*  Generate message to display. */


    sprintf (message, "\
This program uses three knob widgets to balance colors. The three knobs\n\
are used to adjust the primary colors: red, blue, and green.  As the\n\
knobs are adjusted, the background color changes accordingly. To\n\
terminate the program, press the 'Exit' button and then the 'Quit'\n\
button.\0");


  /* Create the compound strings */
    message_string = XmStringCreateLocalized (message);
    button_string = XmStringCreateLocalized ("Close");
    title_string = XmStringCreateLocalized ("knobcolors help");
```

```c
  /*  Create message box dialog. */
    n = 0;
    XtSetArg (args[n], XmNdialogTitle, title_string);  n++;
    XtSetArg (args[n], XmNokLabelString, button_string);  n++;
    XtSetArg (args[n], XmNmessageString, message_string);  n++;
    message_box = XmCreateMessageDialog (parent, "helpbox", args,
n);


    button = XmMessageBoxGetChild (message_box,
            XmDIALOG_CANCEL_BUTTON);
    XtUnmanageChild (button);
    button = XmMessageBoxGetChild (message_box,
            XmDIALOG_HELP_BUTTON);
    XtUnmanageChild (button);


  /*  Free strings and return message box. */
    if (title_string) XmStringFree (title_string);
    if (message_string) XmStringFree (message_string);
    if (button_string) XmStringFree (button_string);
    return (message_box);
}



/*********************************************
 *  QuitCB      - callback for quit button
 ******************************************/
static void
QuitCB (Widget w, XtPointer client_data, XtPointer call_data)
{
 /*  Terminate the application. */
    exit (0);
}



/**********************************************************************
```

```c
 *
 *  GetColor        - function for converting a string into a color
 ***************************************************************************/
static XtArgVal
GetColor(char * colorstr)
{

    XrmValue from, to;

    from.size = strlen(colorstr) +1;
    if (from.size < sizeof(String)) from.size = sizeof(String);
    from.addr = colorstr;
    to.addr = NULL;
    XtConvert(appshell, XmRString, &from, XmRPixel, &to);

    return ((XtArgVal) *((XtArgVal *) to.addr));
}



/***************************************************************
 * CreateColorEditor  -  Create the grid and knob widgets
 ****************************************************************/
static void
CreateColorEditor(void)
{
    register int      n;
    Arg               args[15];
    XmString          string;                  /* temp Xm string */
    WidgetList        children;
    XColor *rgb = &bg_color;
    char* color_string = XtMalloc(sizeof(char)*5);
    int new_color;


    /* Create grid widget */
```

```c
n=0;
XtSetArg(args[n], XmNbackground, bg_color.pixel);  n++;
XtSetArg(args[n], XmNforeground, fg_color.pixel);  n++;
XtSetArg(args[n], XmNtopShadowColor, ts_color.pixel);  n++;
XtSetArg(args[n], XmNbottomShadowColor, bs_color.pixel);  n++;
XtSetArg(args[n], XsmNhorizontalAlignment,
        XsmALIGN_CENTER);  n++;
XtSetArg(args[n], XsmNshowGridLines, True);  n++;
XtSetArg(args[n], XsmNrows, 3);  n++;
XtSetArg(args[n], XsmNcolumns, 3);  n++;
grid = XsmCreateGrid(frame, "grid", args, n);


XtManageChild (grid);


/*
 * Create the three groups of widgets, one each for red, green, and
 * blue
 */


/* Create red label, knob, values & label */
 new_color = rgb->red >> 8;


 string =  XmStringCreateLocalized("R");
 n = 0;
XtSetArg(args[n], XmNlabelString, string); n++;
XtSetArg(args[n], XsmNrowPosition, 0); n++;
XtSetArg(args[n], XsmNcolumnPosition, 0); n++;
redLabel = XmCreateLabel(grid, "redLabel", args, n);


XtManageChild(redLabel);
XmStringFree(string);


n = 0;
XtSetArg(args[n], XmNbackground, bg_color.pixel);  n++;
```

```c
XtSetArg(args[n], XmNforeground, GetColor("maroon")); n++;
XtSetArg(args[n], XsmNmaxValue, 0xff);   n++;
XtSetArg(args[n], XsmNminValue, 0x0);   n++;
XtSetArg(args[n], XsmNknobColor, GetColor("red")); n++;
XtSetArg(args[n], XsmNindicatorColor, GetColor("Blue")); n++;
XtSetArg(args[n], XsmNvalue, new_color); n++;
XtSetArg(args[n], XsmNrowPosition, 1); n++;
XtSetArg(args[n], XsmNcolumnPosition, 0); n++;
XtSetArg(args[n], XsmNturnDelay, 120); n++;
XtSetArg(args[n], XsmNmarginWidth, 1); n++;
XtSetArg(args[n], XsmNmarginHeight, 1); n++;
redKnob = XsmCreateKnob(grid, "redKnob", args, n);

XtManageChild(redKnob);
XtAddCallback(redKnob, XsmNvalueChangedCallback, ChangeRGB_CB,
              (XtPointer) RED);
n = 0;
sprintf(color_string, "%d", new_color);

string =  XmStringCreateLocalized(color_string);
XtSetArg(args[0], XmNlabelString, string); n++;
XtSetArg(args[n], XsmNrowPosition, 2); n++;
XtSetArg(args[n], XsmNcolumnPosition, 0); n++;
redValueLabel = XmCreateLabel(grid, "redValueLabel", args, n);

XtManageChild(redValueLabel);
XmStringFree(string);

/* Create green label, knob, values & label */
new_color = rgb->green >> 8;

string =  XmStringCreateLocalized("G");
n = 0;
XtSetArg(args[n], XmNlabelString, string); n++;
```

```c
XtSetArg(args[n], XsmNrowPosition, 0); n++;
XtSetArg(args[n], XsmNcolumnPosition, 1); n++;
greenLabel = XmCreateLabel(grid, "greenLabel", args, n);


XtManageChild(greenLabel);
XmStringFree(string);


n = 0;
XtSetArg(args[n], XmNbackground, bg_color.pixel);   n++;
XtSetArg(args[n], XmNforeground, GetColor("ForestGreen")); n++;
XtSetArg(args[n], XsmNmaxValue, 0xff);   n++;
XtSetArg(args[n], XsmNminValue, 0x0);   n++;
XtSetArg(args[n], XsmNknobColor, GetColor("Green")); n++;
XtSetArg(args[n], XsmNindicatorColor, GetColor("Red")); n++;
XtSetArg(args[n], XsmNvalue, new_color); n++;
XtSetArg(args[n], XsmNrowPosition, 1); n++;
XtSetArg(args[n], XsmNcolumnPosition, 1); n++;
XtSetArg(args[n], XsmNturnDelay, 120); n++;
XtSetArg(args[n], XsmNmarginWidth, 1); n++;
XtSetArg(args[n], XsmNmarginHeight, 1); n++;
greenKnob = XsmCreateKnob(grid, "greenKnob", args, n);


XtManageChild(greenKnob);
XtAddCallback(greenKnob, XsmNvalueChangedCallback, ChangeRGB_CB,
              (XtPointer) GREEN );
n = 0;
sprintf(color_string, "%d", new_color);
string =  XmStringCreateLocalized(color_string);
XtSetArg(args[0], XmNlabelString, string); n++;
XtSetArg(args[n], XsmNrowPosition, 2); n++;
XtSetArg(args[n], XsmNcolumnPosition, 1); n++;
greenValueLabel = XmCreateLabel(grid, "greenValueLabel",
                  args, n);
```

```c
    XtManageChild(greenValueLabel);
    XmStringFree(string);


    /* Create blue label, knob, values & label */
    new_color = rgb->blue >> 8;


    string =  XmStringCreateLocalized("B");
    n = 0;
    XtSetArg(args[n], XmNlabelString, string); n++;
    XtSetArg(args[n], XsmNrowPosition, 0); n++;
    XtSetArg(args[n], XsmNcolumnPosition, 2); n++;
    blueLabel = XmCreateLabel(grid, "blueLabel", args, n);


    XtManageChild(blueLabel);
    XmStringFree(string);


    n = 0;
    XtSetArg(args[n], XmNbackground, bg_color.pixel);   n++;
    XtSetArg(args[n], XmNforeground, GetColor("navy")); n++;
    XtSetArg(args[n], XsmNmaxValue, 0xff);   n++;
    XtSetArg(args[n], XsmNminValue, 0x0);   n++;
    XtSetArg(args[n], XsmNknobColor, GetColor("Blue")); n++;
    XtSetArg(args[n], XsmNindicatorColor, GetColor("red")); n++;
    XtSetArg(args[n], XsmNvalue, new_color); n++;
    XtSetArg(args[n], XsmNrowPosition, 1); n++;
    XtSetArg(args[n], XsmNcolumnPosition, 2); n++;
    XtSetArg(args[n], XsmNturnDelay, 120); n++;
    XtSetArg(args[n], XsmNmarginWidth, 1); n++;
    XtSetArg(args[n], XsmNmarginHeight, 1); n++;
    blueKnob = XsmCreateKnob(grid, "blueKnob", args, n);


    XtManageChild(blueKnob);
    XtAddCallback(blueKnob, XsmNvalueChangedCallback, ChangeRGB_CB,
                  (XtPointer) BLUE );
```

```c
        n = 0;
        sprintf(color_string, "%d", new_color);
        string =  XmStringCreateLocalized(color_string);
        XtSetArg(args[0], XmNlabelString, string); n++;
        XtSetArg(args[n], XsmNrowPosition, 2); n++;
        XtSetArg(args[n], XsmNcolumnPosition, 2); n++;
        blueValueLabel = XmCreateLabel(grid, "blueValueLabel", args, n);

        XtManageChild(blueValueLabel);
        XmStringFree(string);

        XtFree(color_string);

}


/*********************************************************************
 *    GenerateColors()
 *     Generates new RGB values for foreground, top shadow, and
 *     bottom shadow, and select color based on the background.
 *     Select color is not used in our program, but the Motif color
 *     generation routine expects it and calculates it.
 *     The Colors generated are stored in the red, green, and blue
 *     fields of the XColor structure passed in.
 *     The generated colors are then used to update the color cells
 *     of the ColorSet being edited.
 *********************************************************************/
static void
GenerateColors(void)
{
    XColor colors[4];
    int j=0;

    /* Get the motif1.1 color calculation procedure */
    if (calcRGB == NULL)
```

```c
        calcRGB = XmGetColorCalculation();


    /* Given the background color, calculate the foreground,
       select color, top shadow, and bottom shadow colors */
      (*calcRGB)(&bg_color, &fg_color, &sc_color, &ts_color,
                 &bs_color);


    /* Put those calculated colors in an array */
      colors[j++] =  bg_color;
      colors[j++] =  fg_color;
      colors[j++] =  ts_color;
      colors[j++] =  bs_color;


   /* Go change the colors dynamically */
      XStoreColors(display, colormap, colors, j);
}


/**************************************************************
 *    ChangeRGB_CB()
 *     Called when one of the RGB knobs is moved
 **************************************************************/
static void
ChangeRGB_CB( Widget w, XtPointer client_data, XtPointer call_data
)
{
    int reason_code;
    int value;
    int color;

    reason_code = ((XmAnyCallbackStruct *)call_data)->reason;
    if ( reason_code == XsmCR_VALUE_CHANGED)
    {
        color = (int) client_data;
        value = ((XsmKnobCallbackStruct *)call_data)->value;
```

```c
        /*
         * Shift value -- to make up for knob max of only 0xff
         */
        value <<= 8;
        switch (color)
        {
          case RED:
            bg_color.red = value;
            break;
          case GREEN:
            bg_color.green = value;
            break;
          case BLUE:
            bg_color.blue = value;
            break;
          default:
            return;
        }


        SetKnobs(&bg_color, color);
        GenerateColors();
    }
}


/*****************************************************************
 * SetColors()
 *  Change the label string in the value label widget
 *****************************************************************/
static void
SetColors(Widget valueLabel, char * color_string)
{
    Arg        args[1];
    XmString string;
```



```c
        string =  XmStringCreateLocalized(color_string);
        XtSetArg(args[0], XmNlabelString, string);
        XtSetValues(valueLabel, args, 1);
        XmStringFree(string);
}


/********************************************************************
 *    SetKnobs()
 *      Passed an XColor, updates all knobs.
 ********************************************************************/
static void
SetKnobs(XColor * rgb, int color)
{
    char* color_string = XtMalloc(sizeof(char)*5);
    int new_color;

    switch (color)
    {
        case RED:
          new_color = rgb->red >> 8;
          sprintf(color_string, "%d", new_color);
          SetColors(redValueLabel, color_string);
          break;

        case GREEN:
          new_color = rgb->green >> 8;
          sprintf(color_string, "%d", new_color);
          SetColors(greenValueLabel, color_string);
        break;

        case BLUE:
          new_color = rgb->blue >> 8;
          sprintf(color_string, "%d", new_color);
```

```c
            SetColors(blueValueLabel, color_string);
            break;


      default:
        break;
    }


    XtFree(color_string);
}




/****************************************************************
 *    GetPixel()
 *      Passed in a color string, calls XtConvert, which is an X
 *      toolkit converter that converts a string into a pixel value
 ****************************************************************/
Pixel
GetPixel( Widget widget, char * color_string )
{
    XrmValue from, to;


  /* Determine the size of the string passed in */
    from.size = strlen(color_string) + 1;
    if (from.size < sizeof(String))
        from.size = sizeof(String);
    from.addr = color_string;


  /* Go convert the string into a pixel (i.e. color cell) */
    XtConvert(widget, XmRString, &from, XmRPixel, &to);


  /* Return that pixel */
    return ((Pixel) *((Pixel *) to.addr));
}
```

```c
#include <math.h>
#include "KnobP.h"


/* Defines for mathematic functions used in drawing */
#define   RADIANS(x)   (M_PI * 2.0 * (x) / 360.0)
#define   DEGREES(x)   ((x) / (M_PI * 2.0) * 360.0)
#define   MIN_ANGLE    225.0
#define   MAX_ANGLE    345.0
#define   NUM_SEGS     24
#define   MIN(a,b)     (((a) < (b)) ? (a) :  (b))


#define MIN_KNOB_DIAMETER                   3
#define DEFAULT_DIAMETER                  100
#define DEFAULT_KNOB_MARGIN                 5
#define DEFAULT_KNOB_MARGIN_PERCENTAGE     50


/********     Static Function Declarations    ********/


/* Core class methods */
static void ClassPartInitialize( WidgetClass widget_class) ;
static void Initialize( Widget request, Widget new_w, ArgList args,
                        Cardinal *num_args) ;
static void Destroy( Widget w) ;
static void Resize( Widget w) ;
static void Redisplay( Widget w, XEvent *event, Region region) ;
static Boolean SetValues( Widget old_w, Widget request, Widget
                        new_w, ArgList args, Cardinal *num_args) ;
static void SetValuesAlmost( Widget old_w, Widget new_w,
                        XtWidgetGeometry *request,
                        XtWidgetGeometry *reply);
static XtGeometryResult QueryGeometry( Widget w, XtWidgetGeometry
```

```c
                              *request, XtWidgetGeometry *reply) ;

    /* Primitive class methods */
    static void HighlightKnob( Widget w) ;
    static void UnhighlightKnob( Widget w) ;

    /* Knob class methods */
    static void GetDiameters( Widget w, unsigned int *diameter,
                              unsigned int *inner_diameter) ;
    static void CreateSegments( Widget w) ;
    static void DrawIndicator( Widget w) ;

    /* Resource callprocs */
    static void DefaultKnobColor( Widget, int, XrmValue *);

    /* Action procedures */
    static void TurnKnob( XtPointer closure, XtIntervalId *id) ;
    static void DrawKnob( Widget w) ;
    static void TurnLeft( Widget w, XEvent *event, char **params,
                          Cardinal *num_params) ;
    static void TurnRight( Widget w, XEvent *event, char **params,
                           Cardinal *num_params) ;
    static void ToggleLeft( Widget w, XEvent *event, char **params,
                            Cardinal *num_params) ;
    static void ToggleRight( Widget w, XEvent *event, char **params,
                             Cardinal *num_params) ;
    static void ReleaseKnob( Widget w, XEvent *event, char **params,
                             Cardinal *num_params) ;

    /* Resource list initialization - sets up resource names and values
     * for each resource of this widget.
     */
    static XtResource resources[] = {
    {
```

```c
        XsmNvalueChangedCallback, XmCCallback, XmRCallback,
        sizeof(XtCallbackList),
        XtOffset (XsmKnobWidget, knob.value_changed_callback),
        XmRImmediate, NULL
    },

    {
        XsmNvalue, XsmCValue, XmRInt, sizeof(int),
        XtOffset (XsmKnobWidget, knob.value),
        XmRImmediate, (XtPointer) 0
    },

    {
        XsmNmaxValue, XsmCMaxValue, XmRInt, sizeof(int),
        XtOffset (XsmKnobWidget, knob.max_val),
        XmRImmediate, (XtPointer) 100
    },

    {
        XsmNminValue, XsmCMinValue, XmRInt, sizeof(int),
        XtOffset (XsmKnobWidget, knob.min_val),
        XmRImmediate, (XtPointer) 0
    },

    {
        XsmNturnDelay, XsmCTurnDelay, XmRInt, sizeof(int),
        XtOffset(XsmKnobWidget, knob.turn_delay),
        XmRImmediate, (XtPointer) 50
    },

    {
        XsmNknobColor, XsmCKnobColor, XmRPixel, sizeof (Pixel),
        XtOffset (XsmKnobWidget, knob.knob_color),
        XmRCallProc, (XtPointer) DefaultKnobColor
```

```
  },

  {

    XsmNindicatorColor, XsmCIndicatorColor, XmRPixel, sizeof (Pixel),
    XtOffset (XsmKnobWidget, knob.indicator_color),
    XmRCallProc, (XtPointer) _XmForegroundColorDefault
  },

  {

    XsmNmarginWidth, XmCMarginWidth, XmRHorizontalDimension,
    sizeof (Dimension),
    XtOffset (XsmKnobWidget, knob.margin_width),
    XmRImmediate, (XtPointer) DEFAULT_KNOB_MARGIN
  },

  {

    XsmNmarginHeight, XmCMarginHeight, XmRVerticalDimension,
    sizeof (Dimension),
    XtOffset (XsmKnobWidget, knob.margin_height),
    XmRImmediate, (XtPointer) DEFAULT_KNOB_MARGIN
  },


  {

    XsmNknobMargin, XsmCKnobMargin, XmRDimension, sizeof (Dimension),
    XtOffset (XsmKnobWidget, knob.knob_margin),
    XmRImmediate, (XtPointer) DEFAULT_KNOB_MARGIN_PERCENTAGE
  },
};


/* Synthetic resource list initialization - sets up resource
 * procedures to get called when setting or getting the various
 * resources.  These synthetic resources are used in resolution
 * independence.
```

```c
 */
static XmSyntheticResource syn_resources[] = {
        {
          XsmNmarginWidth,
          sizeof (Dimension),
          XtOffset( XsmKnobWidget, knob.margin_width),
          _XmFromHorizontalPixels,
          _XmToHorizontalPixels
        },

        {
          XsmNmarginHeight,
          sizeof (Dimension),
          XtOffset( XsmKnobWidget, knob.margin_height),
          _XmFromVerticalPixels,
          _XmToVerticalPixels
        }
};



/* Action table - where procedures are mapped to strings */
static XtActionsRec knob_actions[] = {
    {"turn-left",    TurnLeft},
    {"turn-right",   TurnRight},
    {"toggle-left",  ToggleLeft},
    {"toggle-right", ToggleRight},
    {"release-knob", ReleaseKnob},
  };

/* Translation table - where events are mapped to action names */
char defaultTranslations[] = "\
<Key>greater:  toggle-left()\n\
<Key>less:     toggle-right()\n\
```

```
<Key>:            release-knob()\n\
<Btn1Down>:       turn-left()\n\
<Btn3Down>:       turn-right()\n\
<Btn1Up>:         release-knob()\n\
<Btn3Up>:         release-knob()\n\
<FocusIn>:        Focus-in()\n\
<FocusOut>:       Focus-out()\n\
<EnterWindow>: enter()\n\
<LeaveWindow>: leave()";


/* Widget class record initialization - Here we initialize each
 * field of the core, primitive, and knob class parts.
 */
externaldef (xsmknobclassrec) XsmKnobClassRec xsmKnobClassRec = {
{
   (WidgetClass) &xmPrimitiveClassRec, /* superclass         */
      "XsmKnob",                        /* class_name          */
      sizeof(XsmKnobRec),               /* widget_size         */
      NULL,                             /* class_initialize    */
      ClassPartInitialize,              /* class_part_initialize*/
      FALSE,                            /* class_inited        */
      Initialize,                       /* initialize          */
      NULL,                             /* initialize_hook     */
      XtInheritRealize,                 /* realize             */
      knob_actions,                     /* actions             */
      XtNumber(knob_actions),           /* num_actions         */
      resources,                        /* resources           */
      XtNumber(resources),              /* num_resources       */
      NULLQUARK,                        /* xrm_class           */
      TRUE,                             /* compress_motion     */
      XtExposeCompressMaximal,          /* compress_exposure   */
      TRUE,                             /* compress_enterleave */
```



```c
    FALSE,                              /* visible_interest    */
    Destroy,                            /* destroy             */
    Resize,                             /* resize              */
    Redisplay,                          /* expose              */
    SetValues,                          /* set_values          */
    NULL,                               /* set_values_hook     */
    SetValuesAlmost,                    /* set_values_almost   */
    NULL,                               /* get_values_hook     */
    NULL,                               /* accept_focus        */
    XtVersion,                          /* version             */
    NULL,                               /* callback_private    */
    defaultTranslations,                /* tm_table            */
    XtInheritQueryGeometry,             /* query_geometry      */
    XtInheritDisplayAccelerator,        /* display accel       */
    NULL,                               /* extension           */
  },

  {                                     /* Xmprimitive         */
    HighlightKnob,                      /* border_highlight    */
    UnhighlightKnob,                    /* border_unhighlight  */
    XtInheritTranslations,              /* translations        */
    NULL,                               /* arm_and_activate    */
    syn_resources,                      /* syn resources       */
    XtNumber(syn_resources),            /* num syn_resources   */
    NULL,                               /* extension           */
  },

  {                                     /* knob class          */
    GetDiameters,                       /* get_diameters       */
    CreateSegments,                     /* create_segments     */
    DrawIndicator,                      /* draw_indicator      */
    TurnKnob,                           /* move                */
    DrawKnob,                           /* draw                */
    NULL,                               /* extension           */
```

```
        }
    };

    externaldef(xsmknobwidgetclass) WidgetClass xsmKnobWidgetClass =
                            (WidgetClass) &xsmKnobClassRec;
```


Program Listings

```c
/*****************************************************************
 *
 * Core Class Methods
 *
 *****************************************************************/




/*****************************************************************
 *
 * ClassPartInitialize() -
 * The initialization routine for class parts.  It is called for
 * the initialization of this class and each time a new subclass is
 * created for this widget class.  It is called only once per
 * subclass.
 *
 *****************************************************************/
static void ClassPartInitialize(WidgetClass wc)
{
 XsmKnobWidgetClass kc = (XsmKnobWidgetClass) wc;
 XsmKnobWidgetClass sc = (XsmKnobWidgetClass)
                            wc->core_class.superclass;

/* Assign procedures to the classes pointers that inherit these
    procedures */

    if (kc->knob_class.get_diameters == XsmInheritGetDiameters)
       kc->knob_class.get_diameters = sc->knob_class.get_diameters;

    if (kc->knob_class.create_segments == XsmInheritCreateSegments)
       kc->knob_class.create_segments =
                        sc->knob_class.create_segments;
```

```c
        if (kc->knob_class.draw_indicator == XsmInheritDrawIndicator)
            kc->knob_class.draw_indicator =
                            sc->knob_class.draw_indicator;


        if (kc->knob_class.turn == XsmInheritTurn)
            kc->knob_class.turn = sc->knob_class.turn;


        if (kc->knob_class.draw == XsmInheritDraw)
            kc->knob_class.draw = sc->knob_class.draw;


}
/*****************************************************************
 *
 *  Initialize() -
 *  The main widget instance initialization routine.  Verify
 *  resource values and initialize widget instance fields.
 *
 ****************************************************************/

static void Initialize( Widget request, Widget new_w, ArgList args,
                        Cardinal *num_args )
{
    XsmKnobWidget req_kw = (XsmKnobWidget) request;
    XsmKnobWidget new_kw = (XsmKnobWidget) new_w;
    XsmKnobWidgetClass kc = (XsmKnobWidgetClass) XtClass(new_w);
    Dimension min_width, min_height;
    XGCValues values;
    unsigned long valuemask;

    /* Verify resource values */

    /* Verify that the maximum value is not less than or equal to
       zero */
    if (new_kw->knob.max_val <= 0) {
```

                                                          Program Listings

```c
        XtWarning("MaxValue is must be greater than 0, Defaulting
                MaxValue to 1");
        new_kw->knob.max_val = 1;
    }


    /*
     * Verify that the maximum value is not less than the minimum
       value
     */
    if (new_kw->knob.max_val < new_kw->knob.min_val) {
        XtWarning("MaxValue is less than the MinValue, Defaulting
                to 0");
        new_kw->knob.min_val = 0;
    }


    /* Verify that the value is not greater than the maximum value */
    if (new_kw->knob.value > new_kw->knob.max_val) {
        XtWarning("Value is greater than MaxValue, Defaulting to
                MaxValue");
        new_kw->knob.value = new_kw->knob.max_val;
    }


    /* Verify that the value is not less than the minimum value */
    if (new_kw->knob.value < new_kw->knob.min_val) {
        XtWarning("Value is less than MinValue, Defaulting to
                MinValue");
        new_kw->knob.value = new_kw->knob.min_val;
    }


    /* Verify that turn rate is not less than 1 */
    if (new_kw->knob.turn_delay < 1) {
        XtWarning("Turn Delay is less than 1, Defaulting to 1");
        new_kw->knob.turn_delay = 1;
    }
```

```c
/*
 * Knob margin is a percentage of the total knob,
 * thus it must be between 0 and 100.  Because this resource is
 * typed as a dimension (unsigned short), a negative value
 * becomes a large positive, thus this also checks for < 0.
 */

if (new_kw->knob.knob_margin > 100)
{
    XtWarning("Knob Margin must be between 0 and 100");
    new_kw->knob.knob_margin = DEFAULT_KNOB_MARGIN_PERCENTAGE;
}


/*
 * Initialize the minimum required dimensions for the knob
 */

min_width = MIN_KNOB_DIAMETER +
    (2 * (new_kw->knob.margin_width +
        new_kw->primitive.highlight_thickness));
min_height = MIN_KNOB_DIAMETER +
            (2 * (new_kw->knob.margin_width +
    new_kw->primitive.highlight_thickness));

/*
 * If an initial width and height weren't set, initialize
 * a default dimensions; otherwise, verify that the dimensions
 * that were set are at least the minimum dimension.
 */

if (req_kw->core.width == 0)
    new_kw->core.width = DEFAULT_DIAMETER +
```

```c
                              (2 * (new_kw->knob.margin_width +
                    new_kw->primitive.highlight_thickness));
    else
        if (new_kw->core.width < min_width)
            new_kw->core.width = min_width;


    if (req_kw->core.height == 0)
        new_kw->core.height = DEFAULT_DIAMETER +
                            (2 * (new_kw->knob.margin_height +
                    new_kw->primitive.highlight_thickness));
    else
        if (new_kw->core.height < min_width)
            new_kw->core.height = min_height;



    /* Save original calculated width and height for use in query
       geometry */
        new_kw->knob.orig_width = new_kw->core.width;
        new_kw->knob.orig_height = new_kw->core.height;


    /* Initialize internal variables */

    new_kw->knob.num_segments = NUM_SEGS;
    new_kw->knob.segments = (XSegment *) XtMalloc(sizeof(XSegment)
                            * (new_kw->knob.num_segments + 1));


    new_kw->knob.move_clockwise = True;
    new_kw->knob.turning = False;
    new_kw->knob.timer_id = NULL;
    new_kw->knob.angle_offset = 0;


    /* Create initial segments */
```

```c
        (*kc->knob_class.create_segments)(new_w);


    /* Set up graphic context for use in drawing the knob */


    valuemask = (GCForeground | GCBackground);
    values.foreground = new_kw->primitive.foreground;
    values.background = new_kw->knob.knob_color;
    new_kw->knob.gc = XtGetGC(new_w, valuemask, &values);
}



/*********************************************************************
 *
 *   Destroy() -
 *   Clean up allocated resources when the widget is destroyed.
 *   Free any allocated data.
 *
 *********************************************************************/
static void Destroy( Widget w )
{
    XsmKnobWidget kw = (XsmKnobWidget) w;

  /* Free graphics contexts */
    XtReleaseGC( w, kw->knob.gc);

  /* Free allocated data */
    XtFree((char *) kw->knob.segments);

  /* Remove any outstanding timeouts */
    if (kw->knob.timer_id) XtRemoveTimeOut(kw->knob.timer_id);

  /* Remove all callbacks */
    XtRemoveAllCallbacks (w, XsmNvalueChangedCallback);
}
```

```c
/*****************************************************************
 *
 *  Resize() -
 *  Redraw according to when size changes.
 *
 *****************************************************************/
static void Resize( Widget w )
{
    XsmKnobWidgetClass kc = (XsmKnobWidgetClass) XtClass(w);

    /* Recreate any segments based on the new size */
    (*kc->knob_class.create_segments)(w);
}
```

```c
/*****************************************************************
 *
 *  Redisplay() -
 *  Redraw region that go exposed.  Simple and less efficient
 *  expose routines simply redraw the whole widget.  This is an
 *  example of a simple expose routine.
 *
 *****************************************************************/
static void Redisplay( Widget w, XEvent *event, Region region)
{
    XsmKnobWidget kw = (XsmKnobWidget) w;
    XsmKnobWidgetClass kc = (XsmKnobWidgetClass) XtClass(w);

  /* Use the class pointer to redraw the whole knob */
    (*kc->knob_class.draw)(w);

  /* Use the class pointers to highlight or unhighlight the knob */
    if (kw->primitive.highlighted)
        (*kc->primitive_class.border_highlight)(w);
    else
        (*kc->primitive_class.border_unhighlight)(w);
}


/*****************************************************************
 *
 * SetValues() -
 * The procedure is used to verify changes to the resource values.
 * If the resource changes effect the visuals of the widget, the
 * return value of the procedure should be set to True indicating
 * that the expose procedure will be called to redraw the widget.
 * Any changes to the widget's geometry in this procedure will
 * generate a geometry request to its parent.
 *
 *****************************************************************/
```

```c
static Boolean SetValues( Widget old_w, Widget request,
                          Widget new_w, ArgList args,
                          Cardinal *num_args )
{
    XsmKnobWidget old_kw = (XsmKnobWidget) old_w;
    XsmKnobWidget new_kw = (XsmKnobWidget) new_w;
    XsmKnobWidgetClass kc = (XsmKnobWidgetClass) XtClass(new_w);
    Dimension min_width, min_height;
    Boolean redisplay = False; /* flag to determine return value */


    /* Verify changes in resource settings */


    /* Verify that the maximum value is not less than or equal to
       zero */
    if (new_kw->knob.max_val <= 0) {
        XtWarning("MaxValue is must be greater than 0, MaxValue set
                  to 1");
        new_kw->knob.max_val = 1;
    }


    /*
     * Verify that the minimum value is not greater or equal to
     * the maximum value.
     */
    if (new_kw->knob.min_val >= new_kw->knob.max_val) {
        XtWarning("MinValue is greater than or equal to MaxValue,
                  MinValue set to 0");
        new_kw->knob.min_val = 0;
    }


    /* Verify that the value is not greater than the maximum value */
    if ((new_kw->knob.max_val != old_kw->knob.max_val ||
         new_kw->knob.value != old_kw->knob.value) &&
         new_kw->knob.value > new_kw->knob.max_val) {
```

```c
        XtWarning("Value is greater than MaxValue, Changing Value to
                MaxValue");
        new_kw->knob.value = new_kw->knob.max_val;
        redisplay = True;
    }


    /* Verify that the value is not less than the minimum value */
    if ((new_kw->knob.min_val != old_kw->knob.min_val ||
            new_kw->knob.value != old_kw->knob.value) &&
            new_kw->knob.value < new_kw->knob.min_val) {
        XtWarning("Value is less than MinValue, Changing Value to
                MinValue");
        new_kw->knob.value = new_kw->knob.min_val;
        redisplay = True;
    }


    /* Verify that turn rate is not less than 1 */
    if (new_kw->knob.turn_delay < 1) {
        XtWarning("Turn Delay is less than 1, Defaulting to 1");
        new_kw->knob.turn_delay = 1;
    }


    /*
     * Knob margin is a percentage of the total knob,
     * thus it must be between 0 and 100.  Because this resource is
     * typed as a dimension (unsigned short), a negative value
     * becomes a large positive, thus this also checks for < 0.
     */
    if (new_kw->knob.knob_margin > 100)
    {
        XtWarning("Knob Margin must be between 0 and 100");
        new_kw->knob.knob_margin = old_kw->knob.knob_margin;
    }
```

```c
    /* Don't allow a zero size to set */
    if (new_kw->core.width == 0) new_kw->core.width =
                              old_kw->core.width;
    if (new_kw->core.height == 0) new_kw->core.height =
                              old_kw->core.height;


    /* If the color resources change, the graphic context needs to be
       updated. */
    if (new_kw->primitive.foreground !=
        old_kw->primitive.foreground ||
        new_kw->knob.knob_color != old_kw->knob.knob_color) {
        XGCValues values;
        unsigned long valuemask;

        valuemask = (GCForeground | GCBackground );
        values.foreground = new_kw->primitive.foreground;
        values.background = new_kw->knob.knob_color;
        XtReleaseGC( new_w, new_kw->knob.gc);
        new_kw->knob.gc = XtGetGC(new_w, valuemask, &values);
        redisplay = True;
    }


    min_width = MIN_KNOB_DIAMETER +
                (2 * (new_kw->knob.margin_width +
                new_kw->primitive.highlight_thickness));
    min_height = MIN_KNOB_DIAMETER +
                (2 * (new_kw->knob.margin_width +
                new_kw->primitive.highlight_thickness));
    /* Try to retain a minimum height and width */

    if (new_kw->core.width < min_width)
    {
        new_kw->core.width = min_width;
```

```c
        redisplay = True;
    }


    if (new_kw->core.height < min_height)
    {
        new_kw->core.height = min_height;
        redisplay = True;
    }


    /*
     * If any of the following resource values changed, the knob
     * segments needs to be recomputed and the knob needs to be
     * redisplayed.
     */
    if (new_kw->knob.margin_height != old_kw->knob.margin_height ||
        new_kw->knob.margin_width != old_kw->knob.margin_width ||
        new_kw->knob.knob_margin != old_kw->knob.knob_margin ||
        new_kw->knob.max_val != old_kw->knob.max_val ||
        new_kw->knob.min_val != old_kw->knob.min_val ||
        new_kw->core.height != old_kw->core.height ||
        new_kw->core.width != old_kw->core.width ||
        new_kw->primitive.highlight_thickness !=
old_kw->primitive.highlight_thickness) {

        (*kc->knob_class.create_segments)(new_w);
        redisplay = True;
    }


    return(redisplay);
}
```

```c
/****************************************************************
 *
 * SetValuesAlmost() -
 * The procedure is used to negotiate a geometry with the parent.
 * If the change in geometry in the SetValues Procedure failed.
 * Setting the reply->request_mode to zero ends the negotiations.
 *
 ****************************************************************/
static void SetValuesAlmost( Widget old_w, Widget new_w,
                             XtWidgetGeometry *request,
                             XtWidgetGeometry *reply)
{
    XsmKnobWidget new_kw = (XsmKnobWidget) new_w;
    XsmKnobWidget old_kw = (XsmKnobWidget) old_w;
    Dimension min_width, min_height;

    /* If the request failed completely, reset old values and
       return */
    if (reply->request_mode == 0)
    {
        new_kw->knob.margin_width = old_kw->knob.margin_width;
        new_kw->knob.margin_height = old_kw->knob.margin_height;
        request->request_mode = 0;
        return;
    }


    /* All attempts to accommodate size failed */
    if (new_kw->knob.margin_width == 0 ||
        new_kw->knob.margin_height == 0)
    {
        request->request_mode = 0;
        return;
    }
```

```c
        min_width = MIN_KNOB_DIAMETER +
                (2 * (new_kw->knob.margin_width +
                new_kw->primitive.highlight_thickness));
        min_height = MIN_KNOB_DIAMETER +
                (2 * (new_kw->knob.margin_width +
                new_kw->primitive.highlight_thickness));


    /* Reduce margin to accommodate smaller size */
    if ( reply->width < min_width )
    {
        new_kw->knob.margin_width--;
        min_width -= 2; /* minus one pixel on each side of knob */
        request->width = min_width;
    }
    else /* Accept larger size */
    {
        request->width = reply->width;
    }


    /* Reduce margin to accommodate smaller size */
    if (reply->height < min_height)
    {
        new_kw->knob.margin_height--;
        min_height -= 2; /* minus one pixel on each side of knob */
        request->height = min_height;
    }
    else /* Accept larger size */
    {
        request->width = reply->width;
    }
}


/****************************************************************************
```

```c
 *
 *   QueryGeometry() -
 * This procedure is used to negotiate a geometry with the parent
 * when the parent is requesting a preferred size of the child.
 * If the values in the request don't match the values in the
 * reply, we need to return either XtGeometryNo or
 * XtGeometryAlmost.   Use XtGeometryNo if the values in the
 * request match the current values.
 * Note: This procedure is only interested in height and width
 * values.  It will accept any changes to x, y, border width and
 * stacking order.
 *
 **************************************************************************/


static XtGeometryResult QueryGeometry( Widget w,
                                       XtWidgetGeometry  *request,
                                       XtWidgetGeometry *reply)
{
    XsmKnobWidget kw = (XsmKnobWidget) w;

    reply->width = kw->knob.orig_width;
    reply->height = kw->knob.orig_height;
    reply->request_mode = CWWidth | CWHeight;

    /* Return XtGeometryYes if the request matches the reply width
       and height */
    if (((request->request_mode & CWWidth) && request->width ==
            reply->width) &&
        ((request->request_mode & CWHeight) && request->height ==
          reply->height))
            return XtGeometryYes;

    /* Return XtGeometryNo if reply matches our current width and
       height */
```

```c
    if (reply->width == kw->core.width && reply->height ==
        kw->core.height)
            return XtGeometryNo;

    /* Return XtGeometryAlmost if one of the reply fields doesn't
     * match the current or request width or height.
     */
    return XtGeometryAlmost;
}


/******************************************************************
 *
 * Primitive Class Methods
 *
 ******************************************************************/




/*******************************************************************
 *
 * HighlightKnob
 * This is a primitive class procedure for drawing highlight around
 * the knob.  Knob needs a customized one to draw a circular
 * highlight.
 *
 *******************************************************************/
static void HighlightKnob( Widget w )
{
    XsmKnobWidget kw = (XsmKnobWidget) w;
    XsmKnobWidgetClass kc = (XsmKnobWidgetClass) XtClass(w);
    unsigned int outer_diameter, inner_diameter, diameter;
    XGCValues values;
    unsigned long valuemask;
```

```c
    /* Get the diameter */
    (*kc->knob_class.get_diameters)(w, &outer_diameter,
                                    &inner_diameter);


    diameter = outer_diameter + (2 *
            kw->primitive.highlight_thickness);


    /* Change the graphic context to highlight the knob */
    valuemask = (GCLineWidth | GCForeground);
    values.foreground = kw->primitive.highlight_color;
    values.line_width = kw->primitive.highlight_thickness;
    XChangeGC(XtDisplay(kw), kw->knob.gc, valuemask, &values);


    /* Draw the highlight */
    XDrawArc(XtDisplay(kw), XtWindow(kw), kw->knob.gc,
            kw->knob.margin_width, kw->knob.margin_height,
            diameter, diameter, 0, 64*360);


    /* Set flags to indicate that the highlight has been drawn */
    kw->primitive.highlighted = True;
    kw->primitive.highlight_drawn = True;


    /* Change the graphic context back for drawing the knob */
    values.foreground = kw->knob.knob_color;
    values.line_width = 0;
    XChangeGC(XtDisplay(kw), kw->knob.gc, valuemask, &values);
}



/***************************************************************************
 *
 * UnhighlightKnob
 * This is a primitive class procedure for erasing a highlight
```

```c
 * around the knob.  Knob needs a customized one to erase a circular
 * highlight.
 *
 ****************************************************************/
static void UnhighlightKnob( Widget w )
{
    XsmKnobWidget kw = (XsmKnobWidget) w;
    XsmKnobWidgetClass kc = (XsmKnobWidgetClass) XtClass(w);
    unsigned int outer_diameter, inner_diameter, diameter;
    XGCValues values;
    unsigned long valuemask;

    /* Get the diameter */
    (*kc->knob_class.get_diameters)(w, &outer_diameter,
                                       &inner_diameter);


    diameter = outer_diameter + (2 *
            kw->primitive.highlight_thickness);


    /* Change the graphic context to unhighlight */
    valuemask = (GCLineWidth | GCForeground);
    values.foreground = kw->core.background_pixel;
    values.line_width = kw->primitive.highlight_thickness;
    XChangeGC(XtDisplay(kw), kw->knob.gc, valuemask, &values);


    /* Erase the highlight */
    XDrawArc(XtDisplay(kw), XtWindow(kw), kw->knob.gc,
            kw->knob.margin_width, kw->knob.margin_height,
            diameter, diameter, 0, 64*360);


    kw->primitive.highlighted = False;
    kw->primitive.highlight_drawn = False;


    /* Change the graphic context back for drawing the knob */
```


Program Listings

```c
        values.foreground = kw->knob.knob_color;
        values.line_width = 0;
        XChangeGC(XtDisplay(kw), kw->knob.gc, valuemask, &values);


}


/**************************************************************
 *
 * Knob Class Methods
 *
 **************************************************************/


/**************************************************************
 *
 * GetDiameters
 * This knob class method is used to determine the inner and outer
 * diameter of the knob.  The knob draws 3 circles. The outer most
 * circle is for highlighting. The next circle is for drawing the
 * outer edge of the knob.  The margin_width or the margin_height
 * determine the outer edge of the circle.  The knob_margin
 * determines the inner most circle (being a percentage of the
 * knob itself).
 *
 **************************************************************/
static void GetDiameters( Widget w, unsigned int *diameter,
 unsigned int *inner_diameter)
{
    XsmKnobWidget kw = (XsmKnobWidget) w;


    if (kw->core.height - (2 * kw->knob.margin_width) >=
        kw->core.width - (2 * kw->knob.margin_height))
       *diameter = kw->core.width - (2 * (kw->knob.margin_width +
                kw->primitive.highlight_thickness));
    else
```

```c
        *diameter = kw->core.height - (2 * (kw->knob.margin_height +
                    kw->primitive.highlight_thickness));


    if (*diameter < MIN_KNOB_DIAMETER) *diameter =
        MIN_KNOB_DIAMETER;


    *inner_diameter = (*diameter * kw->knob.knob_margin)/100;


    if (*inner_diameter < 1) *inner_diameter = 1;
}



/********************************************************************
 *
 * CreateSegments
 * This knob class procedure is used to create the line segments
 * used in drawing the knob.
 *
 ********************************************************************/
static void CreateSegments( Widget w )
{
    XsmKnobWidget kw = (XsmKnobWidget) w;
    XsmKnobWidgetClass kc = (XsmKnobWidgetClass) XtClass(w);
    unsigned int diameter, inner_diameter;
    unsigned int radius, inner_radius;
    double    angle, cosine, sine, angle_change;
    Position center_x, center_y;
    int       i;
    XSegment  *ptr;


    ptr = kw->knob.segments;


    angle_change = RADIANS(MAX_ANGLE) /
                   (float)(kw->knob.num_segments - 1);
```

```c
    (*kc->knob_class.get_diameters)(w, &diameter, &inner_diameter);

    angle = kw->knob.angle_offset;

    center_x = (diameter >> 1) + kw->knob.margin_width +
               kw->primitive.highlight_thickness;
    center_y = (diameter >> 1) + kw->knob.margin_height +
               kw->primitive.highlight_thickness;

    radius = ((diameter >> 1) * 80)/100;

    if (inner_diameter > 2)
        inner_radius = ((inner_diameter >> 1) * 110)/100;
    else
        inner_radius = 1;

    for (i = 0; i < kw->knob.num_segments; i++) {
        cosine = cos(angle);
        sine   = sin(angle);
        ptr->x1    = (short)(center_x + radius * sine);
        ptr->y1 = (short)(center_y - radius * cosine);
        ptr->x2    = (short)(center_x + inner_radius * sine);
        ptr++->y2 = (short)(center_y - inner_radius * cosine);
        angle += angle_change;
    }
}

/*******************************************************************
 *
 * DrawIndicator
 * This knob class procedure is used to draw the indicator portion
```

```c
 * of the knob.
 *
 ****************************************************************/
static void DrawIndicator( Widget w )
{
    XsmKnobWidget kw = (XsmKnobWidget) w;
    XsmKnobWidgetClass kc = (XsmKnobWidgetClass) XtClass(w);
    unsigned int diameter, inner_diameter;
    unsigned int radius;
    double angle;
    Position center_x, center_y;

    (*kc->knob_class.get_diameters)(w, &diameter, &inner_diameter);

    angle = (RADIANS(MAX_ANGLE) * kw->knob.value)/
            (kw->knob.max_val - kw->knob.min_val) ;

    center_x = (diameter >> 1) + kw->knob.margin_width +
                kw->primitive.highlight_thickness;
    center_y = (diameter >> 1) + kw->knob.margin_height +
                kw->primitive.highlight_thickness;

    radius = ((diameter >> 1) * 93)/100;

    diameter = (diameter * 5)/100;
    if (diameter == 0) diameter = 1;

    center_x += (Position)(radius * sin(angle)) - (diameter >> 1);
    center_y -= (Position)(radius * cos(angle)) + (diameter >> 1);


    XDrawArc(XtDisplay(w), XtWindow(w), kw->knob.gc,
            center_x, center_y, diameter, diameter, 0, 64*360);
```

```c
    XFillArc(XtDisplay(w), XtWindow(w), kw->knob.gc,
      center_x, center_y, diameter, diameter, 0, 64*360);



}




/**************************************************************************
 *
 * TurnKnob
 * This knob class procedure is used in the timeout procedures
 * to show the knob turning.
 *
 *************************************************************************/
static void TurnKnob( XtPointer closure, XtIntervalId *id )
{
    Widget w = (Widget) closure;
    XsmKnobWidget kw = (XsmKnobWidget) w;
    XsmKnobWidgetClass kc = (XsmKnobWidgetClass) XtClass(w);
    XsmKnobCallbackStruct cb;

    if ((kw->knob.value < kw->knob.max_val - 1 &&
        kw->knob.move_clockwise) ||
        (kw->knob.value > 1 && !kw->knob.move_clockwise)) {
            kw->knob.timer_id =
            XtAppAddTimeOut(XtWidgetToApplicationContext(w),
            (unsigned long) kw->knob.turn_delay,
            kc->knob_class.turn, (XtPointer) kw);
    } else {
        kw->knob.turning = False;
    }


    XSetForeground(XtDisplay(kw), kw->knob.gc, kw->knob.knob_color);
    (*kc->knob_class.draw_indicator)(w);
```

```c
    XDrawSegments(XtDisplay(w), XtWindow(w), kw->knob.gc,
                  kw->knob.segments, kw->knob.num_segments);

    if (kw->knob.move_clockwise) kw->knob.value++;
    else kw->knob.value--;

    if (kw->knob.value_changed_callback) {
        cb.reason = XsmCR_VALUE_CHANGED;
        cb.event = NULL;
        cb.value = kw->knob.value;
        XtCallCallbackList(w, kw->knob.value_changed_callback,
                           (XtPointer) &cb);
    }

    kw->knob.angle_offset = (RADIANS(MAX_ANGLE) * kw->knob.value)/
                            (kw->knob.max_val - kw->knob.min_val) ;
      (*kc->knob_class.create_segments)(w);

    XSetForeground(XtDisplay(w), kw->knob.gc,
                   kw->knob.indicator_color);
    (*kc->knob_class.draw_indicator)(w);

    XSetForeground(XtDisplay(w), kw->knob.gc,
                   kw->primitive.foreground);
    XDrawSegments(XtDisplay(w), XtWindow(w), kw->knob.gc,
                  kw->knob.segments, kw->knob.num_segments);

}
```

```c
/*************************************************************
 *
 * DrawKnob
 * This knob class procedure is used to draw the knob.
 *
 *************************************************************/
static void DrawKnob( Widget w )
{
    XsmKnobWidget kw = (XsmKnobWidget) w;
    XsmKnobWidgetClass kc = (XsmKnobWidgetClass) XtClass(w);
    unsigned int diameter, inner_diameter, top_knob_start;

    (*kc->knob_class.get_diameters)(w, &diameter, &inner_diameter);

    /* Bottom of knob */
    XSetForeground(XtDisplay(kw), kw->knob.gc, kw->knob.knob_color);
    XFillArc(XtDisplay(kw), XtWindow(kw), kw->knob.gc,
      (kw->knob.margin_width + kw->primitive.highlight_thickness),
      (kw->knob.margin_height + kw->primitive.highlight_thickness),
       diameter, diameter, 0, 64*360);
    XSetForeground(XtDisplay(kw), kw->knob.gc,
                   kw->primitive.foreground);

    XDrawArc(XtDisplay(kw), XtWindow(kw), kw->knob.gc,
      (kw->knob.margin_width + kw->primitive.highlight_thickness),
      (kw->knob.margin_height + kw->primitive.highlight_thickness),
      diameter, diameter, 0, 64*360);

    top_knob_start = (diameter - ((diameter *
                     kw->knob.knob_margin)/100))/2;

    /* Top of knob */
    XDrawArc(XtDisplay(kw), XtWindow(kw), kw->knob.gc,
             (top_knob_start + kw->knob.margin_width +
```

```c
                        kw->primitive.highlight_thickness),
                    top_knob_start + kw->knob.margin_height +
                    kw->primitive.highlight_thickness),
                    inner_diameter, inner_diameter, 0, 64*360);

        XDrawSegments(XtDisplay(w), XtWindow(w), kw->knob.gc,
                    kw->knob.segments, kw->knob.num_segments);

        XSetForeground(XtDisplay(w), kw->knob.gc,
                    kw->knob.indicator_color);
        (*kc->knob_class.draw_indicator)(w);
        XSetForeground(XtDisplay(w), kw->knob.gc,
                    kw->primitive.foreground);

}
/*******************************************************************
 *
 * Callproc procedures defined to set default settings for
 * resources.
 *
 *******************************************************************/


/*******************************************************************
 *   DefaultKnobColor
 *     Get the default knob color Motif default background color.
 *******************************************************************/
static void
DefaultKnobColor( Widget g, int offset, XrmValue *value )
{
    XmManagerWidget  mw = (XmManagerWidget) XtParent (g);
    static Pixel     pixel;

    value->addr = (XtPointer) &pixel;
    value->size = sizeof (Pixel);
```

```c
    /* Work around for bug in _XmBackgroundColorDefault callproc */
    _XmSetDefaultBackgroundColorSpec(XtScreen(g),
                                     XmDEFAULT_BACKGROUND);

    /* Motif callproc to get default color */
    _XmBackgroundColorDefault (g, offset, value);
}


/****************************************************************
 *
 * Action Procedures
 *
 ****************************************************************/




/****************************************************************
 *
 * TurnLeft
 * An action procedure that is called on a left mouse button press.
 * This procedure will use a timeout to keep the knob turning
 * to the left.
 *
 ****************************************************************/
static void TurnLeft( Widget w, XEvent *event, char **params,
                      Cardinal *num_params )
{
    XsmKnobWidget kw = (XsmKnobWidget) w;
    XsmKnobWidgetClass kc = (XsmKnobWidgetClass) XtClass(w);

    /*
     * As long as the value has not reached the minimum value,
     * continue turning
```

```c
     */
    if (kw->knob.value > kw->knob.min_val) {
        kw->knob.move_clockwise = False;
        kw->knob.timer_id =
                    XtAppAddTimeOut(XtWidgetToApplicationContext(w),
                        (unsigned long) kw->knob.turn_delay,
                            kc->knob_class.turn, (XtPointer) w);
    }
}




/**************************************************************************
 *
 * TurnRight
 * An action procedure that is called on a right mouse button
 * press.  This procedure will use a timeout to keep the knob
 * turning to the right.
 *
 **************************************************************************/
static void TurnRight( Widget w, XEvent *event, char **params,
                    Cardinal *num_params )
{
    XsmKnobWidget kw = (XsmKnobWidget) w;
    XsmKnobWidgetClass kc = (XsmKnobWidgetClass) XtClass(w);

    /* As long as the value has not maxed out, continue turning */
    if (kw->knob.value < kw->knob.max_val) {
        kw->knob.move_clockwise = True;
        kw->knob.timer_id =
                    XtAppAddTimeOut(XtWidgetToApplicationContext(w),
                        (unsigned long) kw->knob.turn_delay,
                            kc->knob_class.turn, (XtPointer) w);
```

```c
        }
}


/******************************************************************
 *
 * ToggleLeft
 * An action procedure that is called on a key press.
 * This procedure will add a timeout to keep the knob turning
 * left.
 *
 ******************************************************************/
static void ToggleLeft( Widget w, XEvent *event, char **params,
                        Cardinal *num_params )
{
    XsmKnobWidget kw = (XsmKnobWidget) w;
    XsmKnobWidgetClass kc = (XsmKnobWidgetClass) XtClass(w);


    /* If the knob has not started turning, added the timeout */
    if (!kw->knob.turning) {
        if (kw->knob.value > kw->knob.min_val) {
            kw->knob.move_clockwise = False;
            kw->knob.timer_id =
                    XtAppAddTimeOut(XtWidgetToApplicationContext(w),
                    (unsigned long) kw->knob.turn_delay,
                    kc->knob_class.turn, (XtPointer) w);
            kw->knob.turning = True;
        }
    } else {
        /*
         * If it is already turning, remove the old timeout and
         * continue turning with a new timeout
         */
```

```c
        if (kw->knob.timer_id) XtRemoveTimeOut(kw->knob.timer_id);

        /* if it was turning left continue the turning, otherwise
           stop. */
        if (kw->knob.move_clockwise) {
            kw->knob.move_clockwise = False;
            kw->knob.timer_id =
                        XtAppAddTimeOut(XtWidgetToApplicationContext(w),
                            (unsigned long) kw->knob.turn_delay,
                             kc->knob_class.turn, (XtPointer) w);
        } else {
            kw->knob.turning = False;
        }
    }
}


/*************************************************************************
 *
 * ToggleRight
 * An action procedure that is called on a key press.
 * This procedure will add a timeout to keep the knob turning
 * right.
 *
 *************************************************************************/
static void ToggleRight( Widget w, XEvent *event, char **params,
                         Cardinal *num_params )
{
    XsmKnobWidget kw = (XsmKnobWidget) w;
    XsmKnobWidgetClass kc = (XsmKnobWidgetClass) XtClass(w);

    /* If the knob has not started turning, add the timeout */
    if (!kw->knob.turning) {
```


Program Listings

```c
            if (kw->knob.value < kw->knob.max_val) {

                kw->knob.move_clockwise = True;

                kw->knob.timer_id =

                        XtAppAddTimeOut(XtWidgetToApplicationContext(w),

                        (unsigned long) kw->knob.turn_delay,

                        kc->knob_class.turn, (XtPointer) w);

        kw->knob.turning = True;

            }

        } else {

            /*

             * If it is already turning, remove the old timeout and

             * continue turning with a new timeout.

             */

            if (kw->knob.timer_id) XtRemoveTimeOut(kw->knob.timer_id);


            /* if it was turning right continue the turning, otherwise

                stop. */

            if (!kw->knob.move_clockwise) {

                kw->knob.move_clockwise = True;

                kw->knob.timer_id =

                        XtAppAddTimeOut(XtWidgetToApplicationContext(w),

                        (unsigned long) kw->knob.turn_delay,

                         kc->knob_class.turn, (XtPointer) w);

            } else {

                kw->knob.turning = False;

            }

        }

    }
```

```c
/******************************************************************
 *
 * ReleaseKnob
 * An action procedure that is called on a mouse button release.
 * This procedure will remove a timeout to stop the knob from
 * turning.
 *
 *****************************************************************/
static void ReleaseKnob( Widget w, XEvent *event, char **params,
                         Cardinal *num_params )
{
    XsmKnobWidget kw = (XsmKnobWidget) w;

    /* Remove the timeout */
    if (kw->knob.timer_id) XtRemoveTimeOut(kw->knob.timer_id);

    kw->knob.turning = False;
}


/******************************************************************
 *
 * Public Convenience Functions
 *
 *****************************************************************/

/*************************************************************
 *
 * XsmCreateWidget() -
 * Knob widget creation convenience routine.
 *
 *************************************************************/


Widget XsmCreateKnob( Widget parent, char *name, ArgList arglist,
                      Cardinal argcount )
```

```c
{
    return (XtCreateWidget(name, xsmKnobWidgetClass,
                           parent, arglist, argcount));
}


/****************************************************************
 *
 * XsmGetKnobValue() -
 * A function to get the knob value quickly.  If a resource value
 * needs to be retrieved frequently, it might be a good idea to
 * have a convenience function like this to avoid costly calls to
 * XtGetValues().  Too many of these functions can be confusing
 * to the application developer.
 *
 ****************************************************************************
/
int XsmGetKnobValue( Widget w )
{
    XsmKnobWidget kw = (XsmKnobWidget) w;


    return(kw->knob.value);
}


/*****************************************************************************
 *
 * XsmSetKnobValue() -
 * A function to set the knob value quickly.  If a resource value
 * needs to be changed frequently, it might be a good idea to
 * have a convenience function like this to avoid costly calls to
 * XtSetValues().  Too many of these functions can be confusing
 * to the application developer.
 *
 *****************************************************************************/
```

```c
void XsmSetKnobValue( Widget w, int value )
{
    XsmKnobWidget kw = (XsmKnobWidget) w;
    XsmKnobWidgetClass kc = (XsmKnobWidgetClass) XtClass(w);

    /* Return if the value doesn't change */

    if (value == kw->knob.value) return;

    /* Verify the changed values */

    if (value > kw->knob.max_val) {
        XtWarning("Value is less than MaxValue, Defaulting to
                MaxValue");
        kw->knob.value = kw->knob.max_val;
    }

    if (value < kw->knob.min_val) {
        XtWarning("Value is greater than MinValue, Defaulting to
                MinValue");
        kw->knob.value = kw->knob.min_val;
    }

    /*
    * If the knob is realized, redraw the knob segments and indicator
    * to indicate the new value.
    */

    if (XtIsRealized(w)) {
      /* erase old indicator */
        XSetForeground(XtDisplay(kw), kw->knob.gc,
                    kw->knob.knob_color);
        (*kc->knob_class.draw_indicator)(w);
        XDrawSegments(XtDisplay(w), XtWindow(w), kw->knob.gc,
```

```c
                    kw->knob.segments, kw->knob.num_segments);


    /* Set new value */
     kw->knob.value = value;


    /* Recreate segments */
     kw->knob.angle_offset = (RADIANS(MAX_ANGLE) *
                                   kw->knob.value)/
                               (kw->knob.max_val - kw->knob.min_val) ;
     (*kc->knob_class.create_segments)(w);


    /* Redraw indicator */
     XSetForeground(XtDisplay(w), kw->knob.gc,
                    kw->knob.indicator_color);
     (*kc->knob_class.draw_indicator)(w);


    /* Redraw segments */
     XSetForeground(XtDisplay(w), kw->knob.gc,
                    kw->primitive.foreground);
     XDrawSegments(XtDisplay(w), XtWindow(w), kw->knob.gc,
                    kw->knob.segments, kw->knob.num_segments);
    } else {
      kw->knob.value = value;
    }


    }
```

Knob.h

```c
#ifndef _XsmKnob_h
#define _XsmKnob_h


/* Always include Xm.h */
#include <Xm/Xm.h>


/* Add extern for C++ applications */
#ifdef __cplusplus
extern "C" {
#endif


/* Resource Names */


#define XsmNvalueChangedCallback    "valueChangedCallback"
#define XsmNindicatorColor          "indicatorColor"
#define XsmNmarginWidth             "marginWidth"
#define XsmNmarginHeight            "marginHeight"
#define XsmNknobMargin              "knobMargin"
#define XsmNknobColor               "knobColor"
#define XsmNmaxValue                "maxValue"
#define XsmNminValue                "minValue"
#define XsmNturnDelay               "turnDelay"
#define XsmNvalue                   "value"


/* Resource Class Names */


#define XsmCValueChangedCallback    "ValueChangedCallback"
#define XsmCIndicatorColor          "IndicatorColor"
#define XsmCMarginWidth             "MarginWidth"
#define XsmCMarginHeight            "MarginHeight"
#define XsmCKnobMargin              "KnobMargin"
```

```c
#define XsmCMaxValue              "MaxValue"
#define XsmCMinValue              "MinValue"
#define XsmCTurnDelay             "TurnDelay"
#define XsmCValue                 "Value"


/* Callback Structs */


typedef struct
{
    int reason;
    XEvent * event;
    int value;
} XsmKnobCallbackStruct;


/* Callback reason for the above callback */


#define XsmCR_VALUE_CHANGED    0


/* Extern the widget class for applications that use
   XtCreateWidget() */


externalref WidgetClass  xsmKnobWidgetClass;


/*
 * To allow applications to use tight type checking, define
 * structures for the widget class and instance pointers
 * specific to this class of widget.
 */


typedef struct _XsmKnobClassRec * XsmKnobWidgetClass;
typedef struct _XsmKnobRec        * XsmKnobWidget;


/********    Public Function Declarations    ********/
```

```c
/* Declare the function that can be used by the application
   developer. */


extern Widget XsmCreateKnob(
                    Widget    parent,
                    char      *name,
                    ArgList   arglist,
                    Cardinal argcount) ;
extern int XsmGetKnobValue(
                    Widget w) ;
extern void XsmSetKnobValue(
                    Widget w,
                    int     value) ;


#ifdef __cplusplus
}  /* Close scope of 'extern "C"' declaration which encloses file.
*/
#endif


#endif /* _XsmKnob_h */
/* DON'T ADD STUFF AFTER THIS #endif */
```

```c
#ifndef _XsmKnobP_h
#define _XsmKnobP_h


/* Include the public header as well as the super class private
   header */


#include "Knob.h"
#include <Xm/PrimitiveP.h>


/*---------------------------------------------------------------*/
/***********************
 * THE KNOB CLASS RECORD *
 **********************/


/*
 * Define class part record.  Be sure to include an extension
 * pointer field for future expansion.
 */


typedef struct {
    XsmGetDiametersProc get_diameters;   /* procedure to draw inner
                                            and outer circles */

    XtWidgetProc        create_segments; /* procedure used to
                                            create handle segments */

    XtWidgetProc        draw_indicator;  /* procedure for drawing
                                            knob indicator */

    XtTimerCallbackProc turn;            /* timeout procedure used
                                            to turn knob */

    XtWidgetProc        draw;            /* procedure for drawing
                                            the knob */

    XtPointer           extension;       /* pointer to extension
```

```c
                                        record used for future
                                        expansion */
} XsmKnobClassPart;


/*
 * Define class record, which includes all superclass parts.
 * Start first with Core, then Primitive, and finally the Knob
 * class part defined above.
 */


typedef struct _XsmKnobClassRec {
    CoreClassPart          core_class;
    XmPrimitiveClassPart   primitive_class;
    XsmKnobClassPart       knob_class;
} XsmKnobClassRec;


/* Define procedure pointers not defined in the Intrinsics. */


typedef void (*XsmGetDiametersProc)(Widget, unsigned int *,
unsigned int *) ;


/* Define inheritance procedures for all knob class procedures. */


#define XsmInheritGetDiameters ((XsmGetDiametersProc) _XtInherit)
#define XsmInheritCreateSegments ((XtWidgetProc) _XtInherit)
#define XsmInheritDrawIndicator ((XtWidgetProc) _XtInherit)
#define XsmInheritTurn ((XtTimerCallbackProc) _XtInherit)
#define XsmInheritDraw ((XtWidgetProc) _XtInherit)


/*------------------------------------------------------------*/
/**************************
 * THE KNOB INSTANCE RECORD *
 **************************/
```

```c
/*
 * Define the instance part record.  Be sure to include all the
 * fields to hold resource values as well as fields for internal
 * variables unique to each instance of a knob widget.
 */


typedef struct _XsmKnobPart {
    XtCallbackList value_changed_callback; /* resource - callback
                                        when value changes */
    int value;                      /* resource - value of the knob */
    int max_val;                    /* resource - maximum value allowed */
    int min_val;                    /* resource - minimum value allowed */
    int turn_delay;                /* resource - the delay before the next
                                    increment */
    Pixel knob_color;              /* resource - the color of the knob */
    Pixel indicator_color;         /* resource - the color of the
                                    indicator */
    Dimension margin_width;        /* resource - determines the outer
                                    edge of */
    Dimension margin_height;       /* the circle. Whichever value is
                                    greater when the dimension is
                                    subtracted from its margin
                                    value determines the knob
                                    diameter. */
    Dimension knob_margin;         /* resource - The percentage from the
                                    knob's outer edge to draw the inner
                                    circle. */
    Dimension orig_width;          /* saves the original dimension */
    Dimension orig_height;         /* saves the original dimension */
    Boolean move_clockwise;        /* indicates direction of turn */
    Boolean turning;               /* indicates whether turning is in
                                    progress */
    GC gc;                         /* graphics context use in graphic
                                    ops */
```

```c
    XSegment *segments;        /* the line segments used for drawing
                                  the handle */
    int num_segments;          /* the number of segments in the above
                                  list */
    XtIntervalId timer_id;     /* the timer id of the timeout used in
                                  turning the knob */
    double angle_offset;       /* used to calculate the segment
                                  positions */
} XsmKnobPart;


/*
 * Define instance record which includes all superclass instance
 * parts.  Start with Core, then Primitive, and finally the Knob
 * instance part defined above.
 */


typedef struct _XsmKnobRec {
    CorePart          core;
    XmPrimitivePart primitive;
    XsmKnobPart       knob;
} XsmKnobRec;

#endif /* _XsmKnobP_h */
/* DON't ADD STUFF AFTER THIS #endif */
```

knob1.c

knob1.c is a very simple program that demonstrates the knob widget. You can
turn the knob in either direction, but because there are no callbacks, nothing
happens. Compare how the knob is used in this program with its use in
knobcolors.c.

```c
#include <stdio.h>

#include <stdlib.h>

#include <X11/Intrinsic.h>

#include "Knob.h"


void
main (
    int             argc,
    String          *argv)
    Widget          shell, knob;
    Display         *display;
    XtAppContext    app_context;
    Arg             args[20];
    int             n;


    /*
     * Initialize the Intrinsics.
     */
    XtToolkitInitialize();
    app_context = XtCreateApplicationContext();
    display = XtOpenDisplay(app_context, NULL, argv[0],
                        "Knob1", NULL, 0, &argc, argv);
    if (!display) {
        printf("Unable to open display\n");
        exit(0);
    }


    /*
```

```c
 * Create shell
 */
n = 0;
XtSetArg (args[n], XmNallowShellResize, True); n++;
shell = XtAppCreateShell(argv[0], NULL,
                         applicationShellWidgetClass,
                         display, args, n);



/*
 * Create a knob widget
 */
knob = XtCreateWidget("knob", xsmKnobWidgetClass, shell,
                      NULL, 0);
XtManageChild(knob);
XtRealizeWidget(shell);
XtAppMainLoop(app_context);

}
```

knobcolors.c

`knobcolors.c` uses three knob widgets in a row column manager. Each knob has two labels: one to identify the color each knob controls, and one to display the current value of each knob. The knob minimum value is set to 0, and the maximum value is set to 255. As the knobs are rotated, the background color changes accordingly.

```c
/*  Xm headers  */
#include <Xm/DialogS.h>
#include <Xm/RowColumn.h>
#include <Xm/Frame.h>
#include <Xm/LabelG.h>
#include <Xm/PushBG.h>
#include <Xm/CascadeB.h>
#include <Xm/MessageB.h>
#include <Xm/MainW.h>
#include "Knob.h"


/* Global defines */
#define CMPSTR(str) \
   XmStringCreateLtoR (str, XmSTRING_DEFAULT_CHARSET)


/* Geometry */
#define HORIZONTAL_SPACING          (Dimension) 30
#define VERTICAL_SPACING                        5
#define TOP_OFFSET                  (Dimension)  5
#define KNOB_HIGHLIGHT_THICKNESS    (Dimension)  2


#define RED        1
#define GREEN      2
#define BLUE       3
#define ALL_COLORS 4


#define BUFFERSZ   1000
```

```c
Widget  appshell;
Widget  frame;
Widget  rowcol;
Widget  redLabel;
Widget  greenLabel;
Widget  blueLabel;
Widget  redKnob;
Widget  greenKnob;
Widget  blueKnob;
Widget  redValueLabel;
Widget  greenValueLabel;
Widget  blueValueLabel;

XColor  bg_color;   /* color structure for the background color */
XColor  fg_color;   /* color structure for the foreground color */
XColor  ts_color;   /* color structure for the top shadow color */
XColor  bs_color;   /* color structure for the bottom shadow
                       color */
XColor  sc_color;   /* color structure for the select color (arm)
                       color */

XmColorProc calcRGB;

Display    *display;

Colormap    colormap;

/* Forward Declarations */
static Widget   CreateHelp();
static void     HelpCB();
static void     QuitCB();
static XtArgVal GetColor();
static void     CreateColorEditor();
```

```c
static void      changRGB_CB();
static void      SetKnobs();
static void      GenerateColors();

Pixel GetPixel();

char *tmpbuf = "#78a0d5";
/*****************************************/
/* Main                                  */
/*****************************************/
void main(argc, argv)
    int      argc;
    char     **argv;
{
    register int n;
    Arg          args[4];
    Widget   main_window, menu_bar, menu_pane, cascade;
    Widget   button;
    Boolean  status;
    unsigned long plane_mask;
    unsigned long *color_cells;
    XtAppContext    app_context;

  /* Initialize the toolkit and open the display */
    appshell = XtAppInitialize(&app_context, "Knobcolors", NULL, 0,
                               &argc, argv, NULL, args, 0);

  /* Get the display */
    display = XtDisplay(appshell);

  /* Get the default colormap for this display */
    colormap = XDefaultColormap(display, XDefaultScreen(display));

  /* Allocate 4 color cells for use with this program: background,
```

```c
                foreground, top shadow, and bottom shadow.  The select color
            won't be used so we don't need to allocate for it. */
        color_cells = (unsigned long *)XtMalloc (
                        4 * sizeof (unsigned long));
        status = XAllocColorCells (display, colormap,
                                    0, &plane_mask, 0, color_cells, 4);


        if(status == False)
        {
            printf(" couldn't allocate enough color cells\n");
            exit(1);
        }
        else
        {
/* Assign the allocated color cells to the correct structure */
            n = 0;
            bg_color.pixel = color_cells[n++];
            bg_color.flags = DoRed | DoGreen | DoBlue;
            fg_color.pixel = color_cells[n++];
            fg_color.flags = DoRed | DoGreen | DoBlue;
            bs_color.pixel = color_cells[n++];
            bs_color.flags = DoRed | DoGreen | DoBlue;
            ts_color.pixel = color_cells[n];
            ts_color.flags = DoRed | DoGreen | DoBlue;
        }


/* Get the RGB value (XColor) of the background */
    XParseColor(display, colormap, tmpbuf, &bg_color);


/* Create main window. */
    main_window = XmCreateMainWindow (appshell, "main1", args, 0);
    XtManageChild (main_window);


/* Create menu bar in main window. */
```

```c
    menu_bar = XmCreateMenuBar (main_window, "menu_bar", args, 0);
    XtManageChild (menu_bar);


/* Create "Exit" pulldown menu. */
    menu_pane = XmCreatePulldownMenu (menu_bar, "menu_pane",
                                      args, 0);


    button = XmCreatePushButtonGadget (menu_pane, "Quit", args, 0);
    XtManageChild (button);
    XtAddCallback (button, XmNactivateCallback, QuitCB, NULL);


    n = 0;
    XtSetArg (args[n], XmNsubMenuId, menu_pane); n++;
    cascade = XmCreateCascadeButton (menu_bar, "Exit", args, n);
    XtManageChild (cascade);


/* Create "Help" button. */
    cascade = XmCreateCascadeButton (menu_bar, "Help", args, 0);
    XtManageChild (cascade);
    XtAddCallback (cascade, XmNactivateCallback, HelpCB, NULL);


    n = 0;
    XtSetArg (args[n], XmNmenuHelpWidget, cascade); n++;
    XtSetValues (menu_bar, args, n);


/*
 * Create a frame widget
 */
    n = 0;
    XtSetArg(args[n], XmNmarginWidth, 15); n++;
    XtSetArg(args[n], XmNmarginHeight, 15); n++;
    frame = XmCreateFrame (main_window, "frame", args, n);
    XtManageChild(frame);
```

```c
    /*  Set main window areas  */
    XmMainWindowSetAreas (main_window, menu_bar, NULL, NULL,
                          NULL, frame);


   /* Generate the foreground, top shadow, and bottom shadow
    * colors based on the background color which was set by
    * XParseColor above. */
    GenerateColors ();


   /* Create the sliders with labels using the generated colors */
    CreateColorEditor ();


    XtRealizeWidget (appshell);


    XtAppMainLoop (app_context);
}



/*-------------------------------------------------------------------
**  HelpCB      - callback for help button
*/
static
void HelpCB (w, client_data, call_data)
Widget      w;              /*  widget id                */
XtPointer   client_data;  /*  data from application    */
XtPointer   call_data;    /*  data from widget class   */
{
    Widget    message_box;  /*  message box              */

   /*  Create help window. */
    message_box = CreateHelp (w);

   /*  Display help window. */
    XtManageChild (message_box);
}
```

```c
/*-----------------------------------------------------------
** CreateHelp    - create help window
*/
static
Widget CreateHelp (parent)
Widget    parent;      /*  parent widget  */
{
    Widget          button;
    Widget          message_box;        /*  Message Dialog  */
    Arg             args[4];            /*  arg list        */
    register int  n;                    /*  arg count       */

    static char   message[BUFFERSZ]; /*  help text       */
    XmString        title_string = NULL;
    XmString        message_string = NULL;
    XmString        button_string = NULL;


 /*  Generate message to display. */

    sprintf (message, "\
This program uses three knob widgets to balance colors. The \n\
three knobs are used to adjust the primary colors: red, blue,\n\
and green.  As the knobs are adjusted, the background color \n\
changes accordingly.  To terminate the program, press the \n\
'Exit' button and then the 'Quit' button.\0");


 /* Create the compound strings */
    message_string = CMPSTR (message);
    button_string =  CMPSTR ("Close");
    title_string =   CMPSTR ("knobcolors help");
```

```c
/*  Create message box dialog. */
   n = 0;
   XtSetArg (args[n], XmNdialogTitle, title_string);   n++;
   XtSetArg (args[n], XmNokLabelString, button_string);   n++;
   XtSetArg (args[n], XmNmessageString, message_string);   n++;
   message_box = XmCreateMessageDialog (parent, "helpbox",
                                        args, n);


   button = XmMessageBoxGetChild (message_box,
                                  XmDIALOG_CANCEL_BUTTON);
   XtUnmanageChild (button);
   button = XmMessageBoxGetChild (message_box,
                                  XmDIALOG_HELP_BUTTON);
   XtUnmanageChild (button);

 /*  Free strings and return message box. */
   if (title_string) XmStringFree (title_string);
   if (message_string) XmStringFree (message_string);
   if (button_string) XmStringFree (button_string);
   return (message_box);
}



/*-----------------------------------------------------------
** QuitCB      - callback for quit button
*/
static
void QuitCB (w, client_data, call_data)
Widget    w;                /*  widget id                 */
XtPointer client_data;  /*  data from application   */
XtPointer call_data;    /*  data from widget class  */
{
 /*  Terminate the application. */
```

```c
    exit (0);
}


/*-------------------------------------------------------------------
**  GetColor       - function for converting a string into a color
*/
static XtArgVal GetColor(colorstr)
char *colorstr;
{
    XrmValue from, to;

    from.size = strlen(colorstr) +1;
    if (from.size < sizeof(String)) from.size = sizeof(String);
    from.addr = colorstr;
    to.addr = NULL;
    XtConvert(appshell, XmRString, &from, XmRPixel, &to);

    return ((XtArgVal) *((XtArgVal *) to.addr));
}




/*-------------------------------------------------------------------
 * CreateColorEditor  -  Create the rowcol and knob widgets
 */
static void
CreateColorEditor()
{
    register int    n;
    Arg             args[15];
    XmString        string;                 /* temp Xm string */
    WidgetList      children;

  /* Create rowcol widget */
    n=0;
```

```c
XtSetArg(args[n], XmNbackground, bg_color.pixel);  n++;

XtSetArg(args[n], XmNforeground, fg_color.pixel);  n++;

XtSetArg(args[n], XmNtopShadowColor, ts_color.pixel);  n++;

XtSetArg(args[n], XmNbottomShadowColor, bs_color.pixel);  n++;

XtSetArg(args[n], XmNentryAlignment, XmALIGNMENT_CENTER); n++;

XtSetArg(args[n], XmNpacking, XmPACK_COLUMN);  n++;

XtSetArg(args[n], XmNorientation, XmHORIZONTAL);  n++;

XtSetArg(args[n], XmNnumColumns, 3);  n++;

rowcol = XmCreateRowColumn(frame,"rowcol", args, n);


XtManageChild (rowcol);


/*
 * Create RGB label gadgets for R, G, B, labels
 */
string =  CMPSTR("R");
n = 0;
XtSetArg(args[n], XmNlabelString, string); n++;
redLabel = XmCreateLabelGadget(rowcol, "redLabel", args, n);
XtManageChild(redLabel);
XmStringFree(string);


string =  CMPSTR("G");
n = 0;
XtSetArg(args[n], XmNlabelString, string); n++;
greenLabel = XmCreateLabelGadget(rowcol, "greenLabel", args, n);
XtManageChild(greenLabel);
XmStringFree(string);


string =  CMPSTR("B");
n = 0;
XtSetArg(args[n], XmNlabelString, string); n++;
blueLabel = XmCreateLabelGadget(rowcol, "blueLabel", args, n);
XtManageChild(blueLabel);
```

```c
    XmStringFree(string);

/*
 * Create the three knob widgets, one each for red, green, and blue
 */
    n = 0;
    XtSetArg(args[n], XmNbackground, bg_color.pixel);   n++;
    XtSetArg(args[n], XmNforeground, fg_color.pixel);   n++;
    XtSetArg(args[n], XsmNmaxValue, 0xff);   n++;
    XtSetArg(args[n], XsmNminValue, 0x0);   n++;
    XtSetArg(args[n], XsmNknobColor, GetColor("red")); n++;
    XtSetArg(args[n], XsmNindicatorColor, GetColor("maroon")); n++;
    redKnob = XsmCreateKnob(rowcol, "redKnob", args, n);
    XtManageChild(redKnob);
    XtAddCallback(redKnob, XsmNvalueChangedCallback, changRGB_CB,
                (XtPointer) RED);

    n--; n--;
    XtSetArg(args[n], XsmNknobColor, GetColor("Green")); n++;
    XtSetArg(args[n], XsmNindicatorColor, GetColor("ForestGreen"));
n++;
    greenKnob = XsmCreateKnob(rowcol, "greenKnob", args, n);
    XtManageChild(greenKnob);
    XtAddCallback(greenKnob, XsmNvalueChangedCallback, changRGB_CB,
                (XtPointer) GREEN );

    n--; n--;
    XtSetArg(args[n], XsmNknobColor, GetColor("Blue")); n++;
    XtSetArg(args[n], XsmNindicatorColor, GetColor("navy")); n++;
    blueKnob = XsmCreateKnob(rowcol, "blueKnob", args, n);
    XtManageChild(blueKnob);
    XtAddCallback(blueKnob, XsmNvalueChangedCallback, changRGB_CB,
                (XtPointer) BLUE );
```

```c
        n = 0;
        redValueLabel = XmCreateLabelGadget(rowcol, "redValueLabel",
                                        args, n);
        XtManageChild(redValueLabel);


        n = 0;
        greenValueLabel = XmCreateLabelGadget(rowcol, "greenValueLabel",
                                        args, n);
        XtManageChild(greenValueLabel);


        n = 0;
        blueValueLabel = XmCreateLabelGadget(rowcol, "blueValueLabel",
                                        args, n);
        XtManageChild(blueValueLabel);


    /* Set the knobs to the bg component of the selected color */
        SetKnobs(&bg_color, ALL_COLORS);
}


/*******************************************************************
 * GenerateColors()
 *     Generates new RGB values for foreground, top shadow,
 *     bottom shadow, and select color based on the background.
 *     Select color is not used in our program but the Motif color
 *     generation routine expects it and calculates it.
 *     The Colors generated are stored in the red, green, and blue
 *     fields of the XColor structure passed in.
 *     The color generation routine will be exported in Motif1.1.
 *     The generated colors are then used to update the color cells
 *     of the ColorSet being edited.
 *******************************************************************/
static void
GenerateColors()
{
```

```c
    XColor colors[4];
    int j=0;


  /* Get the Motif1.1 color calculation procedure */
    if (calcRGB == NULL)
        calcRGB = XmGetColorCalculation();


  /* Given the background color, calculate the foreground,
     select color, top shadow, and bottom shadow colors. */
    (*calcRGB)(&bg_color, &fg_color, &sc_color, &ts_color,
       &bs_color);


  /* Put those calculated colors in an array */
    colors[j++] =  bg_color;
    colors[j++] =  fg_color;
    colors[j++] =  ts_color;
    colors[j++] =  bs_color;


  /* Go change the colors dynamically */
    XStoreColors(display, colormap, colors, j);
}


/*****************************************************************
 * changeRGB_CB()
 *    Called when one of the RGB knobs is moved
 *****************************************************************/
static void
changRGB_CB( w, client_data, call_data )
Widget    w;
XtPointer client_data;
XtPointer call_data;
{
    int reason_code;
    int value;
```

```c
    int color;

    reason_code = ((XmAnyCallbackStruct *)call_data)->reason;
    if ( reason_code == XsmCR_VALUE_CHANGED)
    {
        color = (int) client_data;
        value = ((XsmKnobCallbackStruct *)call_data)->value;

        /*
         * Shift value -- to make up for knob max of only 0xff
         */
        value <<= 8;
        switch (color)
        {
          case RED:
             bg_color.red = value;
             break;
          case GREEN:
             bg_color.green = value;
             break;
          case BLUE:
             bg_color.blue = value;
             break;
          default:
             return;
        }

        SetKnobs(&bg_color, color);
        GenerateColors();
    }
}

static void
SetColors(new_color, color_string, valueLabel, knob_w)
```

   Program Listings

```c
    int new_color;
char *color_string;
Widget valueLabel;
Widget knob_w;
{
    register int  n;
    Arg           args[15];
    XmString      string;


    string =  CMPSTR(color_string);
    XtSetArg(args[0], XmNlabelString, string);
    XtSetValues(valueLabel, args, 1);
    XsmSetKnobValue(knob_w, new_color);
    XmStringFree(string);
}



/****************************************************************
 *    SetKnobs()
 *            Passed an XColor, updates all knobs.
 ****************************************************************/
static void
SetKnobs( rgb, color )
XColor *rgb;
int color;
{
    char* color_string = XtMalloc(sizeof(char)*5);
    int new_color;

    switch (color)
    {
      case RED:
      new_color = rgb->red >> 8;
      sprintf(color_string, "%d", new_color);
```

```c
        SetColors(new_color, color_string, redValueLabel, redKnob);
        break;

    case GREEN:
        new_color = rgb->green >> 8;
        sprintf(color_string, "%d", new_color);
        SetColors(new_color, color_string, greenValueLabel,
                greenKnob);
        break;

    case BLUE:
        new_color = rgb->blue >> 8;
        sprintf(color_string, "%d", new_color);
        SetColors(new_color, color_string, blueValueLabel, blueKnob);
        break;

    case ALL_COLORS:
        new_color = rgb->red >> 8;
        sprintf(color_string, "%d", new_color);
        SetColors(new_color, color_string, redValueLabel, redKnob);
        new_color = rgb->green >> 8;
        sprintf(color_string, "%d", new_color);
        SetColors(new_color, color_string, greenValueLabel,
                greenKnob);
        new_color = rgb->blue >> 8;
        sprintf(color_string, "%d", new_color);
        SetColors(new_color, color_string, blueValueLabel, blueKnob);
        break;

    default:
    return;
    }

    XtFree(color_string);
```

```c
}


/*******************************************************************
 * GetPixel()
 *  Passed in a color string, calls XtConvert which is an X
 *  toolkit converter which converts a string into a pixel value.
 *******************************************************************/
Pixel
GetPixel( widget, color_string )
Widget widget;
char *color_string;
{
    XrmValue from, to;

  /* Determine the size of the string passed in */
    from.size = strlen(color_string) + 1;
    if (from.size < sizeof(String))
        from.size = sizeof(String);
    from.addr = color_string;

  /* Go convert the string into a pixel (i.e. color cell) */
    XtConvert(widget, XmRString, &from, XmRPixel, &to);

  /* Return that pixel */
    return ((Pixel) *((Pixel *) to.addr));
}
```

KnobG.c

KnobG.c is the object code for the knob gadget described in Chapter 5.

```c
#include <math.h>
#include <X11/keysym.h>
#include <Xm/ManagerP.h>
#include "KnobGP.h"


/* Defines for mathematic functions used in drawing */
#define   RADIANS(x)   (M_PI * 2.0 * (x) / 360.0)
#define   DEGREES(x)   ((x) / (M_PI * 2.0) * 360.0)
#define   MIN_ANGLE   225.0
#define   MAX_ANGLE   345.0
#define   NUM_SEGS    24
#define   MIN(a,b)    (((a) < (b)) ? (a) :  (b))


#define MIN_KNOB_DIAMETER                  3
#define DEFAULT_DIAMETER                 100
#define DEFAULT_KNOB_MARGIN                5
#define DEFAULT_KNOB_MARGIN_PERCENTAGE    50


/********    Static Function Declarations    ********/


/* RectObj methods */
static void ClassPartInitialize( WidgetClass widget_class) ;
static void Initialize( Widget request, Widget new_w, ArgList args,
                        Cardinal *num_args) ;
static void Destroy( Widget w) ;
static void Resize( Widget w) ;
static void Redisplay( Widget w, XEvent *event, Region region) ;
static Boolean SetValues( Widget old_w, Widget request, Widget
                          new_w, ArgList args, Cardinal *num_args) ;
static void SetValuesAlmost( Widget old_w, Widget new_w,
```

```c
                                        XtWidgetGeometry *request,
                                        XtWidgetGeometry *reply);
static XtGeometryResult QueryGeometry( Widget w,
                                        XtWidgetGeometry *request,
                                        XtWidgetGeometry *reply) ;
static void GetDiameters( Widget w, unsigned int *diameter,
                                unsigned int *inner_diameter) ;


/* Gadget methods */
static void HighlightKnob( Widget w) ;
static void UnhighlightKnob( Widget w) ;
static void InputDispatch( Widget wid, XEvent *event,
                                Mask event_mask) ;
static void ArmAndActivate( Widget wid, XEvent *event,
                                String *params,
                                Cardinal *num_params) ;
static Boolean VisualChange( Widget wid, Widget cmw, Widget nmw) ;



/* Resource callprocs */
static void DefaultIndicatorColor( Widget, int, XrmValue *);
static void DefaultIndicatorColor( Widget, int, XrmValue *);


/* Knob methods */
static void CreateSegments( Widget w) ;
static void DrawIndicator( Widget w) ;
static void TurnKnob( XtPointer closure, XtIntervalId *id) ;
static void DrawKnob( Widget w) ;


/* Action procs */
static void HandleKey( Widget w, XEvent *event, char **params,
                        Cardinal *num_params) ;
static void ToggleLeft( Widget w, XEvent *event, char **params,
                        Cardinal *num_params) ;
```

```c
static void ToggleRight( Widget w, XEvent *event, char **params,
                         Cardinal *num_params) ;
static void ToggleKnob( Widget w, XEvent *event, char **params,
                        Cardinal *num_params) ;
static void StartKnobTurn( Widget w, XEvent *event, char **params,
                           Cardinal *num_params) ;
static void ReleaseKnob( Widget w, XEvent *event, char **params,
                         Cardinal *num_params) ;


/* Resource list initialization - sets up resource names and values
 * for each resource of this widget.
 */
static XtResource resources[] = {
    {
        XsmNvalueChangedCallback, XmCCallback, XmRCallback,
        sizeof(XtCallbackList),
        XtOffset (XsmKnobGadget, knobg.value_changed_callback),
        XmRCallback, NULL
    },

    {
        XsmNvalue, XsmCValue, XmRInt, sizeof(int),
        XtOffset (XsmKnobGadget, knobg.value),
        XmRImmediate, (XtPointer) 0
    },

    {
        XsmNmaxValue, XsmCMaxValue, XmRInt, sizeof(int),
        XtOffset (XsmKnobGadget, knobg.max_val),
        XmRImmediate, (XtPointer) 100
    },

    {
        XsmNminValue, XsmCMinValue, XmRInt, sizeof(int),
```

                                                              Program Listings

```c
    XtOffset (XsmKnobGadget, knobg.min_val),
    XmRImmediate, (XtPointer) 0
  },


  {
    XsmNturnDelay, XsmCTurnDelay, XmRInt, sizeof(int),
    XtOffset(XsmKnobGadget, knobg.turn_delay),
    XmRImmediate, (XtPointer) 50
  },


  {
    XsmNknobColor, XsmCKnobColor, XmRPixel, sizeof (Pixel),
    XtOffset (XsmKnobGadget, knobg.knob_color),
    XmRCallProc, (XtPointer) _XmBackgroundColorDefault
  },


  {
    XsmNindicatorColor, XsmCIndicatorColor, XmRPixel,
    sizeof (Pixel),
    XtOffset (XsmKnobGadget, knobg.indicator_color),
    XmRCallProc, (XtPointer) _XmForegroundColorDefault
  },


  {
    XsmNmarginWidth, XmCMarginWidth, XmRHorizontalDimension,
    sizeof (Dimension),
    XtOffset (XsmKnobGadget, knobg.margin_width),
    XmRImmediate, (XtPointer) DEFAULT_KNOB_MARGIN
  },


  {
    XsmNmarginHeight, XmCMarginHeight, XmRVerticalDimension,
    sizeof (Dimension),
    XtOffset (XsmKnobGadget, knobg.margin_height),
```

```c
                XmRImmediate, (XtPointer) DEFAULT_KNOB_MARGIN
        },


        {

          XsmNknobMargin, XsmCKnobMargin, XmRDimension,
          sizeof (Dimension),
          XtOffset (XsmKnobGadget, knobg.knob_margin),
          XmRImmediate, (XtPointer) DEFAULT_KNOB_MARGIN_PERCENTAGE
        },
};


/* Synthetic resource list initialization - sets up resource
 * procedures to get called when setting or getting the various
 * resources.  These synthetic resources are used in resolution
 * independence.
 */
static XmSyntheticResource syn_resources[] = {
        {
          XsmNmarginWidth,
          sizeof (Dimension),
          XtOffset( XsmKnobGadget, knobg.margin_width),
          _XmFromHorizontalPixels,
          _XmToHorizontalPixels
        },


        {

          XsmNmarginHeight,
          sizeof (Dimension),
          XtOffset( XsmKnobGadget, knobg.margin_height),
          _XmFromVerticalPixels,
          _XmToVerticalPixels
        }
};
```

```c
    /* Widget class record initialization - Here we initialize each
     * field of the rectobj, gadget, and knob class parts.
     */
    externaldef (xsmknobgadgetclassrec)
            XsmKnobGadgetClassRec xsmKnobGadgetClassRec = {
      {
            /* RectObj Class Rec    */
        (WidgetClass) &xmGadgetClassRec,  /* superclass            */
        "XsmKnobGadget",                  /* class_name            */
        sizeof(XsmKnobGadgetRec),         /* widget_size           */
        NULL,                             /* class_initialize      */
        ClassPartInitialize,               /* class_part_initialize */
        FALSE,                            /* class_inited          */
        Initialize,                       /* initialize            */
        NULL,                             /* initialize_hook       */
        NULL,                             /* realize               */
        NULL,                             /* actions               */
        0,                                /* num_actions           */
        resources,                        /* resources             */
        XtNumber(resources),              /* num_resources         */
        NULLQUARK,                        /* xrm_class             */
        TRUE,                             /* compress_motion       */
        XtExposeCompressMaximal,          /* compress_exposure     */
        TRUE,                             /* compress_enterleave   */
        FALSE,                            /* visible_interest      */
        Destroy,                          /* destroy               */
        Resize,                           /* resize                */
        Redisplay,                        /* expose                */
        SetValues,                        /* set_values            */
        NULL,                             /* set_values_hook       */
        SetValuesAlmost,                  /* set_values_almost     */
        NULL,                             /* get_values_hook       */
```

```c
        NULL,                                   /* accept_focus          */
        XtVersion,                              /* version               */
        NULL,                                   /* callback_private      */
        NULL,                                   /* tm_table              */
        QueryGeometry,                          /* query_geometry        */
        NULL,                                   /* display accel         */
        NULL,                                   /* extension             */
    },


    {                                           /* Gadget Class Rec      */
        HighlightKnob,                          /* border_highlight      */
        UnhighlightKnob,                        /* border_unhighlight    */
        ArmAndActivate,                         /* arm_and_activate      */
        InputDispatch,                          /* input dispatch        */
        VisualChange,                           /* visual_change         */
        syn_resources,                          /* syn resources         */
        XtNumber(syn_resources),                /* num syn_resources     */
        NULL,                                   /* class cache part      */
        NULL,                                   /* extension             */
    },


    {                       /* Knob Gadget Class Rec */
        GetDiameters,                           /* get_diameters         */
        CreateSegments,                         /* create_segments       */
        DrawIndicator,                          /* draw_indicator        */
        TurnKnob,                               /* turn                  */
        DrawKnob,                               /* draw                  */
        NULL,                                   /* extension             */
    }
};


externaldef(xsmknobwidgetclass) WidgetClass xsmKnobGadgetClass =
    (WidgetClass) &xsmKnobGadgetClassRec;
```

```c
/******************************************************************
 * Class Functions
 *
 ******************************************************************/



/******************************************************************
 *
 * ClassPartInitialize() -
 * The initialization routine for class parts.  It is called for
 * the initialization of this class and each time a new subclass is
 * created for this widget class.  It is called only once per
 * subclass.
 *
 ******************************************************************/
static void ClassPartInitialize(WidgetClass wc)
{
    XsmKnobGadgetClass kc = (XsmKnobGadgetClass) wc;
    XsmKnobGadgetClass sc = (XsmKnobGadgetClass)
                            wc->core_class.superclass;

  /* Assign procedures to the classes pointers that inherit these
     procedures */

    if (kc->knobg_class.get_diameters == XsmInheritGetDiameters)
       kc->knobg_class.get_diameters =
                            sc->knobg_class.get_diameters;

    if (kc->knobg_class.create_segments ==
                            XsmInheritCreateSegments)
       kc->knobg_class.create_segments =
            sc->knobg_class.create_segments;
```

```c
    if (kc->knobg_class.draw_indicator == XsmInheritDrawIndicator)
        kc->knobg_class.draw_indicator =
            sc->knobg_class.draw_indicator;


    if (kc->knobg_class.turn == XsmInheritTurn)
        kc->knobg_class.turn = sc->knobg_class.turn;


    if (kc->knobg_class.draw == XsmInheritDraw)
        kc->knobg_class.draw = sc->knobg_class.draw;


}



/****************************************************************************
 *
 * Initialize() -
 * The main widget instance initialization routine.  Verify
 * resource values and initialize widget instance fields.
 *

 ***************************************************************************/

static void Initialize( Widget request, Widget new_w, ArgList args,
                        Cardinal *num_args )
{
    XsmKnobGadget req_kg = (XsmKnobGadget) request;
    XsmKnobGadget new_kg = (XsmKnobGadget) new_w;
    XsmKnobGadgetClass kc = (XsmKnobGadgetClass) XtClass(new_w);
    XmManagerWidget mw = (XmManagerWidget) XtParent(new_w);
    Dimension min_width, min_height;
    XGCValues values;
    unsigned long valuemask;


/* Verify resource values */
```

```c
    /* Verify that the maximum value is not less than or equal
       to zero */
      if (new_kg->knobg.max_val <= 0) {
        XtWarning("MaxValue is must be greater than 0, Defaulting
                  MaxValue to 1");
        new_kg->knobg.max_val = 1;
      }


    /*
     * Verify that the maximum value is not less than the minimum
       value
     */
      if (new_kg->knobg.max_val < new_kg->knobg.min_val) {
        XtWarning("MaxValue is less than the MinValue, Defaulting
                  to 0");
        new_kg->knobg.min_val = 0;
      }


    /* Verify that the value is not greater than the maximum value */
      if (new_kg->knobg.value > new_kg->knobg.max_val) {
        XtWarning("Value is greater than MaxValue, Defaulting to
                  MaxValue");
        new_kg->knobg.value = new_kg->knobg.max_val;
      }


    /* Verify that the value is not less than the minimum value */
      if (new_kg->knobg.value < new_kg->knobg.min_val) {
        XtWarning("Value is less than MinValue, Defaulting to
                  MinValue");
        new_kg->knobg.value = new_kg->knobg.min_val;
      }


    /* Verify that turn delay is not less than 1 */
      if (new_kg->knobg.turn_delay < 1) {
```

```c
        XtWarning("Turn Delay is less than 1, Defaulting to 1");
        new_kg->knobg.turn_delay = 1;
    }


    /*
     * Knob margin is a percentage of the total knob,
     * thus it must be between 0 and 100.  Because this resource is
     * typed as a dimension (unsigned short), a negative value
     * becomes a large positive, thus this also checks for < 0.
     */

    if (new_kg->knobg.knob_margin > 100)
    {
        XtWarning("Knob Margin must be between 0 and 100");
        new_kg->knobg.knob_margin = DEFAULT_KNOB_MARGIN_PERCENTAGE;
    }



    /*
     * Initialize the minimum required dimensions for the knob
     */

    min_width = MIN_KNOB_DIAMETER + (2 *
                (new_kg->knobg.margin_width
                + new_kg->gadget.highlight_thickness));
    min_height = MIN_KNOB_DIAMETER + (2 *
                (new_kg->knobg.margin_width
                + new_kg->gadget.highlight_thickness));

    /*
     * If an initial width and height weren't set, initialize
     * a default dimensions; otherwise, verify that the dimensions
     * that were set are at least the minimum dimension.
     */
```

```c
    if (req_kg->rectangle.width == 0)
        new_kg->rectangle.width = DEFAULT_DIAMETER +
                            (2 * (new_kg->knobg.margin_width +
                                new_kg->gadget.highlight_thickness));
    else
        if (new_kg->rectangle.width < min_width)
            new_kg->rectangle.width = min_width;


    if (req_kg->rectangle.height == 0)
        new_kg->rectangle.height = DEFAULT_DIAMETER +
                                (2 * (new_kg->knobg.margin_height +
                                new_kg->gadget.highlight_thickness));
    else
        if (new_kg->rectangle.height < min_width)
            new_kg->rectangle.height = min_height;




    /* Save original calculated width and height for use in query
       geometry */
        new_kg->knobg.orig_width = new_kg->rectangle.width;
        new_kg->knobg.orig_height = new_kg->rectangle.height;

    /* Initialize internal variables */

new_kg->knobg.num_segments = NUM_SEGS;
new_kg->knobg.segments = (XSegment *) XtMalloc(sizeof(XSegment) *
                            new_kg->knobg.num_segments + 1));

    new_kg->knobg.move_clockwise = True;
    new_kg->knobg.turning = False;
    new_kg->knobg.timer_id = NULL;
    new_kg->knobg.angle_offset = 0;
```

```c
    /* Create initial segments */

    (*kc->knobg_class.create_segments)(new_w);


    /* Set up graphic context for use in drawing the knob */

    valuemask = (GCForeground | GCBackground);
    values.foreground = mw->manager.foreground;
    values.background = new_kg->knobg.knob_color;
    new_kg->knobg.gc = XtGetGC((Widget)mw, valuemask, &values);


    /*  Initialize the interesting input types.  */

    new_kg->gadget.event_mask = XmARM_EVENT | XmACTIVATE_EVENT |
                        XmFOCUS_IN_EVENT | XmFOCUS_OUT_EVENT |
                        XmENTER_EVENT | XmLEAVE_EVENT |
                        XmKEY_EVENT;
}


/****************************************************************
 *
 *  Destroy() -
 *  Clean up allocated resources when the widget is destroyed.
 *  Free any allocated data.
 *
 ****************************************************************/
static void Destroy( Widget w )
{
    XsmKnobGadget kg = (XsmKnobGadget) w;

    /* Free graphics contexts */
    XtReleaseGC( w, kg->knobg.gc);
```

```c
    /* Free allocated data */
    XtFree((char *) kg->knobg.segments);


    /* Remove any outstanding timeouts */
    if (kg->knobg.timer_id) XtRemoveTimeOut(kg->knobg.timer_id);


    /* Remove all callbacks */
    XtRemoveAllCallbacks (w, XsmNvalueChangedCallback);
}


/**************************************************************/
 *
 *  Resize() -
 *        Redraw according to when size changes.
 *
 **************************************************************/
static void Resize( Widget w )
{
    XsmKnobGadgetClass kc = (XsmKnobGadgetClass) XtClass(w);


    /* Recreate any segments based on the new size */
    (*kc->knobg_class.create_segments)(w);
}


/**************************************************************/
 *
 *  Redisplay() -
 *  Redraw region that go exposed.  Simple and less efficient
 *  expose routines simply redraw the whole widget.  This is an
 *  example of a simple expose routine.
 *
 **************************************************************/
static void Redisplay( Widget w, XEvent *event, Region region)
{
```

```c
    XsmKnobGadget kg = (XsmKnobGadget) w;
    XsmKnobGadgetClass kc = (XsmKnobGadgetClass) XtClass(w);


    /* Use the class pointer to redraw the whole knob */
    (*kc->knobg_class.draw)(w);


    /* Use the class pointers to highlight or unhighlight the knob */
    if (kg->gadget.highlighted)
        (*kc->gadget_class.border_highlight)(w);
    else
        (*kc->gadget_class.border_unhighlight)(w);
}




/***************************************************************
 *
 *   SetValues() -
 *   The procedure is used to verify changes to the resource values.
 *   If the resource changes affect the visuals of the widget, the
 *   return value of the procedure should be set to True indicating
 *   that the expose procedure will be called to redraw the widget.
 *   Any changes to the widget's geometry in this procedure will
 *   generate a geometry request to its parent.
 *
 ***************************************************************/
static Boolean SetValues( Widget old_w, Widget request, Widget
                          new_w, ArgList args, Cardinal *num_args )
{
    XsmKnobGadget old_kg = (XsmKnobGadget) old_w;
    XsmKnobGadget new_kg = (XsmKnobGadget) new_w;
    XsmKnobGadgetClass kc = (XsmKnobGadgetClass) XtClass(new_w);
    XmManagerWidget mw = (XmManagerWidget) XtParent(new_w);
```

```c
    Dimension min_width, min_height;
    Boolean redisplay = False; /* flag to determine return value */


    /* Verify changes in resource settings */


    /* Verify that the maximum value is not less than or equal to
       zero */
    if (new_kg->knobg.max_val <= 0) {
        XtWarning("MaxValue is must be greater than 0, MaxValue set
                   to 1");
        new_kg->knobg.max_val = 1;
    }


    /*
     * Verify that the minimum value is not greater or equal to
     * the maximum value
     */
    if (new_kg->knobg.min_val >= new_kg->knobg.max_val) {
        XtWarning("MinValue is greater than or equal to MaxValue,
                   MinValue set to 0");
        new_kg->knobg.min_val = 0;
    }


    /* Verify that the value is not greater than the maximum value */
    if ((new_kg->knobg.max_val != old_kg->knobg.max_val ||
         new_kg->knobg.value != old_kg->knobg.value) &&
         new_kg->knobg.value > new_kg->knobg.max_val) {
        XtWarning("Value is greater than MaxValue, Changing Value to
                   MaxValue");
        new_kg->knobg.value = new_kg->knobg.max_val;
        redisplay = True;
    }


    /* Verify that the value is not less than the minimum value */
```

```c
        if ((new_kg->knobg.min_val != old_kg->knobg.min_val ||
            new_kg->knobg.value != old_kg->knobg.value) &&
            new_kg->knobg.value < new_kg->knobg.min_val) {
        XtWarning("Value is less than MinValue, Changing Value to
                MinValue");
        new_kg->knobg.value = new_kg->knobg.min_val;
        redisplay = True;

    }


/* Verify that turn rate is not less than 1 */
    if (new_kg->knobg.turn_delay < 1) {
        XtWarning("Turn Delay is less than 1, Defaulting to 1");
        new_kg->knobg.turn_delay = 1;

    }


    /*
     * Knob margin is a percentage of the total knob,
     * thus it must be between 0 and 100.  Because this resource is
     * typed as a dimension (unsigned short), a negative value
     * becomes a large positive, thus this also checks for < 0.
     */
    if (new_kg->knobg.knob_margin > 100)
    {
        XtWarning("Knob Margin must be between 0 and 100");
        new_kg->knobg.knob_margin = old_kg->knobg.knob_margin;
    }



/* Don't allow a zero size to set */
    if (new_kg->rectangle.width == 0)
        new_kg->rectangle.width = old_kg->rectangle.width;
    if (new_kg->rectangle.height == 0)
        new_kg->rectangle.height = old_kg->rectangle.height;
```

```c
    /* If the color resources change, the graphic context needs to be
        updated */
    if (new_kg->knobg.knob_color != old_kg->knobg.knob_color) {
        XGCValues values;
        unsigned long valuemask;

        valuemask = (GCBackground );
        values.background = new_kg->knobg.knob_color;
        XtReleaseGC((Widget)mw, new_kg->knobg.gc);
        new_kg->knobg.gc = XtGetGC((Widget)mw, valuemask, &values);
        redisplay = True;
    }


    min_width = MIN_KNOB_DIAMETER +
                (2 * (new_kg->knobg.margin_width +
                 new_kg->gadget.highlight_thickness));
    min_height = MIN_KNOB_DIAMETER +
                (2 * (new_kg->knobg.margin_width +
                  new_kg->gadget.highlight_thickness));

/* Try to retain a minimum height and width */

    if (new_kg->rectangle.width < min_width)
    {
        new_kg->rectangle.width = min_width;
        redisplay = True;
    }

    if (new_kg->rectangle.height < min_height)
    {
        new_kg->rectangle.height = min_height;
        redisplay = True;
    }
```

```
        /*
         * If any of the following resource values changed, the knob
         * segments need to be recomputed and the knob need to be
         * redisplayed.
         */
        if (new_kg->knobg.margin_height != old_kg->knobg.margin_height ||
            new_kg->knobg.margin_width != old_kg->knobg.margin_width ||
            new_kg->knobg.knob_margin != old_kg->knobg.knob_margin ||
            new_kg->knobg.max_val != old_kg->knobg.max_val ||
            new_kg->knobg.min_val != old_kg->knobg.min_val ||
            new_kg->rectangle.height != old_kg->rectangle.height ||
            new_kg->rectangle.width != old_kg->rectangle.width ||
            new_kg->gadget.highlight_thickness !=
            old_kg->gadget.highlight_thickness) {

            (*kc->knobg_class.create_segments)(new_w);
            redisplay = True;
        }


    /*  Initialize the interesting input types.  */

    new_kg->gadget.event_mask = XmARM_EVENT | XmACTIVATE_EVENT |
                            XmFOCUS_IN_EVENT | XmFOCUS_OUT_EVENT |
                            XmENTER_EVENT | XmLEAVE_EVENT |
XmKEY_EVENT;
    return(redisplay);
}


/****************************************************************
 *
 *  SetValuesAlmost() -
 *  The procedure is used to negotiate a geometry with the parent
 *  if the change in geometry in the SetValues Procedure failed.
```

```c
 *   Setting the reply->request_mode to zero ends the negotiations.
 *
 ***********************************************************************/
static void SetValuesAlmost( Widget old_w, Widget new_w,
                             XtWidgetGeometry *request,
XtWidgetGeometry *reply)
{
    XsmKnobGadget new_kg = (XsmKnobGadget) new_w;
    XsmKnobGadget old_kg = (XsmKnobGadget) old_w;
    Dimension min_width, min_height;

/* If the request failed completely, reset old values and return */
    if (reply->request_mode == 0)
    {
        new_kg->knobg.margin_width = old_kg->knobg.margin_width;
        new_kg->knobg.margin_height = old_kg->knobg.margin_height;
        request->request_mode = 0;
        return;
    }


    /* All attempts to accommodate size failed */
    if (new_kg->knobg.margin_width == 0 ||
        new_kg->knobg.margin_height == 0)
    {
        request->request_mode = 0;
        return;
    }


    min_width = MIN_KNOB_DIAMETER +
                (2 * (new_kg->knobg.margin_width +
                 new_kg->gadget.highlight_thickness));
    min_height = MIN_KNOB_DIAMETER +
                (2 * (new_kg->knobg.margin_width +
                 new_kg->gadget.highlight_thickness));
```

```c
    /* Reduce margin to accommodate smaller size */
    if ( reply->width < min_width )
    {
        new_kg->knobg.margin_width--;
        min_width -= 2; /* minus one pixel on each side of knob */
        request->width = min_width;
    }
    else /* accept larger size */
    {
        request->width = reply->width;
    }


    /* Reduce margin to accommodate smaller size */
    if (reply->height < min_height)
    {
        new_kg->knobg.margin_height--;
        min_height -= 2; /* minus one pixel on each side of knob */
        request->height = min_height;
    }
    else /* accept larger size */
    {
        request->width = reply->width;
    }
}


/*****************************************************************************
 * QueryGeometry()
 * The procedure is used to negotiate a geometry with the parent
 * when the parent is requesting a preferred size of the child.
 * If the values in the request don't match the values in the
 * reply, we need to return either XtGeometryNo or
 * XtGeoemtryAlmost.  Use XtGeoemtryNo if the values in the request
 * match the current values.
```

```c
 * Note: This procedure is only interested in height and width
 * values. It will accept any changes to x, y, border width, and
 * stacking order.
 *
 *******************************************************************

static XtGeometryResult QueryGeometry( Widget w,
                                       XtWidgetGeometry *request,
                                       XtWidgetGeometry *reply)
{
    XsmKnobGadget kg = (XsmKnobGadget) w;

    reply->width = kg->knobg.orig_width;
    reply->height = kg->knobg.orig_height;
    reply->request_mode = CWWidth | CWHeight;

    /* Return XtGeometryYes if the request matches the reply width
       and height. */
    if (((request->request_mode & CWWidth) && request->width ==
            reply->width) && ((request->request_mode & CWHeight) &&
        request->height == reply->height))
            return XtGeometryYes;

    /* Return XtGeometryNo if reply matches our current width and
       height. */
    if (reply->width == kg->rectangle.width && reply->height ==
        kg->rectangle.height)
            return XtGeometryNo;

    /* Return XtGeometryAlmost if one of the reply fields doesn't
     * match the current or request width or height.
     */
    return XtGeometryAlmost;
}
```

```c
/******************************************************************
 *
 * HighlightKnob
 * This is a gadget class procedure for drawing a highlight around
 * the knobg.  Knob needs a customized one to draw a circular
 * highlight.
 *
 ******************************************************************/
static void HighlightKnob( Widget w )
{
    XsmKnobGadget kg = (XsmKnobGadget) w;
    XsmKnobGadgetClass kc = (XsmKnobGadgetClass) XtClass(w);
    XmManagerWidget mw = (XmManagerWidget) XtParent(w);
    unsigned int outer_diameter, inner_diameter, diameter;
    XGCValues values;
    unsigned long valuemask;

    /* Get the diameter */
     (*kc->knobg_class.get_diameters)(w, &outer_diameter,
                                      &inner_diameter);

    diameter = outer_diameter + (2 * kg->gadget.highlight_thickness);

    /* Draw the highlight */
    XDrawArc(XtDisplay(kg), XtWindow(kg), mw->manager.highlight_GC,
            kg->rectangle.x + kg->knobg.margin_width,
            kg->rectangle.y + kg->knobg.margin_height, diameter,
            diameter, 0, 64*360);

    /* Set flags to indicate that the highlight has been drawn */
    kg->gadget.highlighted = True;
    kg->gadget.highlight_drawn = True;
```

```c
   /* Change the graphic context back for drawing the knob */
   valuemask = (GCLineWidth | GCForeground);
   values.foreground = kg->knobg.knob_color;
   values.line_width = 0;
   XChangeGC(XtDisplay(kg), kg->knobg.gc, valuemask, &values);
}


/******************************************************************
 *
 * UnhighlightKnob
 * The is a gadget class procedure for erasing a highlight around
 * the knobg.  Knob needs a customized one to erase a circular
 * highlight.
 *
 ******************************************************************/
static void UnhighlightKnob( Widget w )
{
   XsmKnobGadget kg = (XsmKnobGadget) w;
   XsmKnobGadgetClass kc = (XsmKnobGadgetClass) XtClass(w);
   unsigned int outer_diameter, inner_diameter, diameter;
   XmManagerWidget mw = (XmManagerWidget) XtParent(w);
   XGCValues values;
   unsigned long valuemask;

   /* Get the diameter */
   (*kc->knobg_class.get_diameters)(w, &outer_diameter,
                                       &inner_diameter);


diameter = outer_diameter + (2 * kg->gadget.highlight_thickness);

   /* Change the graphic context to unhighlight */
   valuemask = (GCLineWidth | GCForeground);
   values.foreground = mw->core.background_pixel;
   values.line_width = kg->gadget.highlight_thickness;
```

```c
    XChangeGC(XtDisplay(kg), kg->knobg.gc, valuemask, &values);


  /* Erase the highlight */
  XDrawArc(XtDisplay(kg), XtWindow(kg), kg->knobg.gc,
            kg->rectangle.x + kg->knobg.margin_width,
            kg->rectangle.y + kg->knobg.margin_height,
            diameter, diameter, 0, 64*360);


  kg->gadget.highlighted = False;
  kg->gadget.highlight_drawn = False;


  /* Change the graphic context back for drawing the knob */
  values.foreground = kg->knobg.knob_color;
  values.line_width = 0;
  XChangeGC(XtDisplay(kg), kg->knobg.gc, valuemask, &values);


}


/*****************************************************************
 *
 *      ArmAndActivate
 *
 ******************************************************************/
static void
ArmAndActivate( Widget wid, XEvent *event, String *params,
                Cardinal *num_params )
{
      ToggleKnob(wid, event, NULL, NULL);
}


/******************************************************************
 *
 *   InputDispatch
 * This function catches input sent by a manager and dispatches it
```

```c
 * to the individual routines.
 *
 **************************************************************************/
static void
InputDispatch(
        Widget wid,
        XEvent *event,
        Mask event_mask )
{
    XsmKnobGadget kg = (XsmKnobGadget) wid;
    XsmKnobGadgetClass kc = (XsmKnobGadgetClass) XtClass(wid);

    if (event_mask & XmARM_EVENT)
        StartKnobTurn(wid, event, NULL, NULL);
    else if (event_mask & XmACTIVATE_EVENT)
        ReleaseKnob(wid, event, NULL, NULL);
    else if (event_mask & XmKEY_EVENT)
        HandleKey(wid, event, NULL, NULL);
    else if (event_mask & XmENTER_EVENT)
        _XmEnterGadget ((Widget) kg, event, NULL, NULL);
    else if (event_mask & XmLEAVE_EVENT)
        _XmLeaveGadget ((Widget) kg, event, NULL, NULL);
    else if (event_mask & XmFOCUS_IN_EVENT)
        _XmFocusInGadget( (Widget) kg, event, NULL, NULL);
    else if (event_mask & XmFOCUS_OUT_EVENT)
        _XmFocusOutGadget( (Widget) kg, event, NULL, NULL);
}


/**************************************************************************
 *
 * VisualChange
 * This function is called from XmManagerClass set values when
 * the managers visuals have changed.  The gadget regenerates any
 * GC based on the visual changes and returns True indicating a
```

```
 * redraw is needed.  Otherwise, False is returned.
 *
 ********************************************************************/
static Boolean
VisualChange(
        Widget wid,
        Widget cmw,
        Widget nmw )
{
    XsmKnobGadget kg = (XsmKnobGadget) wid ;
    XmManagerWidget curmw = (XmManagerWidget) cmw ;
    XmManagerWidget newmw = (XmManagerWidget) nmw ;

    if (curmw->manager.foreground != newmw->manager.foreground)
    {
        XSetForeground(XtDisplay(kg), kg->knobg.gc,
                       newmw->manager.foreground);
        return (True);
    }

    if (curmw->manager.highlight_color !=
        newmw->manager.highlight_color ||
        curmw->core.background_pixel !=
        newmw->core.background_pixel ||
        curmw->manager.highlight_pixmap !=
        newmw->manager.highlight_pixmap)
            return (True);

    return (False);
}
```

```c
/******************************************************************
 *
 * GetDiameters
 * This knob class method is used to determine the inner and outer
 * diameter of the knobg. The knob draws 3 circles. The outermost
 * circle is for highlighting. The next circle is for drawing the
 * outer edge of the knobg.  The margin_width or the margin_height
 * determine the outer edge of the circle.  The knob_margin
 * determines the innermost circle (being a percentage of the knob
 * itself).
 *
 ******************************************************************/
static void GetDiameters( Widget w, unsigned int *diameter,
                          unsigned int *inner_diameter)
{
    XsmKnobGadget kg = (XsmKnobGadget) w;

    if (kg->rectangle.height - (2 * kg->knobg.margin_width) >=
        kg->rectangle.width - (2 * kg->knobg.margin_height))
        *diameter = kg->rectangle.width - (2 *
        (kg->knobg.margin_width +

kg->gadget.highlight_thickness));
    else
        *diameter = kg->rectangle.height -
                    (2 * (kg->knobg.margin_height +
                    kg->gadget.highlight_thickness));

    if (*diameter < MIN_KNOB_DIAMETER)
        *diameter = MIN_KNOB_DIAMETER;

    *inner_diameter = (*diameter * kg->knobg.knob_margin)/100;

    if (*inner_diameter < 1) *inner_diameter = 1;
```

```c
}

/****************************************************************
 *
 * CreateSegments
 *   This knob class procedure is used to create the line segments
 *   used in drawing the knobg.
 *
 ****************************************************************/
static void CreateSegments( Widget w )
{
    XsmKnobGadget        kg = (XsmKnobGadget) w;
    XsmKnobGadgetClass kc = (XsmKnobGadgetClass) XtClass(w);
    unsigned int        diameter, inner_diameter;
    unsigned int        radius, inner_radius;
    double              angle, cosine, sine, angle_change;
    Position            center_x, center_y;
    int                 i;
    XSegment            *ptr;

    ptr = kg->knobg.segments;

    angle_change = RADIANS(MAX_ANGLE) /
            (float)(kg->knobg.num_segments - 1);
    (*kc->knobg_class.get_diameters)(w, &diameter,
                                &inner_diameter);

    angle = kg->knobg.angle_offset;

    center_x = kg->rectangle.x + (diameter >> 1) +
            kg->knobg.margin_width +
            kg->gadget.highlight_thickness;
    center_y = kg->rectangle.y + (diameter >> 1) +
            kg->knobg.margin_height +
```

```c
                      kg->gadget.highlight_thickness;

    radius = ((diameter >> 1) * 80)/100;


    if (inner_diameter > 2)
        inner_radius = ((inner_diameter >> 1) * 110)/100;
    else
        inner_radius = 1;


    for (i = 0; i < kg->knobg.num_segments; i++) {
        cosine = cos(angle);
        sine   = sin(angle);
        ptr->x1   = (short)(center_x + radius * sine);
        ptr->y1 = (short)(center_y - radius * cosine);
        ptr->x2   = (short)(center_x + inner_radius * sine);
        ptr++->y2 = (short)(center_y - inner_radius * cosine);
        angle += angle_change;
    }
}


/*****************************************************************
 *
 * DrawIndicator
 * This knob class procedure is used to draw the indicator portion
 * of the knobg.
 *
 *****************************************************************/
static void DrawIndicator( Widget w )
{
    XsmKnobGadget kg = (XsmKnobGadget) w;
    XsmKnobGadgetClass kc = (XsmKnobGadgetClass) XtClass(w);
    unsigned int diameter, inner_diameter;
    unsigned int radius;
    double angle;
```

```c
    Position center_x, center_y;


    (*kc->knobg_class.get_diameters)(w, &diameter, &inner_diameter);


    angle = (RADIANS(MAX_ANGLE) * kg->knobg.value)/
                (kg->knobg.max_val - kg->knobg.min_val) ;


    center_x = kg->rectangle.x + (diameter >> 1) +
                kg->knobg.margin_width +
                kg->gadget.highlight_thickness;
    center_y = kg->rectangle.y + (diameter >> 1) +
                kg->knobg.margin_height +
                kg->gadget.highlight_thickness;


    radius = ((diameter >> 1) * 93)/100;


    diameter = (diameter * 5)/100;
    if (diameter == 0) diameter = 1;


    center_x += (Position)(radius * sin(angle)) - (diameter >> 1);
    center_y -= (Position)(radius * cos(angle)) + (diameter >> 1);



    XDrawArc(XtDisplay(w), XtWindow(w), kg->knobg.gc,
                center_x, center_y, diameter, diameter, 0, 64*360);


    XFillArc(XtDisplay(w), XtWindow(w), kg->knobg.gc,
                center_x, center_y, diameter, diameter, 0, 64*360);


}


/*****************************************************************
 *
 * TurnKnob
```

```c
 * This knob class procedure is used in the timeout procedures
 * to show the knob turning.
 *
 ****************************************************************/
static void TurnKnob( XtPointer closure, XtIntervalId *id )
{
    Widget                    w = (Widget) closure;
    XsmKnobGadget             kg = (XsmKnobGadget) w;
    XsmKnobGadgetClass        kc = (XsmKnobGadgetClass) XtClass(w);
    XmManagerWidget           mw = (XmManagerWidget) XtParent(w);
    XsmKnobGadgetCallbackStruct cb;

    if ((kg->knobg.value < kg->knobg.max_val - 1 &&
          kg->knobg.move_clockwise) ||
        (kg->knobg.value > 1 && !kg->knobg.move_clockwise)) {
            kg->knobg.timer_id =
                XtAppAddTimeOut(XtWidgetToApplicationContext(w),
                                (unsigned long) kg->knobg.turn_delay,
                                kc->knobg_class.turn, (XtPointer) kg);
    } else {
        kg->knobg.turning = False;
    }

    XSetForeground(XtDisplay(kg), kg->knobg.gc,
                   kg->knobg.knob_color);
    (*kc->knobg_class.draw_indicator)(w);

    XDrawSegments(XtDisplay(w), XtWindow(w), kg->knobg.gc,
                  kg->knobg.segments, kg->knobg.num_segments);

    if (kg->knobg.move_clockwise)
        kg->knobg.value++;
    else
        kg->knobg.value--;
```

```c
    if (kg->knobg.value_changed_callback) {
        cb.reason = XsmCR_VALUE_CHANGED;
        cb.event = NULL;
        cb.value = kg->knobg.value;
        XtCallCallbackList(w, kg->knobg.value_changed_callback,
                           (XtPointer) &cb);
    }


    kg->knobg.angle_offset = (RADIANS(MAX_ANGLE) * kg->knobg.value)/
                             (kg->knobg.max_val - kg->knobg.min_val) ;
    (*kc->knobg_class.create_segments)(w);


    XSetForeground(XtDisplay(kg), kg->knobg.gc,
                   kg->knobg.indicator_color);
    (*kc->knobg_class.draw_indicator)(w);


    XSetForeground(XtDisplay(kg), kg->knobg.gc,
                   mw->manager.foreground);
    XDrawSegments(XtDisplay(w), XtWindow(w), kg->knobg.gc,
                  kg->knobg.segments, kg->knobg.num_segments);


}


/**************************************************************
 *
 * DrawKnob
 * This knob class procedure is used to draw the knobg.
 *
 **************************************************************/
static void DrawKnob( Widget w )
{
    XsmKnobGadget kg = (XsmKnobGadget) w;
    XsmKnobGadgetClass kc = (XsmKnobGadgetClass) XtClass(w);
```


Program Listings

```c
XmManagerWidget mw = (XmManagerWidget) XtParent(w);
unsigned int diameter, inner_diameter, top_knob_start;


(*kc->knobg_class.get_diameters)(w, &diameter, &inner_diameter);


/* Bottom of knob */
XSetForeground(XtDisplay(kg), kg->knobg.gc,
               kg->knobg.knob_color);
XFillArc(XtDisplay(kg), XtWindow(kg), kg->knobg.gc,
        kg->rectangle.x + (kg->knobg.margin_width +
        kg->gadget.highlight_thickness),
        kg->rectangle.y + (kg->knobg.margin_height +
        kg->gadget.highlight_thickness),
        diameter, diameter, 0, 64*360);
XSetForeground(XtDisplay(kg), kg->knobg.gc,
               mw->manager.foreground);


XDrawArc(XtDisplay(kg), XtWindow(kg), kg->knobg.gc,
        kg->rectangle.x + (kg->knobg.margin_width +
        kg->gadget.highlight_thickness),
        kg->rectangle.y + (kg->knobg.margin_height +
        kg->gadget.highlight_thickness),
        diameter, diameter, 0, 64*360);


top_knob_start = (diameter - ((diameter *
                kg->knobg.knob_margin)/100))/2;


/* Top of knob */
XDrawArc(XtDisplay(kg), XtWindow(kg), kg->knobg.gc,
        kg->rectangle.x + (top_knob_start +
        kg->knobg.margin_width +
        kg->gadget.highlight_thickness),
        kg->rectangle.y + (top_knob_start +
        kg->knobg.margin_height +
```

```c
                kg->gadget.highlight_thickness),

           inner_diameter, inner_diameter, 0, 64*360);


    XDrawSegments(XtDisplay(w), XtWindow(w), kg->knobg.gc,
             kg->knobg.segments, kg->knobg.num_segments);


    XSetForeground(XtDisplay(kg), kg->knobg.gc,
             kg->knobg.indicator_color);
    (*kc->knobg_class.draw_indicator)(w);
    XSetForeground(XtDisplay(kg), kg->knobg.gc,
             mw->manager.foreground);

}
/******************************************************************
 *
 * Callproc procedures defined to set default settings for
 * resources.
 *
 ******************************************************************/


/******************************************************************
 *
 *   DefaultKnobColor
 *        Get the default knob color from parent's background
 *        if the parent is a manager widget; otherwise, get the
 *        Motif default background color.
 *
 ******************************************************************/
static void
DefaultKnobColor( Widget g, int offset, XrmValue *value )
{
    XmManagerWidget    mw = (XmManagerWidget) XtParent (g);
    static Pixel       pixel;
```

```c
        value->addr = (XtPointer) &pixel;
        value->size = sizeof (Pixel);


        if (XmIsManager((Widget) mw))
            pixel = mw->core.background_pixel;
        else
        {
/* Work around for bug in _XmBackgroundColorDefault callproc */
            XmSetDefaultBackgroundColorSpec(XtScreen(g),
                                            XmDEFAULT_BACKGROUND);

            _XmBackgroundColorDefault (g, offset, value);
        }
}


/******************************************************************
 *
 *   DefaultIndicatorColor
 *   Get the default indicator color from parent's foreground
 *   if the parent is a manager widget; otherwise, get the
 *   Motif default background color.
 ******************************************************************/
static void
DefaultIndicatorColor( Widget g, int offset, XrmValue *value )
{
    XmManagerWidget  mw = (XmManagerWidget) XtParent (g);
    static Pixel      pixel;

    value->addr = (XtPointer) &pixel;
    value->size = sizeof (Pixel);

    if (XmIsManager ((Widget) mw))
        pixel = mw->manager.foreground;
```

```c
    else
        _XmForegroundColorDefault (g, offset, value);
}


/***********************************************************************
 *
 * Functions defined in the action table.
 *
 ***********************************************************************/


/***********************************************************************
 *
 * HandleKey
 *   An action procedure that is called on any key press.
 *   This procedure will toggle the key turning in the direction
 *   of the key pressed, '<' turns left and '>' turns right.
 *
 ***********************************************************************/
static void HandleKey( Widget w, XEvent *event, char **params,
                       Cardinal *num_params )
{
    XsmKnobGadget kg = (XsmKnobGadget) w;
    XKeyEvent * k_event = (XKeyEvent *) event;
    KeySym keysym = XKeycodeToKeysym(XtDisplay(w),
                    k_event->keycode, 1);

    if (keysym == XK_less)
        ToggleLeft( w, event, params, num_params );
    else if (keysym == XK_greater)
        ToggleRight( w, event, params, num_params );
}
```

```c
/******************************************************************
 *
 * ToggleLeft
 *   An action procedure that is called on a key press.
 *   This procedure will add a timeout to start the knob
 *   turning left.
 *
 ******************************************************************/
static void ToggleLeft( Widget w, XEvent *event, char **params,
                        Cardinal *num_params )
{
    XsmKnobGadget kg = (XsmKnobGadget) w;
    XsmKnobGadgetClass kc = (XsmKnobGadgetClass) XtClass(w);

   /* If the knob has not started turning, add the timeout */
    if (!kg->knobg.turning) {
      if (kg->knobg.value > kg->knobg.min_val) {
        kg->knobg.move_clockwise = False;
        kg->knobg.timer_id =
            XtAppAddTimeOut(XtWidgetToApplicationContext(w),
                            (unsigned long) kg->knobg.turn_delay,
                            kc->knobg_class.turn, (XtPointer) w);
        kg->knobg.turning = True;
      }
    } else {
      /*
       * If it is already turning, remove the old timeout and
       * continue turning with a new timeout.
       */
      if (kg->knobg.timer_id) XtRemoveTimeOut(kg->knobg.timer_id);

      /* If it was turning left, continue the turning; otherwise,
         stop. */
```

```c
        if (kg->knobg.move_clockwise) {
            kg->knobg.move_clockwise = False;
            kg->knobg.timer_id =
                XtAppAddTimeOut(XtWidgetToApplicationContext(w),
                                    (unsigned long) kg->knobg.turn_delay,
                                    kc->knobg_class.turn, (XtPointer) w);
        } else {
            kg->knobg.turning = False;
        }
    }
}


/**********************************************************************
 *
 * ToggleRight
 * An action procedure that is called on a key press.
 * This procedure will add a timeout to start the knob turning
 * right.
 *
 **********************************************************************/
static void ToggleRight( Widget w, XEvent *event, char **params,
                         Cardinal *num_params )
{
    XsmKnobGadget kg = (XsmKnobGadget) w;
    XsmKnobGadgetClass kc = (XsmKnobGadgetClass) XtClass(w);

    /* If the knob has not started turning, add the timeout */
    if (!kg->knobg.turning) {
        if (kg->knobg.value < kg->knobg.max_val) {
            kg->knobg.move_clockwise = True;
            kg->knobg.timer_id =
                XtAppAddTimeOut(XtWidgetToApplicationContext(w),
                                    (unsigned long) kg->knobg.turn_delay,
                                    kc->knobg_class.turn, (XtPointer) w);
```

```c
            kg->knobg.turning = True;
        }
    } else {
        /*
         * If it is already turning, remove the old timeout and
         * continue turning with a new timeout.
         */
        if (kg->knobg.timer_id) XtRemoveTimeOut(kg->knobg.timer_id);

        /* If it was turning right, continue the turning; otherwise,
           stop. */
        if (!kg->knobg.move_clockwise) {
            kg->knobg.move_clockwise = True;
            kg->knobg.timer_id =
                    XtAppAddTimeOut(XtWidgetToApplicationContext(w),
                                    (unsigned long) kg->knobg.turn_delay,
                                    kc->knobg_class.turn, (XtPointer) w);
        } else {
            kg->knobg.turning = False;
        }
    }
}


/*****************************************************************
 *
 * ToggleKnob
 *   An action procedure that is called on a spacebar key press.
 *   This procedure will toggle the direction for turning.
 *
 *****************************************************************/
static void ToggleKnob( Widget w, XEvent *event, char **params,
                        Cardinal *num_params )
{
    XsmKnobGadget kg = (XsmKnobGadget) w;
```

```c
        if (kg->knobg.move_clockwise)
            kg->knobg.move_clockwise = False;
        else
            kg->knobg.move_clockwise = True;
}


/*******************************************************************
 *
 * StartKnobTurn
 *  An action procedure that is called on a mouse button press.
 *  This procedure will use a timeout to keep the knob
 *  turning.
 *
 ******************************************************************/
static void StartKnobTurn( Widget w, XEvent *event, char **params,
                    Cardinal *num_params )
{
    XsmKnobGadget kg = (XsmKnobGadget) w;
    XsmKnobGadgetClass kc = (XsmKnobGadgetClass) XtClass(w);

  /*
   * As long as the value has not reached the minimum value,
   * continue turning.
   */
    if (kg->knobg.move_clockwise)
    {
        if (kg->knobg.value < kg->knobg.max_val)
            kg->knobg.timer_id =
                XtAppAddTimeOut(XtWidgetToApplicationContext(w),
                                (unsigned long) kg->knobg.turn_delay,
                                kc->knobg_class.turn, (XtPointer) w);
    }
    else
```

```c
    {
        if (kg->knobg.value > kg->knobg.min_val)
            kg->knobg.timer_id =
                    XtAppAddTimeOut(XtWidgetToApplicationContext(w),
                                    (unsigned long) kg->knobg.turn_delay,
                                    kc->knobg_class.turn, (XtPointer) w);

    }


}


/*****************************************************************
 * ReleaseKnob
 *   An action procedure that is called on a mouse button release.
 *   This procedure will remove a timeout to stop the knob from
 *   turning.
 ****************************************************************/
static void ReleaseKnob( Widget w, XEvent *event, char **params,
                         Cardinal *num_params )
{

    XsmKnobGadget kg = (XsmKnobGadget) w;

    /* Remove the timeout. */
    if (kg->knobg.timer_id) XtRemoveTimeOut(kg->knobg.timer_id);

    kg->knobg.turning = False;
}


/*****************************************************************
 * Public Functions
 ****************************************************************/


/*********************************************************
 * XsmCreatKnobGadget() -
 *   Knob widget creation convenience routine.
```

```c
 *
 ************************************************************/

Widget XsmCreateKnobGadget( Widget parent, char *name,
                            ArgList arglist,
                            Cardinal argcount )
{
    return (XtCreateWidget(name, xsmKnobGadgetClass,
                           parent, arglist, argcount));
}


/*******************************************************************
 * XsmGetKnobValue() -
 *  A function to get the knob value quickly.  If a resource value
 *  needs to be retrieved frequently, it might be a good idea to
 *  have a convenience function like this to avoid costly calls to
 *  XtGetValues().  Too many of these functions can be confusing
 *  to the application developer.
 *******************************************************************/
int XsmGetKnobValue( Widget w )
{
    XsmKnobGadget kg = (XsmKnobGadget) w;

    return(kg->knobg.value);
}


/*******************************************************************
 *
 * XsmSetKnobValue()
 *  A function to set the knob value quickly.  If a resource value
 *  needs to be changed frequently, it might be a good idea to
 *  have a convenience function like this to avoid costly calls to
 *  XtSetValues().  Too many of these functions can be confusing
 *  to the application developer.
```

```c
 *
 **********************************************************************/
void XsmSetKnobValue( Widget w, int value )
{
    XsmKnobGadget kg = (XsmKnobGadget) w;
    XsmKnobGadgetClass kc = (XsmKnobGadgetClass) XtClass(w);
    XmManagerWidget mw = (XmManagerWidget) XtParent(w);


    /* Return if the value doesn't change. */

    if (value == kg->knobg.value) return;


    /* Verify the changed values. */

    if (value > kg->knobg.max_val) {
        XtWarning("Value is less than MaxValue, Defaulting to
                MaxValue");
        kg->knobg.value = kg->knobg.max_val;
    }


    if (value < kg->knobg.min_val) {
        XtWarning("Value is greater than MinValue, Defaulting to
                MinValue");
        kg->knobg.value = kg->knobg.min_val;
    }


    /*
     * If the knob is realized, redraw the knob segments and indicator
     * to indicate the new value.
     */

    if (XtIsRealized(w)) {
      /* Erase old indicator. */
        XSetForeground(XtDisplay(kg), kg->knobg.gc,
```

```c
                    kg->knobg.knob_color);
        (*kc->knobg_class.draw_indicator)(w);
        XDrawSegments(XtDisplay(w), XtWindow(w), kg->knobg.gc,
                      kg->knobg.segments, kg->knobg.num_segments);


        /* Set new value. */
        kg->knobg.value = value;


        /* Recreate segments. */
        kg->knobg.angle_offset = (RADIANS(MAX_ANGLE) *
                                  kg->knobg.value)/
                                 (kg->knobg.max_val -
kg->knobg.min_val);
        (*kc->knobg_class.create_segments)(w);


        /* Redraw indicator. */
        XSetForeground(XtDisplay(kg), kg->knobg.gc,
                       kg->knobg.indicator_color);
        (*kc->knobg_class.draw_indicator)(w);


        /* Redraw segments. */
        XSetForeground(XtDisplay(kg), kg->knobg.gc,
                       mw->manager.foreground);
        XDrawSegments(XtDisplay(w), XtWindow(w), kg->knobg.gc,
                      kg->knobg.segments, kg->knobg.num_segments);
    } else {
        kg->knobg.value = value;
    }


}
```

KnobG.h

KnobG.h is the public header file for the knob gadget described in Chapter 5.

```c
#ifndef _XsmKnobG_h
#define _XsmKnobG_h


/* Always include Xm.h */
#include <Xm/Xm.h>


/* Add extern for C++ applications */
#ifdef __cplusplus
extern "C" {
#endif


/* Resource Names */


#define XsmNvalueChangedCallback    "valueChangedCallback"
#define XsmNindicatorColor          "indicatorColor"
#define XsmNmarginWidth             "marginWidth"
#define XsmNmarginHeight            "marginHeight"
#define XsmNknobMargin              "knobMargin"
#define XsmNknobColor               "knobColor"
#define XsmNmaxValue                "maxValue"
#define XsmNminValue                "minValue"
#define XsmNturnDelay               "turnDelay"
#define XsmNvalue                   "value"


/* Resource Class Names */


#define XsmCValueChangedCallback    "ValueChangedCallback"
#define XsmCIndicatorColor          "IndicatorColor"
#define XsmCMarginWidth             "MarginWidth"
#define XsmCMarginHeight            "MarginHeight"
```

```c
#define XsmCKnobMargin            "KnobMargin"
#define XsmCMaxValue              "MaxValue"
#define XsmCMinValue              "MinValue"
#define XsmCTurnDelay             "TurnDelay"
#define XsmCValue                 "Value"


/* Callback Structs */

typedef struct
{
    int      reason;
    XEvent   *event;
    int value;
} XsmKnobGadgetCallbackStruct;


/* Callback reason for the above callback */

#define XsmCR_VALUE_CHANGED     0

/* Extern the widget class for applications that use
   XtCreateWidget() */

externalref WidgetClass        xsmKnobGadgetClass;

/*
 * To allow applications to use tight type checking, define
 * structures for the widget class and instance pointers
 * specific to this class of widget.
 */

typedef struct _XsmKnobGadgetClassRec *XsmKnobGadgetClass;
typedef struct _XsmKnobGadgetRec       *XsmKnobGadget;


/********     Public Function Declarations     ********/
```

```c
/* Declare the function that can be used by the application
   developer. */

extern Widget XsmCreateKnobGadget(
                    Widget parent,
                    char *name,
                    ArgList arglist,
                    Cardinal argcount) ;
extern int XsmGetKnobGadgetValue(
                    Widget w) ;
extern void XsmSetKnobGadgetValue(
                    Widget w,
                    int value) ;

#ifdef __cplusplus
}/* Close scope of `extern "C"' declaration which encloses file. */
#endif

#endif /* _XsmKnobG_h */
/* DON'T ADD STUFF AFTER THIS #endif */
```

KnobGP.h is the private header file for the knob gadget described in Chapter 5.

```
#ifndef _XsmKnobGP_h
#define _XsmKnobGP_h


/* Include the public header as well as the super class private
   header. */


#include "KnobG.h"
#include <Xm/GadgetP.h>


/*-------------------------------------------------------------------*/
/***********************

 * THE KNOB CLASS RECORD *

 ***********************/


/* Define procedure pointers not defined in the Intrinsics. */

typedef void (*XsmGetDiametersProc)(Widget, unsigned int *,
                                          unsigned int *) ;


/* Define inheritance procedures for all knob class procedures. */


#define XsmInheritGetDiameters ((XsmGetDiametersProc) _XtInherit)
#define XsmInheritCreateSegments ((XtWidgetProc) _XtInherit)
#define XsmInheritDrawIndicator ((XtWidgetProc) _XtInherit)
#define XsmInheritTurn ((XtTimerCallbackProc) _XtInherit)
#define XsmInheritDraw ((XtWidgetProc) _XtInherit)


/*

 * Define class part record.  Be sure to include an extension
   pointer field for future expansion.
```

```c
 */

typedef struct {
  XsmGetDiametersProc get_diameters;    /* procedure to inner and
                                           outer circles */
  XtWidgetProc        create_segments;  /* procedure used to
                                           create handle
                                           segments */
  XtWidgetProc        draw_indicator;   /* procedure for drawing
                                           knob indicator */
  XtTimerCallbackProc turn;             /* timeout procedure used
                                           to turn knob */
  XtWidgetProc        draw;             /* procedure for drawing
                                           the knob */
  XtPointer           extension;        /* pointer to extension
                                           record used for future
                                           expansion */
} XsmKnobGadgetClassPart;

/*
 * Define class record, which includes all super class parts.
 * Start first with Core, then Primitive, and finally the Knob
 * class part defined above.
 */

typedef struct _XsmKnobGadgetClassRec {
    RectObjClassPart       rect_class;
    XmGadgetClassPart      gadget_class;
    XsmKnobGadgetClassPart knobg_class;
} XsmKnobGadgetClassRec;

/*-----------------------------------------------------------------/
/************************
 * THE KNOB INSTANCE RECORD *
```

```
***************************/

/*
 * Define the instance part record.  Be sure to include all the
 * fields to hold resource values as well as fields for internal
 * variables unique to each instance of a knob widget.
 */


typedef struct _XsmKnobGadgetPart {
  XtCallbackList value_changed_callback; /* resource - callback
                                          when value changes */
  int value;                 /* resource - value of the knob */
  int max_val;               /* resource - maximum value allowed */
  int min_val;               /* resource - minimum value allowed */
  int turn_delay;            /* resource - the delay before the next
                                increment */
  Pixel knob_color;          /* resource - the color of the knob */
  Pixel indicator_color;     /* resource - the color of the
                                indicator */
  Dimension margin_width;    /* resource - determines the outer
                                edge of */
  Dimension margin_height;   /* the circle. Whichever value is
                                greater when the dimension is
                                subtracrted from its margin
                                value determines the knob
                                diameter. */
  Dimension knob_margin;     /* resource - The percentage from the
                                knob's outer edge to draw the inner
                                circle. */
  Dimension orig_width;      /* saves the original dimension */
  Dimension orig_height;     /* saves the original dimension */
  Boolean move_clockwise;    /* indicates direction of turn */
  Boolean turning;           /* indicates whether turning is in
                                progress */
```

                                                    Program Listings

```c
    GC gc;                    /* graphics context use in graphic
                                 ops */
    XSegment *segments;       /* the line segments used for drawing
                                 the handle */
    int num_segments;         /* the number of segments in the above
                                 list */
    XtIntervalId timer_id;    /* the timer id of the timeout used in
                                 turning the knob */
    double angle_offset;      /* used to calculate the segment
                                 positions */
} XsmKnobGadgetPart;


/*
 * Define instance record which include all superclass instance
 * parts.  Start first with Core, then Primitive, and finally the
 * Knob instance part defined above.
 */


typedef struct _XsmKnobGadgetRec {
    ObjectPart          object;
    RectObjPart         rectangle;
    XmGadgetPart        gadget;
    XsmKnobGadgetPart   knob;
} XsmKnobGadgetRec;


#endif /* _XsmKnobGP_h */
/* DON't ADD STUFF AFTER THIS #endif */
```

knobGcolors.c


```c
/*  Xm headers  */
#include <Xm/DialogS.h>
#include <Xm/RowColumn.h>
#include <Xm/Frame.h>
#include <Xm/LabelG.h>
#include <Xm/PushBG.h>
#include <Xm/CascadeB.h>
#include <Xm/MessageB.h>
#include <Xm/MainW.h>
#include "KnobG.h"


/* Global defines */
#define CMPSTR(str)  XmStringCreateLtoR (str,

                                    XmSTRING_DEFAULT_CHARSET)


/* Geometry */
#define HORIZONTAL_SPACING          (Dimension) 30
#define VERTICAL_SPACING            5
#define TOP_OFFSET                  (Dimension) 5
#define KNOB_HIGHLIGHT_THICKNESS    (Dimension) 2


#define RED             1
#define GREEN           2
#define BLUE            3
#define ALL_COLORS      4


#define BUFFERSZ        1000


Widget  appshell;
Widget  frame;
Widget  rowcol;
```

```c
    Widget   redLabel;

    Widget   greenLabel;

    Widget   blueLabel;

    Widget   redKnob;

    Widget   greenKnob;

    Widget   blueKnob;

    Widget   redValueLabel;

    Widget   greenValueLabel;

    Widget   blueValueLabel;


    XColor   bg_color;    /* color structure for the background color */
    XColor   fg_color;    /* color structure for the foreground color */
    XColor   ts_color;    /* color structure for the top shadow color */
    XColor   bs_color;    /* color structure for the bottom shadow
                             color */
    XColor   sc_color;    /* color structure for the select color (arm)
                             color */


    XmColorProc calcRGB;


    Display *display;


    Colormap colormap;


    /* Forward Declarations */
    static Widget CreateHelp();

    static void HelpCB();

    static void QuitCB();

    static XtArgVal GetColor();

    static void CreateColorEditor();

    static void changRGB_CB();

    static void SetKnobs();

    static void GenerateColors();
```

```c
Pixel GetPixel();

char *tmpbuf = "#78a0d5";
/*****************************************/
/* Main                                  */
/*****************************************/
void main(argc, argv)
    int argc;
    char **argv;
{
    register int n;
    Arg args[4];
    Widget main_window, menu_bar, menu_pane, cascade;
    Widget button;
    Boolean status;
    unsigned long plane_mask;
    unsigned long *color_cells;
    XtAppContext app_context;

  /* Initialize the toolkit and open the display */
    appshell = XtAppInitialize(&app_context, "Knobcolors", NULL, 0, &argc,
                               argv, NULL, args, 0);


  /* Get the display */
    display = XtDisplay(appshell);


  /* Get the default colormap for this display */
    colormap = XDefaultColormap(display, XDefaultScreen(display));


  /* Allocate 4 color cells for use with this program: background,
     foreground, top shadow, and bottom shadow.  The select color
     won't be used so we don't need to allocate for it. */
    color_cells = (unsigned long *)XtMalloc
```

```c
                                          (4 * sizeof (unsigned long));
    status = XAllocColorCells (display, colormap,
                                    0, &plane_mask, 0, color_cells, 4);


    if(status == False)
    {
        printf(" couldn't allocate enough color cells\n");
        exit(1);
    }
    else
    {
/* Assign the allocated color cells to the correct structure */
        n = 0;
        bg_color.pixel = color_cells[n++];
        bg_color.flags = DoRed | DoGreen | DoBlue;
        fg_color.pixel = color_cells[n++];
        fg_color.flags = DoRed | DoGreen | DoBlue;
        bs_color.pixel = color_cells[n++];
        bs_color.flags = DoRed | DoGreen | DoBlue;
        ts_color.pixel = color_cells[n];
        ts_color.flags = DoRed | DoGreen | DoBlue;
    }


/* Get the RGB value (XColor) of the background */
    XParseColor(display, colormap, tmpbuf, &bg_color);


/* Create main window. */
    main_window = XmCreateMainWindow (appshell, "main1", args, 0);
    XtManageChild (main_window);


/* Create menu bar in main window. */
    menu_bar = XmCreateMenuBar (main_window, "menu_bar", args, 0);
    XtManageChild (menu_bar);
```

```c
    /* Create "Exit" pulldown menu. */
    menu_pane = XmCreatePulldownMenu (menu_bar, "menu_pane", args,
0);


    button = XmCreatePushButtonGadget (menu_pane, "Quit", args, 0);
    XtManageChild (button);
    XtAddCallback (button, XmNactivateCallback, QuitCB, NULL);


    n = 0;
    XtSetArg (args[n], XmNsubMenuId, menu_pane); n++;
    cascade = XmCreateCascadeButton (menu_bar, "Exit", args, n);
    XtManageChild (cascade);

 /* Create "Help" button. */
    cascade = XmCreateCascadeButton (menu_bar, "Help", args, 0);
    XtManageChild (cascade);
    XtAddCallback (cascade, XmNactivateCallback, HelpCB, NULL);


    n = 0;
    XtSetArg (args[n], XmNmenuHelpWidget, cascade); n++;
    XtSetValues (menu_bar, args, n);

 /*
  * Create a frame widget
  */
    n = 0;
    XtSetArg(args[n], XmNmarginWidth, 15); n++;
    XtSetArg(args[n], XmNmarginHeight, 15); n++;
    frame = XmCreateFrame (main_window, "frame", args, n);
    XtManageChild(frame);

 /*  Set main window areas  */
    XmMainWindowSetAreas (main_window, menu_bar, NULL, NULL, NULL,
                          frame);
```

```c
    /* Go generate the foreground, top shadow, and bottom shadow
       colors based on the background color which was set by
       XParseColor above */
    GenerateColors();


   /* Create the sliders with labels using the generated colors */
    CreateColorEditor();


    XtRealizeWidget (appshell);


    XtAppMainLoop (app_context);
}



/*-------------------------------------------------------------
**   HelpCB        - callback for help button
*/
static
void HelpCB (w, client_data, call_data)
Widget      w;              /*  widget id                */
XtPointer   client_data;  /*  data from application    */
XtPointer   call_data;    /*  data from widget class   */
{
    Widget    message_box;  /*  message box              */

  /*  Create help window. */
    message_box = CreateHelp (w);

  /*  Display help window. */
    XtManageChild (message_box);
}
```

```c
/*-----------------------------------------------------------
** CreateHelp   - create help window
*/
static
Widget CreateHelp (parent)
Widget    parent;    /* parent widget  */
{
    Widget         button;
    Widget         message_box;       /* Message Dialog */
    Arg            args[4];           /* arg list       */
    register int   n;                 /* arg count      */

    static char    message[BUFFERSZ];  /* help text      */
    XmString       title_string = NULL;
    XmString       message_string = NULL;
    XmString       button_string = NULL;


  /* Generate message to display. */


    sprintf (message, "\
This program uses three knob widgets to balance colors. The three knob\n\
are used to adjust the primary colors: red, blue, and green.  As the\n\
knob are adjusted, the background color changes accordingly.  To\n\
terminate the program, press the `Exit' button and then the `Quit'\n\
button.\0");


  /* Create the compound strings */
    message_string = CMPSTR (message);
    button_string = CMPSTR ("Close");
```

```c
    title_string = CMPSTR ("knobcolors help");

  /*  Create message box dialog. */
    n = 0;
    XtSetArg (args[n], XmNdialogTitle, title_string);  n++;
    XtSetArg (args[n], XmNokLabelString, button_string);  n++;
    XtSetArg (args[n], XmNmessageString, message_string);  n++;
    message_box = XmCreateMessageDialog (parent, "helpbox",
                                          args, n);

    button = XmMessageBoxGetChild (message_box,
                                     XmDIALOG_CANCEL_BUTTON);
    XtUnmanageChild (button);
    button = XmMessageBoxGetChild (message_box,
                                     XmDIALOG_HELP_BUTTON);
    XtUnmanageChild (button);

  /*  Free strings and return message box. */
    if (title_string) XmStringFree (title_string);
    if (message_string) XmStringFree (message_string);
    if (button_string) XmStringFree (button_string);
    return (message_box);
}



/*------------------------------------------------------------
**   QuitCB      - Callback for quit button
*/
static
void QuitCB (w, client_data, call_data)
Widget     w;            /*  widget id               */
XtPointer  client_data;  /*  data from application   */
XtPointer  call_data;    /*  data from widget class  */
{
```

```c
    /*  Terminate the application. */
    exit (0);

}


/*-----------------------------------------------------------------
**  GetColor       - Function for converting a string into a color
*/
static XtArgVal GetColor(colorstr)
char *colorstr;
{
    XrmValue from, to;

    from.size = strlen(colorstr) +1;
    if (from.size < sizeof(String)) from.size = sizeof(String);
    from.addr = colorstr;
    to.addr = NULL;
    XtConvert(appshell, XmRString, &from, XmRPixel, &to);

    return ((XtArgVal) *((XtArgVal *) to.addr));
}


/*-----------------------------------------------------------------
 * CreateColorEditor  -  Create the rowcol and knob widgets
 */
static void
CreateColorEditor()
{
    register int    n;
    Arg             args[15];
    XmString        string;                 /* temp Xm string */
    WidgetList      children;

  /* Create rowcol widget */
```

```c
n=0;
XtSetArg(args[n], XmNbackground, bg_color.pixel);   n++;
XtSetArg(args[n], XmNforeground, fg_color.pixel);   n++;
XtSetArg(args[n], XmNtopShadowColor, ts_color.pixel);   n++;
XtSetArg(args[n], XmNbottomShadowColor, bs_color.pixel);   n++;
XtSetArg(args[n], XmNentryAlignment, XmALIGNMENT_CENTER); n++;
XtSetArg(args[n], XmNpacking, XmPACK_COLUMN);   n++;
XtSetArg(args[n], XmNorientation, XmHORIZONTAL);   n++;
XtSetArg(args[n], XmNnumColumns, 3);   n++;
rowcol = XmCreateRowColumn(frame,"rowcol", args, n);

XtManageChild (rowcol);

/*
 * Create RGB label gadgets for R, G, B, labels
 */
string =  CMPSTR("R");
n = 0;
XtSetArg(args[n], XmNlabelString, string); n++;
redLabel = XmCreateLabelGadget(rowcol, "redLabel", args, n);
XtManageChild(redLabel);
XmStringFree(string);
string =  CMPSTR("G");
n = 0;
XtSetArg(args[n], XmNlabelString, string); n++;
greenLabel = XmCreateLabelGadget(rowcol, "greenLabel", args, n);
XtManageChild(greenLabel);
XmStringFree(string);

string =  CMPSTR("B");
n = 0;
XtSetArg(args[n], XmNlabelString, string); n++;
blueLabel = XmCreateLabelGadget(rowcol, "blueLabel", args, n);
XtManageChild(blueLabel);
```

```c
    XmStringFree(string);

/*
 * Create the three knob widgets, one each for red, green, and blue
 */
    n = 0;
    XtSetArg(args[n], XsmNmaxValue, 0xff);  n++;
    XtSetArg(args[n], XsmNminValue, 0x0);  n++;
    XtSetArg(args[n], XsmNknobColor, GetColor("red")); n++;
    XtSetArg(args[n], XsmNindicatorColor, GetColor("maroon")); n++;
    redKnob = XsmCreateKnobGadget(rowcol, "redKnob", args, n);
    XtManageChild(redKnob);
    XtAddCallback(redKnob, XsmNvalueChangedCallback, changRGB_CB,
                                              (XtPointer) RED);


    n--; n--;
    XtSetArg(args[n], XsmNknobColor, GetColor("Green")); n++;
    XtSetArg(args[n], XsmNindicatorColor, GetColor("ForestGreen"));
    n++;
    greenKnob = XsmCreateKnobGadget(rowcol, "greenKnob", args, n);
    XtManageChild(greenKnob);
    XtAddCallback(greenKnob, XsmNvalueChangedCallback, changRGB_CB,
                  (XtPointer) GREEN );


    n--; n--;
    XtSetArg(args[n], XsmNknobColor, GetColor("Blue")); n++;
    XtSetArg(args[n], XsmNindicatorColor, GetColor("navy")); n++;
    blueKnob = XsmCreateKnobGadget(rowcol, "blueKnob", args, n);
    XtManageChild(blueKnob);
    XtAddCallback(blueKnob, XsmNvalueChangedCallback, changRGB_CB,
                  (XtPointer) BLUE );


    n = 0;
    redValueLabel = XmCreateLabelGadget(rowcol, "redValueLabel",
```

```c
                              args, n);
        XtManageChild(redValueLabel);


        n = 0;
        greenValueLabel = XmCreateLabelGadget(rowcol, "greenValueLabel",
                              args, n);
        XtManageChild(greenValueLabel);


        n = 0;
        blueValueLabel = XmCreateLabelGadget(rowcol, "blueValueLabel",
                              args, n);
        XtManageChild(blueValueLabel);


     /* Set the knobs to the bg component of the selected color */
        SetKnobs(&bg_color, ALL_COLORS);
    }


/********************************************************************
 *      GenerateColors()
 *         Generates new RGB values for foreground, top shadow,
 *         bottom shadow, and select color based on the background.
 *         Select color is not used in our program, but the Motif color
 *         generation routine expects it and calculates it.
 *         The Colors generated are stored in the red, green, and blue
 *         fields of the XColor structure passed in.
 *         The color generation routine will be exported in Motif1.1.
 *         The generated colors are then used to update the color cells
 *         of the ColorSet being edited.

 ********************************************************************/
static void
GenerateColors()
{
    XColor colors[4];
```

```c
    int j=0;

    /* Get the Motif1.1 color calculation procedure */
    if (calcRGB == NULL)
        calcRGB = XmGetColorCalculation();

    /* Given the background color, calculate the foreground, select
       color,
        top shadow, and bottom shadow colors */
    (*calcRGB)(&bg_color, &fg_color, &sc_color, &ts_color,
                &bs_color);

    /* Put those calculated colors in an array */
    colors[j++] =  bg_color;
    colors[j++] =  fg_color;
    colors[j++] =  ts_color;
    colors[j++] =  bs_color;

    /* Go change the colors dynamically */
    XStoreColors(display, colormap, colors, j);
}


/******************************************************************
 *    changeRGB_CB()
 *        Called when one of the RGB knobs is moved
 ******************************************************************/
static void
changRGB_CB( w, client_data, call_data )
Widget    w;
XtPointer client_data;
XtPointer call_data;
{
    int reason_code;
    int value;
```

```c
    int color;

    reason_code = ((XmAnyCallbackStruct *)call_data)->reason;
    if ( reason_code == XsmCR_VALUE_CHANGED)
    {
        color = (int) client_data;
        value = ((XsmKnobGadgetCallbackStruct *)call_data)->value;

        /*
         * Shift value -- To make up for knob max of only 0xff
         */
        value <<= 8;
        switch (color)
        {
          case RED:
             bg_color.red = value;
             break;
          case GREEN:
             bg_color.green = value;
             break;
          case BLUE:
             bg_color.blue = value;
             break;
          default:
             return;
        }

        SetKnobs(&bg_color, color);
        GenerateColors();
    }
}

static void
SetColors(new_color, color_string, valueLabel, knob_w)
```

```
    int new_color;
char *color_string;
Widget valueLabel;
Widget knob_w;
{
    register int      n;
    Arg               args[15];
    XmString string;

    string =  CMPSTR(color_string);
    XtSetArg(args[0], XmNlabelString, string);
    XtSetValues(valueLabel, args, 1);
    XsmSetKnobValue(knob_w, new_color);
    XmStringFree(string);
}


/****************************************************************
 *    SetKnobs()
 *            Passed an XColor, updates all knobs.
 ****************************************************************/
static void
SetKnobs( rgb, color )
XColor *rgb;
int color;
{
    char* color_string = XtMalloc(sizeof(char)*5);
    int new_color;

    switch (color)
    {
        case RED:
            new_color = rgb->red >> 8;
            sprintf(color_string, "%d", new_color);
            SetColors(new_color, color_string, redValueLabel,
```


Program Listings

```c
                redKnob);
        break;


    case GREEN:
        new_color = rgb->green >> 8;
        sprintf(color_string, "%d", new_color);
        SetColors(new_color, color_string, greenValueLabel,
                greenKnob);
        break;


    case BLUE:
        new_color = rgb->blue >> 8;
        sprintf(color_string, "%d", new_color);
        SetColors(new_color, color_string, blueValueLabel,
                blueKnob);
        break;


    case ALL_COLORS:
        new_color = rgb->red >> 8;
        sprintf(color_string, "%d", new_color);
        SetColors(new_color, color_string, redValueLabel,
                redKnob);
        new_color = rgb->green >> 8;
        sprintf(color_string, "%d", new_color);
        SetColors(new_color, color_string, greenValueLabel,
                greenKnob);
        new_color = rgb->blue >> 8;
        sprintf(color_string, "%d", new_color);
        SetColors(new_color, color_string, blueValueLabel,
                blueKnob);
        break;


    default:
        return;
```

```c
    }

    XtFree(color_string);
}


/*****************************************************************
 *  GetPixel()
 *  Passed in a color string, calls XtConvert, which is an X
 *  toolkit converter that converts a string into a pixel value.
 *****************************************************************/
Pixel
GetPixel( widget, color_string )
Widget widget;
char *color_string;
{
    XrmValue from, to;

  /* Determine the size of the string passed in */
    from.size = strlen(color_string) + 1;
    if (from.size < sizeof(String))
        from.size = sizeof(String);
    from.addr = color_string;

  /* Go convert the string into a pixel (i.e. color cell) */
    XtConvert(widget, XmRString, &from, XmRPixel, &to);

  /* Return that pixel */
    return ((Pixel) *((Pixel *) to.addr));
}
```

Makefile

You can use the Makefile listed below for any of the new widgets and their sample
programs. Again, all the widgets and programs were created on a Hewlett-Packard Model 9000 Series 700 workstation running HP-UX version 9.0, X11R5, and
Motif 1.2. You may have to change some of the variables to reflect your system's
characteristics and paths.

```
TOP = /usr


CURDIR = .


CC = cc
CDEBUGFLAGS = +O1


RM = rm -f


LIBDIR = $(TOP)/lib
INCLUDEDIR = $(TOP)/include


MOTIFLIBDIR = $(LIBDIR)/Motif1.2
TOOLKITLIBDIR = $(LIBDIR)/X11R5
MATHLIB = -lm


LIBS = -L$(MOTIFLIBDIR) -L$(TOOLKITLIBDIR) -lXm -lXt -lX11
$(MATHLIB)


INCLUDES = -I. -I$(INCLUDEDIR)/Motif1.2 -I$(INCLUDEDIR)/X11R5


ANSI_DEFINES = -Aa -D_HPUX_SOURCE


DEFINES = $(ANSI_DEFINES)
CFLAGS = $(CDEBUGFLAGS) $(INCLUDES) $(DEFINES)


OBJS1 = Knob.o
```

```
OBJS2 = KnobG.o
OBJS3 = Grid.o Knob.o

PGM1 = knob1
PGM2 = knobcolors
PGM3 = gadgetcolors
PGM4 = gridcolors

OBJECTS = $(OBJS2) $(OBJS3)
PGMS = $(PGM1) $(PGM2) $(PGM3) $(PGM4)

all: $(PGMS)

.c.o:
$(CC) $(CFLAGS) -c $*.c

clean:
$(RM) *.o $(PGMS) core

sample: sample.o
$(CC) -o $@ $@.o $(LIBS)

knob1: knob1.o $(OBJS1)
$(CC) -o $@ $@.o $(OBJS1) $(LIBS)

knobcolors: knobcolors.o $(OBJS1)
$(CC) -o $@ $@.o $(OBJS1) $(LIBS)

gadgetcolors: gadgetcolors.o $(OBJS2)
$(CC) -o $@ $@.o $(OBJS2) $(LIBS)

gridcolors: gridcolors.o $(OBJS3)
$(CC) -o $@ $@.o $(OBJS3) $(LIBS)
```

```
Knob.o: $(CURDIR)/Knob.h $(CURDIR)/KnobP.h
$(CC) $(CFLAGS) -c Knob.c


Grid.o: $(CURDIR)/Grid.h $(CURDIR)/GridP.h
$(CC) $(CFLAGS) -c Grid.c


KnobG.o: $(CURDIR)/KnobG.h $(CURDIR)/KnobGP.h
$(CC) $(CFLAGS) -c KnobG.c
```

sample.c

This program is a very simple example of a widget program, designed as an introduction or refresher to programming with the Motif widgets. It consists of a pushbutton widget and a label widget contained in a bulletin board widget.

```c
/**-----------------------------------------------------------------
 ***   sample.c
 ***
 ***-------------------------------------------------------------*/


/*  Include files  */

#include <stdio.h>
#include <Xm/Label.h>
#include <Xm/PushB.h>
#include <Xm/BulletinB.h>


/*  Functions defined in this program  */

void main();
void activateCB(); /* Callback for the pushbutton */


/*  Global variables  */

XmString btn_text;   /* button label pointer for compound string */
XmString label_text;  /* label pointer for compound string */


/*----------------------------------------------------------
** main - Main logic for xmbutton
*/
void main (argc,argv)
int argc;
```

```c
    char **argv;
    {
        Widget          toplevel;       /*  Shell widget           */
        Widget          bboard;         /*  Bulletin board widget */
        Widget          button;         /*  Pushbutton widget      */
        Widget          label;          /*  Label widget           */
        Arg             args[10];       /*  arg list               */
        register        int n;          /*  arg count              */
        XtAppContext app_context;       /*  application context    */


    /*  Initialize the toolkit, create application context, open
            display, and create a toplevel shell */
        toplevel = XtAppInitialize (&app_context, "Sample", NULL, 0,
                    &argc, argv, NULL, args, 0);


    /*  Create a bulletin board widget for the pushbutton and label */
        n = 0;
        bboard = XmCreateBulletinBoard (toplevel, "bboard", args, n);


    /*  Manage the bulletin board widget */
        XtManageChild (bboard);


    /*  Create a compound string for the pushbutton label */
        btn_text = XmStringCreateLtoR("Exit", XmSTRING_DEFAULT_CHARSET);


    /*  Set up an arglist for the pushbutton widget */
        n = 0;
        XtSetArg (args[n], XmNlabelString, btn_text);  n++;


    /*  Create the push button widget */
        button = XmCreatePushButton (bboard, "button", args, n);


    /*  Manage the pushbutton widget */
        XtManageChild (button);
```

```c
    /*  Create a compound string for the label widget text */
    label_text = XmStringCreateLtoR("Hello, World!",
                                     XmSTRING_DEFAULT_CHARSET);


    /*  Set up an arglist for the label widget */
    n = 0;
    XtSetArg (args[n], XmNlabelString, label_text);   n++;


    /*  Create the label widget */
    label = XmCreateLabel (bboard, "label", args, n);


    /*  Manage the pushbutton widget */
    XtManageChild (label);


    /*  Free the compound string memory */
    XmStringFree (btn_text);
    XmStringFree (label_text);


    /*  Add a callback  */
    XtAddCallback (button, XmNactivateCallback, activateCB, NULL);


    /*  Realize widgets  */
    XtRealizeWidget (toplevel);


    /*  Process events  */
    XtAppMainLoop (app_context);
}


/*-----------------------------------------------------------
**  activateCB - callback for button
*/
void activateCB (w, client_data, call_data)
    Widget    w;                    /*  widget id              */
```


Program Listings

```c
    XtPointer    client_data;  /*  data from application  */
    XtPointer    call_data;    /*  data from widget class */
{
/*  Print message and terminate program  */
  printf ("Pushbutton Activated.\n");
  exit (0);
}
```

Sample

Sample is the defaults file used with `sample.c`. You can place this in the directory /usr/lib/X11/app-defaults or in your home directory.

```
!    app-defaults file for sample.c
!
!    general appearance and behavior defaults
!
*keyboardFocusPolicy:    POINTER
*fontList:               HelvB12
*shadowThickness:        3
!
!  BulletinBoard resources
!
*bboard.resizePolicy     RESIZE_NONE
*bboard.height:          150
*bboard.width:           250
!*bboard.background:      sky blue
!
!  PushButton resources
!
!*XmPushButton.foreground:  midnight blue
!*XmPushButton.background:  goldenrod
*XmPushButton.borderWidth:  0
*XmPushButton.height:       30
*XmPushButton.width:        100
*XmPushButton.x:            75
*XmPushButton.y:            90
!
!  Label resources
!
!*label.foreground:    midnight blue
!*label.background:    goldenrod
```

```
*label.borderWidth:    0
*label.height:     30
*label.width:      100
*label.x:          75
*label.y:          30
```

Appendix B Motif Representation Types

This appendix contains a list of currently valid Motif representation types. See Chapter 2 for more information.

```
XmRAlignment

XmRAnimationMask

XmRAnimationPixmap

XmRAnimationStyle

XmRArrowDirection

XmRAtomList

XmRAttachment

XmRAudibleWarning

XmRAvailability

XmRBackgroundPixmap

XmRBlendModel

XmRBooleanDimension

XmRBottomShadowPixmap

XmRButtonType

XmRCallbackProc

XmRChar

XmRCharSetTable

XmRChildHorizontalAlignment

XmRChildPlacement

XmRChildType

XmRChildVerticalAlignment

XmRCommandWindowLocation
```

XmRCompoundText

XmRDefaultButtonType

XmRDeleteResponse

XmRDialogStyle

XmRDialogType

XmRDoubleClickInterval

XmRDragInitiatorProtocolStyle

XmRDragReceiverProtocolStyle

XmRDropSiteActivity

XmRDropSiteOperations

XmRDropSiteType

XmRDropTransfers

XmRExtensionType

XmRFileTypeMask

XmRFontList

XmRGadgetPixmap

XmRHighlightPixmap

XmRHorizontalDimension

XmRHorizontalInt

XmRHorizontalPosition

XmRIconAttachment

XmRImportTargets

XmRIndicatorType

XmRItemCount

XmRItems

XmRKeySym

XmRKeySymTable

XmRKeyboardFocusPolicy

XmRLabelType

XmRListMarginHeight

XmRListMarginWidth

XmRListSizePolicy

XmRListSpacing

XmRManBottomShadowPixmap

XmRTransferStatus

XmRTraversalType

XmRUnitType

XmRUnpostBehavior

XmRValueWcs

XmRVerticalAlignment

XmRVerticalDimension

XmRVerticalInt

XmRVerticalPosition

XmRVirtualBinding

XmRVisibleItemCount

XmRVisualPolicy

XmRWhichButton

XmRXmBackgroundPixmap

XmRXsmtringCharSet

XmRXsmtringTable

This appendix contains a list of Motif functions you might need when writing your own widgets. Some of these functions were used in the knob, grid, and knob gadget. All the functions listed will undergo a name change in Motif 2.0, and the new name is listed at the end of each description.

_XmClearBorder

`_XmClearBorder` clears the border highlight and/or the widget shadows.

```
#include <Xm/DrawP.h>

extern void _XmClearBorder(Display *display,
                           Window    w,
                           Position  x,
                           Position  y,
                           Dimension width,
                           Dimension height,
                           Dimension shadow_thick) ;
```

display — The display where the window is rendered (use `XtDisplay(widget)`).

window — The widget's window (use `XtWindow(widget)`).

x,y — The location of the upper left corner of the area where the highlight or shadow is to be cleared. For clearing the highlight, the values should be 0,0. For clearing the shadow, they should be the value of the widget's highlight thickness.

width, height — The width and height of the area of the widget to be cleared. For clearing the highlight, the values should be the width and height of the widget. For clearing the shadows, they should be the width and height of the widget minus the widget's highlight thickness.

thickness — The thickness of what is being erased. Set it to the highlight thickness if the highlight is being cleared and to the shadow thickness if that is what is being cleared.

Future versions of Motif (post 1.2) will change the name of `_XmClearBorder` to `XmeClearBorder`.

_XmConfigureObject

_XmConfigureObject changes the location and/or dimensions of a widget or gadget.

```
#include <Xm/XmP.h>
extern void _XmConfigureObject( Widget g,
                                Position x,
                                Position y,
                                Dimension width,
                                Dimension height,
                                Dimension border_width) ;
```

g — The widget or gadget child to be reconfigured.

x,y — The new location of the child.

width — The new width of the child.

height — The new height of the child.

border_width — The new border_width of the child.

Future versions of Motif (post 1.2) will change the name of _XmConfigureObject to XmeConfigureObject.

_XmDrawArrow

_XmDrawArrow draws the arrows in the shape of a triangle with shadows for use in widgets such as the scrollbar widget.

```
#include <Xm/DrawP.h>

extern void _XmDrawArrow( Display *display,
                          Drawable d,
                          GC top_gc,
                          GC bot_gc,
                          GC cent_gc,
                          Position x,
                          Position y,
                          Dimension width,
                          Dimension height,
                          Dimension shadow_thick,
                          unsigned char direction) ;
```

display — The display where the window is rendered (use `XtDisplay(widget)`).

drawable — The drawable to which the arrow will be drawn (use `XtWindow(widget)`).

top_gc — The graphics context used to draw the top shadow.

bottom_gc — The graphics context used to draw the bottom shadow.

center_gc — The graphics context used to draw the area in the center of the arrow.

x,y — The location of the upper left corner of the bounding box in which the arrow will be drawn.

width, height — The width and height of the bounding box in which the arrow will be drawn.

shadow_thick — The thickness of the shadows to be drawn around the arrow.

direction — Indicates the direction to draw the arrow (either XmARROW_UP, XmARROW_DOWN, XmARROW_LEFT, or XmARROW_RIGHT)

Future versions of Motif (post 1.2) will change the name of `_XmDrawArrow` to `XmeDrawArrow`.

_XmDrawDiamond

_XmDrawDiamond draws a diamond with a shadow for use in widgets like the toggle button.

```
#include <Xm/DrawP.h>

extern void _XmDrawDiamond( Display *display,
                            Drawable d,
                            GC top_gc,
                            GC bottom_gc,
                            GC center_gc,
                            Position x,
                            Position y,
                            Dimension width,
                            Dimension height,
                            Dimension shadow_thick,
                            Dimension fill) ;
```

display — The display where the window is rendered (use `XtDisplay(widget)`).

drawable — The drawable to which the diamond will be drawn (use `XtWindow(widget)`).

top_gc — The graphics context used to draw the top shadow.

bottom_gc — The graphics context used to draw the bottom shadow.

center_gc — The graphics context used to draw the area in the center of the diamond.

x,y — The location of the upper left corner of the bounding box in which the diamond will be drawn.

width, height — The width and height of the bounding box in which the diamond will be drawn.

shadow_thick — The thickness of the shadows to be drawn around the diamond.

fill — Indicates whether to include a one pixel margin between the diamond filled area and the shadows. A 0 indicates that the margin will be used, a non-zero indicates that the fill area in the diamond should be drawn all the way to the shadows.

Future versions of Motif (post 1.2) will change the name of `_XmDrawDiamond` to
`XmeDrawDiamond`.

_XmDrawHighlight

_XmDrawHighlight draws the border highlight of the widget for use with keyboard traversal.

```
#include <Xm/DrawP.h>

extern void _XmDrawHighlight( Display *display,
                              Drawable d,
                              GC gc,
                              Position x,
                              Position y,
                              Dimension width,
                              Dimension height,
                              Dimension highlight_thick,
                              int line_style) ;
```

display — The display where the window is rendered (use `XtDisplay(widget)`).

drawable — The drawable to which the highlight will be drawn (use `XtWindow(widget)`).

gc — The graphics context used to draw the highlight.

x,y — The location of the upper left corner of the highlight to be drawn around the widget.

width, height — The width and height of the highlight to be drawn.

highlight_thick — The thickness of the highlight to be drawn around the widget.

Future versions of Motif (post 1.2) will change the name of `_XmDrawHighlight` to `XmeDrawHighlight`.

_XmDrawSeparator

_XmDrawSeparator draws line-based separators.

```
#include <Xm/DrawP.h>
extern void _XmDrawSeparator( Display *display,
                              Drawable drawable,
                              GC top_gc,
                              GC bottom_gc,
                              GC separator_gc,
                              Position x,
                              Position y,
                              Dimension width,
                              Dimension height,
                              Dimension shadow_thick,
                              Dimension margin,
                              unsigned char orientation,
                              unsigned char separator_type) ;
```

display — The display where the window is rendered (use `XtDisplay(widget)`).

drawable — The drawable to which the separator will be drawn (use `XtWindow(widget)`).

top_gc — The graphics context used to draw the top shadow. The location of this shadow depends on the orientation and type of shadow.

bottom_gc — The graphics context used to draw the bottom shadow. The location of this shadow depends on the orientation and type of shadow.

separator_gc — The graphics context used to draw the area in the center of the separator.

x,y — The location of the upper left corner of the separator.

width, height — The width and height specifies the dimensions of the separator.

shadow_thick — The thickness of the shadows to be drawn around the separator. This is only used in shadowed type separators (see *separator_type*).

margin — Indicates the space between the separator lines and the shadow.

orientation — The orientation of the line (XmVERTICAL or XmHORIZONTAL).

separator_type — The type of separator to be drawn, one of the following:

> XmSHADOW_ETCHED_IN
>
> XmSHADOW_ETCHED_OUT
>
> XmSHADOW_ETCHED_IN_DASH
>
> XmSHADOW_ETCHED_OUT_DASH
>
> XmSINGLE_LINE
>
> XmDOUBLE_LINE
>
> XmSINGLE_DASHED_LINE
>
> XmDOUBLE_DASHED_LINE

Future versions of Motif (post 1.2) will change the name of `_XmDrawSeparator` to `XmeDrawSeparator`.

_XmDrawShadows

_XmDrawShadows draws a shadow around a widget.

```
#include <Xm/DrawP.h>
extern void _XmDrawShadows( Display *display,
                            Drawable drawable,
                            GC top_gc,
                            GC bottom_gc,
                            Position x,
                            Position y,
                            Dimension width,
                            Dimension height,
                            Dimension shadow_thick,
                            unsigned int shadow_type) ;
```

display — The display where the window is rendered (use `XtDisplay(widget)`).

drawable — The drawable to which the shadow will be drawn (use `XtWindow(widget)`).

top_gc — The graphics context used to draw the top shadow.

bottom_gc — The graphics context used to draw the bottom shadow.

x,y — The location of the upper left corner of the shadow.

width, height — The width and height specifies the dimensions of the shadow.

shadow_thick — The thickness of the shadows to be drawn around the drawable.

shadow_type — The type of shadow to be drawn, one of the following:

      XmSHADOW_OUT

      XmSHADOW_IN

      XmSHADOW_ETCHED_OUT

      XmSHADOW_ETCHED_IN

Future versions of Motif (post 1.2) will change the name of `_XmDrawShadows` to `XmeDrawShadows`.

_XmFocusIsInShell

_XmFocusIsInShell determines whether a widget's shell parent has the keyboard focus.

```
#include <Xm/XmP.h>
```

```
extern Boolean _XmFocusIsInShell( Widget widget) ;
```

widget — The target widget use to check if its shell widget parent that has the keyboard focus.

_XmFocusIsInShell returns True if the shell parent of the widget has the keyboard focus; otherwise, False.

Future versions of Motif (post 1.2) will change the name of _XmFocusIsInShell to XmeFocusIsInShell.

_XmFromHorizontalPixels

_XmFromHorizontalPixels converts from pixels to the unit type defined by XmUnitType for the horizontal dimension resources (width and margin_width). Used with synthetic resource definitions to provide resolution independence.

```
#include <Xm/XmP.h>

extern void _XmFromHorizontalPixels( Widget widget,

                                     int offset,

                                     XtArgVal *value) ;
```

widget — Specifies the widget where the XmNunitType resource is specified.

offset — Specifies the offset into the resource field of the widget's instance record.

value— Specifies the value of the resource in pixels and returns the value in the specified unit type.

Future versions of Motif (post 1.2) will change the name of _XmFromHorizontalPixels to XmeFromHorizontalPixels.

_XmFromVerticalPixels

_XmFromVerticalPixels converts from pixels to the unit type defined by `XmNunitType` for the vertical dimension resources (e.g. height and margin_height). Used with synthetic resource definitions to provide resolution independence.

```
#include <Xm/XmP.h>

extern void _XmFromVerticalPixels( Widget widget,

                                   int offset,

                                   XtArgVal *value) ;
```

widget — Specifies the widget where the `XmNunitType` resource is specified.

offset — Specifies the offset into the resource field of the widget's instance record.

value — Specifies the value of the resource in pixels and returns the value in the specified unit type.

Future versions of Motif (post 1.2) will change the name of `_XmFromVerticalPixels` to `XmeFromVerticalPixels`.

_XmGetDefaultDisplay

_XmGetDefaultDisplay retrieves the default display. It is used when a widget is not available for use with XtDisplay.

```
#include <Xm/VendorSP.h>
```

```
extern Display * _XmGetDefaultDisplay( void );
```

You must have created vendor shell widget in order to successfully use this procedure.

Future versions of Motif (post 1.2) will change the name of _XmGetDefaultDisplay to XmeGetDefaultDisplay.

_XmGetNullCursor retrieves a transparent cursor used in drag and drop visuals.

```
#include <Xm/ScreenP.h>
```

```
extern Cursor _XmGetNullCursor( Widget w) ;
```

widget — Specifies the widget used to get display information. Any instantiated widget will work.

Future versions of Motif (post 1.2) will change the name of _XmGetNullCursor to XmeGetNullCursor.

_XmGetPixmapData

_XmGetPixmapData retrieves information from a pixmap in the image cache.

```
#include <Xm/XmP.h>
extern Boolean _XmGetPixmapData( Screen *screen,
                                 Pixmap pixmap,
                                 char **image_name,
                                 int *depth,
                                 Pixel *foreground,
                                 Pixel *background,
                                 int *hot_x,
                                 int *hot_y,
                                 unsigned int *width,
                                 unsigned int *height) ;
```

screen — Used with the pixmap to get the cache entry for the screen.

pixmap — Specifies the pixmap to search for in the cache.

image_name — Returns the image name of the cached pixmap.

depth — Returns the depth of the pixmap.

foreground — Returns the foreground of the pixmap.

background — Returns the background of the pixmap.

hot_x — Returns the pixmap `hot_x`.

hot_y — Returns the pixmap `hot_y`.

width — Returns the width of the pixmap.

height — Returns the height of the pixmap.

_XmGetPixmapData returns True if the pixmap is in the image cache; otherwise, it returns False.

Future versions of Motif (post 1.2) will change the name of _XmGetPixmapData to XmeGetPixmapData.

_XmGetTextualDragIcon

_XmGetTextualDragIcon returns the drag icon used in dragging textual data. Used with XmDragStart to provide the appropriate drag visual.

```
#include <Xm/DragIconP.h>
```

```
extern Widget _XmGetTextualDragIcon( Widget w);
```

w — Specifies the widget used to get screen information in creating the drag icon. Any instantiated widget is valid.

Future versions of Motif (post 1.2) will change the name of _XmGetTextualDragIcon to XmeGetTextualDragIcon.

_XmMicroSleep pauses execution for the given number of seconds.

```
#include <Xm/XmosP.h>

extern int _XmMicroSleep( long secs) ;
```

secs - Specifies the length of the pause.

Future versions of Motif (post 1.2) will change the name of _XmMicroSleep to XmeMicroSleep.

_XmStringsAreEqual

_XmStringsAreEqual compares two strings to see if they are equivalent. It is used to compare motif constants with resource string values. The constants have the "Xm" prefix stripped and are converted to lower case prior to the comparison.

```
#include <Xm/XmP.h>

extern Boolean _XmStringsAreEqual( register char *in_str,

                                   register char *test_str) ;
```

in_str — Specifies one of two string to be compared. The leading "Xm" (case ignored) is removed from the string. The rest of the string is changed to lower case.

test_str — Specifies the second of the two string to be compared. The string must not have the "Xm" prefix and must be all lower case.

_XmStringsAreEqual returns True if the strings (once converted) are equivalent.

Future versions of Motif (post 1.2) will change the name of _XmStringsAreEqual to XmeNamesAreEqual.

_XmNavigChangeManaged

_XmNavigChangeManaged handle keyboard focus changes when there are changes in the visibility of the child widgets. Used in ChangeManaged class procedures to forward changes in the managed state of the child widgets.

```
#include <Xm/XmP.h>
```

```
extern void _XmNavigChangeManaged( Widget widget) ;
```

widget — The manager widget whose child has changed its managed state.

Future versions of Motif (post 1.2) will change the name of `_XmNavigChangeManaged` to `XmeNavigChangeManaged`.

_XmOSGetHomeDirName

_XmOSGetHomeDirName retrieves the full pathname to the user's home directory.

```
#include <Xm/XmosP.h>
```

```
extern String _XmOSGetHomeDirName( void) ;
```

_XmOSGetHomeDirName returns the internal pointer to the pathname of the user's home directory. Don't free this pointer.

Future versions of Motif (post 1.2) will change the name of _XmOSGetHomeDirName to XmeGetHomeDirName.

_XmRedisplayGadgets

_XmRedisplayGadgets redisplays the gadget children of a manager widget. It is typically called in the manager widget's expose class procedure.

```
#include <Xm/XmP.h>
extern void _XmRedisplayGadgets( Widget widget,

                                 register XEvent *event,

                                 Region region) ;
```

widget — Specifies the manager widget that needs to have its children redisplayed.

event — Specifies the expose event passed into the manager's expose class procedure.

region — Specifies the region that has been exposed. Setting this to NULL causes all the gadgets to be redisplayed.

Future versions of Motif (post 1.2) will change the name of _XmRedisplayGadgets to XmeRedisplayGadgets.

_XmStringUpdateWMShellTitle

`_XmStringUpdateWMShellTitle` updates the window manager title.

```
#include <Xm/XmP.h>
extern void _XmStringUpdateWMShellTitle( XmString xmstr,
                                         Widget shell) ;
```

xmstr — Specifies the XmString for the new title.

shell — Specifies the widget that is a subclass of WMShell, which is the shell that needs the title change.

Future versions of Motif (post 1.2) will change the name of `_XmStringUpdateWMShellTitle` to `XmeStringUpdateWMShellTitle`.

_XmToHorizontalPixels

_XmToHorizontalPixels converts from the unit type specified in the resource XmNunitType to the number of pixels in the horizontal dimension. It is the reverse converter to _XmFromHorizontalPixels. It is used with synthetic resource definitions to provide resolution independence.

```
#include <Xm/XmP.h>

extern void _XmFromHorizontalPixels( Widget widget,

                                     int offset,

                                     XtArgVal *value) ;
```

widget — Specifies the widget where the XmNunitType resource is specified.

offset — Specifies the offset into the resource field of the widget's instance record.

value — Specifies the value of the resource in the specified horizontal pixels and returns the value in the unit type specified in the resource XmNunitType.

Future versions of Motif (post 1.2) will change the name of _XmToHorizontalPixels to XmeToHorizontalPixels.

_XmToVerticalPixels converts from the unit type, specified in the resource XmNunitType, to the number of pixels in the vertical dimension. It is the reverse converter to _XmFromVerticalPixels. Used with synthetic resource definitions to provide resolution independence.

```
#include <Xm/XmP.h>

extern void _XmFromVerticalPixels( Widget widget,

                                        int offset,

                                        XtArgVal *value) ;
```

widget — Specifies the widget where the XmNunitType resource is specified.

offset — Specifies the offset into the resource field of the widget's instance record.

value — Specifies the value of the resource in the specified vertical pixels and returns the value in the unit type specified in the resource XmNunitType.

Future versions of Motif (post 1.2) will change the name of _XmToVerticalPixels to XmeToVerticalPixels.

_XmVirtualToActualKeysym

`_XmVirtualToActualKeysym` retrieves the keysym associated with a virtual keysym. If more than one keysym matches the virtual keysym, an array of keysyms and modifiers are returned.

```
#include <Xm/VirtKeysP.h>
extern void _XmVirtualToActualKeysym( Display *display,
                                      KeySym virtKeysym,
                                      KeySym *actualKeysymRtn,
                                      Modifiers *modifiersRtn) ;
```

display — Specifies the display (use XtDisplay(widget)),

virtKeysym — Specifies the virtual keysym to be translated.

actualKeysymRtn — Returns a pointer to the array of actual keysyms that match the virtual keysym.

modifiersRtn — Returns a pointer to the array of modifiers that match the virtual keysym. This array parallels the keysym array.

Future versions of Motif (post 1.2) will change the name of `_XmVirtualToActualKeysym` to `XmeVirtualToActualKeysym`.

The syntax of `XmeVirtualToActualKeysym()` changes in future versions to:

```
extern int XmeVirtualToActualKeysyms( Display       *display,
                                      KeySym        virtualKeysym,
                                      XmKeyBinding  *physicalKeysyms)
```

Where `XmKeyBinding` is a struct that contains keysym and modifier pairs defined as follows:

```
typedef struct {
        KeySym        keysym;
        Modifiers     modifiers;
} XmKeyBindingRec, *XmKeyBinding;
```

_XmWarning generates a Motif style warning to standard error.

```
#include <Xm/XmP.h>
extern void XmeWarning( Widget widget,
                                char *message)
```

widget — Specifies the widget where the warning occurs.

message — Specifies the message to accompany the warning.

Future versions of Motif (post 1.2) will change the name of _XmWarning to XmeWarning.

Glossary

Action

An event that is bound to a function by a translation. The function is called when the event occurs.

Action Table

A list of functions and their corresponding string equivalents that bind the actions to a translation table.

Callback

A function or procedure in an application that is invoked as the result of some action on the widget. For example, an application with a pushbutton widget will probably have a function or procedure to be invoked when the pushbutton is "pressed."

Callback Structure

A structure containing information about the widget that invoked the callback and the event that caused the callback to be invoked. The name of the structure is used as the third parameter of callback function call.

Chained Method

Methods of the same name that belong to both superclasses and widget classes, and that are executed in sequence when the widget class method is called. An example of this is the set values methods defined in the various classes.

Class

An object-oriented programming term used to identify widget types. There are a number of different classes, and together they form a hierarchy. Lower classes can inherit the attributes of higher classes.

Class Part Record

A structure that defines the widget class part.

Class Record

A structure that defines the widget class. It is composed of pointers to the widget class part records.

Defaults File

A file of default values for the widgets in an application. This file can be located in the directory /usr/lib/X11/app-defaults, your home directory, or a directory specified by the environment variables XFILESEARCHPATH, XUSERFILESEARCHPATH, and XAPPLRESDIR.

Event

An occurrence of possible interest to an application. The application is notified of the event's occurrence by the X Server, which stores information about the event in a data structure that is made available to the application. Examples of events are "pressing" a pushbutton widget, entering a window, and leaving a window. See Table 2-1 in Chapter 2.

Function

A subroutine that returns one or more values, unlike a procedure, which returns no values.

Gadget

An object similar to a widget but without a window of its own. A gadget must rely on its parent for its window. In addition, a gadget does not support translations, popup children, or event handlers.

Inheritance Procedure

Methods and procedures belonging to a widget class that can be inherited by widgets that are subclassed from this widget.

Instance

A unique separate occurrence of a widget belonging to a specific widget class. Each instance has its own instance record but share the widget class record.

Instance Part Record

A structure that defines each unique instance of a widget.

Instance Record

A structure similar to a widget class record, except that where widgets of the same class share the widget class record, they have their own instance record.

Method

An object-oriented term for function or procedure. For our purposes, a method is a function or procedure that is declared in the widget class record.

Motif

A library of user interface components called widgets and gadgets that is built on top of Xlib and the Xt Intrinsics. See Chapter 1.

Multiple Inclusions

The potential for including a header file more than once, which is overcome by inserting certain lines of code at the beginning and end of a header file.

Private Header File

A widget header file normally used only by widgets that are subclassed from the widget in question. The private header file consists of structures that define the widget class and instance records.

Procedure

A function that does not return any values.

Public Header File

A widget header file used by applications that use the widget. It consists of the widget class name, resource strings, callback structures, and public function declarations.

QueryOnly Request

A geometry request in which the requesting widget is "just asking" to see what the manager's reply will be. It doesn't intend to actually make a change. Normally, this is used only by manager widgets.

Resource

An attribute of a widget or gadget that affects some aspect of the widget, such as size, position, background color, or foreground color. You can set values into resources in several ways.

Resource String

An alternate name for a widget resource. Typically, it is the resource name with the first three or four letters (XmN or XsmN) dropped. Resource strings are defined in the widget's public header file, and the names thus defined can be used by an application programmer to set values into the resources.

Subclass

The process by which a widget class is derived from a higher class. For example, XmFrame is subclassed from Manager.

Superclass

Any of several higher-level widget classes upon which all the other classes depend. These are generally considered to be Core, XmGadget, Constraint, Composite, Manager, and Primitive.

Synthetic Resource

A resource description for preprocessing resources prior to Initialize, SetValues, and GetValues routines. It is used primarily to convert resolution independent resources for a unit type other then pixel into pixel for use with X. The Motif superclass widgets XmGadget, XmManager, and Primitive each have a resource called `XmNunitType`, which provides the basic support for resolution independence. See the description of this resource in the man page for any of the foregoing superclass widgets.

Translation

A translation ties an event to an action name.

Translations Table

A list of translations that apply to a particular widget.

Widget

A user interface object made up of data structures and functions that make use of the Xlib and Xt Intrinsics functions. It may or may not have a visible window, depending on its intended use. Examples of widgets that have a window are the pushbutton, toggle button, and frame. Examples of widgets that do not have a window are Shell, TopLevelShell, and ApplicationShell.

Widget Class Record

A structure that defines the widget class. It is composed of the class structures of higher-level widgets from which the current widget is subclassed. For example, the pushbutton widget class record is composed of class part records for Core, Primitive, and Label, in addition to its own class part.

Xlib

One of the two libraries (the other is the Xt Intrinsics) that form the basis for the X Window System. Xlib consists of a number of low-level functions and procedures that you can use to write programs for the X Window System.

Xt Intrinsics

One of the two libraries (the other is Xlib) that form the basis for the X Window System. The Xt Intrinsics consists of a number of functions and procedures that you can use to write programs for the X Window System.

Index